PROPERTY OF

D0762763

Research Methods in Social Work

Research Methods in Social Work

FIFTH EDITION

David Royse
University of Kentucky

THOMSON

BROOKS/COLE

Australia • Brazil • Canada • Mexico • Singapore • Spain
United Kingdom • United States

THOMSON

BROOKS/COLE

Research Methods in Social Work, **Fifth Edition**
David Royse

Acquisitions Editor: Dan Alpert
Development Editor: Tangelique Williams
Assistant Editor: Ann Lee Richards
Editorial Assistant: Stephanie Rue
Technology Project Manager: Julie Aguilar
Marketing Manager: Meghan McCullough
Marketing Assistant: Teresa Marino
Marketing Communications Manager: Shemika Britt
Project Manager, Editorial Production: Christy Krueger
Creative Director: Rob Hugel

Art Director: Vernon Boes
Print Buyer: Nora Massuda
Permissions Editor: Roberta Broyer
Production Service: ICC Macmillan Inc./Gunjan Chandola
Copy Editor: Michelle Gaudreau
Cover Designer: Larry Didona
Cover Image: © Photodisc Red/Getty Images
Cover Printer: Thomson West
Compositor: ICC Macmillan Inc.
Printer: Thomson West

COPYRIGHT © 2008, 2003 Thomson Brooks/Cole, a part of
The Thomson Corporation. Thomson, the Star logo, and Brooks/
Cole are trademarks used herein under license.

ALL RIGHTS RESERVED. No part of this work covered by
the copyright hereon may be reproduced or used in any form or
by any means—graphic, electronic, or mechanical, including
photocopying, recording, taping, web distribution, information
storage and retrieval systems, or in any other manner—without
the written permission of the publisher.

Printed in the United States of America
1 2 3 4 5 6 7 11 10 09 08 07

Library of Congress Control Number 2006937043

ISBN-13: 978-0-495-11566-3
ISBN-10: 0-495-11566-5

Thomson Higher Education
10 Davis Drive
Belmont, CA 94002-3098
USA

For more information about our products, contact us at:
Thomson Learning Academic Resources Center
1-800-423-0563
For permission to use material from this text or product,
submit a request online at
http://www.thomsonrights.com
Any additional questions about permissions can be
submitted by e-mail to
thomsonrights@thomson.com

Contents

CHAPTER 5 | Research Designs for Group Comparisons   114

CHAPTER 6 | Understanding and Using Research Instruments   145

CHAPTER 10 | Unobtrusive Approaches to Data Collection: Secondary Data and Content Analysis   243

CHAPTER 11 | Qualitative Research   269

Preface

TO THE STUDENT

Research Methods in Social Work, Fifth Edition, is an introductory textbook and has been written for both undergraduate and graduate social work students. When I first started teaching research methods, there was not a good selection of books available for social work students. In fact, my program at that time used a research textbook written by a sociologist. Because sociologists do not always have the same interests or values as social workers, I set to work on a textbook that would have examples and illustrations from social work journals—one that reveals social work literature and entices students to explore it. I didn't want to lose students with too many technical details—especially students who might find the topic intimidating. My goal was to demystify research and help students to see that research really is understandable. My plan was to provide all that was essential and nothing that didn't directly relate in a useful way.

The first edition was printed in 1991, and over the years it has been gratifying to hear students comment that my writing style makes the content easy to grasp. Perhaps its readability stems from the fact that with that first edition I pilot-tested the material with my own students—furnishing them with spiral-bound copies of the manuscript to read. (Well, at least they didn't have to buy a book for the course that semester.) Since I still use this book in my own teaching, I'm constantly updating and trying to polish sections where students hit snags.

At the end of each chapter you will find questions with answers for self-review. These aren't intended to test every concept, but serve as a quick check to see if you are comprehending most of what you read. I encourage you to take the time to look up some of the references and Web sites throughout the book. The more you put into your learning, the more you will get out of it.

TO THE INSTRUCTOR

I have tried to make this book as complete a resource as possible given the page limitations. That is, you'll find questions for class discussion, potential assignments, and a host of readings that can be used to add a little zip to lectures. A quick look at this edition will reveal that it contains templates for suggested assignments at the end of each chapter. This feature has several advantages.

First, unlike assignments made orally in class that can result in homework submissions of vastly different quality (students may hear something different than was intended), the proposed exercises provide all the guidance needed in black and white—reducing confusion about what you actually meant when making the assignment.

Second, having the exercises already developed saves the instructor preparation time and affords a variety of ways that content can be highlighted. I've supplied multiple exercises for each chapter, enabling you to choose one or several for students to complete—depending on the class's understanding of the content, length of your course, and so forth. Students may copy all or portions of the exercises on separate sheets of paper with their submitted responses. Alternatively, you may also employ the exercises in class and have students pencil their thoughts directly into their books as they participate in classroom activities.

Third, exercises that are not assigned give students additional opportunities to try out their understanding of the material on their own. At the same time, the range of exercises allows you to be considerate of different learning styles while finding meaningful ways to assist students with the material being covered.

I've designed these exercises with active learning principles in mind, and you have many options for teaching with them. Some of the suggested assignments lend themselves to small group work in class; others can be done individually during a class period or outside of class. They vary in the length of time needed for completion; some exercises will require several hours and others can be finished in 15 minutes or less. With the exception of the first two (at the end of Chapter 1), which serve as "icebreakers" that foster interaction among students and allow them to get to know each other, what the exercises have in common is that they involve students in applying the research knowledge they have been acquiring.

CHANGES TO THE FIFTH EDITION

My orientation to the exploration of social problems is unapologetically quantitative. That is, I believe that science moves forward with careful and accurate measurements, that objectivity is crucial, that concepts need to be operationally defined, that generalizability is desired, and that it is necessary to be able to speak with some confidence about one's findings—meaning that statistical analysis is vitally important as evidence that findings are not a strange quirk but real and likely to be reproducible by other researchers. On a 10-point continuum with 1 being the most qualitative and 10 being the most quantitative, I would place myself at about a 7 or 8 in terms of my quantitative orientation. In previous editions, I did not go to any great lengths to help students see that a qualitative researcher might have a different way of approaching the study of the same social problem.

Increasingly, I have come to believe that it is valuable to acknowledge (and help students see) that there can be more than one way to find answers to the questions that we need to address. Indeed, there is much to be learned from qualitative approaches. Diversity of perspective brings great strength. While this book is still primarily quantitative in direction and guidance, what readers will discover is that in this edition I have attempted to provide a more rounded and alternate (qualitative) way of thinking about social work research.

My goal is to help students become more flexible in their thinking about how to plan and collect data for their investigations. In Zen Buddhism there is an expression something to the effect that a wheel has many spokes, but all of them lead to the center. Although I might, characteristically, begin a study using a quantitative approach, I am not so rigid as to believe that my way is the only way. After reading this book it is my hope that readers will come away with a great many more "tools" in their research toolboxes because they will be able to think in the "language" of both qualitative and quantitative researchers.

ACKNOWLEDGMENTS

The author's appreciation goes to the following reviewers for their helpful critiques of the manuscript: William Cloud, University of Denver; Gail M. Folaron, Indiana University–Purdue University of Indianapolis; Steve Kapp, University of Kansas; and Stephen Marson, University of North Carolina–Pembroke.

BIOGRAPHICAL INFORMATION

Besides this book, David Royse is the author of another research text: *Program Evaluation: An Introduction* (Brooks/Cole, 2006) as well as books on data analysis, field instruction, emotional abuse, and teaching tips for college instructors. He has been at the University of Kentucky since 1985.

Introduction

CHAPTER 1

WHERE DOES RESEARCH START?

Have you ever noticed that unanswered questions, riddles, and mysteries surround us? If we were face-to-face in a classroom, I'd ask you to take a minute or two to think about some of the questions percolating in the back of your mind that have never been satisfactorily answered. I'm not talking about questions like "I wonder what's for supper?" or "Who on earth did Jimmy go out with last night?" but larger questions like "Is heredity or environment the more powerful influence in alcohol dependence?" or "To what extent do most victims of child abuse recover from their trauma?"

For some of you, life's mysteries involve specific individuals and their behavior. You may wonder why a favorite cousin committed suicide in the prime of his life, or why Aunt Martha can't seem to quit drinking. Maybe you have grown up with a schizophrenic parent or sibling and wonder if you somehow unintentionally contributed to their illness.

Research seeks to provide answers to life's enigmas by exploring questions that originate from people just like yourself. You see, ideas for suitable research projects often stem from our own life experiences or observations. Allow me to give you a brief illustration.

Close to the end of a spring semester several years ago, I was concluding a lecture on qualitative research methods. (Qualitative research methods seek to help the investigator understand the experience or viewpoint of another person or group of people.) As I typically do during that lecture, I introduced material from Clifford Beers's book, *A Mind That Found Itself* (1910). Beers was a college student around the turn of the century who, after breaking up with his fiancé, began losing his mind. He kept a diary of the events that occurred during this period of his life—he talks, for instance, of feeling a compulsion to jump out of a third-floor window, at the same time knowing that it was a crazy thought.

"What would it be like," I asked the class, "to feel torn between wanting to injure yourself and knowing that those thoughts were crazy? To be unable to stop obsessing about something?" I had the class's attention, but paused for a moment to switch examples.

In a recent series of articles on child abuse our local newspaper had portrayed a number of officials (judges, lawyers, and, yes, social workers) who had not done enough to protect vulnerable children. Most students probably were familiar with the newspaper accounts, but I wanted to impress on them that knowledge of the statistics and facts about child abuse is quite different from the experience of abuse.

"What would it be like," I asked the class, "to be chained in a dark, damp basement as a child? To have your cries of hunger ignored by your parents—or worse, to be sexually abused on a filthy mattress on the cold concrete floor? Would you understand child abuse any differently than you do now? How might living in that situation provide you with knowledge that you wouldn't get just by reading a book or journal article?"

A student raised her hand and when I acknowledged her, she simply pointed to the student beside her. Even from the front of the classroom, I could see that something was unusual about Frank. As the whole class turned to look at him, he sat rigid, eyes glazed over. I walked closer and called his name several times. There was no response. Gently I reached over and tugged on his sleeve. Again, there was no indication that Frank recognized he was the focus of the class's attention. I shook Frank harder. Nothing. I checked for blink and startle reflexes . . . He had none.

My first thought was that he was having some sort of seizure, although I had never seen one quite like it. After what seemed like an eternity, someone suggested that we look in his wallet to see if it contained any emergency medical information. It did. We found the number of a clinical social worker whose office wasn't too far from campus.

With the card in my hand, I sprinted to the nearest pay phone on the next floor and dialed the number. I insisted that the receptionist immediately connect me with the therapist. A few seconds later, the social worker confirmed that Frank became temporarily catatonic from time to time; not all of his triggers had been identified. However, she assured me, Frank usually recovered on his own within twenty minutes to an hour.

I went back to the classroom and found my students anxiously gathered around Frank, watching for some blink or sigh, some indication that he was in the land of the living. The bell rang, signaling the end of class. Anticipating that another class would be coming into our classroom, I asked a student to help me lift Frank to see if we could assist him in walking out of the classroom. Frank was still unresponsive and it was like lifting a 150-pound bag of potatoes. Rather than risk dropping him, we decided to leave Frank in his seat.

Several students volunteered to stay with Frank, but I encouraged them to go on to their own classes, assuring them that I would remain behind. About this time, I looked back at Frank and noticed a single tear slipping down his cheek. He blinked his eyes and turned his head as if to acquaint himself with his surroundings. "Are you okay?" I asked. Frank responded by nodding his head. It took a few more minutes for Frank to compose himself enough to walk to my car so that I could take him to his therapist.

I saw Frank again about a week later when he took his final exam. He did well, and finished in the top third of the class.

Frank had been a victim of nightmarish child abuse. Something I had said, some image I evoked, summoned a flood of memories so painful that Frank's catatonia had resulted. But Frank's experience also had an effect on me. Maybe not that afternoon, but shortly thereafter, I began wondering about the extent to which other students in social work might have been impaired by early childhood or dysfunctional family experiences. That thought spun off others—could early childhood experiences affect the choice of social work as a career? Could unfortunate childhood experiences affect our satisfaction with life as adults? That remarkable experience with Frank fueled my curiosity about a whole set of questions I had never seriously contemplated before and was the catalyst for several research projects and a book on emotional abuse.

In the first project (Royse, Rompf, & Dhooper, 1991) my colleagues and I contributed questions to a statewide survey (a quantitative approach) and asked respondents if there were problems such as child abuse, mental illness, or substance abuse in their families of origin. We used that information to see if those who experienced such problems were less satisfied with their lives than those without that exposure. Not only were they less satisfied with their lives, they also tended to make less money—suggesting that trauma in their early life had affected them as adults.

In another survey (Rompf & Royse, 1994), we asked students the same family-of-origin questions along with some others to see if these experiences had influenced the students to choose social work as a career.

But then I did something much more in the vein of quality research. As a result of learning firsthand about emotional abuse from a faculty member who had experienced some truly awful emotional abuse from her own mother, I became interested in learning more about the topic and began interviewing victims of abuse to collect their stories. I then incorporated that information into a book that didn't quote numbers or percentages (which would have been consistent with a quantitative approach), but which simply told the stories as a way of helping other people (even victims) to understand that emotional abuse can be experienced in an infinite number of ways. Why was this important? Because victims of abuse live in homes where abuse is normalized. They sometimes don't know that the craziness that goes on there doesn't occur in every home.

For instance, an attractive, intelligent woman told me that, during her teens, if her date was a few minutes late her mother would say something like, "If you were only more attractive, your date would be on time." Even though the young woman didn't think she was unattractive, she had two choices: either she believed that others found her unattractive, or her own mother was a malicious liar. From those interviews I wove a book (now out of print) entitled *How Do I Know It's Abuse? Identifying and Countering Emotional Mistreatment from Friends and Family Members* (Royse, 1994).

As a researcher you always have a choice in how you go about learning about a phenomenon. To give a simple explanation, sometimes it makes sense to do a survey and other times interviewing a handful of people about their experiences seems to be the way to go. As we progress through this book you'll get a better idea about the strengths and weaknesses of both the qualitative and quantitative approaches. If you already see that both perspectives could be valuable, then be reassured that it is often possible to use both in the same project (an approach often called "mixed methods"). Researchers seldom face an "either-or" situation in terms of having to use only a quantitative or qualitative approach.

I shared this information from my own experiences to show how life experiences can influence and lead to the questions that researchers want to answer. Researchers collect and interpret data to find an explanation to some question or phenomenon that they don't understand. While social workers don't always think of themselves as detectives, both social work practitioners and researchers are actually sleuths.

Consider the young man who says he can't keep a job. He's had seven jobs in the last three years, lasting an average of six months at each place. Does he have a substance abuse problem or some underlying mental illness, or has he just run into a string of hard-to-live-with bosses? The social worker looks for clues in a client's speech, dress, or behavior that can assist her in making an assessment. These data can then be interpreted by the social worker or others and may become part of treatment planning or used to judge the success of a program.

Our life experiences may raise a host of different questions for each of us. Here's another example: A paraplegic MSW student once remarked in class that few professionals know how to talk to people with disabilities. He speculated that because their training had taught them not to ask questions for which they do not need answers, professionals often did not inquire as to how he lost the use of his legs. As a result, they often made erroneous assumptions— and in doing so, failed to get to know him as a person. "I would much rather," he said, "have them ask, 'What happened to you?' so that I can explain something about me as a person. As I tell them about my former career as an electronics engineer and the airplane crash, they begin to know me as a human being. I'm no longer some vegetable in a wheelchair."

As he talked, I realized that other people with disabilities may feel as he did. And—you guessed it—a number of questions about disability and disabled people's preferences with regard to disclosing information about it began forming in my mind. Later, the two of us combined our knowledge and conducted a study (Royse & Edwards, 1989). While our investigation was not definitive by any means, it did provide some initial evidence suggesting that disabled people are frequently open to disclosing information about their disabilities. It was a small study that produced only one piece of evidence, but that was nevertheless a starting place for other interested researchers (possibly people like yourself) to build on.

Unanswered questions, riddles, and mysteries surround us and provide the stimuli for research. Over the years, I've lost track of the number of students who've come to me to explore some particular research interest. Those able to conceptualize their projects clearly, and those with lots of perseverance (willingness to revise and rewrite), have sometimes been rewarded by seeing their efforts published in professional journals. Who creates knowledge for social workers? Individuals like you. The research process can (and should) start with your interests, experiences, questions, and your healthy curiosity.

HOW RESEARCH RELATES TO PRACTICE

Social work is an exciting career choice. Students select this profession because they like people and want to help them with such problems as domestic abuse, mental illness, alcohol dependence, and homelessness. As a consequence, social work students are often eager to soak up instruction that will assist them in becoming better counselors or practitioners. They approach practice-oriented courses with enthusiasm and vigor. All goes well until they learn that they must take a research course (sometimes two courses) as part of the requirements for a degree. Immediately some students are resentful. "Research!" they say. "Why do I have to take research?" "I don't want to do research. I want to work with the severely mentally ill." Variations of this point of view are: "I want to work with children" and "I want to work with adolescents who have eating disorders."

Why, then, must social work students study research? Consider a few examples that will demonstrate its usefulness to practitioners of social work.

1. You are asked to direct an HIV/AIDS prevention program. The goal of the program is to supply adolescents with information about how to avoid contracting the AIDS virus. After several months you are convinced that the participants in your program are now more knowledgeable about this issue and that their sexual behavior will reflect what they have learned. How would you convince others of the success of your intervention?

2. You are hired by an agency that provides counseling to families in which children have been sexually assaulted by a family member. You are assigned to work with the offenders. Counseling seems to go well with your first several clients, and now several want to return to their families. How would you go about providing evidence that your intervention was effective—that it was safe to reunite the family members?

3. You manage services in a community agency for people with chronic mental illness and have approached a local foundation in order to obtain funding for an exciting new program that matches clients with volunteers. The foundation asks how you will evaluate the success of the proposed program.

In each of these three examples, some research skills are required—skills that can be applied to other problems and concerns. It is not hard to imagine other projects that might come your way when you are interning or working as a social worker.

SOCIAL WORK STUDENTS AND RESEARCH

Although a few students are delighted to be in their first research course because they are eager to acquire the tools that will allow them to investigate some area of interest, many more do not see the necessity for the course. In fact, Epstein (1987) has observed that "no other part of the social work curriculum has been so consistently received by students with as much groaning, moaning, eye-rolling, bad-mouthing, hyperventilation, and waiver strategizing as the research course" (p. 71). Epstein has cited other studies that document social work students' disinterest in research—what he calls the "resistance phenomenon" (Dane & Epstein, 1985; Kirk & Fisher, 1976; Rosenblatt, 1968).

Briar (1980) has noted a widespread belief among social workers that the same person cannot be both a good researcher and a good practitioner. He continues:

> The personal qualities believed to make a good researcher are seen as handicaps for a practitioner, and the reverse also has been said to be true. The stereotypes are familiar. Researchers are supposedly intellectual, rational, unfeeling creatures who lack the sensitivity to understand the subtle nuances that are of primary concern to practitioners. Practitioners are purported to be intuitive, sensitive, creative persons more akin to artists than scientists; they emphasize the importance of seeing clients as whole persons who should not be subjected to the categorization and atomization that research allegedly requires. It is easy, of course, to show that these stereotypes are invalid, but such beliefs, although less prevalent than they once were, continue to influence the relationship between practice and research in social work. (p. 31)

Unlike psychology, which adopted the Scientist-Professional Training Model shortly after World War II, the dual emphasis on research and practice has not received the same emphasis in social work until fairly recent times. Educators know that students are still exposed to and supervised by social workers who do not conduct any research or evaluate their own practice. These individuals are not the best role models for students and, unfortunately, they perpetuate the myth that social workers do not need research skills.

Having taught research courses for many years, it is quite apparent to me that many students come into social work because they are math phobic. That is, they fear mathematical concepts and quantification. These students are math avoiders and have selected social work because they believe that there will be fewer required courses in research and statistics here than elsewhere.

Why do students choose the career of social work? It's another one of those mysteries. As I told a class not too long ago, there are two things we know for sure: (1) as long as you are a social worker, you'll never run out of work, and (2) they'll never pay you all that you deserve. However, it is also clear that at least some students choose this field because of their anxiety about math. A small study of our own bachelor of social work (BSW) students found that they rated themselves significantly more anxious on a 24-item Mathematics Anxiety Rating Scale than did a cross-section of undergraduates (Royse & Rompf, 1992). More recently, Bob Green and his Virginia colleagues (2001) conducted a study and once again found that social work graduate students reported more research anxiety, computer anxiety, and generally believed that research was less important to their profession than a comparison group of graduate students in psychology and business. However, Hyduk and Large (1999) discovered that among master of social work (MSW) students, those who had participated in prior research projects showed a decrease in fear of research compared to those with no prior participation.

Blame it on your high school algebra teacher or a bad experience in seventh-grade math, but for whatever reason, a sizeable proportion of students coming into this field not only want to help vulnerable populations but also want to do it with as little involvement with research and statistics as possible. Educators know this, and it is our secret agenda to try and change your thinking about the need to acquire research skills. Don't say I didn't warn you. In this age of accountability, students simply do not have the option of choosing *not* to acquire a basic understanding of research.

WHY RESEARCH IS REQUIRED

There are several reasons why you, as a social work student, should take at least one research course. First of all, both as a student and as a social worker you will be reading journal articles and technical reports in which research results are presented. You need to have an ability to distinguish good research from bad, and to be able to evaluate the strengths and weaknesses of the published research. Research studies can be biased or flawed for a lot of different reasons, and you might not be able to detect these reasons without a basic under-standing of research methodology. To make effective use of research that you encounter, whether in journals or unpublished reports produced in your agency, you need to know something about how proper research is conducted.

Like it or not, we are all consumers of research. We hear the results of studies or polls on the television and radio, and we read about studies that are reported in newspapers, magazines, and journals. How do you know if these studies are any good? Could you identify a poorly designed study? What criteria would you use? One bestseller that used thousands of questionnaires to support its conclusions has been called the "functional equivalent of malpractice for surveys." Just because something finds its way into print does not mean that it is based on good research or scholarship. Learn to be a skeptical reader. Ask questions of what you read. Do the findings seem consistent with what you know about the subject? Even a little knowledge of research will help you become a more informed consumer of the information you routinely encounter both in print and on the Internet.

Being an *informed consumer* will lead you to evaluate the reported research and enable *you* to make more substantial contributions when you are called on to disseminate knowledge in your everyday practice. Social workers are often required to prepare reports, conduct in-service training, or make workshop presentations. Information you pull together will be shared not only with fellow professionals but also with clients and the community. As you make greater use of professional journals, you will find that you need an understanding of research in order to comprehend fully what is being reported.

Second, social workers are accountable for their interventions. As a professional, you must be able to determine whether the intervention you are using with a client is making any difference. Could you demonstrate that the client is improving? Or, at the very least, could you show that your intervention has not harmed the client? Even if you are not interested in conducting research on a large scale, you owe it to your clients and yourself to be able to evaluate your practice with them. A research approach discussed in this book, the single system design, will help you evaluate your practice with individual clients.

Accountability is important on another level. Social service agencies vary enormously in size and may employ several to hundreds of social workers. Taxpayers, governmental agencies, and funding sources, such as United Way organizations, often expect social service agencies to conduct or provide evaluation research on such issues as client utilization of the agency's services and the effects or outcomes of the services provided. Agencies must show that they are meeting the needs of their target populations, that their clientele feel satisfied with services, and that the agency's operation is productive and efficient.

A recent newspaper article (Freking, 2006) proclaimed that the federal government's antidrug ad campaign has not been shown to deter children from using drugs. Since 1998 the government has spent about $1.2 billion on television, print, and radio ads but the research company paid to evaluate the success of this campaign found that the ads had "no significant favorable effects" and didn't deter children from trying marijuana or getting them to stop smoking. Unfortunately, it was concluded that more 12- to 13-year-olds and girls were trying the drug after seeing the ads. Knowing just these results from the evaluation, would you recommend that more money be poured into these antidrug ads?

Suppose you become a program director or manager in a social service organization and the executive director wants you to begin a new program. The director insists that the program must have a good evaluation system built into it. Would you know how to go about evaluating a social service program? Would you know a poor evaluation if you saw one? Programs are sometimes funded with the provision that they demonstrate some impact on the problem. This provision usually means that research in some form or fashion is required. Faced as we are with major social problems and fairly limited amounts of monies that can be applied to these problems, it is incumbent on social workers to create and maintain programs that have the best success rates.

As a new social worker fresh from the university, you might be asked to conduct research to meet some reporting or accreditation requirement. Occasionally, students tell me how surprised they were on their first jobs when they were assigned a research project—especially when it was not even discussed during the initial employment interview. Would you be more interested in learning how to conduct research if you knew you would be responsible for conducting research or evaluating a program in your next job?

Third, the Council on Social Work Education (CSWE), a national, nongovernmental accreditation and standard-setting organization for baccalaureate and master's degree programs, requires research as one of the five required professional content areas. In order for the institution's program to be accredited by CSWE, each college and university that grants degrees in social work must periodically submit documentation attesting to the fact that it conforms with curriculum policy. The council's curriculum policy requires that social work students (at both the BSW and MSW levels) understand that "a spirit of inquiry" and "informed criticism" are the bases of scientific thinking and lead to the acquisition of knowledge and the application of that knowledge in practice. Research content is expected to help students learn the critical appreciation and use of research and program evaluation as they learn the methods for evaluating service delivery in all areas of practice. The clear expectation is that students will move from a position of only being able to consume research to being able to evaluate practice systematically.

A fourth reason you are in a research class is because of this language in the National Association of Social Workers' Code of Ethics (1996):

SECTION 5.02

(a) Social workers should monitor and evaluate policies, the implementation of programs, and practice interventions.

(b) Social workers should promote and facilitate evaluation and research to contribute to the development of knowledge.

(c) Social workers should critically examine and keep current with emerging knowledge relevant to social work and fully use evaluation and research evidence in their professional practice.

The Code of Ethics asserts that we have a responsibility for both evaluating practice and building knowledge. Research improves our practice and allows us to test new innovations.

As professional social workers, we must advocate for our clients by conducting research on social policies at the state and national levels. While it may seem unlikely that you would ever be involved in such research, consider for a moment the extent to which most social workers are affected by state and national policies. Some of these policies are good and some could use modification. How might you go about convincing legislators and government officials that cutting funds to social services will have an adverse effect on your client population? Can you see the value of having "hard data" to show skeptics how many people depend on certain social services and how their lives might be affected if funds were cut? The profession needs researchers who can show that cuts in social service programs ultimately result in greater tax burdens. I am convinced that greater funding for social services will come as social workers are better able to demonstrate that adequate levels of social services are cost-effective for reducing or eliminating some of the major social problems facing us today.

Also, you need to be comfortable with both consuming and conducting research because otherwise you may not be practicing the most effective treatment available. Myers and Thyer (1997) have raised the issue this way: "A client sees a clinical social worker about a psychosocial disorder for which there is a treatment that has been demonstrated effective through repeated, well-designed outcome studies. Does the client have the right to receive this validated treatment, or does the social worker have the latitude to provide another, unsupported treatment?" (p. 288). Most of us would probably agree that clients deserve the best intervention available, not one that is delivered simply because "that's the way I have always treated this problem" or "this is what I learned 30 years ago in graduate school."

Social workers who do not keep current on the literature and research in their fields are in danger of practicing primitive, if not incompetent, social work. Interventions are not equally effective, and social workers need to be able to inform clients why, on the basis of empirical studies, one particular treatment is recommended over another. Although Myers and Thyer (1997) list 13 different psychosocial disorders (for example, bulimia, chronic pain, social phobia) and the empirically validated treatments for them, it is also apparent that such knowledge has not been developed for all the problems clients may bring. This is where you come in. As a social worker who can understand as well as conduct research, you will be able to identify those interventions that should be used with specific client groups and those that shouldn't. You have an ethical obligation to do as much.

Along this line, Gambrill (1995) argues that an empirically based social work practice exposes fraud and quackery and those practitioners who make questionable claims of effectiveness. I like that notion—that social work professionals should be consumer advocates for the interventions our clients receive. And how does one advocate for effective programs without data?

At this point in your career, evaluating policies and attempting to build knowledge may not interest you, but once you are engaged in practice full time you may make discoveries—perhaps you will want to report on the effectiveness of some new treatment approach or exciting innovation that you have devised. There might be a conference in sunny Orlando that would be interested in your making a presentation, or a journal that would like to have your article on the intervention. In other words, you need competence in research methods to help you achieve your potential as a contributing member of the social work profession. There will be times when even the most thoroughly convinced "I've-always-wanted-to-be-just-a-clinician" wishes that he or she understood a little more about research. By knowing research, you position yourself to reach higher goals and even to increase your income. For instance, some social workers become managers and administrators within their agencies or districts; others develop copyrighted instruments or interventions that are sold commercially; still others become nationally recognized experts, consultants, and even faculty!

JUNK SCIENCE

Anyone who has ever spent time searching for information on the Internet soon discovers a lot of self-proclaimed "experts" out there whose opinions aren't worth two dead penlight batteries. There are, for instance, supposed nutritional supplements based on exotic herbs that are dangerous to one's health. This is not to say that their advocates aren't bright, or don't mount convincing arguments occasionally, but what they often attempt to pass off as scientific fact is an assortment of false claims, opinions, and biased data while ignoring the findings of others with whom they disagree. Their data may be distorted or presented in such a way as to lead to an erroneous conclusion. While statistics are often the hallmark of good, scientific studies, their presence does not necessarily mean that the reader can turn off his or her brain and suspend more in-depth thinking about the problem.

For instance, a recent report by the Centers for Disease Control (CDC) found that black people die of fires at twice the rate of white people. That statistic does not prove that blacks use more candles than whites, smoke in bed more frequently, or are more careless around fire. The statistics that say 2.63 blacks per 100,000 population die from fires compared to 1.18 whites does not explain that people living in poverty tend to live in older housing with fewer smoke detectors. Since many blacks live in cities, they may be more likely to live in apartments in multistoried buildings that are harder to get out of in emergencies. And also, arson rates are higher in big cities (e.g., some suspicious fires could be set by drug dealers or criminals who want to retaliate for reporting them to police). Thus, a statistic by itself is a single piece of information; it should not be taken as an entire explanation or proof of one's pet hypothesis.

By the end of the book you should become skeptical of information found on the Internet or in reports or testimony which does not help you to know how the "facts" were determined or the data gathered. If quantitative data are being presented, you'll know that legitimate researchers generally follow agreed-upon principles for conducting scientific studies that involve posing plausible explanations, testing hypotheses, describing a methodology for gathering data that others can follow, and examining the reliability and validity of the data they collect. Both qualitative and quantitative manuscripts submitted to journals for publication or professional conferences are reviewed by other researchers and experts who point out problem areas. These people are also empowered to vote to reject those papers that have flawed methodology and/or apparent bias—such as data that are selectively interpreted to fit the author's point of view. The test of a good study is when other researchers who were not involved with the project agree that it makes a contribution to our understanding of a phenomenon.

Fabricated research (this includes studies that have been made up as well as those in which the findings have been purposely distorted or slanted to support an author's claims) can be difficult to spot if you assume that everything appearing in print must be true. Challenge those outrageous claims and look at how the "evidence" was gathered. If you employ fabricated or false research in making decisions about your clients, you could be held responsible—possibly even charged with malpractice. Social work students need to know the difference between good and bad research. As Katzer, Cook, and Crouch (1998) note, "In all of the social sciences the literature contains more errors and erroneous conclusions than the average nonresearcher is usually led to believe" (p. 6).

Here are some questions to help you evaluate Internet information.

- Who is the author? Does he or she have credibility? (Sometimes academic degrees lend respectability but they may also be purchased from phony universities on the Internet. More important is whether the author has published findings in respectable academic or scholarly journals. Be suspicious of information where the author's name is not given and where contact information such as street and city addresses are missing.)
- What is the author's perspective? (The author's bias may be very apparent or subtle. However, objective writing usually includes both sides of an argument—including those perspectives that don't support the author's claims.)
- Who or what is the publishing source? (If the author is affiliated with an university or widely recognized organization such as the American Cancer Society, then the source may be more credible than if the domain comes from the ".com" or corporate world where someone is attempting to make money from readers of the Web site.)
- What is the supporting documentation? (Internet articles that do not support their claims with legitimate studies listed in a bibliography or references—that you can check out for yourself—are to be avoided. Scholarly writers know it is important to inform their readers about the pertinent studies and literature on the topic that they have identified. If there is no—or very little—companion or comparison literature, then you the reader should be distrustful. Documentation includes the data that findings are based on. The "evidence" being provided to you should contain sufficient details that you can conclude if the author is talking, for instance, about a 2%, 22%, or 62% phenomenon.)
- How did you find this information? (If you were surfing for information and were directed to a Web site from another site that has dubious origins and doubtful claims, don't be surprised if the content of the second

Web site is also untrustworthy. Web sites found by using Internet search engines will not necessarily bring you the most reliable information. When the quality of information is important, specialized search engines associated with university libraries (e.g., MEDLINE®, PsycINFO®, etc.) will supply scholarly articles that have been reviewed by professionals in the field—a process called peer review—and will be the most honest and authoritative information available.)

Evidence-Based Practice

Social work educators want their students to be skilled, expert practitioners. We have a vested interest in your success, but we can't do it all. Our profession's future depends on you becoming the most competent practitioner possible. Accountability is required of all social workers and it mandates that you not be ineffective or make problems worse. In recent years most professions have embraced the concept of **Evidence-Based Practice** (EBP). EBP involves the use of interventions which have been shown to be beneficial to clients. The central notion is that practitioners shouldn't use interventions simply because they are comfortable with them or because "that's the way the agency has always done it," but instead social workers employ the treatments that have been shown to be clinically relevant because scientific investigations have evaluated them.

In choosing interventions, the social worker should ask questions such as, "What has been shown to work with this type of problem?" Or, "What intervention is the most effective with this type of client?" Questions of this type will lead the practitioner to information which has to be assessed in terms of whether it is credible, methodologically sound, from a well-respected source, and convincing in terms of what is known about success and prior interventions with the client group. Most importantly, the intervention is not applied without evaluating the clients' progress so that it can be determined if the intervention really is effective at the local level. We must show that our activities are in the client's best interest—that they are ethical, goal-directed, effective, and efficient (Rosen, 2003).

Much more in the way of being accountable is expected of today's practitioner. To prepare yourself to be the most conscientious and evidence-based practitioner, you'll need to learn, at a minimum, how to sort the "junk" from the good science so that you can apply the strongest research-supported interventions it in your practice. Allow this book to show you how to recognize good and poor data collection methods and research designs. Try to view research as a tool that can help you solve problems or support your suspicions and hypotheses.

Perhaps the best way to acquire the stance of viewing research as a useful tool is to think about a question or problem that you would like to investigate. This question should be one that interests you—one that piques your curiosity. Keep this question in the back of your mind as each new chapter is presented. As you read, think about how that information could be harnessed to answer your question, but also how you can use that technique or approach to make you the best possible social work practitioner.

One of the characteristics of social work research is that it is applied; it seeks knowledge that will improve the lives of our clients and make this world a little bit of a better place. Research begins when people like you develop questions from real-life situations and observations of human nature and social problems, and become concerned about the lack of answers. In some instances, a thorough search of library resources may provide needed information. But if it does not, you may have identified a gap in our knowledge base. Social work has no shortage of problems needing additional investigation, and many opportunities exist for you as a researcher to make important contributions to our field. If you had the time and the funding to explore one unanswered question, what would it be?

KEY TERM

Evidence-Based Practice (EBP)

SELF-REVIEW

(Answers at the end of the book)

1. The Scientist-Professional Training Model is closely associated with which discipline:
   a. social work
   b. psychology
   c. anthropology
   d. theology
2. List five reasons discussed in this chapter why social work students should study research methods.
3. What is the purpose of the Council on Social Work Education?
   a. accreditation of social work programs
   b. peer training of social work educators
   c. marketing of social work programs
4. T or F. The NASW Code of Ethics requires social workers to monitor and evaluate their practice, their programs, and the policies that shape their interventions.
5. Summarize what "empirically based practice" means.
6. What is the chief characteristic of social work research?
7. Where does research start?

QUESTIONS FOR CLASS DISCUSSION

1. What are your fears about taking a research class?
2. What do you hope to learn from this class?
3. What experiences have you had that might help in this class? Describe any research-related experiences you may have had.

4. What are the problems that might develop when a profession's knowledge base and research lag behind its practice?

5. As a class, make a list of problems and questions that you think need to be researched.

6. Have you ever come across a piece of research that you thought was worthless? Why did you have this opinion?

7. What stereotypes do you have about researchers?

8. In what ways could research be used to affect a local, state, or national policy that you think needs to be changed?

9. Discuss ways you might go about investigating the success of the programs in the three examples at the beginning of this chapter (HIV awareness, sexually abused children, and persons with chronic mental illness).

10. Make a list of reasons why it is important for social workers to engage in empirically based practice.

RESOURCES AND REFERENCES

Beers, C. (1910). A mind that found itself: An autobiography. New York: Longmans, Green & Co.

Briar, S. (1980). Toward the integration of practice and research. In David Fanshel (Ed.), *Future of social work research*. Washington, DC: National Association of Social Workers, 31–37.

Dane, E., & Epstein, L. (1985). A dark horse in continued education programming at the postmaster's level: Monitoring and evaluation skills for social workers in middle management. *Journal of Continuing Social Work Education, 3(2)*, 3–8.

Epstein, L. (1987). Pedagogy of the perturbed: Teaching research to the reluctants. *Journal of Teaching in Social Work, 1(1)*, 71–89.

Freking, K. (2006). Anti-drug ads called ineffective. The Cincinnati Enquirer, August 26, 2006, A10.

Gambrill, E. (1995). Behavioral social work: Past, present, and future. *Research on Social Work Practice, 5*, 460–484.

Green, R. G., Bretzin, A., Leininger, C., & Stauffer, R. (2001). Research learning attributes of graduate students in social work, psychology, and business. *Journal of Social Work Education, 37(2)*, 333–341.

Hyduk, C. A., & Large, S. J. (1999). Factors that influence fear of research in MSW students: Implications for social work educators. *ARETE, 23*, 1–9.

Katzer, J., Cook, K. H., & Crouch, W. W. (1998). *Evaluating information: A guide for users of social science research*. Boston: McGraw-Hill.

Kirk, S., & Fisher, J. (1976). Do social workers understand research? *Journal of Education for Social Work, 2(1)*, 63–71.

Myers, L. L., & Thyer, B. A. (1997). Should social work clients have the right to effective treatment? *Social Work, 42*, 288–298.

National Association of Social Workers (1996). *Code of ethics*. Washington, DC: Author.

Rompf, E. L., & Royse, D. (1994). Choice of social work as a career: Possible influences. *Journal of Social Work Education, 30*, 163–171.

Rosen, A. (2003). Evidence-based social work practice: Challenges and promise. *Social Work Research, 27*, 197–208.

Rosenblatt, A. (1968). The practitioners' use and evaluation of research. *Social Work, 13*, 53–59.

Royse, D. (1994). *How do I know it's abuse? Identifying and countering emotional mistreatment from friends and family members*. Springfield, IL: CC Thomas.

Royse, D., & Edwards, T. (1989). Communicating about disability: Attitudes and preferences of persons with physical handicaps. *Rehabilitation Counseling Bulletin, 32(3)*, 203–209.

Royse, D., & Rompf, E. L. (1992). Math anxiety: A comparison of social work and non-social work students. *Journal of Social Work Education, 28(3)*, 270–277.

Royse, D., Rompf, E. L., & Dhooper, S. S. (1991). Childhood trauma and adult life satisfaction in a random adult sample. *Psychological Reports, 69*, 1227–1231.

ASSIGNMENT 1.1: Who Are the Students in This Research Class?

Objective: *To introduce you to each other and to demonstrate, on a beginning level, how patterns and themes exist within a collection of data.*

The Task: Interview two people from your research class that you don't know, asking them the following questions. (Your instructor may want to pool all of the responses from class to see if any common elements or themes emerge. Learn the names of those you interview.)

Respondent #1   Respondent #2

1. Have you completed any other research courses?
   If yes, how many?

2. Name one skill, talent, or life experience you have
   that a researcher might find useful.

3. How important would you say that it is for social
   workers to know how to conduct research? (Use a scale
   from 1 to 10, with 1 equaling *not very important* and
   10 equaling *very important*.)

4. Why have you chosen to be a social worker?

5. What is one thing you hope to acquire from this class?

6. What is your favorite food, movie, or song?

_____
Student's Name

ASSIGNMENT 1.2: Where Does Research Start?

Objective: *To help you apply forthcoming content in the book to a specific problem, population, or intervention; and to introduce you to the instructor.*

Scenario: Imagine that a wealthy philanthropist has agreed to fund your salary for one year, providing that you conduct research about some problem that concerns social workers.

1. What question or problem would you investigate?

2. Give a rationale explaining why you think that problem is more important than any others.

3. How would you go about conducting research on the problem or question?

4. What do you think you would need to learn?

5. List three facts relating to this problem that you already know.

2 CHAPTER | The Way Research Proceeds

Research in the social sciences usually results from a real problem someone has encountered. The process is logical and similar to the problem-solving model so familiar to social workers. You may be surprised to find that the research process is not much different from the way that you normally go about finding solutions. This chapter will provide an overview of the various steps.

The research process (sometimes called the scientific method) is based on the assumptions that the natural world is essentially orderly and that observed phenomena have some stimulus or cause. If the laws of nature are not haphazard in their operation, then it follows that laws that govern the phenomena we observe can be learned. Our knowledge about the world is obtained through the use of a logical sequence of steps. It is only when we don't know very much about a phenomenon that there seem to be no discernible laws. The more we know about something, the better we can see certain laws or principles in action. Let's take an example of a problematic situation suggested by Leedy (1974) that illustrates a research-like process.

You leave your home to go to class. You are running a little bit late and are in a hurry. You put the key in your car's ignition and turn it. Nothing happens. At first you don't believe your bad luck, turning the key again and again. Nothing happens. You pull the key from the ignition and look at it to make sure that it's the right key. You try again. Nothing. At this point you almost immediately pose questions to yourself. Did I leave the lights on? Is there enough gas? You select a logical explanation and begin the "research" process. Suppose you have a notion that you left the car lights on all night.

You can test the hypothesis of a weak battery by turning on the car's radio or headlights. If they work, then you can assume that the battery still has a charge, and you can move on to another hypothesis. You remember telling your brother to put gas in the car, and you wonder whether or not he did. You look at the fuel indicator and see that it registers "Full." Does the gauge work properly? Assuming it does, you move on to the next hypothesis: Perhaps your 10-year-old car is in need of spark plugs, or isn't in gear. Those of you who have had the experience of owning an old car could probably proceed with such hypotheses longer than anyone else would be interested. The point is that questions needing investigation flow from the problematic situation. As this example reveals, research involves an orderly thought process that moves from what is known to what is not known. Numerous and varied hypotheses may be tested. Information gained leads to the consideration of other questions or hypotheses.

THE SCIENTIFIC METHOD: A.K.A. THE QUANTITATIVE RESEARCH PROCESS

As illustrated in the example above, the research process is composed of a few relatively simple steps or stages. For instructional purposes, these steps are presented as being sequential. However, sometimes they occur out of order. For instance, once a question is formulated, we might start thinking about how to collect the necessary data before we go to the library to start a literature search.

This chapter presents what is generally known as the traditional "scientific method" and is generally the approach followed by quantitative researchers. You should know, however, that qualitative researchers are not locked into following these steps in quite the same way. After discussing the research process steps in the quantitative tradition, we'll then examine each step from the qualitative perspective.

Step 1: Posing a Question or Stating a Hypothesis

Before you can begin conducting research you often must limit yourself to one question (or at least to a small set of related questions) or one specific topic to investigate. Ideas may emerge from observations of clients, personal experiences, discussions with colleagues, or reading the literature pertinent to a certain topic. Research questions often stem from a problem to be solved or wanting to better understand some behavior. At least initially, the question or questions that drive the study might be somewhat broad. For example, you might want to know why students drop out of college.

Research questions may come about as a result of **deduction** (where knowledge of a theory or general principle allows you to make a prediction or an application to a single specific case). Deductive studies often involve testing some hypothesis. Or, research questions may stem from induction. **Induction** or inductive thinking is where your observations about a case or cases seem to suggest a theory or set of principles. For instance, let's say you are a social work intern in a children's hospital and receive a 2-year-old child who has been eating crumbling plaster in his dilapidated apartment. This may cause you to wonder if this problem is widespread. What is causing it? Is it boredom, lack of adult supervision, or hunger? If this case motivated you to want to find out more by collecting data and looking for a pattern, then you would be going about the research inductively. Induction goes from the specific to the general.

Unlike research questions in other disciplines, questions in social work generally stem from problems that actually need to be solved. We tend as professionals to be inductive rather than deductive thinkers because our research tends to have more of an applied focus.

Once a question has been roughly posed or drafted, it will often need to be restated as a researchable question. Not all questions can be answered, and the purpose of research is to generate information that can be verified by others. "Why is there suffering?" is an example of a question best left to philosophers or theologians. Social scientists in the quantitative tradition are interested in concrete, tangible, objective findings that can be **replicated** (reproduced) by others.

Sometimes, however, it is possible to give a slightly different emphasis to an expansive question like "Why is there suffering?" and thereby make it a researchable question. "How do children with leukemia explain the origin of their illnesses?" is a question that could be investigated. Often, very broad questions can be narrowed down by considering specific manifestations of the problem or how you would go about collecting data.

There is a definite knack to developing a good question. If too few words are used, the question tends to be too large to investigate. "What causes child abuse?" is an example of a research question that needs to be narrowed down. There is nothing wrong with wanting to provide answers to such questions, but practically speaking, the research needed to answer them would be well beyond the resources of most undergraduate or graduate students. As you read about child abuse, you will discover that the role of certain factors has already been demonstrated. It is usually better to ask questions that allow you to examine a specific theory or perhaps a small part of the problem. A better question might be "Were child abusers abused themselves as children?" or "Do perpetrators of child abuse tend to be chemically dependent?"

Questions that are asked in research studies are often very specific. This specificity is reflected in the titles of journal articles. Browse through an issue of *Research on Social Work Practice*. The articles will demonstrate how narrowly focused the studies are. Hypotheses and research questions will be precisely worded. The research process starts with *either* a question to be answered *or* with a hypothesis to be tested. Most students find it easier to understand the research process in terms of asking questions rather than testing hypotheses. However, a **hypothesis** is simply a formal version of a hunch or speculation that usually is based on some theory. A good hypothesis is one that clearly expresses a statement that can be empirically tested about the relationship of two or more variables. Data are gathered to see if they will *support* the hypothesis. (Social scientists don't *prove* hypotheses.)

Hypotheses and research questions are both legitimate starting points for the research process as long as they are not frivolous or unethical. One's hypothesis can be converted into a research question and vice versa, as seen below:

> *Example of a hypothesis:* Adolescent female athletes are more likely to disclose an eating disorder than females not involved in athletics.
>
> *Example of a research question:* Are eating disorders reported more often by adolescent female athletes or adolescent females not participating in organized athletic competition?

Elaborate studies may have several major hypotheses as well as a number of minor hypotheses.

Occasionally **null hypotheses** are used. These state that there is no difference between the groups being compared (for example, adolescent males are no more impulsive than adolescent females). Researchers sometimes hope to find sufficient evidence to allow for *rejection* of the null hypothesis. The researcher does not have to believe that there is no difference or no relationship in order to state a null hypothesis.

> *Example of a null hypothesis:* Female adolescents who participate in organized sports are no more likely to report eating disorders than female adolescents who are not involved in athletics.

When you write hypotheses, aim for precision and avoid the "you" construction as in this example:

> *Poor:* The lower the education level, the more likely you are to be unhappy. If you come from a broken family, you are less likely to be happy.
>
> *Better:* Adults with less than 12 years of education will have lower life satisfaction scores than adults who have completed 12 or more years of education.

Hypotheses, like research questions, may be developed from theories, literature, or interactions with colleagues or clients. Hypotheses might not always be stated but might emerge from exploratory or qualitative studies to be tested in future research.

The Importance of Theory   Theories vary considerably in their complexity, their perspective or orientation, and the amount of evidence that can be mustered to support them. For a good example of how various theories from different disciplines might be used to explain a social phenomenon, consider the concept of altruism—why are some people more altruistic than others?

Checklist for Evaluating Hypotheses

- Does it make a clear statement? Do you understand it? Poor hypothesis: *Cancer survivors will have different feelings about the relationships in their lives.*

- Is it specific, not vague? Can you determine who the research subjects will be and how the relationship will be tested? Poor hypothesis: *Previous accident victims will demonstrate a more conservative approach.*

- Does one variable seem to influence or affect another variable? (Is there a direction to the relationship?) Poor hypothesis: *There will be a difference in motivation scores and length of time on the job.*

- Would a research project testing the hypothesis be realistic and feasible to conduct? Poor hypothesis: *The amount of verbal abuse that older adults have received in their lifetimes will be proportionate to the self-images that they draw while doodling at restaurants waiting for their food to arrive.*

- Would an investigation of the hypothesis add important new information to our knowledge base? Poor hypothesis: *The minutes spent in real, meaningful conversation among first-year college students will be directly related to the minutes spent dreaming the night before.*

According to social learning theory, altruism might be acquired by children who learn it from generous role models. However, sociobiologists might argue that an "altruist" gene developed because sharing behavior promotes greater survival of the species. From a psychological standpoint, altruism might be explained because it serves some inner, egoistic motive. From this perspective, even helping others may result in some self-benefit (for example, a positive mood state).

The research you do, or at least the way you go about it, is strongly influenced by your theoretical orientation. If you assume that altruism is caused by one's genetic inheritance, then the types of questions you'll explore will be vastly different from those you'd employ if your assumption is that people learn altruism by observing others. Your theoretical orientation directs your attention to events that are assumed to be important and allows you to ignore those that are expected to be irrelevant. A good theory explains, organizes, and predicts (Munson, 1983). It allows you to go beyond the known facts, suggesting what you might expect in the future and allowing you to integrate the facts you already have. From theories we conceptualize and create hypotheses—a process that might lead to new interventions.

A good theory focuses attention, saves effort, and builds on existent knowledge. Theories lead to predictions about the world in which we operate and might be likened to mental maps that suggest avenues or directions.

Why is a theoretical framework so important? Let me give you an example from a practicum seminar that I led one summer. As was our custom, the students each took about ten minutes at the beginning of class to report the progress of their clients or to share something new they had learned in the previous week. When it was Marcie's turn, she reported working with an alcoholic client who was heavily into denial. He maintained that he did not have a drinking problem, although he was beginning to have some liver complications, and that he could quit drinking any time he wanted. Since she wasn't making much headway with him, Marcie, noticing that her client was a chain smoker, asked if he could give up cigarette smoking as a way of showing that he could quit drinking. She reasoned that he might be more willing to quit drinking once he realized that he could live without cigarettes.

"Marcie," I asked when she had finished her account, "where did that intervention come from?"

"What do you mean?" she asked.

"Who has suggested that asking clients to give up their cigarettes helps them give up alcohol?"

"Well," she said, looking skyward for inspiration, "no one that I can think of. I thought of this all by myself."

"What happens," I asked, "if your client tries to quit smoking but fails? Could that experience convince him that he couldn't quit drinking even if he wanted to?"

"Oh," she said, her face blushing. "I didn't think of that."

At that point, we began a discussion about the importance of theory and how it can help guide our efforts, whether we are researchers or direct service practitioners. Theories are equally valuable to both. Practitioners employ theories in their interventions, and these theories provide guidelines or suggest techniques, as well as offer explanations of observed phenomena.

It should also be noted that theories have often emerged from value orientations. This principle can be seen most sharply when we look at dated, historical theories like those of Freud and the way he viewed women and children. Bettelheim's (1967) blaming autism on "cold" mothers who happened to be career-oriented is also an infamous example. It makes one wonder: What theories that we currently hold precious will be discarded 20 or 30 years from now? More recently, Emery (2005) has commented on the lack of evidence supporting the "Parent Alienation Syndrome." He cautions us that while clinical experience provides fertile ground for "creative hypotheses," at the same time we must keep in mind that "case studies are valuable for generating hypotheses but not for confirming hypotheses" (p. 10). Theories provide guides for thinking about the interrelationship of various factors in causing or stimulating a problem. We should not, however, overlook the fact that theories evolve over time and either get richer or they go out of vogue because researchers can't find sufficient evidence to support them.

Although logical positivists (quantitatively oriented researchers) strive to be "objective" so that their science can be "value-free," in some ways it's like trying to scoop a cup of sunlight. Social and cultural values do affect our learning, the people we become, the questions we want to explore, the explanations of phenomena that we attend to and those that we ignore. Our values affect our research at every level—theories, hypotheses, choice of methodologies and variables, data analysis strategies—whether we are conscious of our values or not.

Are our observations and views of the world influenced by our education? Our ethnicity or gender? Our religion, social class, past experiences? What do you think?

Sidebar: How Selective Attention Affects Point of View

A couple of summers ago I was visiting a quaint historical village in the Eastern part of the United States. I asked the driver of the car, a college graduate,

"Is there is much diversity in this town?"
"Oh, yes," she said, "we have doctors, lawyers, college professors—a little bit of everything."

What kind of findings do you think the driver of car might have reported if we had asked her to conduct a study of the diversity in her community? How might her cultural values be different from yours?

Step 2: Reviewing the Literature

Once you have a question or hypothesis in mind, the second step is to review the professional literature to see what others have already written about the topic. There are many good reasons for learning as much as possible about your subject before beginning to conduct a study. A careful review of the literature can save you a lot of unnecessary work and prevent you from wasting your time studying a problem that has already been thoroughly investigated.

As you discover how others have studied the problem, approaches that you hadn't considered may be suggested. You may find new instruments or ways for measuring your **dependent variable.** (The dependent variable is the topic of your investigation—what you are trying to explain or predict. More on this later in the chapter.) And, a solid review of the literature will help you ground your research interest and possible findings within a theoretical framework. Finally, acquainting yourself with the literature can provide you with data to compare with your own findings. Particularly if you are evaluating the success of an intervention, you may want to know how successful other approaches have been.

Journals sometimes have a particular theoretical orientation that influences the articles they publish. Sometimes this "slant" is very apparent—as in this example:

> The patient was a 40-year-old male who reported at age 3 he had gone into his parents' bedroom and seen his father's leg draped over his mother. The memory was associated with narcissistic rage. . . . Interpretation of the erotic transference allowed the patient to work through the anxiety associated with his sexual feelings and understand the Oedipal issues surfacing in his struggle with his career choice.

One thing is for sure—often you will find so much literature on a topic that you are certain to have a large number of titles to choose from. In fact, the amount of literature available may be almost unmanageable. For instance, there is so much literature on schizophrenia, it would take years to read all the relevant journal articles and books. Once again we can see the utility of having a research question that is relatively narrow in its focus. How might this topic be narrowed down? (Hints: By searching for explanations of etiology or genetic evidence; examining diagnostic criteria for different types of schizophrenia; looking at the use of specific antipsychotic drugs for treatment; studying psychosocial intervention and management or the history of institutional treatment of schizophrenia; or focusing on relapse by searching for partial hospitalization or day treatment programs; and, finally, by limiting the search to specific populations or age groups.)

Starting a Literature Search   There are several ways to begin a literature search; you might use only one approach or many, depending on your success in finding relevant articles of interest. If you love to browse in libraries, a laidback approach is to check the subject index to find where the books on your topic are located. Then examine the books on those shelves. As you review these books, you may find references to other books or journals.

The method I sometimes use is to go to specific journals that I know publish articles on the subject of my literature review. For instance, *Child Abuse and Neglect: An International Journal* would be a logical place to start if one wanted to find journal articles on child abuse. You might also look at *Child Welfare* and skim the table of contents in issues of the last two years. If you find several articles of interest, they almost always direct you to additional journal articles or studies that you can use to further explore what is known about your question. Journals tend to be very specialized so you should not assume, for instance, that if *Social Work* carried no articles on child abuse last year—that no other journal would either.

A third (and perhaps best) approach when you want to conduct a serious search of the literature is to use the various bibliographic databases available at your university. For instance, PsycINFO is comprehensive and a good place to begin searching for just about any topic in the social sciences. You probably can access it electronically through your university. Similarly, *Social Work Abstracts* will be a good source of articles on topics that are of special interest to social workers—such as adoption and foster care topics. Some libraries will carry a regular subscription to *Social Work Abstracts* and it will be kept in the periodical section. Other schools may make it available electronically. Examples of other databases that can be searched by computer are:

ERIC—For information on education-based concerns (for example, school dropouts, adolescent pregnancies, learning disorders).

MEDLINE—For articles on medical-related problems (for example, depression, autism, attention-deficit hyperactivity disorder, anorexia).

InfoTrac® College Edition—Contains both abstracts and full-text articles.

First Search®—This is a database of databases. Your library may subscribe to all of them or to a selected set. Some of the databases contained in First Search include Article1st, Contents1st, Books in Print, Dissertation Abstracts, NewsAbs, SocioAbs, SocSciAbs, and WorldCat.

Don't make the assumption that all databases are the same, that if there was nothing on "long-term care ombudsmen" in ERIC, there would be nothing in MEDLINE. As Kemp and Brustman (1997) have noted, while there is duplication, databases will vary in terms of the number of relevant matches—some producing stronger results than others. If you don't find a sufficient number of resources in one database, consult another. Another useful strategy is to search using different terms—"nursing home ombudsmen" or even "ombud" instead of "long-term care ombudsmen" might be useful. Use of a long string of key words will generally limit the number of "hits." Shorter terms are usually better for receiving the best pool of articles.

The world of electronic databases changes rapidly, which is good news for you. It is quicker and easier to search for literature by computer than ever before. Computerized databases abound and many more exist than I have attempted to list. LexisNexis, for example, could be useful if you are interested in a topic usually associated with the criminal justice system (e.g., home incarceration). And your reference librarian will know of other specialized databases on such topics as AIDS, child abuse, or gerontology if you ask.

If you have never searched by computer for professional literature, don't be intimidated. Most of the databases operate from menus and are simple enough that even beginners can use them. Once you learn your way around, you are likely to encounter just one problem: finding too much literature.

If your search comes back with thousands of "hits," then your topic is much too broad. Here are your options for narrowing the topic down:

- Add key words (for example, "suspensions *and* high school" not just "suspensions").
- Skim the most current titles to determine if other key words may eliminate some of the citations that do not interest you.
- Limit the search by language, year, or type of publication.
- Skim the titles and/or abstracts for those articles that are themselves reviews of the literature on your topic.

If you find barely any literature, here are a few tips:

- Substitute synonyms (for example, try "adolescent" instead of "teenager").
- Think categorically (for example, "parenting styles," "disciplinary techniques").
- Go further than the most recent three years (for example, five or seven years).
- Check your spelling (for example, "bulimia" not "bulemia").
- Use fewer words ("parenting" rather than "parental disciplinary styles").
- Look in a different database.
- Try variations of the key words ("juvenile delinquent" and "teen").

If you can find a recent article that has already surveyed the literature on your topic, it will save you a great deal of time. While you may still want to read the studies cited in that paper, you can use your time more effectively if you can locate a review article than if you have to review all of the literature yourself. For instance, Kessler, White, and Nelson (2003) have authored "Group Treatments for Women Sexually Abused as Children: A Review of the Literature and Recommendations for Future Outcome Research." Onwuegbuzie and Wilson (2003) have examined what we know about statistics anxiety in "Statistics Anxiety: Nature, Etiology, Antecedents, Effects, and Treatments—a

Comprehensive Review of the Literature." Thaxton, Emshoff, and Guessous (2005) have examined a number of studies in "Prostate Cancer Support Groups: A Literature Review."

You can't always tell by the title, however. The title of the article, "The Prevention of Mental Disorders in Children and Adolescents: Future Research and Public Policy Recommendations" by Dulmus and Rapp-Paglicci (2000) doesn't sound like a literature review but is described in the abstract as being one that examines the research on the prevention of mental illness in children and adolescents.

Even if you don't discover titles or abstracts clearly suggesting a review of the literature on your topic, most articles in professional journals will contain some survey of the literature. Whether the article contains an extensive or more restricted list of references will depend somewhat on the journal and the nature of the article. It is likely, however, that the literature review stopped two years or more before the article was published. (It may take an article three to ten months to be examined by a journal's reviewers, and even if no revisions are required of the author, many journals have a backlog of a year or longer before a manuscript is published.) So, even if you find a rather complete review of the literature in an article published in 2006, the author's references may not include any sources published later than 2005 and possibly 2004. Odds are, however, that you won't be so lucky as to find one article that does all your library work for you.

While some information databases may contain book titles, do not be surprised if all of the references produced from a computer search are found in journals (many of which you may not have known existed). New knowledge in a field is often first introduced or reported in journal articles. Unlike magazines that are written largely for public entertainment, journals report studies and new thinking about old problems for students, professionals, and scholars. Journals usually lack vivid graphics and multicolor advertisements.

An information database like InfoTrac College Edition may mix some professional journal articles with magazines like *Newsweek* and *Time*. While these sources are useful for providing current statistics about social problems and experts' opinions, they are not considered professional literature. Many instructors will not count magazine or newspaper articles when students are given the assignment of preparing a bibliography on a special topic.

A number of social work journals are listed on the next page to help you become familiar with some of the important journals in our profession. This listing is by no means comprehensive. Many more journals exist than could conveniently be listed here, and the number of new journals has increased in recent years. Also, many specialized journals (for example, *Crime and Delinquency, Gerontologist, Evaluation Review*) are not listed but may be of interest to some students.

Such journals as these and other specialized journals allow for in-depth reporting and discussion of a topic because they are written for a specific audience. Typically, a journal article starts with a literature review or a historical overview of the problem and then explains the current study. At the end of the article, the findings are discussed in terms of implications for professionals. An article may also identify areas where future research should be

Selected Social Work Journals

Administration in Social Work

Affilia: Journal of Women and Social Work

Arete

Child and Family Social Work

Child Welfare

Clinical Social Work Journal

Families in Society

Health and Social Work

International Journal of Social Welfare

Journal of Applied Social Sciences

Journal of Gerontological Social Work

Journal of Multicultural Social Work

Journal of Social Service Research

Journal of Social Welfare

Journal of Social Work Values and Ethics

Journal of Social Work Education

Journal of Sociology and Social Welfare

Journal of Teaching in Social Work

Policy & Practice of Public Human Services

Research on Social Work Practice

School Social Work Journal

Smith College Studies in Social Work

Social Service Review

Social Work

Social Work Abstracts

Social Work in Education

Social Work with Groups

Social Work in Health Care

Social Work Research

Source: www.socialworker.com/jswve

directed. Contrast this format with the coverage of a report in a newspaper article or a magazine; often these accounts do not explain the investigator's approach (the methodology), the sample size, and how the data were analyzed, or address future studies that are still needed. You should get all of this information in a journal article. At the end, you should be able to make a conclusion about the worth of a study.

As you become more familiar with the literature relevant to your research question, you will be able to refine your question and might even decide to modify it. You may delight to discover that researchers have suggested that the study you are planning is desperately needed. Even if it is not so directly stated, you may find gaps in our knowledge about the problem that interests you. These are fertile areas where you as a social worker can make an important contribution with your research.

The necessity for immersing yourself in the literature cannot be emphasized strongly enough. Research builds on the accumulated efforts of all those laboring to expand our knowledge and correct our misconceptions. But to make a contribution in the social sciences, we first must be familiar with what is known about the problem. When you read the literature on a topic as a social work researcher, you are reading for a purpose. You are trying to discover:

- What do the majority of the studies conclude?
- What theories have attempted to explain the phenomenon?

- What interventions have been tried?
- What instruments have been used to assess the problem?
- What are the gaps in our knowledge about the problem?
- What additional research needs have been identified?

Step 3: Developing a Research Design

A research design is something like a blueprint. It outlines the approach to be used to collect the data. It describes the conditions under which the data will be collected; how the subjects or respondents will be selected; what instrument will be used; and generally provides information about the who, what, when, where, and how of the research project.

The research design should be carefully thought out to ensure that the information you obtain will be the information you need to support or reject your hypothesis. In developing a research design, ask yourself, "What do I need to know?" and then "How will I go about gathering the information?" The answers to these two questions will guide the development of a research design.

For now, research designs can be classified as fitting one of three broad categories:

1. Exploratory designs
2. Descriptive designs
3. Explanatory designs

Exploratory research designs are used with topics about which very little information is available. For example, the first studies on the psychosocial impact of AIDS on the lives of gay men were important even if they involved only a relatively small number of respondents. Because these exploratory studies are responsive to new concerns or to areas that have not been subjected to research, they tend to be more tentative and small scale (small samples). Their findings are not conclusive or definitive, and, as a consumer of the information resulting from an exploratory design, you may get ideas for further areas of inquiry. Generating research questions and hypotheses for additional investigation, in fact, is the main value of exploratory studies in the quantitative tradition. Qualitative investigators may conduct exploratory studies to understand or explain some process or activity.

The idea for some exploratory research might start when you discover something about a client—say, a homeless street teen reports a history of childhood sexual abuse. From there you might gather data from a few similar clients to see if they fit the same pattern. If they also affirm childhood abuse, you might then want to expand your inquiry and conduct a descriptive study to provide a profile of these clients that allows you to generalize your findings.

Descriptive studies in the quantitative tradition are large-scale efforts that attempt to characterize a population group (for example, the homeless) in a definitive way. Because the studies want to provide precise information, for instance, on what proportion of the homeless are single women, women with children, Vietnam vets, persons of color, and so on, they will be noted for the large numbers of people they survey. They report data largely in terms of percentages and proportions and will be concerned with questions like "How many clients. . . ." This descriptive purpose may result from an agency's need to understand its client population better, to compare its caseload today with the "typical client" from five years ago, or to make comparisons with client groups in other agencies or other parts of the country. Typically, these studies are quite concerned with the issue of **representativeness** and go to great lengths to ensure that their samples look very much like the population from which they were drawn.

Qualitative investigators may also conduct studies to describe a group (e.g., inmates on Death Row) but they are not usually concerned with percentages, proportions, or reporting from a large sample of persons who were interviewed or surveyed.

Explanatory studies are experiments in which hypotheses from certain theories are tested and control or comparison groups are often used. An explanatory study might be conducted, for instance, to investigate whether cognitive behavior therapy is more effective than prescription medicine for persons with sleep disorders.

Frequently, the studies we want to conduct as social workers are exploratory. We may read about or attend a workshop on some new treatment approach and want to implement it. However, because we're not entirely sure that it will work with our clients, we realize the importance of initially involving only a small group of clients—and then if it is effective, expanding the number of clients who would receive it. On other occasions, it makes sense to conduct a small-scale exploratory study because if our hunch is correct, then a foundation or other funding source might provide the resources to launch a more thorough descriptive or explanatory study.

Sometimes it is difficult to know how many subjects are required by a particular type of research design. Although this is an issue we will be discussing in more depth later (particularly in Chapter 8), for now the best advice is to plan your study to be roughly comparable to similar studies being reported in the journals you have been reading. Having a small number of subjects is not likely to jeopardize the potential of your manuscript being published if your project explores a topic never previously investigated. If, however, you are planning a more elaborate study in an area where a good deal of research exists, then sample size is much more crucial.

Group research designs are discussed in Chapter 5. In that chapter, you'll learn that designs employing random assignment of subjects and control groups can produce information in which we can place a great deal of confidence. You'll also learn about situations that rob us of the ability to determine if it was our intervention (or some other factor) that made a difference in the lives of our clients. Research designs are obviously important and design considerations will be discussed in practically every chapter.

Ultimately, your choice of a research design will be largely determined by the problem you are studying, the type and amount of data available to you, and how you choose to examine the data.

Example of an Exploratory Study

Who are trash pickers? How much money do they make per day? Because no prior study had investigated those who gather aluminum cans from dumpsters and garbage cans, a convenience sample of these individuals were interviewed for the study. Some of the findings were that:

- Eighteen percent were homeless.
- Twenty-four percent had been hospitalized for emotional or mental health problems.
- Thirty-six percent said can collecting supplemented Social Security or some form of a disability or pension payment.

- Fifty-two percent had never held a job that provided hospitalization insurance.
- Sixty-four percent reported drinking "some" or "a lot" during the past month.
- Seventy-six percent said they couldn't find another job or that they were disabled or too old for other employment (the average age was 51 with a range that went from 19 to 77).
- The average amount of money made on a "good day" was $4.00.
- Forty-four percent were judged to be impaired from alcoholism, mental retardation, or psychosis.

Source: Royse, D. (1987). Homelessness among trash pickers. *Psychological Reports, 60,* 808–810.

Step 4: Operationalizing

In everyday conversation we easily accept concepts that are somewhat vague because we think we understand what they mean. For instance, in most conversations we all understand the terms "heavy," "frequent," and "problem" drinker to mean the same thing. However, researchers must be precise about the concepts employed in their studies; this precision is called developing **operational definitions**. The way one researcher defines problem drinking for the purposes of a study may be quite different from the way another investigator defines the concept.

One study might define problem drinker as a person who drank to the point of intoxication six times or more in the past year; another may identify problem drinkers in terms of the presence of two or more negative consequences (for example, arrests for drunken driving, loss of relationships, trouble at work or school). A third study could focus on the number of times an individual drinks per week (for example, three or four times) or on the symptoms normally associated with alcoholism (alcohol-induced memory lapses, drinking before noon). Still another study may ask significant others to rate their loved ones' drinking on a continuum with numerical values representing low and high levels of the behavior. It should be apparent to you that how you define your variables (such as "problem drinker") has considerable impact on who is included or excluded from participation in the study.

As a researcher you have the freedom to use the operational definitions employed by other researchers or to revise and improve on them. If you want to compare your results to those findings produced by another researcher, then you will want to use the same methodology, operational definitions, and data-gathering instruments. When you do, you are **replicating** (reproducing) that study for the purpose of comparison with your local clients or population.

Before you can begin to collect data, you must operationally define your variables so precisely that no one would have any problem understanding exactly what is being measured or observed. To take an example, if you are working to reduce the incidence of child abuse in a community, you must define what constitutes child abuse. There are many ways to go about this, but it might make sense to count the number of new episodes of child abuse reported by the local child protective service. We know, however, that the number of child abuse investigations only reflects the tip of the iceberg—that most acts of abuse are never reported. But other methods, such as surveying families and asking respondents about the acts of abuse in their families, are problematic, too. Even if you settle on counting the official reports of abuse processed by the child protective service, you still would need to define for the readers of your report whether you are counting the total number of abuse incidents or the number of *substantiated* cases of abuse. Operationally defining your variables well requires you to have a good knowledge of your subject.

The way we operationalize our variables has a direct bearing on what our research can potentially reveal and what use we can make of the data. Imagine you have designed a new intervention for persons with a gambling addiction. It would be easy to claim success if your clients had absolutely no relapses over a 20-year period. Unfortunately, most social workers cannot wait that long to conclude that an intervention was effective. We need results much sooner than that. What if we were to use a 14- or 30-day follow-up period? It is entirely possible there would be no relapses if our observation period is narrow enough. Suppose we define successful intervention as meaning no relapses within six months? Within a year? During the 36 months following intervention? We would very likely discover that the longer time frame we observe for relapses, the more will be discovered. In other words, it would be possible to conclude that the intervention was a total success when it was not—if we observe for too brief a period. What is a reasonable period of time? This decision is where your knowledge of the subject and of the literature comes in. Other studies will provide tools and benchmarks that can help with your investigation.

Constructing operational definitions requires us to think conceptually about what we want to measure. Homelessness is a topic that often needs to be defined better. Anybody can be locked out of a house and have to sleep in a car for a night. That's not homelessness as we usually think about it. What about the 16-year-old adolescent whose stepfather throws him out and who has to live with friends for five or six days? To take another situation: Would you be homeless even if you have a roof over your head but have no running water or electricity?

Social workers deal with a lot of intangible concepts. We might talk about Susan's low self-esteem, and we all tend to know what that means. Similarly, we may have a client who is depressed, one who has school phobia, and still another who is passive-aggressive. We have to deal with differences in intelligence and motivation, power, social status, and pathology. All abstract concepts must become operationalized if they are to be employed as variables in research projects.

Independent variables such as age, gender, race, marital status, political affiliation, and religion tend to be easier for us to operationalize than dependent variables. **Independent variables** are variables that are suspected to influence, affect, or cause the event or situation that you are studying. For example, prior hospitalizations for mental illness or alcoholism might be important independent variables to help explain or predict the problem of homelessness. Students find it useful to remember that independent variables generally precede the dependent variable in time.

In experimental settings, independent variables are those that the researcher can manipulate or control. For example, in studying the effect of positive reinforcement on the retention of research terminology, the researcher might decide to examine the usefulness of candy as a reinforcement for each new vocabulary term learned. The amount, type, and timing of the receipt of the candy are controlled by the researcher and could be considered independent variables. The number of vocabulary items retained would be the dependent variable. The dependent variable as the effect or impact of the stimulus depends upon the independent variable of appreciation of candy.

Dependent variables are those that the researcher is most interested in explaining or illuminating. For instance, to explain why some cancer survivors live longer than others with the same diagnosis, the dependent variable would be the months or years that the cancer patient lived with the disease. A range of interesting independent variables such as optimism, religious belief, social support, compliance with medical recommendations, or diet might help explain any differences in longevity that were observed. (These would be in addition to the demographics of age, race, gender, etc.). In this example, the researcher is trying to see what might cause or contribute to some cancer survivors living longer than others. In other words, longevity might *depend* upon some factor like social support.

Dependent variables in one study may be used as independent variables in another study. For instance, you could start off your research career by studying the level of self-esteem in ninth-grade boys. In a subsequent study, you may wish to use those self-esteem scores to predict juvenile delinquency (which is now the dependent variable).

It is not always easy to determine whether a variable of interest to a researcher is independent or dependent without knowing more about the study (Neuman, 1997).

Operationalizing Involves Measurement   One of the keys to understanding social science research is the notion that if a thing can be defined, then it can be measured. If we can precisely define concepts such as depression and anxiety, for example, then we can measure how much less a client is depressed or anxious after intervention. Since problems brought to social workers are often vague and ambiguous, it is helpful to collect data in order to determine how much clients improve. Just how anxious is the client? How severe is the depression? Social workers design or use instruments to measure the extent of such problems. These instruments provide quantifiable (numerical) values for problems like depression so that we can discuss relative levels of depression and talk more precisely about those who are very depressed and those who are somewhat less depressed. Simply stated, **measurement** is the process of quantifying states, traits, attitudes, behaviors, and theoretical concepts.

The importance of measurement is revealed in two axioms of treatment formulated by social worker Walt Hudson (1978): The first states: "If you cannot measure the client's problem, it does not exist." The second, a corollary of the first, states: "If you cannot measure the client's problem, you cannot treat it" (p. 65). Clinicians and researchers alike must be able to precisely assess (measure) clients' problems. Without precise measurement, it may be impossible to show that clients have improved as a result of intervention. Researchers often attempt to obtain this precision by using scales and instruments when they operationalize their variables.

A **scale** is a cluster or group of statements or questions (items) that are designed to measure a single concept. Social scientists constantly work on and develop new scales to measure more accurately concepts of interest to them. It is not unusual for scales to be revised over time. Also, you will find that investigators may approach a concept in different ways, so scales measuring the same general concept may vary in length, in the type of item used, and in the response categories available to the subject. For example, it is possible to find a 10-item self-esteem inventory, a 25-item one, and others several times that length.

Scales can be developed to measure many different kinds of problems or concepts. Social workers Joel Fischer and Kevin Corcoran (2000) have collected 400 brief scales, which they refer to as "rapid assessment instruments," for social workers to use with problems commonly encountered in clinical practice. Complete scales, as well as information on the scales' availability, primary reference, scoring, and other essential information, are found in their reference book, which contains many interesting and useful scales to use for research projects and for evaluating one's practice. For illustrative purposes, several examples of scales can be found in Chapter 6 and in the appendices.

It is likely that sometime in your life you have been asked to complete a questionnaire that used a **Likert scale** (sometimes referred to as a five-point scale). A Likert scale is a standard set of response choices usually in this format:

5 Strongly Agree

4 Agree

3 Undecided

2 Disagree

1 Strongly Disagree

There is nothing sacred about these particular categories. For instance, you may encounter a scale where clients self-reporting on how much various symptoms bother them might use

0 Not at all

1 Slightly

2 Somewhat

3 Very much

4 Extremely

Likert scales are not limited to only five response choices and can contain an odd or even number of categories. What characterizes a Likert scale is the attempt to standardize categories. By employing the same descriptors each time and assigning them numerical values, responses to multiple items on a scale can be summed to create a single overall score.

When you as a researcher begin to look at scales that have been constructed to measure abstract concepts like marital satisfaction and emotional abuse, you will discover that scales vary enormously in how well they measure the concept they were designed to assess. We'll discuss this topic further in Chapter 6; however, for now you need to know that you always have the option to operationalize a concept in terms of a single-item scale. This option involves naming the concept and then anchoring it at a minimum of two (three is better) points. (See the examples in Figure 2.1.)

Even children can respond to single-item scales. A colleague once told me that whenever her children wanted to stay home from school she asked, "On a scale from one to ten, how sick are you?" She said they soon learned that saying eight, nine, or ten would probably mean a visit to the doctor. A six or seven would probably result in their getting their temperature taken, and maybe a Tylenol or two. If they said "four" or "five," then Mom might

Emotional Abuse

Rate how much you have felt "put down" by your partner in the last week:

	None				*Some*				*Quite a Bit*	
	1	2	3	4	5	6	7	8	9	10

Fear of Injury

Rate the extent to which you fear injury from your partner:

	No Fear				*Moderate*				*Extreme Fear*	
	1	2	3	4	5	6	7	8	9	10

Figure 2.1 | Examples of Single-Item Scales

give them some special attention or ask what was going on at school (for example, maybe the child had a special report due and was experiencing some butterflies).

Many social workers first realize that they have to operationalize certain concepts when they begin to develop a questionnaire for use within their agencies. Some early advice for when you have to operationalize such common variables as age, education, and income—try to think ahead to the use you will be making of the data. Will you need to report average age, average income? If you use *categories* instead of asking for actual age or income, then you are precluded from getting averages. So, if you would like to know that the average client was 26.4 years old and earned $17,585 per year, then *don't* set up overlapping response categories like the following examples:

WHAT WAS YOUR FAMILY'S INCOME LAST YEAR?

Under $10,000

Under $25,000

Under $40,000

Under $50,000

WHAT IS YOUR PRESENT AGE?

Adolescent (18 and under)

Young Adult (18 to 30)

Adult (30 to 45)

Middle-Aged Adult (45 to 65)

Any operationalizing or measurement of a concept should meet the test of clarity. It would do little good to create an age category, for instance, of "pre–middle age," or "old old" if there was confusion as to what ages went into these groupings. A concept (for example, emotional exhaustion) has not been operationally well defined if you don't know or can't tell who is and who isn't emotionally exhausted.

Often, behaviors are very indicative of the concepts we want to measure. For instance, a racist might attend white supremacist meetings or tell ethnic jokes, a sexist might use "girls" in speech when referring to women. Some students find it helpful to think of operationalizing concepts in terms of behaviors that you could detect from watching a videotape. A "good" student might be one who studies at his or her desk at least four hours a day; an emotionally neglectful mother might be one who never touches, hugs, or kisses a young child.

You don't have to have a scale to operationally define a concept: it's just that scales tend to allow for more possibilities so that gradations (think of a continuum running from low to high) of the concept can be measured. Does it make sense to try to distinguish persons who are a little sexist from those who are profoundly sexist in their thinking?

Step 5: Collecting Data

This step is sometimes referred to as conducting or implementing the study. Depending on your research design, you interview people, mail out questionnaires, or begin to procure data that have already been published (such as suicide rates, marriages, divorces, or births by county and year).

This phase of the research process is obviously important. Without data you will have nothing to analyze or report. If your choice of methodology was well-considered, it will not allow for an extreme amount of bias to influence your findings.

Researchers strive to eliminate **bias** from their studies. Bias is an outside contaminant that tends to produce some distortion from what is actually occurring in the data, causing us to make erroneous conclusions about reality. For instance, clients who fear that they might lose their services or their therapists might not be completely honest and instead tell the researcher what they think she or he wants to hear. This results in inaccuracy. Bias can be conscious or unconscious, glaring or subtle, and may creep in and affect the research process at various points. For instance, in developing a questionnaire you might inadvertently use all masculine pronouns and offend female readers. Offended respondents, if they are angry, may not respond to the questionnaire as you had intended. Complex instructions (which might be confusing to persons with less than a high school education) can also result in data that are strongly affected (biased) by education or reading level. While we all have values and biases of our own, researchers should strive to keep their studies as free from bias as possible. A biased data collection instrument can give information that does not produce a true picture or representation of the attitudes or behaviors you are investigating.

Bias can also result from the way we select interviewees or respondents. This type of bias commonly happens when not enough thought has been given to the sampling design. For example, suppose you are interested in getting social work majors to evaluate their undergraduate program. You decide, because it is convenient for you, to go to a nearby men's dormitory and interview all of the social work majors you can find. Obviously, if you base your study on just the interviews from that one dorm, you will have ignored all female social work majors. Your study, then, will be very biased, as female social work students may have different experiences and evaluations of the social work program.

The way, the time of day, and the place you collect your data can have major effects on the outcome of your study. Suppose you go to a neighborhood supermarket to conduct a survey on attitudes about abortion. You choose to do your interviewing on Mondays, Wednesdays, and Fridays for two weeks during the hours between 9:00 A.M. and 4:00 P.M. However, a friend tells you that a better day to go is Saturday because everyone is more talkative. When should you collect your data?

Had you interviewed solely on Mondays, Wednesdays, and Fridays until 4:00 P.M., you may have discovered that your study underrepresented those persons who generally are at work during those hours. By interviewing persons who buy their groceries only on Saturday, you may collect a group of respondents who are employed Monday through Friday. The older, retired, or unemployed persons could be underrepresented. One approach could yield respondents who would likely be older and possibly more conservative, while the other could result in younger, potentially more liberal respondents. If you choose to do your interviewing on Sunday mornings between 10:00 A.M. and noon, what segment of the population would be underrepresented?

Some research questions or populations of interest determine how the data will be collected. Because homeless persons do not have telephones and may not have an address to which mail could be sent, it would be ludicrous to attempt a mail or telephone data collection procedure with this population. Pragmatic considerations such as the amount of time available for conducting the study, the amount of money that can be spent, the availability of subjects, and the ease of locating them all have a direct bearing on the way researchers go about collecting their data and the research design chosen.

Bias is generally minimized as survey samples approach **representativeness,** that is, as samples more closely resemble the larger population being studied. Typically, we draw respondents randomly (so that everyone has a chance of being selected) in order to create representative samples and minimize bias. There can be many sources of bias, but in the conduct of research, objectivity is the proper and necessary stance. You want your data to be as free from bias as possible.

Studies that are free from bias generally have much greater generalizability than those with overt bias. **Generalizability** means how well the findings from a specific study fit another situation. Let's say that I think that my spaghetti sauce is the greatest in the world. I invite my aunt Bessie over to try it. She agrees that it is the best she has ever tasted. My wife also agrees. Even the kids like it. I then decide that I am ready to sell it across the country. Is it reasonable to assume from a small sample of family members that enough of the American public would buy my spaghetti sauce to justify spending all my savings to market it? In this instance I would have been guilty of **overgeneralization.** In other words, I would be assuming too much and going beyond what the data would support.

Suppose that you are interested in predicting an upcoming presidential election. You ask all the social work majors in your college or university how they will vote. In this instance, a much larger sample is involved, but will your findings indicate which candidate will win the national election? The answer is probably not. Why? Because social work majors do not adequately represent a cross-sampling of American voters. For one thing, social work majors probably tend to be more liberal and younger than the average voter. Social work majors at any one school may or may not represent the opinions of other students attending the same school. Similarly, you probably could not predict a national election based on interviews of all the residents of several retirement centers located in South Carolina. However, depending on the size of your sample and how the retirement centers were selected, you might be able to discover the candidate most preferred by older adults living in retirement centers in South Carolina.

As a rule, you can generalize only to the specific universe of people who are interviewed, observed, or surveyed in your study. If you draw an unbiased national sample, then you can speak to the attitudes or preferences of the nation. If you draw an unbiased sample from all the adults in a given state, then you can speak about the knowledge or attitudes of adults residing in that particular state. An unbiased sample from a large city will allow you to speak only about the citizens of that city. For instance, if you had data from a sample of adults living in Las Vegas, Nevada, concerning their attitudes toward prostitution—it would not be responsible to assume that the data were representative of attitudes in other American cities.

Studies that are relatively free of bias are the wheels that allow science to move forward. By allowing us to generalize our findings to similar populations, they improve our knowledge and guide our practice. And while the ideal is to have a bias-free study representative of the population being studied from which we can generalize to similar populations, in reality our data collection methods are often compromised.

I once attended a conference that brought together researchers and chronically mentally ill people who had been studied for four years as part of a special project that provided them with peer counseling and other new interventions—in addition to what they normally received. The principal investigator, armed with charts and transparencies, began explaining that the battery of eight different psychological tests administered before and after the project began showed no significant changes. He was a little perplexed by this, but took the tack of justifying the findings by saying that at least the chronically mentally ill people in the study weren't any worse off. There were a couple of snickers from the audience, and after a few minutes, one of the consumers revealed a possible reason why the psychological tests hadn't found any changes. He said that some in his group had been afraid that if they answered honestly they could ultimately lose their disability checks!

So while the investigators had gone to great lengths to protect their study from known sources of bias by using such procedures as random assignment of consumers to the different intervention groups and sensitive instruments, some of the subjects, acting in their own self-interest, appeared to have biased the findings on their own. I suspect the researchers had not prepared for this turn of events. Who would have? The researchers knew that the information they were collecting from individuals in the study would not be shared with any governmental agencies. They may even have explained this to their subjects. However, to individuals who had much less education and were not informed about what researchers actually do with their data, integrity of the research was less important than preserving the few resources available to them.

Keep this story in mind as you plan your research projects. At each stage of the research process, consider how bias might creep into your study and what you could do to minimize it. If you anticipate problems, you may wish to strengthen your design or change the way you collect your data or operationalize your dependent variable.

Step 6: Analyzing and Interpreting the Data

Once you have finished collecting the data, you are then ready to analyze it. One of the purposes of analysis is to express the data in a way that is "mentally digestible." It may be easy to present detailed responses from three or four individuals, but when you have more than five responses, full descriptions become very cumbersome. Further, it is awkward, if not impossible, to display information from a large number of persons (for example, 50 or more) without summarizing the data in some fashion.

Why summarize the data? Which of the following statements do you find easier to understand?

1. The ages of respondents in Group A were: 12, 14, 15, 12, 13, 14, 12, 13, and 14.
2. The average age of respondents in Group A was 13 years.

Basically, we summarize in order to comprehend the information that we have gathered. Your hypothesis may suggest ways that you can summarize, categorize, or organize your data. For instance, if your hypothesis is that women voters are more supportive than men of tax levies that directly benefit persons with low income, your data naturally suggest two divisions: male and female voters. In your analysis, you will compare and contrast the voting behavior of males and females on specific social service election issues.

Analysis is a logical process that begins with looking at the raw data. For example, you will first want to determine how many persons of each sex, race, or age grouping completed your questionnaires. More than likely, you will then order or arrange your data in some fashion. If you looked at several elections in different years, you might array the data by year of the election. You may begin to notice a trend, for example, of women being more supportive of social service issues or you may identify patterns or directions that have not been suggested in the literature. Sometimes the data are hard to interpret, and the findings are not intuitively obvious.

Interpreting the data is made easier by comparing your findings with those of other studies. Perhaps your respondents are more or less knowledgeable than those in a study that you found during the literature search. Published program evaluations might provide useful benchmarks for comparing the success of the local agency's program.

Occasionally, research findings portrayed as pie or bar charts (see Figure 2.2 and Figure 2.3) or even maps shaded to indicate high or low densities of one variable or another are useful for helping others understand the results of your study. However, statistical methods may also be needed to determine if there is a significant difference between two or more groups.

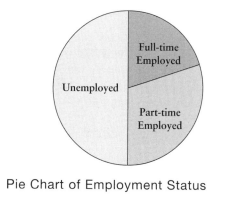

Figure 2.2   Pie Chart of Employment Status

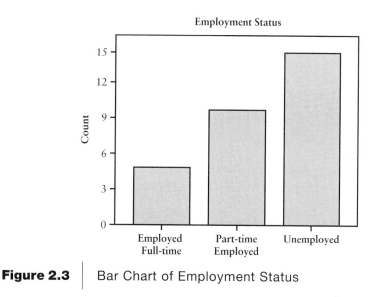

Figure 2.3   Bar Chart of Employment Status

Statistics aid in the interpretation of data. With the advent of computer technology, the computation of statistical tests has become relatively easy.

Chapter 13 presents most of the statistics that you'll need to know to begin to analyze your data. That chapter will present a quick overview of descriptive statistics (for example, measures of central tendency like mean and median) and inferential statistics (for example, t tests and one-way analysis of variance). Descriptive statistics help us understand how much our variables vary (like the range of years between the oldest and youngest participants). Inferential statistics are used to test hypotheses about differences between groups and to aid us in understanding the probabilities of obtaining our results by chance. Graphs and charts can help readers quickly digest some fact or trend in the data.

Step 7: Writing the Report

Once the data have been collected and analyzed, the final step is preparing your findings in such a way that they can be made available to others. There may be times when a memorandum to your supervisor or director summarizing the results of your study will be adequate. If you received funding for the research, it is very likely that you will be required to write a report of your findings. If what you found was especially interesting, you may want to submit your findings to a professional journal. Journals, even those in different fields, tend to be organized in the same format as research reports.

The first part of a research report, the Introduction, puts the research question or hypothesis in context (a description of the extent or severity of the problem, the length of time it has been a problem, what is generally known or believed about the problem) and reviews the important studies found in the literature.

The next section, Methods, is an explanation of the research methodology—how the data were collected, which variables were included and how they were operationalized, and who the subjects were, their characteristics, and how they were recruited. Enough information should be presented so that others can follow what you did and replicate the study.

The third section, Results, presents what was actually learned from the study. Tables and graphs may be employed to visually demonstrate differences and to help with comparisons. Findings from statistical tests are often reported. Qualitative researchers may use tables or graphs but seldom report statistical results. Instead, qualitative reports will be characterized by thick, descriptive detail and actual quotes from those they've talked with that illuminate or characterize the participants in their studies.

Finally, the Discussion section addresses the implications of your findings, speculates why those particular results were obtained, and suggests how future research in this area might be conducted.

It almost goes without saying that many fine research reports are filed away or relegated to dusty shelves because the social work investigators did not exert a little extra effort and prepare the report for publication in a journal or as a paper for a professional symposium. In order to rectify this situation, the last chapter of this textbook, Chapter 14, will focus on writing about research.

THE QUALITATIVE PERSPECTIVE

Thus far this chapter has presented the research process from a quantitative orientation. Now it is time to view the same process from the perspective of a qualitatively oriented researcher.

Step 1: Posing a Question or Stating a Hypothesis

Qualitative researchers often do not state hypotheses ahead of time and their research questions may not be as specific or as narrowly focused as the quantitative researchers. Instead, the qualitative researchers explore a more general question. For instance, they may want to interview refugees from Sudan's Darfur region to learn what conditions were like in the refugee camps. The goal here might be to gather information that could lead to better solutions to the problems of living in the camps. Or, the qualitative researchers may be interested in documenting the atrocities that occurred and forced people to leave their homes. While qualitative researchers may have hypotheses that "drive" their explorations, these hypotheses are not always stated or prominent. For example, the qualitative researcher may believe that the armed militias were conducting genocide rather than just battling over disputed territory. Interviews with refugees could confirm that assumption.

In qualitative research the first step involves identifying a topic, a problem, a phenomenon, or a group of people of interest. Generally, an initial question or small set of questions may serve as the core or catalyst. In qualitative research, the investigator may start with a small set of questions which may lead to others during, say, an interview. On the other hand, quantitative researchers often have a well-defined set of questions or prepared standardized instruments and tend not to deviate from these.

Qualitative interviewers tend to ask broad, open-ended questions like "What daily challenges to mental health does living in a refugee camp present?" or "How do you maintain your mental health in a refugee camp? What strategies do you employ?" These questions, then, produce lots of narrative and tend not to lend themselves to precise measurement (e.g., a single group average score on the Beck Depression Inventory) that would identify quantitatively oriented research. Qualitative researchers can have hypotheses, but they tend to emerge from the study of the group in question rather than coming from outside one's own data collection.

Step 2: Reviewing the Literature

While the quantitative researcher would normally never begin a research project without becoming very familiar with the relevant body of literature, the qualitative researcher is less constrained. In qualitative research there is no requirement that a literature review comes before the data collection. Some qualitative researchers consult the literature after they have collected their data so that previous studies don't "cloud" or influence the new study with the possible misconceptions or erroneous conclusions of others. Agar (1980) noted that a thorough literature review "introduced a lot of unnecessary noise into my mind as I tried to learn about being a heroin addict from 'patients' in the institution" (p. 25). Qualitative researchers try to empty their minds of preconceptions and prejudices—to become "open" to alternative ways of thinking about and viewing the world.

Instead of attempting to read journal articles and books to become more informed about the topic of the proposed research, the qualitative researcher may become more familiar with the topic by talking with others who have worked with the group of interest or who are knowledgeable about them. They may also decide to delve into the literature and to read the quantitatively researched reports skeptically, looking for questions that weren't answered or explored well.

Similarly, qualitative researchers may be guided by some underlying theory (e.g., black feminist theory), but, unlike quantitatively oriented researchers, they are not required or probably as likely to test aspects of a given theory.

Step 3: Developing a Research Design

Qualitative researchers tend to rely heavily on personal interviews and participant observation. Thus, while quantitatively oriented researchers are concerned about sample size and obtaining a representative sample, qualitative researchers do not have the same level of concern about these issues. Qualitative researchers do not use the group research designs with the random assignment and pre- and posttesting that will be elaborated on further in Chapter 5. It is not that qualitative researchers are forbidden from using these procedures, it is that they aren't interested in the same kinds of questions, as a rule, that their quantitative counterparts want to explore.

How research subjects or participants are recruited is an issue for both the qualitative and quantitative researcher. Similarly, both types of researchers will be concerned with both informing participants about their rights as research subjects and receiving the participants' consent. (There will be more about this in Chapter 3 when we discuss ethical research practices.)

Step 4: Operationalizing

Instead of operationalizing dependent and independent variables and trying to find instruments that would allow for precise measurement of these variables, the qualitative researcher would likely be more concerned with specifying the site where the data collection will take place. The site can consist of a particular village, the place where a street gang gathers, or a location (such as a hospital emergency room). Often, the site is described in narrative form in terms of both its history and the participants or residents of that place. These informants are the inside "experts" on the culture or group who are willing to share their everyday experiences and interpret events for the qualitative researcher. Sometimes it is necessary to build rapport and long-term relationships with insiders before meaningful data collection can begin. Could a qualitative researcher use a standardized instrument if he or she wanted to? The answer is: yes, of course. However, the use of paper-and-pencil data collection instruments (as discussed later in Chapter 6) is much more characteristic of the quantitative researcher than the qualitative one.

Step 5: Collecting Data

The qualitative researcher can choose to be an observer or a participant-observer. For instance, if the researcher was investigating life in a homeless shelter, the choice of role as a data collector might involve (a) securing permission to observe the homeless individuals as they come into the shelter; (b) securing permission to interview them there; or (c) deciding to give the appearance of being homeless in order to request services from (and meet the inhabitants of) the shelter. In the first instance the researcher might volunteer to work in the shelter or could even obtain employment there—providing a legitimate role for interacting with the residents. If the researcher decided to be a participant-observer, he or she might spend several weeks out on the streets to get a real feel for the problems and life of the homeless.

Data collection involves virtually everything the qualitative researcher sees, hears, or smells—information from all the senses can be recorded to describe that particular culture. The interviews that are conducted can be structured, but more commonly they are not and would occur on the street or in the shelter—anywhere the homeless might congregate. The answers received to a question might lead to an entirely different set of questions (often unanticipated) as the researcher attempts to learn about the homeless lifestyle or a particular individual's life. The research processes of qualitative researchers have much more fluidity than those of quantitative researchers.

One important issue to resolve is whether the interviews can or should be taped. As you can imagine, sometime the informants might be uncomfortable or extremely suspicious of the qualitative researcher's motives in wanting to record conversations—particularly if they are engaged in illegal activities. Unlike the quantitative researcher who usually obtains written responses to questionnaires or makes use of standardized instruments for raw data, the qualitative researcher herself is most often the data collection instrument. Thus, it is critical to be able to take notes (called field notes) or to be able to access the content of interviews. Taped interviews are usually prepared as written transcriptions and these serve, too, as the data to be analyzed.

Qualitative researchers do not expend much energy worrying about representativeness of the sample; sample size also is not an issue. Generalizability may or may not be a concern as again, the focus is somewhat different. The quantitative researcher is often looking for statistical significance; she wants to have confidence in the numbers (means or ranges) produced. The quantitative researcher relies on counting, measuring, and analyzing numbers. In qualitative research, however, there is little or no use made of statistics. While counting may be employed, it is not the major emphasis. Qualitative researchers desire to explore the detail, richness, and depth of the human experience. They want to know the answers to questions like: what would it be like to live as a homeless person? To be a social worker in a psychiatric emergency room? To be an illegal immigrant trying to find employment? The qualitative researcher seeks to understand social relationships and patterns of interaction. Anecdotal accounts are used to describe the world of the people being investigated.

For the qualitative researcher, generalizability comes from the trustworthiness of the informants and the thick, descriptive detail that is provided. **Triangulation** (collecting information using multiple techniques or from a variety of sources) is also a way to ensure that the findings are credible, accurate, and have validity. There are other ways that qualitative investigators attempt to eliminate bias and improve generalizability in their studies, and these will be discussed in Chapter 6. From qualitative studies, larger, more quantitative surveys or research projects may develop.

Step 6: Analyzing and Interpreting the Data

The next-to-the-last step in qualitative research is analyzing the data. As with quantitative methods, the qualitative researcher is looking for patterns. However, the qualitative researcher transcribes interviews and reads his field notes to look for categories, themes, or topics that allow for grouping and organizing the information. For instance, if you had conducted interviews with street gang members, you might logically begin to group together relevant parts of their conversations on such topics as their views about the police, girlfriends and boyfriends, guns, drugs, family, and school. In this example the qualitative researcher might also be seeking norms of behavior—unwritten rules of conduct that govern the gang members. The qualitative researcher is never really sure what the interviews or observations might turn up, and so the data being analyzed usually are not of the type that would allow for statistical analysis. Computer software exists to help the researcher analyze the text of interviews, recorded conversations, or documents. (There will be more on this in Chapter 11.)

Step 7: Writing the Report

Qualitative research is generally reported in a much more narrative style than quantitative research is. There very likely will be no statistics or averages, and very few numbers involved in qualitative research reports. Instead, they will read more like an in-depth journalistic account, such as you might find in the newspaper. Lots of details describing the participants or their world will be present, as will many of their quotes. Unlike the tradition of quantitative research, the qualitative researcher may use a lot of "I" language as in this brief sample from a student's account:

> My first night in the homeless shelter was the worst. Besides the overpowering body odor from those lying beside me on the floor, someone stole my shoes after I lapsed into a light sleep around 2:00 A.M. That's why most of the men used their shoes for pillows—to keep others from taking them.

SOCIAL WORK RESEARCH AND PRACTICE

While it is often the case that we think of social work practice and research as completely separate and distinct, they both share a logical problem-solving process. They both, for instance, start with a focus on a problem, proceed through some review of its extent and history, develop a plan for addressing it, implement the plan, and then evaluate the research process. In Figure 2.4 you

Research Process	Task-Centered Process
Starts with a problem, question, or hypothesis	Starts with a client's problem
Review of the literature	History taking, identification of resources, strengths, networks
Development of research and operationalizing of variables	Negotiate a contract
Data collection	Begin intervention
Data analysis	Evaluation of intervention
Final report	Termination/summary report

Figure 2.4 | Comparison of the Research Process and the Task-Centered Process

can see for yourself the similarities between the research process and the task-centered or problem-solving process used by social workers.

Even the step that might seem the strangest to you, operationally defining variables, is part and parcel of what social workers must do in everyday practice. A man who could have benefited from counseling once told some friends that his wife didn't respect him. What does that mean? Unless he gives us some additional information, we are clueless as to what exactly upsets him. A skilled social worker would possibly ask such questions as "When do you feel that you are not respected? What is your wife doing or saying?" In gathering more details, the social worker finds out how the client has defined (operationalized) the term "respect."

If you look for areas of overlap between research and practice, you surely will find them—because they use the same general approach. The research process is no more complicated than the problem-solving model you will use as a social worker. It is not an artificial contrivance designed to make life difficult, but an orderly and logical process that should be almost second nature to you.

KEY TERMS

deduction	dependent variable	measurement	overgeneralization
induction	representativeness	scale	triangulation
replicated	operational definitions	Likert scale	
hypothesis	replicating	bias	
null hypotheses	independent variables	generalizability	

SELF-REVIEW

(Answers at the end of the book)

1. List the seven steps in the research process.
2. T or F. The following is a null hypothesis: Math majors do not have higher grade point averages than chemistry majors.
3. In the following hypothesis, what is the dependent variable? "Men arrested for assault and battery are more impulsive than men arrested for public intoxication."
4. What is the major characteristic of descriptive studies?
5. Operationally define "good student."
6. In a study of men arrested for assault and battery, what would be some logical independent variables that would describe this group?
7. A scale is designed to measure a single _____.
8. T or F. A true/false response set on a questionnaire is not an example of a Likert scale.
9. Researchers strive to eliminate which of the following from their studies?
   a. theories
   b. dependent variables
   c. bias
   d. representativeness
10. T or F. Betsy interviewed 10 students from her research methods class about the President's job performance. As a result of this study she thinks she can speak to what most Americans think about the topic. This is a case of overgeneralizing.
11. Betsy found a correlation of .35 between her research subjects' ages and their monthly income. In her own words, she says that younger subjects tend to have less money and older subjects tend to have more. Is this a correct interpretation of the correlation coefficient?
12. Identify which of the following are good or poor hypotheses and state a reason for your answer.
   a. Altruism varies in different groups of people.
   b. In terms of values, there is no comparison between MSW and BSW students.
   c. Tobacco smoking seems to have detrimental health effects.
   d. Fatalistic attitudes about the benefit of treating cancer affect survivability rates.
13. T or F. Qualitative researchers demand hypotheses of each other.
14. Briefly explain the role that a literature review would have for the qualitative researcher.
15. T or F. Qualitative researchers are extremely concerned about sample size in their studies.
16. T or F. The quantitative researcher is more concerned with operationalizing than the qualitative researcher.
17. Which group of researchers (qualitative or quantitative) is more likely to use unstructured personal interviews?

18. Which group of researchers is more likely to use statistical analysis?
19. Which group of researchers is more likely to write a report that reads like an lengthy newspaper story?

QUESTIONS FOR CLASS DISCUSSION

1. Practice developing hypotheses and research questions on the following list of topics:
   a. alcoholism
   b. effective psychotherapy
   c. fear of open spaces
   d. depression
   e. social drinkers
   f. racist attitudes
   g. heavy cigarette smokers
2. Take a hypothesis or research question from Question 1 and convert it into a null hypothesis.
3. Identify as many theories used by social work practitioners as you can.
4. Identify the dependent variables in the following studies:
   a. Alcoholism in Young Adults: The Role of Parents' Drinking Behavior
   b. Repeat Pregnancies among Unmarried Teen Parents
   c. Increasing Child Support Payments with Two New Interventions
   d. Do All-Nighters Pay Off? An Examination of Test Scores and Cram-Studying Techniques in First-Year College Students
   e. Weight Gain in a Sample of Anorexics Receiving Cognitive Therapy
5. Operationally define a "bad marriage" so that a clinical social worker could locate couples who might benefit from a new 12-week intervention designed to help those with troubled marriages.
6. Operationally define each of the following:
   a. a humorous television program
   b. an educational television program
   c. an offensive television program
7. What do you like about how a qualitative researcher might go about conducting a study?
8. Brainstorm examples of how bias could affect a study.
9. Look around the classroom. In how many different ways do your classmates vary? Make a list of as many different independent variables as may be represented by the diversity of characteristics found among your classmates.
10. Bloom and Fischer (1982) have written about aspects of the scientific practitioner and conceptualized practice "as a problem-solving experiment, a research project in which little or nothing is assumed" (p. 19). Discuss the similarities that you see between a research process and the kind of work you would like to do as a practitioner of social work.
11. Make a side-by-side comparison of the differences between qualitative and quantitative research.

RESOURCES AND REFERENCES

Agar, M. (1980). *The professional stranger: An informal introduction to ethnography.* New York: Academic Press.

Bettelheim, B. (1967). *The empty fortress: Infantile autism and the birth of the self.* New York: Free Press.

Bloom, M., & Fischer, J. (1982). *Evaluating practice: Guidelines for the accountable professional.* Englewood Cliffs, NJ: Prentice Hall.

Corcoran, K., & Fischer, J. (2000). *Measures for clinical practice* (2nd ed.). New York: Free Press.

Dulmus, C. N., & Rapp-Paglicci, L. A. (2000). The prevention of mental disorders in children and adolescents: Future research and public policy recommendations. *Families in Society, 81(3),* 294–303.

Emery, R. E. (2005). Reader Commentary: Parental Alienation Syndrome: Proponents bear the burden of proof. *Family Court Review, 43(1),* 8–13.

Hudson, W. W. (1978). Notes for practice: First axioms of treatment. *Social Work, 23(1),* 65–66.

Kemp, B. E., & Brustman, M. J. (1997). Social policy research: Comparison and analysis of CD-ROM resources. *Social Work Research, 21,* 111–119.

Kessler, M. R., White, M. B., & Nelson, B. S. (2003). Group treatments for women sexually abused as children: A review of the literature and recommendations for future outcome research. *Child Abuse and Neglect, 27(9),* 1045–1061.

Leedy, P. D. (1974). *Practical research: Planning and design.* New York: Macmillan.

Munson, C. (1983). *An introduction to clinical social work supervision.* New York: Haworth Press.

Neuman, W. L. (1997). *Social research methods: Qualitative and quantitative approaches.* Boston: Allyn & Bacon.

Onwuegbuzie, A. J., & Wilson, V. A. (2003). Statistics anxiety: Nature etiology, antecedents, effects and treatments: A comprehensive review of the literature. *Teaching in Higher Education, 8(2),* 195–209.

Thaxton, L., Emshoff, J. G., & Guessous, O. (2000). Prostate cancer support groups: A literature review. *Journal of Psychosocial Oncology, 23(1),* 25–40.

ASSIGNMENT 2.1: Developing Hypotheses and Research Questions

Objective: *To develop competency in recognizing and writing good hypotheses and research questions.*

Once you have a topic in mind that you want to explore, an early step in the research process is to state a formal hypothesis or research question. It can't be vague or unclear, but must tell the reader precisely what you would like to investigate. In the space provided below, take an idea and state it so that it would be capable of guiding a research project. Then, slightly rephrase the same idea as a research question.

My hypothesis is:

My hypothesis stated as a research question is:

The dependent variable in both the hypothesis and research question is:

The dependent variable would be operationally defined as:

ASSIGNMENT 2.2: Conducting a Literature Review

Objective: *To acquire experience in searching for relevant professional literature.*

In this exercise go into one of the databases that specializes in professional journal articles: PsycINFO, Social Work Abstracts, MEDLINE, etc. Look for five articles that would help you with your hypothesis in Assignment 2.1. Look for such things as theories that attempt to explain why the social problem exists, gaps in our knowledge about the problem, approaches that have been used to study the problem, or results of interventions that have been tried. You may have to skim or read more than five articles in order to find useful ones for your area of interest.

1. What is the topic on which you want to find literature?

2. What key word(s) will you use? _____ (the initial term)
   List all other key words you will use:

3. *On another sheet of paper* that you will attach to this one, list the full citation of the articles that you found. Use APA style (author, year, title of article, title of journal). In the space below, write *one sentence* that explains what each article contributes to your knowledge about the proposed research you might want to conduct some day.

   Article 1:

   Article 2:

   Article 3:

   Article 4:

   Article 5:

4. Which database(s) did you use in your literature search?

ASSIGNMENT 2.3: Impressions from Conducting Literature Searches

Objective: *To help you learn about differences in databases and search engines; to allow the instructor opportunity to address difficulties and problems in locating pertinent literature.*

1. What was the most important thing you learned from conducting your literature search?

2. What did you find frustrating?

3. How was searching for professional literature different from going into a search engine such as Google?

4. Did you discover it was necessary to narrow down your research topic? How did you do this?

5. Did you see any patterns or themes in the literature? What were they?

6. What journals tend to be carrying the articles most relevant to your topic?

ASSIGNMENT 2.4: Reading a Professional Journal Article

Objective: *To acquire experience in reading and using professional journal articles.*

Evaluate one of the journal articles that you found in your literature search, doing it along the following lines. (*Note*: Your instructor may want you to attach a photocopy of your article to this page.)

Give the full citation of the article. Does the article:

1. State a research question or hypothesis? What is it?

2. Discuss an obvious dependent variable? How is it operationalized?

3. Mention at least one theory? Which one(s)?

4. Have, in your opinion, a solid literature review? How many references are there?

5. Describe a research design? What is the research design?

6. Use statistical procedures to analyze the data? What procedures are used?

Ethical Thinking and Research

Before going much further in learning how to conduct research, we must have a good understanding about what does and doesn't constitute ethical research practice. Without this foundation, researchers run the risk of ruining their reputations or that of the agencies that employ them and could even unintentionally harm their research subjects. While most social workers would never do anything that they knew would be viewed by others as unethical, problems can arise whenever we assume that others think like we do—and they don't. An ethical dilemma develops anytime we have to choose—not between a right and a wrong—but between two arguably correct but conflicting courses of action. Thus, while we all know that it is generally wrong to lie, and though we believe that the ethical researcher would always want to inform his or her research subjects about the nature of the study, does this means that we can *never* deceive in the interest of research? What if there is no other way to conduct the research? Here are several examples of potential ethical problems. Decide if you think the researcher is doing something unethical.

1. Maria wants to learn experientially how society treats our senior citizens. She has a friend who can create latex wrinkles on her face and they've found clothing and a wig that guarantee that she'll look like an 80-year-old. Is Maria being unethical if she doesn't tell the people she encounters that she is really only 23 years old?

2. Conover's (1987) interest was in illegal immigrants: what plans and decisions they made, how they survived, and what they experienced. He crossed the U.S.-Mexican border with a group of Mexicans and was later arrested in the United States for driving a car for the immigrants (they didn't have driver's licenses). Although aiding and abetting these temporary workers may have been illegal, was it unethical?

3. Wellons (1973) engaged in some brilliant, creative research. Knowing about the powerful effect of negative labeling (sometimes known as the self-fulfilling prophecy), Wellons gave workshop supervisors positive but untruthful labels for a group of trainees with mental retardation. He told the supervisors certain supervisees could be expected to "blossom" in intelligence and workshop performance. And sure enough, one month later the experimental group of adult trainees not only had a higher level of productivity but also showed gains in intelligence. There were no changes in the control group. Even though deception was used, was this research unethical?

You begin to see the problem. Ethical dilemmas thrive in those gray areas that are in-between totally right and totally wrong. Sometimes research cannot be conducted without deception. The purist might argue that deception should never be used, but what if the research could benefit society? Should we prevent research in instances where subjects are not informed precisely of the study's purpose? And before you answer that, consider this—are we obligated to inform even those participating in medical research that they will be receiving a placebo, not the new experimental drug?

Heated controversies occasionally arise because of disagreements over what constitutes an unethical act. A final example involves a researcher (Coughlin, 1988) who submitted to 146 journals in social work and related fields a fabricated study of the benefits of temporarily separating asthmatic children from their parents. One version of the article claimed that social work intervention benefited the children. A second version indicated that the intervention had no effect. On acceptance or rejection of the manuscript, the study's investigator notified the journal of the real purpose of his study—to collect data on whether there was a tendency among journals to accept articles that confirm the value of social work intervention.

The controversy arose when an editor of the *Social Service Review* lodged a formal complaint against the author with the National Association of Social Workers. The author believed that the review procedures of journals ought to be investigated because of their potential influence in determining what will be printed. Some argue that the author should not have initiated such a large-scale deception of journals, but how does one investigate the hypothesis that professional journals have a bias that constitutes "prior censorship" without using a little deception? In many instances of unethical research, harm or potential for harm is apparent. Yet who was injured in this example? (To read more about this episode and Coughlin's subsequent research, see Epstein, 1990, 2004).

HISTORICAL CONTEXT

Guidelines to protect the subjects of research originated with the Nuremberg trials after World War II, which, among other areas of concern, examined the Nazis' medical experiments on prisoners. Nazi physicians conducted cruel and harmful experiments on human subjects. Some of their experiments, for example, were designed to determine how long it was possible for human subjects to live in ice water. Prisoners were subjected to conditions that literally froze them. Female prisoners were ordered to warm the frozen subjects with their naked bodies in order to determine if more subjects lived with slow thawing than with quick thawing. Other prisoners (including children) were injected with diseases such as typhus, malaria, and epidemic jaundice in order to test vaccines. To test antibiotics, human beings were wounded and had limbs amputated. Grass, dirt, gangrene cultures, and other debris were rubbed into the wounds so that the injuries would simulate those received on the battlefield. To simulate the problems of high altitude flying, test chambers were created where oxygen was removed and the effect of oxygen starvation on humans studied. Other prisoners of the Nazis were given intravenous injections of gasoline or various forms of poison to study how long it would take them to die. These involuntary subjects experienced extreme pain, and of those few who lived, most suffered permanent injury or mutilation.

These and other atrocities resulted in what became known as the Nuremberg Code—a set of ethical standards by which research with human subjects can be judged. Organizations such as the World Medical Association subsequently developed their own guidelines (The Declaration of Helsinki) for distinguishing ethical from unethical clinical research. The American Medical Association and other groups endorsed the Declaration or developed similar guidelines.

Despite awareness of the Nazi atrocities and the development of ethical guidelines for research by a number of organizations and professional associations, unfortunate incidents in this country in which subjects were experimented on without their permission have occurred. Less than 10 years ago newspapers began carrying headlines such as "Families of Radiation Victims to Get Settlement." The U.S. Department of Energy had just acknowledged that, between 1945 and 1947, 12 individuals were involved in government-sponsored human radiation experiments without their permission. The government paid the one survivor and the 11 other families $400,000 each to settle a lawsuit brought because plutonium injections were given without the recipient's knowledge or consent. In some instances, more than 600 rads of radiation were given—enough to cause bone cancer. It was also revealed that prisoners in Washington and Oregon were irradiated between 1963 and 1971. These experiments violated the first principle of the Nuremberg Code:

> Before the acceptance of an affirmative decision by the experimental subject there should be made known to him the nature, duration, and purpose of the experiment; the method and means by which it is to be conducted; all inconveniences and hazards reasonably to be expected; and the effects upon his health or person which may possibly come from his participation.

The National Commission for the Protection of Human Subjects in Biomedical and Behavioral Research *(The Belmont Report)* identified these three ethical principles for research on humans in 1978:

Beneficence—Maximizing good outcomes for humanity and research subjects while minimizing or avoiding risk or harm.

Respect—Protecting the autonomy of all persons, treating them with courtesy and respect including those who are not completely autonomous (for example, children, the mentally incompetent).

Justice—Ensuring that reasonable, nonexploitative, and well-considered procedures are administered fairly; that the distribution of costs and benefits is fair (for example, those bearing the risks of research should receive the benefit). (Sieber, 1992, p. 18)

In the 1960s in New York, a physician injected cancer cells into 22 geriatric patients. Some were informed orally that they were involved in an experiment, but were not told that they were being given injections of cancer cells. No written consent was acquired, and some patients were incompetent to give informed consent. Later it was learned that the study had not been presented to the hospital's research committee and that several physicians directly responsible for the care of the patients involved in the study had not been consulted (Faden & Beauchamp, 1986).

Another notorious case involved a sample of men with syphilis. In 1932, 400 mostly poor and illiterate black males with tertiary stage syphilis—most of whom lived in Tuskegee, Alabama—were informed that they would receive free treatment for their "bad blood." In actuality, these men received no treatment for syphilis. They received free physical exams, periodic blood testing, hot meals on examination days, free treatment for minor disorders, and a modest burial fee for cooperating with the investigators.

The researchers (supported by the Public Health Service) were interested only in tracing the pathological evolution of syphilis. Although the study was reviewed several times by Public Health Service officials and was reported in 13 articles in prestigious medical and public health journals, it continued uninterrupted until 1972, when a reporter exposed the study in the *New York Times*. The survivors were given treatment for their disease only after this publicity. After the story broke, the Department of Health, Education, and Welfare appointed an advisory panel to review the study. Not until 1975 did the government extend treatment to subjects' wives who had contracted syphilis and their children born with congenital syphilis (Jones, 1981).

Public outcry over the Tuskegee Syphilis Study and other abuses led Congress in 1974 to pass the National Research Act (Public Law 93-348), which requires any organization involved in the conduct of biomedical or behavioral research involving human subjects to establish an institutional review board (IRB) to review the research to be conducted or sponsored. This act also created the National Commission for the Protection of Human Subjects of Biomedical and Behavioral Research. In October 1978, this commission produced recommendations for public comment. The Department of Health, Education, and Welfare (HEW) refined the recommendations and, in 1981, issued them as regulations for research being conducted with its funds. In 1983, specific regulations protecting children were incorporated. On May 16, 1997 President Clinton apologized on behalf of the nation to the survivors of the Tuskegee Syphilis Study and their survivors saying that what the United States Government did was an "outrage" and "shameful."

The impact of these standards was that colleges, universities, hospitals, and other organizations engaging in research and receiving federal funds from HEW (now the Department of Health and Human Services) and other selected departments established institutional review boards (sometimes called human subjects committees) to review and oversee research conducted by investigators affiliated with their organizations. Under some circumstances, the IRBs review students' proposed research as well. These review boards have the authority to approve, disapprove, or modify research activities covered by the regulations, to conduct a continuing review of research involving human subjects, to ensure that there is an informed consent process, and to suspend or terminate the approval of any research.

INSTITUTIONAL REVIEW BOARDS

Institutional review boards are now firmly established as our society's "watchdogs," protecting human subjects from risky or harmful research. This policy does not mean that IRBs prevent all unethical research practices. They cannot monitor research that is covert or not brought to their attention. However, research today is monitored more rigorously than 20 or so years ago. Currently, organizations that receive federal funding and conduct research (such as universities and hospitals) are required to have IRBs to review proposed studies of human subjects.

Researchers begin the process of getting IRB approval by obtaining an application and preparing a description of their project. This narrative containing the research methods and procedures, the benefits and risks, the hypotheses, the recruitment of the subjects, the consent form, and so forth is called the **protocol.** Protocols vary in length and format depending on the planned research and the procedures established by the local IRB. There are three levels of review, from the most cursory (the exempt status), to expedited, to full review.

Federal regulations allow for some kinds of research to be exempted from a full review by the IRB. Research projects that qualify for **exempt status** are those that contain very little or no risk to the research subjects.

Those exempt activities most applicable to social work are

1. Research conducted in educational settings, such as research on normal educational practices involving instructional strategies or effectiveness of instructional techniques, curricula, or classroom management methods.
2. Research involving the use of educational tests (cognitive, diagnostic, aptitude, achievement) if information taken from these sources is recorded in such a manner that subjects cannot be identified directly or through

identifiers—and if any disclosure of the subjects' responses outside the research would not place the subjects at risk of criminal or civil liability or be damaging to the subjects' financial standing, employability, or reputation.

3. Research involving survey or interview procedures and observation of public behavior, if such research meets the conditions specified in (2).

4. Research involving the collection or study of existing data, documents, or records if these sources are publicly available or if the information is recorded by the investigator in such a manner that subjects cannot be identified directly or through identifiers linked to the subjects.

5. Research and demonstration projects approved by the federal department that examine public benefit of service programs.

6. Research involving survey or interview procedures when the respondents are elected or appointed public officials or candidates for public office.

These criteria mean that survey research is exempt from IRB review unless identifying information is collected and unless the disclosure of such information may cause harm to the subjects (Oakes, 2006).

Exemptions may not always be available from IRBs. In such an instance, the researcher will complete a lengthier application and usually is required to appear before the IRB to make a presentation or to respond to questions. Most IRBs will not grant exemptions to research involving certain **vulnerable populations** (e.g., children, prisoners, the mentally disabled, and economically or educationally disadvantaged persons), or when there is deception of subjects or use of techniques that expose the subject to discomfort or harassment beyond levels normally encountered in daily life. Further, exemption is not usually available when the information obtained from medical records is recorded in such a way that subjects can be identified directly or through identifiers linked to the subjects. However, some local IRBs may be more lenient than others.

Generally speaking, students are not required to seek approval from institutional review boards when their research projects are primarily for educational purposes (for example, an assignment to interview a small sample of people in order to learn about interviewing, recording data, or other aspects of the research). However, if the project involves living human subjects and is likely to contribute to generalizable knowledge (that is, research that is likely to be of publishable quality), students ought to seek IRB approval. Normally, student projects with the greatest potential for generating generalizable knowledge are doctoral dissertations and some master's theses. The test that IRBs apply to research projects are these: (1) Is the proposed study designed to be a systematic investigation? And (2) is the goal of the proposed study to add to or produce generalizable knowledge? The proposed data-gathering activity must meet both of these tests in order to be appropriate for IRB review (Amdur, Speers, & Bankert, 2006).

When research activities are of minimal risk—defined as "the probability and magnitude of harm or discomfort anticipated in the research are not greater in and of themselves than those ordinarily encountered in the daily life or during performance of routine physical or psychological examinations or tests" (Oki & Zaia, 2006)—then they may qualify for **expedited review.**

Practice Note: The Health Insurance Portability and Accountability Act (HIPAA)

The Health Insurance Portability and Accountability Act, better known by the acronym of HIPAA, has changed the way research data are collected and individuals in health care settings are informed about research efforts and their right to privacy. The "Privacy Rule" is that portion of HIPAA that addresses the protection of individually identifiable health information and regulates access and disclosure of this information. Protected health information (PHI) as defined by HIPAA amounts to all personally identifiable health information that is kept, held, and transmitted by health care providers, insurance providers/payers, or clearinghouses (referred to as covered entity [CE]). This federal law is very specific and has large penalties (ranging from $100 per violation to up to $250,000 in fines and 10 years in jail for those who sell, transfer, or use PHI for commercial advantage, personal gain, or malicious harm) for those who violate its requirements.

HIPAA defines 18 data elements as individually identifiable health information. Examples are admission and discharge dates, date of death, birth date, medical record numbers, account numbers, photographic images, and any other unique identifying number, characteristic or code. Access to these and other protected health information items must be obtained through a disclosure authorization unless the information is de-identified by removing names, telephone numbers, and all individually identifiable health information including all geographic subdivisions smaller than a state. (The first three digits of a zip code may be used if at least 20,000 people live in that area.)

The written authorization form must provide a description of the protected health information that is to be used or disclosed, the names of those making the request to disclose the information, the purpose of the research, the expiration date of the research effort, signatures of both parties (researcher and participant), information about the participant's right to revoke the authorization, and a statement that health care or service delivery is not contingent upon signing the authorization. Under HIPAA, participants in research from health care facilities have a right to access information about themselves.

HIPAA requirements mean that the health care researcher must often obtain what amounts to two separate informed consents: one that meets the IRB's standards and one that conforms with HIPAA requirements for the authorization of disclosure of information for a specific purpose. According to Muhlbaier (2006) about 50% of the time authorization and consent documents are separated and 50% of the time they can be combined—but this is an institutional decision and not the researcher's decision. In some instances, the IRB may grant a waiver for authorization (for instance, to conduct research on decedents).

In summary, here, for research purposes, is a quick overview of HIPAA:

- Contacting patients to recruit them as participants in a study will require a partial waiver from the appropriate IRB.
- Medical information without identifiers (de-identified data) must be collected and stored in a database by the hospital or health facility—not by the researcher wanting access to the data.
- Limited databases can contain ages, dates, and zip codes when no other personally identifiable items are obtained but a limited data-use agreement with the facility must be created.
- When it is not possible or practical to contact those eligible to participate in a study, a waiver of individual authorization must be sought from the IRB.
- When you want to contact individual consumers of health care services to interview them or review their medical information, they must sign individual authorizations that have been approved by the appropriate IRB.

Resources for more information on HIPAA can be found at http://privacyruleandresearch.nih.gov and http://www.hhs.gov/ocr/hipaa/guidelines/research.pdf.

Expedited reviews are usually conducted by a single member of the IRB or a subcommittee. A study that might involve drawing a blood sample could be considered minimal risk in the life of a normal, healthy individual.

Proposed research activities which do not fit into the exempted or expedited review categories discussed above are then subjected to a full committee review.

GENERAL GUIDELINES FOR ETHICAL RESEARCH

Social workers do not, as a rule, get involved in biomedical or other research where invasive procedures or physical harm to subjects is likely to occur. Research conducted by social workers involves surveys and interviews that require a certain amount of cooperation from the participants in the study. The risks to the subjects of social work research generally derive from the possibility that a third party will violate confidentiality and cause the subject physical, psychological, social, or economic harm. This threat is particularly acute for those subjects engaged in or with past histories of illegal acts.

When questionnaires are used or interviews are conducted with adults who are not in a vulnerable population, the principle of "implied consent" is applied. The act of participation is seen as giving informed consent. In these instances, IRBs do not require written documentation that subjects gave their consent. However, a problem arises when potential subjects feel that they cannot refuse to participate. If these subjects are clients (for example, persons on probation or parole, or recipients of some form of public assistance), they may not feel free to refuse without putting themselves in some jeopardy. Consultation with an institutional review board can come in handy in this type of situation. The IRB may suggest alternative ways to collect data or to reduce any implied coercion by informing potential subjects of their rights in writing. (A written consent form that specifies clearly that the potential subject has the right to refuse participation without any penalty or loss of service is often required. An example of such a form is shown in Figure 3.1) Social workers must be alert to the possibility that encouraging their clients to participate in research could be perceived as coercion. Since social workers are often "gate-keepers" of services, clients could feel pressured into participating in order to gain access to or continue receiving services.

If you are employed at a small agency that does not have its own IRB and you have questions about a proposed research or evaluation project, you might try contacting the IRB at the nearest university for consultation. To help you understand how they make their decisions and go about the process of weighing risks against benefits, the following guidelines are presented.

Guideline 1: Research Subjects Must Be Volunteers

Social work research is not something imposed on involuntary subjects. All of those participating in a research effort should freely decide to participate. No coercion of any kind should be used to secure participants for a study.

All subjects must be competent enough to understand their choice. If they are not able to comprehend fully (for example, if they are under the age of majority), then their legal caretakers must give permission, and the subjects must also **assent**. Even if parents give permission for their children to partici-pate in a research project, the children may still refuse to participate. The subject's right to self-determination is respected, and any research subject is free to withdraw from a study at any time.

Outpatient Drug Treatment Program After-Care Study

I _____ have been asked to participate in a research study under the direction of Ellen Samovar, M.S.W., the Principal Investigator, whose phone number is (231) 555-0000.

Purpose:
I understand that the purpose of this study is to examine the success of the Outpatient Drug Treatment Program in which I am participating—to learn why clients start and stop using drugs and what factors may influence these decisions.

Duration and Location:
I understand the study will take place at the ODTP offices on 717 South First Street. Further, I understand that the study will take about 60 minutes of my time and that I will be interviewed in a private office.

Procedures:
I will be asked to answer questions about my social and psychological well-being, relationships, employment, drug use, and illegal activities. In addition, I will be asked to provide a urine sample to test for evidence of drugs in my system and will be given a Breathalyzer to test for alcohol.

Risks/Discomforts:
It has been explained to me that some of the interview questions are very personal, involving drug and criminal behavior and may cause some discomfort in answering them.

Benefits:
I understand that the benefits from participating in this study may help researchers and those involved in public policy better understand the factors that lead to the starting and stopping of drug use.

Confidentiality:
I understand that a research code number will be used to identify my responses from those of other clients and that my name, address, and other identifying information will not be directly associated with any information obtained from me. A master listing of persons participating in the study and their identifying information will be kept in a secure location under lock and key except when being used by select staff. Further, I understand that a certificate of confidentiality has been obtained from the Department of Health and Human Services (DHHS) that protects investigators from being forced to release any of my data, even under a court order or a subpoena. When results of this study are published, my name or other identifying information will not be used.

Payments:
I will be paid $50 for my time and cooperation. If I stop early, I understand that I will be paid an amount appropriate to the time I have spent.

Right to Withdraw:
I understand that I do not have to take part in this study, and my refusal to participate will involve no penalty or loss of rights to which I am entitled. I may withdraw from the study at any time without fear of losing any services or benefits to which I am entitled.

Signatures:
I have read this entire consent form and completely understand my rights as a potential research subject. I voluntarily consent to participate in this research. I have been informed that I will receive a copy of this consent should questions arise and I wish to contact Ms. Samovar or the University of Somewhere's Institutional Review Board (555-555-5555) to discuss my rights as a research subject.

_____	_____
Signature of Research Subject	Date
_____	_____
Signature of Witness	Date
_____	_____
Signature of Investigator	Date

Figure 3.1 | Informed Consent to Participate in a Research Study

The use of written consent forms helps assure that research subjects know that they are volunteers. These forms provide brief, general information about the nature of the research, the procedures to be followed, and any foreseeable risks, discomforts, or benefits; and they indicate that the research subject is free to withdraw consent and to discontinue participation in the project at any time without penalty or loss of benefits. Consent forms generally contain the name of someone to contact should there be questions about the research or the subject's rights.

Guideline 2: Potential Research Subjects Should Be Given Sufficient Information About the Study to Determine Any Possible Risks or Discomforts as Well as Benefits

"Sufficient information" includes an explanation of the purpose of the research, the expected duration of the subject's participation, the procedures to be followed, and the identification of those procedures that might be experimental. The exact hypothesis does not have to be given away; it can be stated generally. However, the researcher must be specific about procedures that will involve the research subjects. If there are potential risks, these must be identified. Subjects should be given the opportunity to raise and receive answers to any questions at any time about the study or procedures that will be used.

The types of risks resulting from social work research might be psychological, physical, legal, or economic. Psychological risks could result from any procedures that cause research subjects to leave with lowered self-esteem and a sense that they aren't as smart as others (for example, feeling "stupid" to have been a victim of abuse). Similarly, researchers need to be cognizant that certain participants might become depressed if questions awaken painful memories. As they deem it appropriate, IRBs may ask researchers to provide information to research subjects about whom they can contact if they have intrusive or recurring memories (e.g., the local community mental health center's phone number).

Physical risks might occur to research subjects. For instance, if questionnaires were mailed to the homes of women who had surreptitiously attended a support group for battered spouses, their violent partners may discover this and punish them for their efforts to get help.

Legal risks are those associated with illegal behaviors—drug use, child abuse, stealing, or other illegal activities. Just as a social worker would do at the beginning of treatment, researchers must inform adults that if they reveal child abuse in an interview, the investigator is obligated to report it to the appropriate authorities. The most common risk here, however, is that a subject's confidentiality may be compromised if the researcher receives a subpoena or if personal identifiers are used and someone talks about sensitive material outside of the project.

Economic risks could occur if, for example, employees reveal that they are taking drugs or if they are surveyed about the work climate within their

Practice Note: Anonymity and Confidentiality

Anonymous responding means that the research participant cannot be identified by any means or by any person. When anonymity is promised, not even the researcher should be able to associate a response with a particular individual. Researchers need to be sensitive to the issue that participants can sometimes be recognized not from their personal identifiers like addresses and social security numbers but from socio-demographic information. For instance, a small agency might employ one female Asian-American or only one Ph.D. who is 50 years of age. With small samples of research subjects, researchers might want to use broad categories for such variables as age, education, ethnic groupings, and years of experience in order to keep from identifying persons with unique characteristics.

Confidentiality means that the potentially sensitive or private information is being supplied with the understanding that the research participant's identity, although known to the researcher, will be protected. Sometimes it is necessary to know a research participant's name, address, phone number, or social security number in order to match current information with medical records, prior offenses, or when pre- and posttesting of an intervention are being done. Where it is necessary to know the identities of research subjects, investigators routinely use a coding scheme so that personally identifying information is not contained on clients' survey forms, assessment forms, and so on. The listing that links code numbers with individuals' names is always kept in a secure, locked area except when being used.

agency—particularly if they criticize a supervisor or boss and this information wasn't carefully protected. The IRB's job is to think not only about the direct risks but also about the indirect or remote possibilities.

Benefits may be conceptualized as those that obviously reward the subject (such as cash payments, small incentives), those that result in subjects acquiring some type of insight or learning (e.g., learning better nutritional habits), and those that provide some worthwhile information (e.g., needs assessment regarding expanded bus service) for a service-providing organization or community in which the subject lives. Researchers quite often appeal to subjects' altruism and state that the project will advance scientific knowledge. Sometimes a final report of the project is offered to those subjects who voluntarily participated.

Finally, note that informed consent means that language used to inform the prospective research subjects should be not only age appropriate (an especially important consideration with children) but also free of jargon and technical/professional terms that an average person might not understand. A good guideline to use might be to try not to exceed a ninth- or tenth-grade reading level with adult client populations. Further, using "I" language seems to make the informed consent easier to understand than use of the second or third person.

Guideline 3: No Harm Shall Result as a Consequence of Participation in the Research

Social work researchers are not likely to propose research that would result in evident harm to their subjects. But one's perspective on harmful effects should not be limited to the active participants in a study. Punch (1986) related a dilemma that he faced. A group of female students wanted to study the reactions of police officers to reports of rape. In order to conduct this study, they would have had to fabricate stories. While data might have revealed that the police were not as sensitive as they should have been, Punch objected to the study on several grounds. First, there could have been legal repercussions for filing false police reports. Second, subsequent disclosure might have made the police distrustful of researchers. But most important, it might have led police to be skeptical of legitimate claims of sexually assaulted women. The benefits did not seem to outweigh the risks and the potential harm to others that could result.

Unethical research can result in harm to succeeding generations. For instance, the Tuskegee Study has been offered as one of the reasons why few African-Americans participate in research trials (Gamble, 1993). IRBs serve to prevent any potential exploitation of subjects.

Researchers have a responsibility to identify and to minimize harm or risk of harm that might befall the research subjects. And researchers should constantly monitor the subjects for harmful effects of the research. Subjects should not go away from a study feeling that they possess undesirable traits. Often, debriefings are used to inform subjects about the study and to neutralize negative feelings once participation in a project has concluded. Sometimes it is useful to point out that "most subjects" responded in a certain way. For example, if one were studying fears that people have, it might be useful to let participants in the study to know afterwards that most students dread public speaking or that males are not "sissies" if they fear snakes—another common fear.

Guideline 4: Sensitive Information Shall Be Protected

This guideline suggests that no harm to research subjects should result from improper handling of information. The privacy of research subjects may be protected in the following ways:

- Allowing subjects to respond anonymously
- Separating identifying information from the research data by using special coding and keeping the master list secure
- Stressing the importance of protecting confidential material

It is not always possible for subjects to respond anonymously—for example, when you have a situation in which you have administered both pretests and posttests and need to match individuals' scores to check for improvement. However, it is sometimes possible to invent a special code that is easy for subjects to remember and still protect their anonymity. Such a code might consist of the first four letters of the subject's mother's maiden name and the last four digits of the subject's social security number. Even a code this simple will help guard against the accidental recognition or identification of your subjects.

Practice Note: Research and Persons with Alzheimer's Disease

Research involving patients with Alzheimer's disease is fraught with ethical problems. Because their illness destroys cognitive abilities, most lack the capacity to understand an informed consent process, and even if they do, they may forget that they have given consent. Further, there are no well-accepted standards for determining when individuals with Alzheimer's disease have lost the capacity to give consent. Even mildly cognitively impaired older subjects experience difficulty in understanding consent information (High, 1992).

If the patient with Alzheimer's disease is unable to understand the consent process, informed consent is generally obtained from the next-of-kin or legal guardian. In any case, assent from the subject is still sought (High, Whitehouse, Post, & Berg, 1994).

Quantitative researchers report their research findings in the aggregate (group means and totals), which offers a great deal of protection to subjects who would not want to be connected to their responses. However, sometimes researchers wish to use a particularly apt comment (especially when open-ended questions have been employed) to summarize or illustrate the sentiments of the respondents. The caution here is to never report anything from which an individual subject could be identified. For instance, it would be a serious mistake to use the following quote to show the depth of employees' feelings about a new director in a study of job satisfaction at a county-run social service agency:

> I've been working abuse investigation longer than anyone else here—22 years—and I can say, without any doubt in my mind, that our new executive director is all fluff and no substance. He doesn't have a clue about how to do his job; I'm not sure he would even recognize an abused child if he saw one.

Another protection available to clients for when an "outside" researcher makes a request to collect information beyond what may be available from agency files—is for the *agency* to contact the former or present clients. Then, if they give permission, client names, addresses, or phone numbers might be released to the researcher. Finally, agencies sometimes ask researchers and those working with privileged communications to sign a written pledge of confidentiality.

Besides these basic guidelines, most IRBs are insistent that clients not be confused by service providers who are also collecting research data from their clients. To help keep things clear, service providers are usually asked not to recruit research subjects directly themselves—or to administer questionnaires or conduct research interviews with their clients—but instead to employ assistants for these purposes. This separation prevents clients from feeling subtle coercion to participate in a study and thus avoids placing the professional helper in a **dual relationship** of being both a researcher and a direct service provider. This kind of dual role can cause confusion in clients as to the nature of the "true" interest of the social worker.

Practice Note: Clinical Trials and African-Americans

Clinical trials are usually medical research projects where volunteers are divided into two or more groups and are designed to test the effectiveness and safety of new medical interventions (medications or medical devices). The control group generally does not receive the new intervention but gets a placebo (inert substance or activity) or the "tried-and-true" approach.

Clinical trials allow researchers to determine if a new medication or treatment is better than the old one and make available promising new treatments to persons for whom the old medicines, surgery, or treatments did not work. However, the chief drawback is that the studies almost always require random assignment of the research participants. That is, one can't choose to be in the group receiving the new treatment or in the "tried-and-true" group. Usually, research subjects don't learn until after their treatment or the study is finished which group they were in. Of course if they begin to feel or do better, they might guess that they received the new intervention. Other benefits of the clinical trials are that because of the experimental nature of the treatment, the cost to the patient may be reduced or even be free, and also the patient can feel that he or she is making a contribution to humanity.

Because there are race-related differences in responses to drugs for both medical and psychiatric symptoms, there has been a growing awareness of the need to recruit persons of color and to ensure that they are represented in clinical trials research. However, many African-Americans display a lack of trust with the white research establishment because of such historical events as the Tuskegee Syphilis Study. According to Mason (2005), health care social workers have been recruiting and providing support services for clinical researchers and have also been involved in publicizing the need for universal research participation. Mason describes some techniques designed to increase trust, such as allowing possible participants to meet the research team and asking the potential participants: "Is there anything in your beliefs that makes you not want to participate?" She also recommends giving potential participants biographies of the research team and reprints of published articles. To learn more about this topic, read Mason (2005). Another article along this line using the qualitative approach of focus groups has been published by Corbie-Smith, Thomas, Williams, and Moody-Ayers (1999).

POTENTIAL ETHICAL PROBLEMS IN RESEARCH

Deception

One of the thorniest ethical problems facing researchers in the social sciences has to do with deception. Generally speaking, deception should not be employed unless there is no other way to collect the necessary data or to study the phenomenon. Thus, deception might be acceptable if without it respondents would be too embarrassed, ashamed, or defensive to respond truthfully.

Some researchers avoid deception of clients or vulnerable populations by the creative use of simulations in which subjects (such as college students) are asked to imagine themselves in a particular role or setting—and then to respond as if the situation were real. In a study of the qualities that make someone a "good" therapist, subjects might, for instance, be shown video clips of "therapists" in action and then asked to choose the one they would want if they had a problem that could benefit from counseling. In such a study, actors might be used to simulate actual therapists and clients.

At times, the informed consent document that subjects must read and sign alerts them to the possibility that some deception may be involved. At other times, the IRB can decide to waive the right of subjects to be fully informed until after data has been obtained from the subject(s). IRBs generally require debriefing of the research subjects whenever any deception is employed.

Because it is important that the deception does not cause subjects to lose confidence in science or the scientific process, IRBs also expect that subjects should be given ample opportunity to have their questions answered about the project at the time of the debriefing, and, if they choose to do so, subjects are allowed to withdraw their own data from the study.

Should you use deception? Clearly, you should not if someone could be harmed or could go away from the study with a feeling of having been degraded or exploited. For this reason, the decision to use deception should not be made without consultation with others. As part of this process, alternative methodologies for studying the problem should be considered. But, as indicated earlier, sometimes the best way to study a problem depends on deception. An example comes to mind: Suppose you want to study racism but you know that if you approach the topic directly, most individuals would see your intent and construct their answers to minimize their racist opinions. However, suppose you inform your subjects that you are conducting a study on humor and you will be giving them 50 different jokes to see which ones they thought were the funniest. Couldn't this mild deception allow you to investigate racist values without alerting subjects to your real intent? The answer, of course, is yes.

For additional information on this topic you may want to refer to Fisher (2005).

Denial of Treatment

Another problem is that sometimes social workers who contemplate research think that the use of a control group may be unethical because clients would be denied services. It would indeed be unethical to deny beneficial services to clients strictly for the purpose of research.

But there are ways to obtain control groups without being unethical. For instance, if we wanted to evaluate a new program or intervention, we could compare clients receiving the new or experimental intervention against those who receive the usual set of services. In this scenario, there would be no denial of services. Some clients would get a slightly different intervention or set of services than those clients normally receive. This situation could be to their advantage.

In those agencies or programs with long waiting lists, researchers might consider as a control group those clients next in line for services. In fact, clients on a waiting list might appreciate a periodic contact with an agency representative (even if it is limited to the administration of a pretest and posttest), because it would constitute evidence that they have not been forgotten by the agency and that they are still actively queued for services. If these clients had similar problems (such as alcoholism), it might be possible to distribute educational pamphlets or materials to them while they were waiting for service. This group of clients could be considered to be receiving an educational intervention. While it may be a weaker or milder intervention than they would later receive, it would be better than nothing and may help the researcher feel better about gathering data from them. Comparisons could be made to the waiting list clients (the control group) and those who received the new intervention (the experimental group).

Another way to obtain a control group would be to compare your program participants with the clientele of a similar program or agency. While the groups would not be equivalent (since random assignment wasn't possible), at least you would have initial evaluative data. Still another "natural" comparison group could be found in that group of clients who keep one or two appointments, then drop out of treatment. This group could be compared with those individuals who complete the intervention. These examples are only some of the ways in which control groups can be identified without denying treatment.

Compensation

Is the practice of paying respondents or research subjects unethical? While reimbursing subjects for costs incurred (such as babysitting, time away from work, transportation) seems reasonable, questions arise whenever participation includes a *large* financial incentive. The guideline here is to avoid giving incentives that are so large or excessive that they constitute "undue inducement." When large financial rewards are offered for research subjects, the risk increases that some individuals may fabricate information in order to become eligible for money. Should you reimburse subjects for time lost from work and their time for commuting to the agency to participate in research? Generally, this level of compensation would not be viewed as excessive. Sometimes when subjects are followed over several years (longitudinal design), an incentive is built in (for example, a $50 bonus) if they participate in all of the scheduled follow-ups. Increasingly, lotteries have become popular as incentives. Typically, there is a cash prize that every respondent/participant becomes eligible to win.

Existing Data—Records Research Without Clients' Consent

Although many community mental health centers and other such agencies routinely request clients to sign consent forms at intake in the event that a researcher or program evaluator will need to look at their records some day, many agencies do not use consent forms unless their clients might be contacted for a specific study.

Suppose you wanted to do research within a state psychiatric hospital to determine if more bipolar personality disorders were being diagnosed in a recent year than 10 years ago. In such a situation, would you be prevented from conducting research because clients did not give their permission for you to perform archival research involving their records? Probably not, if you are a legitimate researcher and have the approval of an institutional review board.

As a student or faculty member, you would go first to your own university's institutional review board, stating your research objectives, how you would collect the data, and so forth. The IRB is likely to request that you submit a letter of support from the state hospital. Then, you will still need to contact the hospital's human subjects committee. The study ought to be approved if it is to be viewed as useful or having scientific merit.

Archival research of this type is not generally viewed as having any real potential for harming subjects. Further, in some localities the information you want might even be a matter of public record. Even so, some agencies may have you sign an agreement of confidentiality before allowing you access to their records. Remember that existing data is viewed by IRBs as data that are or have been routinely collected. It does *not* refer to data that may be collected at some time in the future.

FINAL THOUGHTS

Even though it is good practice and most often required that researchers seek approval from an institutional review board, some still argue that it is a waste of time for the knowledgeable and ethical researcher who will not be doing any harm. However, to bypass review boards entails a certain risk—as revealed in the following case of a university-based investigator who did not get approval for a controversial questionnaire administered within a school district. Although lots of data had already been collected, to avoid hostile parental reaction and a possible lawsuit, a school official shredded several hundred already completed questionnaires (Schilling, Schinke, Kirkham, Meltzer, & Norelius, 1988). You can imagine how much time was lost—to say nothing about damage to the research project and possibly someone's career. Ultimately, the researcher is responsible for the ethics of the research effort. Even with the approval of an institutional review board or other advisory group, the researcher must constantly be vigilant to prevent any harm or potentially unethical act from occurring.

While the thought of preparing a research protocol or appearing before an institutional review board might be somewhat intimidating, another way to see the process is as a review by concerned peers—individuals who really want good research to be produced. Their suggestions and comments may well improve your project.

As social workers, we really don't have an option not to engage in research and evaluation activities. The National Association of Social Workers' Code of Ethics requires us to evaluate our policies, programs, and interventions—to develop professional knowledge while protecting our research participants. A relevant section of the code addressing ethics in research and evaluation is reproduced in Figure 3.2.

Although it is not uncommon to worry whenever one is seeking IRB approval, if you have been open and honest about how the study will be conducted, you should have nothing to fear. If the IRB wants certain

5.02 EVALUATION AND RESEARCH

(a) Social workers should monitor and evaluate policies, the implementation of programs, and practice interventions.

(b) Social workers should promote and facilitate evaluation and research to contribute to the development of knowledge.

(c) Social workers should critically examine and keep current with emerging knowledge relevant to social work and fully use evaluation and research evidence in their professional practice.

(d) Social workers engaged in evaluation or research should carefully consider possible consequences and should follow guidelines developed for the protection of evaluation and research participants. Appropriate institutional review boards should be consulted.

(e) Social workers engaged in evaluation or research should obtain voluntary and written informed consent from participants, when appropriate, without any implied or actual deprivation or penalty for refusal to participate; without undue inducement to participate; and with due regard for participants' well-being, privacy, and dignity. Informed consent should include information about the nature, extent, and duration of the participation requested and disclosure of the risks and benefits of participation in the research.

(f) When evaluation or research participants are incapable of giving informed consent, social workers should provide an appropriate explanation to the participants, obtain the participants' assent to the extent they are able, and obtain written consent from an appropriate proxy.

(g) Social workers should never design or conduct evaluation or research that does not use consent procedures, such as certain forms of naturalistic observation and archival research, unless rigorous and responsible review of the research has found it to be justified because of its prospective scientific, educational, or applied value and unless equally effective alternative procedures that do not involve waiver of consent are not feasible.

(h) Social workers should inform participants of their right to withdraw from evaluation and research at any time without penalty.

(i) Social workers should take appropriate steps to ensure that participants in evaluation and research have access to appropriate supportive services.

(j) Social workers engaged in evaluation or research should protect participants from unwarranted physical or mental distress, harm, danger, or deprivation.

(k) Social workers engaged in the evaluation of services should discuss collected information only for professional purposes and only with people professionally concerned with this information.

(l) Social workers engaged in evaluation or research should ensure the anonymity or confidentiality of participants and of the data obtained from them. Social workers should inform participants of any limits of confidentiality, the measures that will be taken to ensure confidentiality, and when any records containing research data will be destroyed.

(m) Social workers who report evaluation and research results should protect participants' confidentiality by omitting identifying information unless proper consent has been obtained authorizing disclosure.

(n) Social workers should report evaluation and research findings accurately. They should not fabricate or falsify results and should take steps to correct any errors later found in published data using standard publication methods.

(o) Social workers engaged in evaluation or research should be alert to and avoid conflicts of interest and dual relationships with participants, should inform participants when a real or potential conflict of interest arises, and should take steps to resolve the issue in a manner that makes participants' interests primary.

(p) Social workers should educate themselves, their students, and their colleagues about responsible research practices.

Figure 3.2 | NASW Code of Ethics

Source: Copyright 1996, National Association of Social Workers, Inc., *NASW Code of Ethics.* Reprinted with permission.

Practice Note: Conducting Research with Children

Federal legislation has been proposed (The Family Privacy Act) that would require explicit written consent from parents (active consent) before minors could participate in any research containing sensitive questions including: sexual behavior; illegal, antisocial, or self-incriminating behavior; and psychological problems. Presently, IRBs can waive active parental consent by requiring researchers to send home information to parents giving them the option to refuse their child's participation.

The new legislation would prevent IRBs from allowing passive consent. This new policy could present a problem for researchers as typically 40% to 50% of parents fail to respond to mailed or student-delivered active consent forms; and further, minority students and those from single-parent households are underrepresented in samples requiring active parental consent (Dent, Sussman, & Stacy, 1997).

There can be a host of ethical problems associated with conducting research with children. Gensheimer, Ayers, and Roosa (1993) have identified several of these in discussing a prevention program designed for children of alcoholics. They point out that the very act of recruiting these children, whether by teacher referral or child self-selection after viewing a special film, places them in a situation where "labeling is almost assured." Another problem is that requiring informed consent from parents may prevent at-risk children from entering the program, because such children might fear being harmed by a parent who would be opposed to their participation. Still another question is: How much coaching or prompting is ethical? Could children—even with parental permission—truly feel that they could choose not to participate when teachers and other adults in the school were encouraging them to be involved?

procedures to be tightened up, they will make recommendations in writing. While it is true that investigations asking for certain sensitive information could be stressful for some clients, rarely is that a problem. When a protocol involves a vulnerable population, for example, interviewing sexual assault victims, IRBs may ask that researchers provide their subjects with the phone numbers and addresses of counseling agencies or rape crisis centers. The vast majority of studies proposed by social work researchers pose very little risk to research subjects.

Besides, it should not be overlooked that being a research subject can have positive effects. In clinical interventions, subjects may gain from new therapeutic procedures. Even if that doesn't occur, subjects may feel that the research is important and that they have made a contribution that will be of help to others. Participants may experience an increase in self-worth because they feel honored to have been selected to participate in "research." Sometimes participants receive some form of remuneration, and they appreciate it—even inconsequential amounts. Another consideration is that some research projects are interesting. Participants don't mind giving their opinions or sharing their insights. These examples are just some of the benefits to research participants.

INTERNET RESOURCES

Several federal offices provide tutorials for the purpose of educating researchers about protecting human subjects. The National Institutes of Health Web site (http://cme.nci.nih.gov) has self-assessment questions at the end of each unit

Practice Note: Unethical Use of Evaluation

Almost all of the social workers I have known have struck me as being ethical. For the most part, they have been concerned with such issues as protecting clients' confidentiality and privacy. However, even social workers can engage in unethical behavior when they allow their ambition to run unchecked.

Earlier in my career I was the director of research and evaluation for an agency that funded contract agencies to provide mental health services. As part of my job, I was asked to evaluate a particular agency and its director. There were rumors that the director was playing too much tennis during business hours and that he wasn't managing the agency well.

I went about the evaluation by contacting key professionals in the community who either had been or should have been making referrals to the agency. I obtained a mixed bag of comments. While it was evident that the agency could have done better in some areas, it also did some things reasonably well. I knew that the way the results were presented could affect whether or not the director continued in that position.

Since the instructions to me had been vague, I chose to present the findings in a formative manner rather than in a summative style. I attempted to make a balanced presentation and, insofar as possible, to let the data speak for itself. I did not feel comfortable concluding what the policymakers should do in this situation. Had they been kindly disposed toward the agency director, some of the findings from the evaluation would have been seen as providing constructive suggestions for change. Other statements would have provided positive strokes for the agency and its staff. However, there were political shenanigans going on.

The director of the counseling agency felt that the evaluation of the agency was an undeserved and unwarranted affront and soon resigned. At the funding agency, the individual who had been the strongest critic of the outgoing director, the one who had pushed the hardest for an evaluation of the agency, applied for the director's position and was subsequently hired.

I came away with a firm sense of having been used to oust the former agency director. The new agency director (the individual who had advocated for an evaluation of the outgoing director) had a master's degree in social work and would have been incensed if anyone suggested that something "unethical" had been done. What do you think? Is the act of causing an evaluation to be conducted unethical? At what point was something unethical done?

---

and informs you of correct and incorrect responses. The U.S. Department of Health and Human Services, Office for Human Research Protections, has a self-guided instructional tutorial without the self-assessment questions (http://ohrp.osophs.dhhs.gov/educmat.htm). Both sites will allow you to print out a certificate of completion when finished with the brief courses.

Qualitative Research Notes

At this point you probably have enough knowledge about qualitative research to know that it often has a very different perspective on data gathering and research design. For instance, qualitative researchers seldom use the term "research subjects" but much more often speak of research "participants." Thus, qualitative researchers do not see themselves as "using" other human beings as some kind of experimental guinea pigs. Rather, they prefer to observe and interview and to allow the data to flow from whatever stories or accounts the participants or key informers choose to tell. The research then is an elevation of these stories or explanations. Along this line, oral history interviews, particularly those that are collecting information for biographies, would not warrant IRB review as they are not designed to contribute generalizable knowledge (Gallant & Bliss, 2006).

The potential risks that participants in qualitative research might experience are ordinarily negligible because there is little possibility of medical intervention or treatment that could have the outcome of injury or death. Among the risks might be violation of privacy; breach of confidentiality; sanctioning bad or illegal behavior (i.e., an adult studying adolescent drug use may convey the attitude that their behavior is acceptable); harm to self-image, dignity, or data collection; or presentation of results in such a way that the individuals being studied do not feel respected (Gallant & Bliss, 2006).

A special uniqueness of qualitative research is that even with an interview schedule (list of questions the interviewer wants to use), responses to questions may well lead to other questions that weren't anticipated at the beginning of the study—and so the issue of informed consent and subjects' knowing exactly what they'll be asked can be problematic. Thus, it is possible that the interviewer could uncover a reportable event such as child or elder abuse although that was not the intent of the interviewing or participant observation.

KEY TERMS

protocol	vulnerable populations	assent
exempt status	expedited review	dual relationship

SELF-REVIEW

(Answers at the end of the book)

1. T or F. Legitimate researchers using archival or existing data pose very little risk of causing harm.
2. T or F. Social workers are required by their Code of Ethics to evaluate programs and interventions.
3. T or F. When parents grant permission for their children to be interviewed or tested in a research project, these children cannot refuse to participate.
4. T or F. Institutional review boards cannot refuse to grant permission for researchers if there is no harm to participants and also no scientific merit.
5. T or F. Deception can never be used in a research study involving participants under the age of 21.
6. T or F. Separate signed informed consent statements are usually not used with mailed surveys.
7. The research proposal describing the methods and procedures, recruitment of subjects, the consent form, and so forth is called the _____ _____.
8. _____ means the research participant cannot be identified by any means or any person.

9. _____ means that sensitive or private information may be linked to personally identifying information but is supplied with the understanding that the participant's identity will be protected.

10. T or F. *Every* potential research subject has the right to refuse to participate and may even choose to quit in the middle of a project without being assessed any penalty or losing any benefits.

11. T or F. A researcher would not have an obligation to report to potential research subjects that a new intervention available as a clinical trial had never been shown to be efficacious with humans—because this could dramatically reduce the number of persons who would volunteer.

12. Name one way that qualitative research might vary from quantitative research when viewed from an ethics perspective.

13. T or F. Under the HIPAA regulations, research participants can give verbal consent over the phone for their medical records to be released to a qualified and legitimate researcher affiliated with a hospital.

QUESTIONS FOR CLASS DISCUSSION

1. Discuss situations in which it would be acceptable to involve people in research without their knowledge.

2. A researcher wants to interview children in families where there has been a hospitalization for mental illness within the past three years. Discuss the potential ethical issues that will have to be addressed.

3. A researcher is interested in observing family functioning in families that have experienced a recent suicide. What precautions would the researcher need to take to ensure that no psychological or emotional harm resulted from the interviews?

4. A doctoral student conducting a confidential study of terminally ill patients in a hospice program finds that 15% of the patients are contemplating suicide. Discuss what can and should be done with this information. For instance, should family members be informed?

5. A researcher wants to investigate the emotional consequences of abortion. Because of the difficulty in getting access to the names and addresses of women who have had abortions, the researcher proposes a sampling design based on referrals from women who know of other women who have had abortions. What are the ethical issues involved in the use of this design?

6. Which of the four guidelines for conducting ethical research is of paramount importance? Why?

7. What might be some of the ethical issues with regard to obtaining research participants from the Internet? (See Keller and Lee, 2003, for an article on this topic.)

8. Discuss the HIPAA regulations from a researcher's perspective. Does the act greatly complicate data collection? Does the protection it provides for protecting health care information offset the challenges it creates for the researcher?

RESOURCES AND REFERENCES

Amdur, R. J., Speers, M., & Bankert, E. (2006). Identifying intent: Is this project research? In Elizabeth A. Bankert and Robert J. Amdur (Eds.), *Institutional Review Board: Management and function.* Subury, MA: Jones and Bartlett Publishers.

Annas, G. J., & Grodin, M. A. (1992). *The Nazi doctors and the Nuremberg code: Human rights in human experimentation.* New York: Oxford University Press.

Bankert, E. A. & Amdur, R. J. (Eds.). (2006). *Institutional Review Board: Management and function.* Subury, MA: Jones and Bartlett Publishers.

Caplan, A. L. (1992). Twenty years after. The legacy of the Tuskegee syphilis study: When evil intrudes. *Hastings Center Report, 22(6),* 29–32.

Conover, T. (1987). *Coyotes: A journey through the secret world of America's illegal aliens.* New York: Random House.

Corbie-Smith, G., Thomas, S. B., Williams, M. V. & Moody-Ayers, S. (1999). Attitudes and beliefs of African-Americans toward participation in medical research. *Journal of General Internal Medicine, 14,* 537–546.

Coughlin, E. K. (1988). Scholar who submitted bogus article to journals may be disciplined. *Chronicle of Higher Education,* Nov. 2, A7.

Dent, C. W., Sussman, S. Y, & Stacy, A. W. (1997). The impact of a written parental consent policy on estimates from a school-based drug use survey. *Evaluation Review, 21,* 698–712.

Desroches, F. (1990). Tearoom trade: A research update. *Qualitative Sociology 13(1),* 39–61.

Edgar, H. (1992). Twenty years after. The legacy of the Tuskegee syphilis study: Outside the community. *Hastings Center Report, 22(6),* 32–35.

Epstein, W. M. (1990). Confirmational response bias among social work journals. *Science Technology and Human Values, 15,* 9–38.

Epstein, W. M. (2004). Confirmational response bias and the quality of the editorial processes among American social work journals. *Research on Social Work Practice, 14(6),* 450–458.

Faden, R. R., & Beauchamp, T. L. (1986). *A history and theory of informed consent.* New York: Oxford University Press.

Fisher, C. B. (2005). Deception research involving children: Ethical practices and paradoxes. *Ethics and Behavior, 15(3),* 271–287.

Gallant, D. R., & Bliss, A. (2006). Qualitative social science research. In Elizabeth A. Bankert and Robert J. Amdur (Eds.), *Institutional Review Board: Management and function.* Subury, MA: Jones and Bartlett Publishers.

Gamble, V. (1993). A legacy of district: African-Americans and medical research. *American Journal of Preventive Medicine, 9,* 35–38.

Gensheimer, L. K., Ayers, I. S., & Roosa, M. W. (1993). School-based prevention interventions for at-risk populations. *Evaluation and Program Planning, 16,* 159–167.

High, D. M. (1992). Research with Alzheimer's disease subjects: Informed consent and proxy decision making. *Journal of the American Geriatrics Society, 40,* 950–957.

High, D. M., Whitehouse, P. J., Post, S. G., & Berg, L. (1994). Guidelines for addressing ethical and legal issues in Alzheimer's disease research: A position paper. *Alzheimer Disease and Associated Disorders, 8,* 66–74.

Hornblum, A. M. (1998). *Acres of skin: Human experiments at Holmesburg Prison.* New York: Routledge.

Humphreys, L. (1970). *Tearoom trade: Impersonal sex in public places.* Chicago: Aldine.

Jones, J. H. (1981). *Bad blood: The Tuskegee syphilis experiment.* New York: Free Press.

Keller, H. E., & Lee, S. (2003). Ethical issues surrounding human participants research using the Internet. *Ethics & Behavior, 13(3),* 211–219.

King, P. A. (1992). Twenty years after. The legacy of the Tuskegee syphilis study: The dangers of difference. *Hastings Center Report, 22(6),* 35–38.

Mason, S. E. (2005). Offering African-Americans opportunities to participate in clinical trials research: How social workers can help. *Health and Social Work, 30(4),* 296–304.

Martin, J., & Knox, J. (2000). Methodological and ethical issues in research on lesbians and gay men. *Social Work Research, 24,* 51–60.

Milgram, S. (1977). Ethical issues in the study of obedience. In S. Milgram (Ed.), *The individual in a social world.* Reading, MA: Addison-Wesley.

Muhlbaier, L. H. (2006). Health Insurance Portability and Accountability Act and research. In Elizabeth A. Bankert and Robert J. Amdur (Eds.), *Institutional Review Board: Management and function.* Subury, MA: Jones and Bartlett Publishers.

Oakes, J. M. (2006). Survey research. In Elizabeth A. Bankert and Robert J. Amdur (Eds.), *Institutional Review Board: Management and function*. Subury, MA: Jones and Bartlett Publishers.

Oki, G. S. F., & Zaia, J. A. (2006). In Elizabeth A. Bankert and Robert J. Amdur (Eds.). *Institutional Review Board: Management and function*. Subury, MA: Jones and Bartlett Publishers.

Punch, M. (1986). *The politics and ethics of fieldwork*. Beverly Hills, CA: Sage.

Schilling, R. F., Schinke, S. P, Kirkham, M. A., Meltzer, N. J., & Norelius, K. L. (1988). Social work research in social service agencies: Issues and guidelines. *Journal of Social Service Research*, *11(4)*, 75–87.

Sieber, J. E. (1992). *Planning ethically responsible research: A guide for students and internal review boards*. Newbury Park, CA: Sage.

Wellons, K. (1973). *The expectancy component in mental retardation*. (Doctoral dissertation, University of California, Berkeley.)

ASSIGNMENT 3.1: The Ethical Implications of Research

Objective: *To provide the student the experience of reflecting about the ways that data collection can intersect with ethical concerns.*

In the late 1960s, a sociologist, Laud Humphreys, reported his study of homosexual activity occurring in "tearooms," or public restrooms. He volunteered to be a "watchqueen"—that is, to serve as a lookout for the individuals engaged in this form of sexual activity. In order to obtain additional demographic information about homosexual men, Humphreys recorded the license numbers of their cars and traced the men to their homes. A year later, he posed as a health service interviewer and collected personal information from them. It could be argued that his research was important for its contribution to our understanding of this type of behavior. He found, for instance, that only a small percentage of his subjects were members of the gay community. Many were married men. Humphreys certainly was guilty of deception and invading the private lives of the subjects. Read Laud Humphreys' *Tearoom Trade* (1970), and then prepare a response to this question: "Do the benefits of Humphreys' research outweigh the methods he used?" If that book is not available to you, try to obtain the journal article by Frederick Desroches entitled, "Tearoom Trade: A Research Update" (1990). (See the reference list at the end of the chapter for the publication information of both of these titles.)

1. Take a position, pro or con, on the issue of Humphreys' *Tearoom Trade* study. Based on what you have learned about research ethics, explain why you feel that the study should or should not have been conducted.

ASSIGNMENT 3.2: Developing a Draft Informed-Consent Form

Objective: *To obtain practice in writing an informed consent form.*

Contact the institutional review board at your college or university and obtain a sample informed-consent form. If they do not make these available, then use the example provided in this chapter in order to write your own in a "participant-friendly" style. Address the questions below as you think about the safeguards needed for some *fictitious* study that you could propose.

What is the purpose of the study?

Why am I being invited to take part in this research?

Who is conducting the study?

What will I be asked to do?

Where is the study going to take place and how long will it last?

Are there any possible risks or discomforts?

Will I benefit from taking part in this study?

Do I have to take part in this study?

Do I receive any payment or rewards for taking part in the study?

Who will see the information I give?

ASSIGNMENT 3.3: Preparing an IRB Exemption Request

Objective: *To obtain experience in succinctly explaining research plans on a required form.*

Contact the institutional review board at your college or university and obtain the instructions (or the form) that researchers use to request permission to have their activities exempted from full IRB review. In order to complete this task, you will need to: (a) list research objectives, (b) describe the characteristics of the population from which you will be drawing your subjects, (c) describe your plans for recruiting the research subjects, and (d) detail the activities or procedures that will pertain to the subjects. If there are any potential risks to the subjects, these will also have to be described. Your instructor may want to you to write your responses here as a draft before or in lieu of using the IRB form.

1. List your research objectives:

2. Describe the characteristics of the subject population such as gender, age ranges, ethnic background, and whether they have any special status (e.g., minors, prisoners, mentally disabled):

3. Describe your plans for recruiting subjects:

4. Briefly describe the research procedures that will be applied to the human subjects:

5. Describe any potential physical, psychological, social, legal, or other risks to the research:

4 CHAPTER | Single-System Designs

Single-system designs are easy to use and understand, even with a limited understanding of research methodology. They provide practitioners with immediate, inexpensive, and practical feedback on whether their clients are improving.

Unlike the quantitative approaches that we will study later that involve groups of clients and assist us in understanding the "average" client, single-system designs focus on an individual client and his or her situation. Single-system designs are easiest to explain when the client has a specific behavior, like binge eating, that will be the focus of intervention. However, social work practitioners are not limited to applying these designs only to individual clients. Single-system designs can be used to evaluate the progress being made by a community, an organization, a family, or even a couple receiving marital counseling.

Advocates of single-system designs argue that information about specific clients is often obscured in studies where clients are grouped together, that one might learn little about an individual client—perhaps only whether a client did better or worse than average. However, single-system designs "personalize" the research by looking at a client's particular behavior over time. Before we learn how to develop single-system designs (also known as $N = 1$ research, single-case evaluation, and single-subject designs) for our clients, let's first consider their history.

THE ORIGIN OF SINGLE-SYSTEM DESIGNS

The study of individual cases has long been a part of the richness of the social sciences. For more than a century, case studies have been conducted in behavioral research. Bromley (1986) has stated that, in fact, the case study method goes back even further, to "remote origins in human social history" (p. 39). Prior to the development of statistics for group comparisons, research in the social sciences consisted almost entirely of descriptive case studies and reflections on them. Case studies were useful for illustrating to one's colleagues and students how problems requiring remedial action could be approached with specific theories or interventions.

Although these studies seldom employed any quantification of dependent variables, a number of important discoveries have come from observing individuals. Several examples will serve to demonstrate this point. Using nonsense syllables and himself as the subject, Ebbinghaus made major discoveries regarding principles of human learning. (We learn more efficiently in the morning than in the evening, for instance.) Pavlov's basic findings were obtained from the study of single animals and later were replicated with other single animals. Piaget's theories derived from observations of his own children. From Freud's discussion of specific cases to 11-month-old little Albert becoming conditioned to fear a white rat, generalizations from single subjects have played significant roles in helping us understand human behavior.

Individual case studies have appeared with some frequency throughout social science literature, and case examples or vignettes of cases are not uncommon today in medical and law journals. However, case studies vary greatly in their format, content, and organization. As statistical tests of comparison were developed and widely accepted, case studies fell out of favor with researchers in the social sciences. The use of control groups and group statistical comparisons is now firmly established in the social sciences, and the objective or quantitative methods of measurement used with these studies have led to changes among those researchers conducting case studies.

The emergence of single-system designs in the 1960s and 1970s has been attributed to their use by B. F. Skinner and other practitioners of behavior modification. With a focus on a specific target behavior, single-system designs were well suited for practitioners interested in demonstrating that their interventions were effective. Unlike the descriptive case studies of prior years, which relied heavily on subjective assessments of change, single-system studies today use objective measures to document that change has occurred. In fact, they may be very quantitative in appearance, and do not resemble the heavily narrative case studies of previous years except for the fact that they focus on one individual.

Single-system designs were developed primarily in response to dissatisfaction with group research designs for clinical practice situations and provide an alternative to the group designs usually associated with the conduct of research in the social sciences.

SINGLE-SYSTEM DESIGNS AND PRACTICE

Single-system designs can be thought of as a bridge between research and practice. How is this possible? Imagine for a moment that it is sometime in the future. You have made it through the social work program and are now employed as a therapist in a mental health agency. Your next appointment is a college student in her twenties. As she explains why she has sought counseling, you begin to see a pattern of symptoms suggestive of depression. You have worked with depressed persons before and feel that you can help this woman. Go forward in time another 10 weeks. The young woman is now interested in terminating treatment. How would you determine whether your counseling was successful? Would you calculate the number of times she smiled during your last several sessions? Would her body posture indicate her level of depression? Her plans for the future? While you might have an intuition that you had helped her, could you empirically document this for a supervisor or program director? How would you go about evaluating your own practice?

This example of the depressed young woman comes from Berlin's (1983) description of a practitioner involved in both research and practice with the same client. Berlin describes how a single-system design was employed by the practitioner to evaluate intervention with a 22-year-old part-time graduate student who had overwhelming feelings of sadness and despair.

Because the client's symptoms suggested depression, the therapist asked the client to complete a short, 20-item standardized scale (the CES-D) that measured depression. The client scored 45 on this scale, suggesting that she was clinically depressed. Treatment goals were then developed. Berlin was able to track the client's progress by administering the CES-D each time she met with the client. When you view these test results on a graph over the several weeks of treatment, it is easy to see that the client's level of depression fell dramatically during this time and remained low one month after termination. Figure 4.1 demonstrates this visually in the graph used by Berlin.

Even a cursory glimpse at this graph or at the others in this chapter will convince you that single-system graphs are often easy to comprehend. This simplicity is the essence of single-system designs—the visual presentation of a client's progress.

A CLOSER LOOK AT THE SINGLE-SYSTEM DESIGN

If you look closely at Figure 4.1, the several component parts needed for a single-system design can be detected. Note that a single **target behavior** (the dependent variable) was identified. In this instance, the problem was the client's depression, and the practitioner's interventions were oriented toward reducing that depression. Berlin chose an objective instrument to measure the level of depression being experienced by the client but it would also have been possible to monitor improvement with behavioral measures of depression. For instance, the client may have had crying spells, restless sleep, poor appetite, and loneliness. The selection of a target behavior, such as frequent

CES-D Depression Scores and Daily Average Self-Criticism Scores

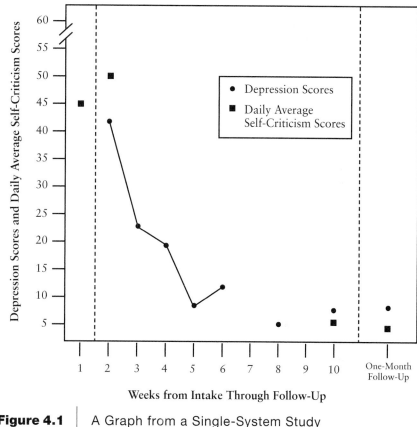

Figure 4.1 | A Graph from a Single-System Study

Source: Berlin, S. B. (1983). Single-case evaluation: Another version. *Social Work Research and Abstracts,* 19(1), 9. Copyright © National Association of Social Workers, Inc. Reprinted with permission.

crying spells, could have been used had there been no objective instrument available for detecting changes in the depression.

Note that no complicated statistical procedures were used, just a simple graph to record (with repeated measurements) the client's improvement over time. (Although it is possible to use statistical procedures to check for statistically significant differences in improvement, this is not a requirement or a necessity for most single-system designs.) The arrangement of the data chronologically on the graph is easy to interpret and follows from the research design. Ideally, data are collected before the intervention begins. The preintervention data are called the **baseline** and allow for comparisons to be made with the behavior during and after intervention.

Retrospective (or reconstructed) baselines are memory-based estimates of the severity of a problem, or could, in some instances, be based on actual data that already exist, such as a report card indicating grades or absences from school. Concurrent baselines are measurements of the problem that are begun sometime after intake assessment.

STARTING A SINGLE-SYSTEM STUDY

The first step in developing a single-system study is to choose a behavior to monitor. This may be a difficult decision, but sometimes it is obvious which behavior needs to be targeted: If you have a client who has been arrested for driving while intoxicated, and this is the second arrest in six months, it is clear that you have a client who needs to change his or her drinking behavior. Similarly, it would be apparent that a child with school phobia needs to decrease the number of days absent from school. Some clients need to demonstrate greater assertiveness; others need to learn to handle their destructive anger. Generally speaking, you will be working with clients to either increase or decrease certain behaviors. However, there can be as many as five different ways to think about how to modify behavior. Sundel and Sundel (1993) have suggested that social workers can help the client: (1) acquire a behavior, (2) increase the strength or frequency of a behavior, (3) maintain a behavior, (4) decrease a behavior, or (5) completely suppress a behavior.

There will not be one target behavior that can be selected for all your clients. Examples of behaviors that can be easily monitored include:

- Increasing a child's positive interactions with peers
- Reducing a child's fear of the dark
- Helping a shy adult become more assertive
- Reducing amount of time spent watching television
- Improving reading comprehension
- Decreasing a compulsive behavior
- Managing anger outbursts better
- Losing weight
- Managing money better
- Procrastinating less

Behaviors to be monitored in a single-system study must necessarily follow from the treatment plan prepared for that individual client. Even though most social workers are not behaviorists, and the goals for their clients may be fairly broad, single-system designs can be used in nonbehavioral treatment, providing that the client's final goals can be stated in measurable terms.

The selection of the appropriate problem to be influenced by the intervention is obviously very important. When choosing a target behavior, keep the following considerations in mind:

1. *Target behaviors should come from the client.* To select problems that are not attuned to clients' perceptions of their problems risks premature termination. Although some clients may have a secret agenda for seeking help or other

problems that may be revealed after a trusting relationship has been established, the best place to start is with the problem the client has identified as being most significant. This may require some prioritizing of the client's problems.

Along this line, it may be helpful to use the following criteria to help rank the problems mentioned by clients: (1) problems that are the most immediate concern; (2) problems that have the most negative consequences for the client, the client's significant other, or society if not handled immediately; (3) problems that have the highest probability of being corrected quickly, thus providing an experience of success; and (4) problems that require handling before other problems can be dealt with (Sundel & Sundel, 1993). Ideally, the social worker and the client should reach mutual agreement regarding the major concern and focus of the intervention.

2. *Vaguely stated problems are difficult to measure.* Select behaviors that are concrete and observable. Avoid any behavior that might be difficult to detect or about which there might be disagreement as to whether it was happening or not.

Choose behaviors that can be counted, observed, or quantified. You may have to help your client move from an ambiguous description of the problem to a more precise definition. For instance, "nervousness" is a vague complaint, but associated with it may be several observable behaviors such as nail biting, overeating, stuttering, episodes of gastrointestinal attacks, or excessive use of antacids, that could be used as surrogate measures of the nervousness. You could count the number of antacids consumed in a day, the number of stuttering episodes, or the number of calories ingested per day. Whenever possible, target behaviors should be so well defined that others would have little difficulty in observing or recording them.

Start with the presenting problem, and then explore how that problem manifests itself. Let's say that a woman tells you that her husband doesn't respect her. You cannot use "lack of respect" as a target behavior, because the term is too broad and not immediately associated with any specific behaviors. You need to find how the client experiences this problem. What specific behaviors illustrate the problem of lack of respect? She could mean that her husband walks away while she is talking. You want to identify the actions that indicate to the woman that her husband does not respect her. From these specific behaviors, choose one or two to focus on during the intervention.

In Berlin's example, a short standardized instrument was available for use. What happens if the therapist knows of no instrument suitable for measuring a problem like depression, anxiety, or other vaguely stated concerns? The therapist has only two choices: review the literature and attempt to find such an instrument, or select specific target behaviors suggested by the client's particular set of problems.

For example, suppose a married couple comes to you because they are arguing almost daily. They are interested in saving their marriage; however, both are assertive, strong-willed individuals. The obvious target behavior is the number of arguments that they have. What led the couple to therapy? The wife (who happens to be a bookkeeper) kept a record of the number of arguments that the couple had over the past 14 days. The frequency of these arguments was disturbing to both of them, and they agreed to seek help.

In this instance, the baseline was readily available to the therapist, and the couple were in agreement that they wanted to reduce the number of arguments that had been occurring. While an instrument would not be needed, one that measured marital satisfaction could be used. If the marital counseling is successful, then it is reasonable to assume that a graph illustrating the number of arguments would show fewer arguments after intervention than during the baseline period.

Sometimes clients describe problems like fear of dying or loneliness that seem to be more of a mental state, more attitudinal than behavioral. In instances like these, you may want to consult Corcoran and Fischer's (2000) *Measures for Clinical Practice* to obtain scales that objectively measure client death anxiety or loneliness. However, even these conditions are likely to be associated with problem behaviors. The person who is afraid of dying may be having panic attacks, insomnia, or be unable to concentrate at work or school. The individual who is experiencing loneliness may need to change introverted, reclusive behaviors and increase social contacts by joining clubs, bowling leagues, coed volleyball teams, hobby groups, and so on. As a practitioner you have to decide what behaviors to monitor and how to monitor improvement. The challenge is always to operationalize so specifically that there is little doubt when change or improvement is occurring.

Not only will vaguely stated problems create difficulties when you attempt to measure them, but so can rather specific events (for example, hearing voices or having delusions) if your client doesn't always report these or if they are not observable by others. Certainly, clients are able to self-report on behaviors or problems that are not noticeable to others, but I would not select these for measurement with a single-system design unless the client was strongly motivated to alleviate the problem and could be trusted to report with accuracy. The easiest problems to measure are those that are easily recognized by others and repetitive. (For instance, I once heard of a client in a residential treatment program who took 10 or more long showers a day.)

Frequency of an event is not the only way of measuring problem behavior like a couple's arguments. In a different situation the therapist might have suggested that the length (or duration) of the arguments be monitored. Or the intensity (magnitude) of the arguments might have been recorded. Minor verbal disagreements might not be counted; only those of the foot-stomping, door-slamming variety would qualify. Residents of a group home who live with someone showering 10 times a day might be just as unhappy if "Mr. Clean" took fewer showers but stayed in 35 minutes each time, using up all the hot water.

The practitioner has quite a bit of freedom in choosing what to measure, how to measure, and even who should do the recording.

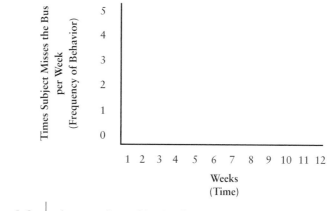

Figure 4.2 | Incomplete Single-System Graph

However, the target behavior should suggest itself from the client's description of the problem. The behavior should be an activity that a client agrees is important to count or record. Clients should be able to see how change in the target behavior contributes to improving their problem situation.

3. *Target behaviors are monitored over time.* Graphs are useful tools for portraying changes in behavior. Graphs need not be drawn on engineering or graph paper; you can draw vertical and horizontal lines that intersect at a right angle and calibrate or demarcate the lines in a way that has meaning and indicates how much of the activity is occurring during the observation period (see Figure 4.2).

On the *vertical line* (or *y-axis*), plot the number of times (frequency) the target behavior occurs. You need to have a rough idea how often the behavior is occurring in order to devise a scale to show its pattern. For instance, if little Pablo misses his bus three times in one week, the vertical axis should record the range of lowest and greatest number possible of these incidents. Since it is unlikely that he could miss his bus more than five mornings a week, the range of these episodes would be 0 to 5.

Some thought needs to go into the selection of the behavior or the problem being counted on the vertical axis. Because missing a bus might be a matter of oversleeping, you might want to target the number of times that little Pablo gets to bed on time the night before. Or, if he is a little older and sets his own alarm clock, the number of times that he oversleeps. Both of these could be legitimate target behaviors for intervention.

Notice the emphasis on counting behaviors. It would be less useful to chart the actual times that little Pablo awakens (for example, 7:04 A.M.) since his problem might be one of procrastination and not oversleeping. On the other hand, if his difficulty is getting to bed on time, the vertical axis might be constructed to show the number of minutes past his bedtime that he is late each evening. Counting intervals of time such as minutes spent

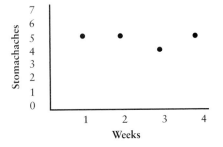

Figure 4.3 | An Example of a Developing Baseline

dressing or eating breakfast (if Pablo tends to dawdle) might also be appropriate for the vertical axis.

The *horizontal line* (or *x-axis*) is used to portray the behavior as it occurs over time. Whether you decide to use hours, days, or weeks as the unit of time depends on the behavior itself. If you were working with a 12-year-old who was having stomachaches because of school phobia and this tended to happen once a day (10 minutes before the school bus arrived), it would be better to count the number of times a week that the stomachaches occurred than to keep hourly records. A baseline graph of the stomachaches in a month prior to the intervention might resemble the one in Figure 4.3.

This graph shows that the child complained of stomach problems five times (corresponding to the five school days) the first week that a record was kept, five times the second and fourth weeks, but only four times in the third week when there was a school holiday. In this example, we know that the symptoms are occurring every school day. The child missed having a stomachache only once on a school day during a 28-day period. This is a well established or *stable pattern* of behavior. If intervention is effective, a pattern of improvement will be readily observable. Contrast this pattern with a target behavior that is unpredictable (where there is no discernible pattern). Suppose that the child had one stomachache the first week, none the second week, five stomachaches during the third week, and none during the fourth week. This would be an erratic pattern where we might want a longer baseline to help us understand what is going on. Instead of school phobia, the child's stomach problems might be due to food allergies that are triggered by specific foods that are not eaten seven days a week.

It is difficult to provide a rule about how long the baseline period should be. Much depends on how often the behavior is occurring and how stable this pattern is. A behavior that occurs relatively infrequently probably is not a useful behavior to choose for monitoring because it will be hard to see any patterns. Similarly, behavior that varies a great deal will not make a good target behavior. Choose a behavior that is fairly dependable in its occurrence. The behavior can vary in frequency, but this variation should not have "wild swings."

Here are several guidelines concerning the length of the baseline (Bloom, Fischer, & Orme, 2003):

- It should be long enough to be useful in assessing the client's problems.
- It should be stable enough to allow you to make some estimates about its frequency if there were no intervention.
- Three observations during baseline are considered a minimum, but this number is often insufficient and 10 baseline points is recommended if it is ethically and practically possible.

Stable patterns are characterized by little variability in the data—for instance, the absence of big peaks and valleys. However, the length of the baseline should be tempered by the availability of data and concern about not unduly delaying intervention.

You don't have to wait five or six weeks to construct a baseline. Suppose a mother comes to you because she is concerned that her 5-year-old is still wetting the bed. You ask, "About how often does this happen?" If the mother says, "About every night" or "Almost every night," then the baseline is established and you can begin with the assumption that bed wetting is occurring about 30 times a month. Even if it is actually happening only 27 or 25 times a month, the obvious goal is to decrease these incidents to zero times a month.

Baseline data can come from various sources. You might find ample reference to the occurrence of the target behavior in the progress notes made during a client intake or therapy session, or the client may have kept some informal records or have a good memory, or there may be official records (for example, elementary school absences). In U.S. society, documentation is often readily available. A baseline for a spouse whose drinking behavior results in days missed from work, for example, might be obtained by looking at paycheck stubs. In some instances, clients can keep logs or self-report on the occurrence of the target behavior. In other situations, someone else will need to monitor the behavior. These decisions are individually determined by a knowledge of the client's abilities and situation.

A good argument for using existing records or data for the baseline is that the very act of counting or measuring a behavior during the baseline phase may begin to change the client's behavior (especially if the client is self-reporting and motivated to improve) even before the intervention is implemented. Self-reporting, though generally regarded as reliable, does have a reactive effect in that clients' behavior might change when they know they are being observed. Needless to say, self-monitoring data will give a false picture if the client is motivated to misrepresent the extent or severity of the problem.

As can be seen in Figure 4.4, the behavior during the baseline period is usually separated from the behavior during the intervention phase by a vertical dotted line.

4. *The last step in developing a single-system study is selecting a design.* Of the many single-system designs from which to choose, only a few of those

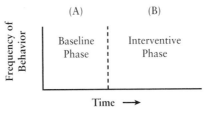

Figure 4.4 | Essential Components of a Single-System Design

judged to be the most useful to practitioners are presented here. As you read the balance of this chapter, you may find yourself liking some designs because you feel that you could comfortably use them. Other designs may strike you as impractical (or worse) because they seem more suited for experimental labs and require greater control over the client system than you feel that you have or ought to have. One design (the AB) is likely to meet most of your needs. But other designs may be more appropriate for specific cases or for when you want greater assurance that it was your intervention and not some other factor that had the desired effect.

TYPES OF DESIGNS

The Case Study or B Design

The case study, as we have already mentioned, is familiar to students. Case studies are sometimes called uncontrolled case studies because they lack baseline measures and use anecdotal information rather than objective measures of the target behavior. These designs are therefore seriously limited in that they do not permit conclusions that the intervention caused the change in the client's behavior. (Other forces or influences may have been at work in addition to the intervention.) What's more, there is no guarantee that the findings from a case study will fit any other cases (Gilgun, 1994).

However, these designs are simple to conceptualize, don't require pre-planning, and are possible to start once intervention has begun. Although they can't ascribe causation or rule out competing explanations, they can describe client progress.

With the beginning of intervention, the practitioner begins keeping records on how much the client changes or improves. No attempt is made to compare the behavior at the end of the intervention with its baseline (because there was none). This design can be used with any theoretical orientation, and its value is the feedback it provides. However, the case study has a number of serious limitations: Lack of systematic observation and standardization of assessment, no baseline measures, and little control of the treatment variable (the intervention may involve several simultaneous procedures). Furthermore, case studies rely heavily on anecdotal information that may rest on a heavily biased

Practice Note: Sudden Infant Death Syndrome

In 1972, five case reports of Sudden Infant Death Syndrome (SIDS) occurring in only three families were described by a physician, Alfred Steinschneider, in the journal *Pediatrics*. Twenty-five years later, a book, *The Death of Innocents: A True Story of Murder* by Richard Firstman and Jamie Talan (1997), raised important questions about how a seriously flawed study could have shaped medical thinking all those years.

Even today, Steinschneider's theories about sleep apnea are considered influential, although the editor of *Pediatrics*, Jerold Lucey, noted in the journal, "We never should have published this article. . . . The patients studied were murdered. They were not SIDS patients . . . some physicians still believe SIDS runs in families. It doesn't—murder does" (1997, p. A77). In one of the families Steinschneider included in his case reports, the mother was convicted recently of smothering all five of her children.

The impact of this book and Dr. Lucey's apology (he was also the editor of *Pediatrics* in 1972) will likely result in medical examiners becoming much more resistant to concluding that SIDS was responsible for an infant's death—particularly when it is the second one within a family.

SIDS kills about 3,500 infants a year, about 2,000 a year fewer than in the years before 1992, when doctors began recommending that parents put babies on their backs to sleep. The overwhelming majority of SIDS deaths are not thought to be infanticide. However, a study in Massachusetts found evidence of parental abuse in more than one-third of 155 babies treated for "near-SIDS" episodes or studied because siblings had died of SIDS. Of those who died from SIDS in 1996, about 3% had siblings who also reportedly died from it (*USA Today*, September 26, 1997; October 28, 1997). This example points out the necessity for researchers to not allow themselves to become blinded by their theories, and the importance of continuing to search for other explanations. It cautions against concluding too much from a small number of cases.

---

presentation, and because of the focus on one individual, the results cannot be generalized to other situations.

Though they lack scientific rigor, case studies are useful for several reasons: They are a source of hypotheses about human behavior and techniques for working with clients, they have a strong persuasive appeal in illustrating a particular point, and they stimulate us to examine rare phenomena (Kazdin, 1992).

A fascinating case study is found in Russ Rymer's *Genie: An Abused Child's Flight from Silence* (1993). This book reveals a great deal about the effects of extreme childhood neglect and abuse on personality and language. It narrates the discovery of a 13-year-old girl who, weighing 59 pounds, was incontinent, could not chew solid food, could not cry or focus her eyes beyond 12 feet, and had no perception of heat and cold. Her productive vocabulary was limited to "Stopit," "Nomore," and several other shorter negatives. And yet she was described as having incredible curiosity, energy, and personality. For most of her life, Genie had been confined alone in a small bedroom, harnessed to an infant's potty chair and beaten if she made any noise. Case studies like this can be riveting to read. However, often they are devoid of pertinent information that would give us a basis for comparison. In this case, the child's father was convinced that she was mentally retarded and would die before the age of 12, but what was her IQ before she was socially and physically deprived? Although she was making good progress, how much she could achieve was hard to predict.

While case studies may be educational and useful from a pedagogic standpoint, they generally are not considered to be formal research methodologies. When we are responsible for the intervention for a complex, difficult, or particularly puzzling client or family, it is often beneficial to build on the simple case study model by constructing a baseline and observing target behaviors. When we add these features, the simple case study becomes a single-system design, capable of providing objective evidence that our treatment did or did not benefit the client.

The AB Design

The basic **AB design** (see Figure 4.5) is the single-system design most often used by social work practitioners and researchers. The A portion of the design is the baseline measurement (for example, the client's scores on a scale assessing depression). The B part of the design is the data collected during the treatment phase. Because of its simplicity, the AB design is virtually unlimited in its applicability in social work. This is perhaps its greatest strength. It reveals changes in behavior—if they occur. Unfortunately, changes in behavior that are detected with this design do not "prove" that the intervention was responsible. Alternative explanations such as the occurrence of other events during intervention (for example, leaving a stressful job, the birth of a child, over-the-fence counseling by a neighbor, or maturation of the client) may account for changes in the client's behavior. These alternative or rival explanations are difficult to rule out with the basic AB design. Most practitioners, however, would be happy with the client's success and would not worry about alternative explanations. While the AB design may not adequately control for competing explanations, it provides a useful way of examining whether there has been an improvement since intervention began.

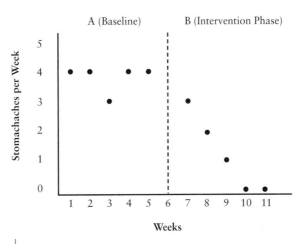

Figure 4.5   Illustration of an AB Design Graph

The ABA and ABAB Designs

These two designs are sometimes called withdrawal, reversal, or experimental single-system designs because they employ a second period of nonintervention, another baseline condition in order to show that the intervention was responsible for the observed effect on the target behavior. These designs are concerned with whether the effect of the intervention will continue or be maintained. After the intervention (B) has been completed or substantially delivered, treatment is withdrawn or stopped, and the target problem is monitored to see what direction it takes.

The second (A) phase in an **ABA design** is like the first A phase in that behavior is recorded during a period of no intervention. This is not to suggest that you as a practitioner should purposely withdraw treatment for "research" purposes; that would be an unethical practice. The second A phase could legitimately come about following termination. (Berlin mailed a depression scale to the client as a follow-up measure one month after treatment. Look back to Figure 4.1 for an example of this graph.)

Because of practice-related concerns about ending client contact during a nonintervention phase, Bloom, Fischer, and Orme (2003) do not recommend this design for most practice situations. However, if the second A phase comes about as a follow-up to intervention, or for other therapeutically sound reasons, this design might be useful and ought not be overlooked.

Each phase of the classical single-system design (AB) is repeated twice in the **ABAB design.** As in the ABA design, treatment is withdrawn or removed in the second baseline (A phase) in order to see if the target behavior will return to its original level (prior to intervention). There may be valid reasons for a second period of nonintervention, both practical—for example, the therapist's vacation—and therapeutic—for example, a trial period of three weeks between appointments to wean a "dependent" client away from intervention. After the second baseline period, the treatment is reintroduced. Unlike the ABA design, the study ends during an intervention phase, which makes it more appealing from an ethical standpoint.

Because the client serves as his or her own control, the ABAB design is an experimental design and provides some assurance that the intervention actually was responsible for any changes in behavior. In this sense, the ABAB design is a stronger and more powerful design than the AB and ABA designs. If the same effects are shown during the second AB (replication) phase, then there is less likelihood that outside influences (alternative explanations) were responsible. The ABAB is a strong design for those who are interested in contributing to the knowledge base by experimentally demonstrating that some intervention is effective.

However, use of the ABAB design is not always practical. In fact, if the first treatment phase reduced the behavior to acceptable levels for the client and others concerned, it is likely that all involved persons would feel that the intervention was a success. Termination would occur, and the therapist would be given a new client to add to his or her caseload. There would be little reason to introduce intervention again unless the client made another request. In fact, the more successful the intervention, the less likely it will be that the behavior would return to its initial baseline (A) level.

The ABAB design may not feel comfortable to many practitioners because they are painfully aware of the shortage of staff or the long lists of clients patiently waiting for help with their problems. Even though the second baseline could come about naturally (vacations, hospitalizations, and so on), the ABAB design may still seem excessive or a luxury unavailable to many practitioners.

The ABAB design is best thought of as a design to be used for knowledge building. It is a design that enables thorough testing of an intervention and reduction of alternative explanations for the client's improvement. This design is what you would use if you were sure that a given intervention worked and you wanted to document or publish your success in some sort of formal way.

The ABC and ABCD Designs

Practitioners know well that sometimes the intervention that you start with doesn't work, is not valued by the client, or does not appear to be working as fast as it should. In these situations, major changes are made in the treatment plan. Another intervention might be started or multiple modalities employed.

The **ABC** or **"successive interventions"** design permits the practitioner to respond with different interventions when needed and still allows for monitoring the effects of these interventions. In this scheme, the effects of the second intervention are identified as (C). The effects of the third intervention are (D), and so on.

Since there is no return to a baseline between the second and third (or even fourth) interventions, these successive intervention designs do not allow the practitioner to determine which interventions caused the changes in the behavior. Even though it might appear that the first intervention (B) didn't work, but that the second intervention (C) did, it could be that the accumulative or interactive effects of both B and C resulted in the change. Although colleagues and the client may be duly impressed with these changes, strictly speaking, conditions were not controlled enough for any sort of formal statement of causality.

Even if this design tends to fall short of the experimenter's expectations, it is appealing to practitioners because intervention is often modified in practice and different techniques are used in the course of therapy. If everyone is happy that the behavior has changed in the desired direction, and success is in the air, neither client nor practitioner may need greater "proof" that the interventions worked. Figure 4.6 shows an example of an **ABCD design** found in the social work literature.

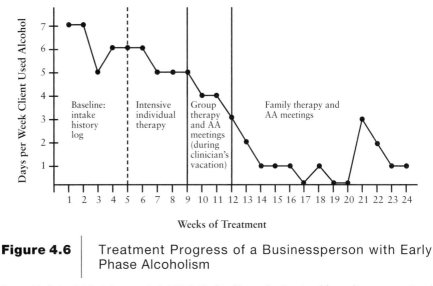

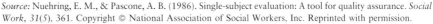

Figure 4.6 | Treatment Progress of a Businessperson with Early Phase Alcoholism

Source: Nuehring, E. M., & Pascone, A. B. (1986). Single-subject evaluation: A tool for quality assurance. *Social Work, 31*(5), 361. Copyright © National Association of Social Workers, Inc. Reprinted with permission.

Multiple Baseline Designs

Single-system designs known as **multiple baseline designs** may be used when you are working with several clients who have the same problem and who receive the same intervention. For instance, suppose you are employed as a social worker in a nursing home and the staff begins to complain about a problem of urinary incontinence with three wheelchair-bound residents who have organic brain disorders. You've recently read an article describing the use of an intervention involving praise and cookies for patients like this that resulted in a decrease in urinary accidents. The staff is eager to participate and soon begin collecting baseline data.

Keeping true to the standards on which single-system designs are based, the intervention starts first with Mr. Smith. Only when there is clear indication of improvement is the intervention applied to the second resident, Mrs. Wright. And then only when she shows improvement can the intervention be applied to the third resident. When success is achieved with all three residents, this becomes the basis for inferring that the intervention caused the observed changes following the "principle of unlikely successive coincidences" (Bloom, Fischer, & Orme, 2003). The shorthand notation for a **multiple baseline across subjects design** is $A_1A_2A_3B$.

You can see in Figure 4.7 that multiple baseline designs have baselines of unequal length and that intervention does not begin in the second graph until change has been shown with the first client.

A **multiple baseline across behaviors design** can be employed if a single client has two, three, or more problems that are likely to respond to the same

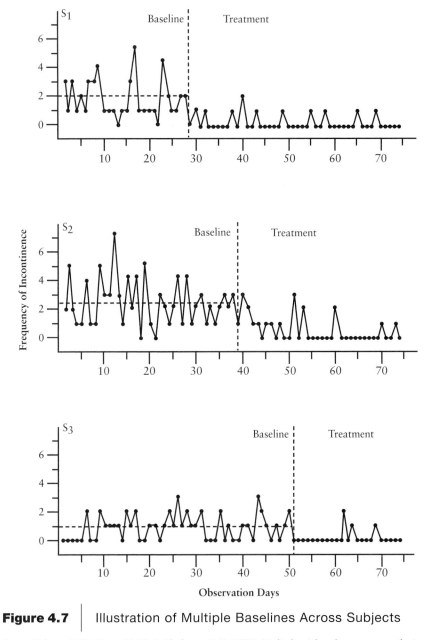

Figure 4.7 | Illustration of Multiple Baselines Across Subjects

Source: Pinkston, E. M., Howe, M. W., & Blackman, D. K. (1987). Medical social work management of urinary incontinence in the elderly: A behavioral approach, *Journal of Social Service Research*, 10 (2, 3, 4), 188. Copyright © Haworth Press, Inc. Reprinted with permission.

intervention. If the client has three target problems, then the notation would reflect the three separate baselines and one intervention and would be $A_1A_2A_3B.$ Note that the notation for both multiple baseline designs (across subjects and behaviors) is the same.

For instance, suppose you are working with a 15-year-old in a residential treatment facility for youth. Alberto has been abused by a stepfather, is not doing well in school, and has poor impulse control, which gets him into frequent fights. He defies authority, is uncooperative with staff, and boasts of several instances of grand theft auto as well as smoking marijuana for the past two years. Alberto is bright and personable, capable of finishing high school, and possibly able to succeed in college. But where do you start?

Following the principles we learned earlier, baselines need to be started on all of the targeted behaviors. Let's say that his social worker and Alberto first attempt to reduce the incidence of fighting with residents at the treatment center. When there is progress there, another behavior like being less defiant of authority might be attempted, and then when there is progress with that one, getting Alberto to apply greater effort toward his schoolwork.

Practitioners may want to consider the multiple baseline designs because of the inferences that can be made about the effectiveness of treatment. An intervention that produces strong rates of change across various behaviors or with different clients is showing generalizability or **external validity.** In other words, these designs provide evidence that the intervention was responsible for the improvement. The assumption is that other social workers who employ this intervention should also expect to find the same beneficial effects with their clients.

However, it is also possible that a multiple baseline across behaviors design could seem too impractical or unwieldy to use. Often, social workers find it necessary to begin working on several of the client's problems at once. There simply is not the luxury of time to address problems sequentially with an adequate baseline for each that began with the monitoring of the first behavior. In real life, Alberto would likely receive more than one intervention (for example, individual therapy, group therapy for impulse control, 12-step group meetings, as well as token economy or other various treatments). Given the multiple interventions, it may make more sense to think of monitoring Alberto's behavior with a series of AB designs. Teachers in the school program would probably keep their own graphs, as would Alberto's probation officer, his social worker at the treatment center, and possibly the social worker managing his case for the state.

VALIDITY AND RELIABILITY CONSIDERATIONS

Characteristics of the design chosen can affect what you as a practitioner conclude about the success or effectiveness of the intervention. Some SSRD designs are more rigorous than others and allow one to eliminate more of the alternative explanations and thus to come closer to concluding that it was the intervention that made the difference. **Internal validity** is concerned with whether the intervention was the cause of the observed change. When a study

Table 4.1 | Threats to the Internal Validity of Single-System Research Designs

Threat	What the Investigator Must Question or Consider
1. History	Did anything happen during the study period beyond the investigator's control which might have had an effect or influence?
2. Maturation	Did the change occur because the individual grew older, developed, or became more experienced with the passing of time?
3. Instrumentation	Did the measurement process change during the course of the study?
4. Testing	Did simply having the individual complete tests or questionnaires, tally behavior, or reflect about it have an effect by sensitizing him or her to the occurrence of the behavior? Might behavior change because one knows that one's behavior is being monitored?
5. Mortality	Did some clients drop out of the study with the result that the group at the end didn't closely resemble the group at the beginning?
6. Statistical Regression	Were there extreme scores at the beginning of the study which might naturally be expected to be less extreme later—even if there had been no intervention?
7. Contamination/Diffusion	Was there the possibility that the clients being studied benefited from learning from clients enrolled in other programs or from other sources?

has good internal validity, then one can place more confidence in the finding that it really was the intervention and not some other extraneous variable (e.g., nutritional supplements or an exercise program) that made the difference. Several common threats to the internal validity of single-system research design are listed in Table 4.1. Consider whether these threats might have caused or contributed to the finding that the intervention was successful or not.

External validity in single-system research designs is concerned with whether the findings from the study can be generalized elsewhere—to clients with similar problems in other settings, to other practitioners who use the same intervention. In other words, can the results be reproduced? This would be particularly important, for instance, if you had developed a new intervention and wanted practitioners in other states or countries to adopt it. There are several ways in which the external validity of a study can be affected. For example, if a supervisor trains three or more staff in a new intervention for clients with identical problems, and if at case closing vastly different results are obtained, then the investigator might want to consider whether the intervention might have been applied differently. The investigator might want to ask if there was variation in the way key components of the intervention were stressed or emphasized. If the intervention is sensitive to differences in the practitioner's experience or training, then that variable might need to be examined—as well as differences in the clients themselves with regard to such variables as age, sex, education, etc. The idea here is that powerful interventions should produce the same type of result with similar clients—no matter whether they live in Alabama, Arkansas, or Alaska. The trick, of course, is to make sure that the intervention is applied in the same way in each location. Sometimes is this referred to as the **fidelity of the intervention.** Providing staff with training manuals describing the intervention protocol improves the fidelity of the intervention and can also increase the likelihood that an intervention's effectiveness can be replicated in other locations—that the results can be generalized. Changing the way an intervention is intended to be delivered is analogous to an individual deciding to take her prescribed medicine at different intervals (once a day instead of three times) or in a different dosage (four pills at once instead of the prescribed one at a time); in other words, it is not a good thing.

External validity in the quantitative research tradition is generally sought by obtaining a representative sample of the population through random sampling. However, with single-system designs there very rarely is a random selection of clients for the study, and so the main threat to the external validity of these studies comes from the lack of representativeness with the client, problem, or situation that is the focus of the evaluation (Bloom, Fischer, & Orme, 2003). The issue is that without random selection and with a very small sample (e.g., $n = 1$), it is difficult to know how well one client being evaluated resembles other clients with the same problem.

Reliability is concerned with the ability to repeat or reproduce the measurements or observations that are made during a study. For instance, if you and Tamatha are observing Fernando during math class and you see that he was distracted 12 times, but Tamatha counts only 6 times, the measurement process does not have very good reliability. In such a situation, it might be helpful to agree upon a definition of what it means to be distracted. Even better would be a printed list where the distracted behaviors (e.g., looking out the window, doodling, putting his head on the desk, etc.) could be tallied. The amount of agreement between two observers is referred to as **interobserver reliability** and could be expressed as a percentage of agreement or a correlation. The higher the reliability, the better. Generally, one would hope to achieve agreement at least 75% to 80% of the time.

STATISTICAL ANALYSIS

Statistical analysis (for example, average number of observed behaviors in the baseline and intervention phases) can be conducted with specialized software such as SPSS and SAS commonly found in universities. Calculation/analysis programs can also be found on the Internet with a little looking or can be performed with Excel®. Bloom, Fischer, & Orme (2003) have even included statistical software for single-system designs on a CD-ROM in their book. They discuss computing chi-square, the *t* test, and the three-standard deviation band approach to determine if there are significant statistical differences as a result of intervention. However, there is a debate about statistical autocorrelation that needs to be mentioned if one is planning on conducting statistical tests.

Most statistical tests are based on the assumption that observations or measurements are independent; that is, that each stands alone, that knowledge of one measurement does not lead you to predict the order or magnitude of the next measurement. (You can think about this as the next measurement being free to move either higher, lower, or not at all; that it is not locked into to being directly predictable from the previous measurement.) However, since the data from single-system designs are made in a succession or series over time, the measurements may be correlated (not independent). For instance, if a client was obsessed with exercising and was increasing her minutes of jogging by 12 minutes each day, it would be possible to predict day seven by knowing the minutes she exercised on day six. With this simple example it is possible to "see" the autocorrelation: it would follow a pattern that looked something like 36 minutes on day three, 48 minutes on day four, 60 minutes on day five, 72 minutes on day six, and 84 minutes on day seven. Such data are considered to be dependent upon each other as opposed to being independent values. Patterns such as these are not always easy to spot. The good news is that the strength of the relationship—how much the values of a variable depend upon the values of prior observations or measurements—can be assessed with statistical tools and this quantitative expression is known as autocorrelation. Autocorrelation in the data is believed to increase the possibility of making **Type I and Type II errors** (concluding that the intervention was effective when it wasn't or not effective when it really was). To be brief, the debate is whether or not single-system designs yield correlated or independent data. (For a larger discussion of this topic see Matyas and Greenwood, 1997.) Even low levels of autocorrelation can lead to the erroneous conclusions by inflating the value of the statistics used to detect differences between the baseline and intervention periods. If you suspect that the data in your single-system graph are auto-correlated, then it would be a good idea to consult Bloom, Fischer, and Orme (2003) in order to test for autocorrelation.

Cooper (1990) has demonstrated the use of one of the simplest statistical approaches for analyzing data from a client with obsessive-compulsive disorder. The client was a young woman with pervasive ritualistic behavior, such as rinsing in the shower for 45 minutes and counting gulps of liquid when swallowing. Figure 4.8 shows how Cooper used a celeration line to understand the behavior was accelerating and to reveal where it would have been without intervention.

You can construct a celeration line easily once an adequate baseline is obtained (note the 10 baseline points in Figure 4.8). Begin by dividing the baseline in half, and then divide each of these in half so that the baseline has four equal quarters. If you have an even number of baseline points you will need to draw your lines between data points. If there is an odd number, draw through the middle point.

Once this is done, compute an average or mean frequency for each half of the baseline. These means are then marked on the one-quarter and third-quarter indicator lines and a line is drawn connecting them and extending in both directions.

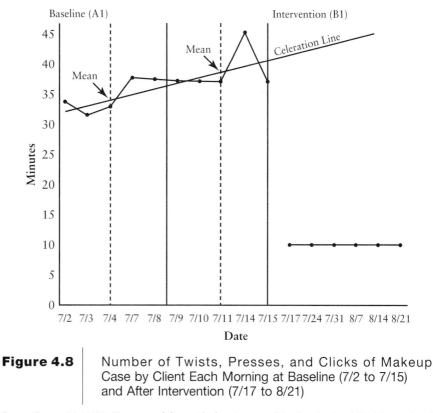

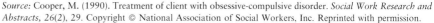

Figure 4.8 | Number of Twists, Presses, and Clicks of Makeup Case by Client Each Morning at Baseline (7/2 to 7/15) and After Intervention (7/17 to 8/21)

Source: Cooper, M. (1990). Treatment of client with obsessive-compulsive disorder. *Social Work Research and Abstracts, 26*(2), 29. Copyright © National Association of Social Workers, Inc. Reprinted with permission.

The celeration line that crosses the line indicating when intervention begins shows what you could expect of the behavior or event if there were no intervention. Bloom, Fischer, and Orme (2003) explain further procedures so that interested practitioners can determine if a statistically significant change has occurred.

Statistics usually are not needed with single-system designs. Because these designs rely on graphs and visual inspection, "eyeballing" and clinical significance are all that is usually needed to establish that improvement occurred. However, the results from these tests at best only rule out a chance occurrence and do not eliminate rival explanations or permit conclusive causal inferences. Sometimes unusually high or low data points affect these statistical techniques and can produce results that are contradictory. Clearly, the ideal situation would be a single-system graph in which an intervention's success (or not) was visually obvious.

Rubin and Knox (1996) caution us about ambiguity in single-system designs. They found ambiguous outcomes in 7 of 23 graphs where male

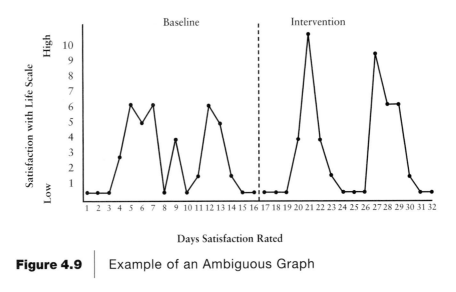

Figure 4.9 | Example of an Ambiguous Graph

adolescent sex offenders were self-monitoring on prosocial behaviors and in 7 of 16 graphs where parents were reporting on their sons' antisocial behaviors. The point is this: You should be prepared for the possibility of obtaining unstable, indistinct baselines. These might be recognized by improvement that begins during the baseline, and by cyclical periods of no problematic behaviors during the intervention phase except for a few high spikes. An example is provided in Figure 4.9 of an ambiguous single-system graph.

If you look closely at Figure 4.9, you'll note that although the spikes are higher during the intervention period, the client actually experiences only one more day than in baseline when his satisfaction with life was self-reported as either 2 or lower. Also, during the 16 days after baseline, the client experienced only two more days when he rated his satisfaction with life a 6 or higher. With this figure, it could be argued that something of an optical illusion creates the notion of successful treatment.

ADVANTAGES AND DISADVANTAGES OF SINGLE-SYSTEM DESIGNS

Single-system designs have a lot to offer social workers for several reasons. First of all, single-system designs readily lend themselves to clinical practice situations. If a social worker wants to objectively evaluate his or her practice, single-system designs do not require either control groups or large groups of clients in order to demonstrate that the intervention is working.

Second, single-system designs are not disruptive to the treatment process. In fact, they support and complement practice nicely by focusing on specific treatment goals or problems. Often, they serve to clarify or confirm a worker's

Practice Note: Gender and Ethnicity

There is a strong possibility that the clients chosen and even the target behaviors selected for single-system design research may be influenced by gender and ethnicity considerations. Nelsen (1994) has suggested that female clients may be more likely to be asked to participate in single-system designs than males. Do you expect females in this society to be more compliant? To be less assertive and more in touch with their feelings?

Conversely, social workers who are not of the same ethnic background probably are less likely to involve minority clients in this type of research because of concern that they may be accused of being insensitive to cultural issues. Nelsen (1994) observes, "The practitioner who avoids asking out of anxiety about practitioner-client ethnic differences also misses an opportunity to address differences that should be discussed at some point in treatment" (p. 146).

Evaluation is intrinsic to good practice (Bloom & Orme, 1993), and single-system designs are perhaps the most practical means for monitoring client improvement. Because there is always the possibility that our interventions can have iatrogenic effects, there is no ethical alternative to monitoring what is happening with our clients (Mattaini, 1996). (An iatrogenic disorder is any adverse mental or physical condition induced in a patient by the effects of treatment.) Competent practice demands that we make every effort to be aware of our biases that may affect clients, and to inform ourselves about those who differ from us in ethnicity, national origin, race, color, gender, and sexual orientation. And insofar as it is possible, we ought to involve the client in defining the problem and assisting with the data collection (Bloom & Orme, 1993).

initial assessment of a client. Furthermore, these designs are constructive in that they provide continuous feedback to the practitioner as well as the client. There is no need to wait until the treatment has ended to determine progress. Many clients have "failure" identities and need to be reassured that they are progressing. Single-system designs can visually demonstrate the progress that has been made. These designs do not take control away from the practitioner or involve denial of service to those in a control or comparison group.

Third, single-system designs do not normally require computers, knowledge of statistics, or clerical help in compiling data. These designs do not require that you develop a hypothesis to test. In short, they are not burdensome to one's practice. They are easy to use and understand. Last, they are theory-free. That is, they can be applied regardless of the worker's theoretical application. For social workers who are interested in some form of accountability, but not able to undertake large-scale research projects, there is much to recommend single-system studies.

On the other hand, these designs have some major limitations. A considerable one is the problem of generalization. Even though one uses a rigorous single-system design and clearly demonstrates that the intervention worked, there will still be those skeptics who say, "So? Maybe you worked well with this one client. Show me that your approach works with lots of clients." A social worker or counselor could be very effective with a single client and yet ineffective with the rest of the caseload.

A number of practical problems sometimes emerge during the use of single-system designs. Ideally, all phases should be of equal length, yet realistically an intervention might be longer than the baseline or longer in one phase (the

Practice Note: Impediments to Using Single-System Designs

Laura Epstein has written this wonderfully evocative line, "Practitioners need research to put reason and order into the madness of practice" (1996, p. 113). For those students who have yet to experience full-time work in a social service agency, it is difficult to prepare you for the job stress and sometimes urgency with which complex decisions must be made—sometimes with insufficient information. It would be terrific if every practitioner had enough time on the job to thoughtfully plan and reflect on every client's progress. Realistically, though, there is seldom enough time to do all that needs to be done. Even though single-system designs are not as labor intensive as the group research designs (to be discussed in a later chapter), they still demand *some* time—and may not be utilized because they are a lower priority than addressing pressing client needs. In fact, having the time to do them might be considered a luxury in some

settings. Along this line, Corcoran (1993) has identified the following practical impediments to using single-system designs:

- Lack of time to do single-system designs
- Availability of suitable measures or instruments
- Settings (for example, acute care hospitals) not amenable to single-system designs

Additionally, the multiproblem constellation of problems that clients bring to social service agencies do not always lend themselves to single-system research designs. Clients' problems are often not discrete and well defined but convoluted and intricately involved. Further, agencies that are attempting to show policymakers and funding sources that intervention does have an impact are much more likely to use aggregate (group) data than single-study designs (SSDs).

B phase) than another phase (the C phase). In actual practice, it is unlikely that all phases would be the same length. Other problems are encountered when we know the baseline behavior is not stable but must start intervention immediately or when several have to be applied simultaneously.

Another problem is that even experienced practitioners may be hard-pressed to think of situations in which they would deliberately withdraw or remove an intervention that is working just to show that it is the intervention that was responsible for the change in behavior. As a consequence, some of the more experimental single-system designs (for example, ABAB) may be viewed by practitioners with disdain or lack of interest.

THE CHOICE AND USE OF SINGLE-SYSTEM DESIGNS

There are many more single-system designs than could be practically presented in this chapter. For instance, Kazi and Wilson (1996) discuss the **ABBC design** where the intervention B is discovered to be relatively feeble and is combined with another intervention, C. Bloom, Fischer, and Orme (2003) have identified even more varieties of designs. Single-system designs allow for the creative adaptation and changes in intervention that occur naturally in social work practice. One cannot employ the excuse, "I can't find the right design for my client." Whether it is simple or complex, the right design is out there, waiting to be used.

The single-system design that is "best" to use depends on how much evidence you feel that you need to rule out alternative explanations for improvement; it is also dictated by the target behaviors or problems identified in the treatment plan. Knowledge of the client and his or her problems is an important consideration in the choice of a design. For instance, you wouldn't want to attempt an ABAB design with a client who agrees to a maximum of three contacts. With another client, you may feel that it is important to monitor three or more target behaviors. With single-subject designs, you have a great deal of flexibility. As a general guideline, however, let your knowledge of the client dictate the design rather than choosing a design and attempting to find a client who conforms to it. If we were all to wait for the "ideal" client to come along before beginning to evaluate our practice, not much evaluation would get done.

It is important not to forget that the purpose and best use of single-system designs is to identify whether a client is progressing. These designs cannot explain why an intervention isn't working. Their purpose is only to inform you about whether the intervention is succeeding.

It requires a certain amount of self-discipline to conduct research. One has to be conscientious about keeping records and monitoring changes in behavior. For many practitioners whose agencies do not require formal evaluation, it is easier to use subjective determinations ("I think the client is doing better"; "The client is acting more appropriately"; "I feel that the couple is getting along better"). However, subjective judgments do not advance the profession or build practice knowledge. Single-system designs can help you to discover what works under which circumstances.

Single-system designs have practical value and can benefit you and your clients. You may find that if you make use of them, you gain an appreciation for empirical research and are more willing to engage in it. As a practicing social worker, you will surely find that you are too busy to attempt a single-system design for every client. That's understood. However, unless you make an effort to evaluate some clients, you'll soon forget how to go about it. What do I recommend? Simply that you use a single-system design with your most difficult clients. You'll keep your skills fresh and your supervisor happy, and you'll be able to determine objectively whether or not these clients are making progress.

KEY TERMS

target behavior

baseline

AB design

ABA design

ABAB design

ABC

successive
   interventions design

ABCD design

multiple baseline
   designs

multiple baseline across
   subjects design

$A_1A_2A_3B$

multiple baseline
   across behaviors
   design

external validity

internal validity

fidelity of the
   intervention

reliability

interobserver reliability

Type I and Type II
   errors

ABBC design

SELF-REVIEW

(Answers at the end of the book)

1. T or F. A single-system design *must* contain a baseline.
2. T or F. In a single-system design, time is recorded on the vertical axis.
3. How many baselines does the design ABA contain?
4. Which design is better for knowledge building, the ABCD or the ABAB?
5. Which design was used in the management of incontinence among the elderly in a nursing home?
   a. ABA
   b. ABAB
   c. ABCD
   d. $A_1A_2A_3B$
6. What makes for an ambiguous graph on either the baseline or intervention side?
7. List the advantages of using a single-system design.
8. What is the major limitation of single-system designs?
9. Besides the fact that it involves more than one client, how is the multiple baseline across subjects design different from the traditional AB design?
10. Why should social workers use single-system designs?
11. What keeps social workers from using single-system designs?
12. If data in a single-system graph are so predictable that you can predict a data point from knowing the preceding value, the observations are probably not _____.
13. Name five threats to the internal validity of a single-system design.
14. External validity is concerned with what?
15. What is the largest threat to the external validity of a single-system design?

QUESTIONS FOR CLASS DISCUSSION

1. Think again about the discussion of the 12-year-old who had stomachaches. Why wouldn't you want to graph the behavior in terms of times per day? (*Hint:* Make a graph on the blackboard showing the reduction at the end of the intervention from one episode per day to none per day.)
2. Is there more than one way graphs can show lack of improvement? Choose a target behavior and draw suggestions from the class that demonstrate lack of improvement.
3. Why is the ability to operationalize target behaviors important for single-subject designs?
4. What would be a good argument for monitoring more than one target behavior with a client?
5. Think about how to set up a graph for a particular target behavior. Would there be advantages in graphing positive behaviors (e.g., number of days on the job) rather than negative behaviors (e.g., days of work missed)?

6. A coworker tells you that she has just completed a single-system design on a family that has received intervention for seven months. She is pleased with what she has done and brings a graph to show you.
   a. What would be your initial reactions about her competence?
   b. Can the single-subject design "prove" that your coworker is an excellent social worker? Why or why not?
7. With a multiple baseline across subjects design, what is the reason for waiting for a change in the behavior of the first subject before beginning intervention on the second? Can you think of any reasons why intervention shouldn't be started on all three subjects at the same time?
8. Odette is failing the ninth grade. At a conference with her mother, Odette's teachers said that she simply was not studying or turning in any homework. The family's social worker wants to develop a single-subject design to monitor the effect of requiring Odette to study two hours every afternoon before the television can be turned on. The social worker is planning to have the vertical axis show "yes" or "no" regarding the completion of two hours of study time every afternoon. Could this design be improved? How?
9. What is wrong with this single-subject design?

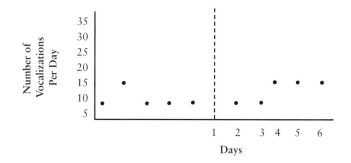

10. What steps could you take to try and protect the fidelity of an intervention?

RESOURCES AND REFERENCES

Barrett, M. D., & Wolfer, T. A. (2001). Reducing anxiety through a structured writing intervention: A single-system evaluation. *Families in Society, 82(4)*, 355–362.

Berlin, S. B. (1983). Single-case evaluation: Another version. *Social Work Research and Abstracts, 19(1)*, 3–11.

Bloom, M., Fischer, J., & Orme, J. G. (2003). *Evaluating practice: Guidelines for the accountable professional*. Englewood Cliffs, NJ: Prentice-Hall.

Bloom, M., & Orme, J. (1993). Ethics and the single-system design. *Journal of Social Service Research, 19*, 161–180.

Brophy, G. (2000). Social work treatment of sleep disturbance in a 5-year-old boy: A single-case evaluation. *Research on Social Work Practice, 10*, 748–758.

Bromley, D. B. (1986). *The case-study method in psychology and related disciplines*. New York: John Wiley & Sons.

Cooper, M. (1990). Treatment of a client with obsessive-compulsive disorder. *Social Work Research and Abstracts, 26(2)*, 26–32.

Corcoran, K. J. (1993). Practice evaluation: Problems and promises of single-system designs in clinical practice. *Journal of Social Service Research, 18*, 147–160.

Corcoran, K., & Fischer, J. (2000). *Measures for clinical practice.* New York: Free Press.

Firstman, R., & Talan, J. (1997). *The death of innocents: A true story of murder.* New York: Bantam.

Epstein, L. (1996). The trouble with the researcher-practitioner idea. *Social Work Research, 20(2)*, 113–118.

Gilgun, J. F. (1994). A case for case studies in social work research. *Social Work, 39*, 371–380.

Kazdin, A. E. (1992). *Research design in clinical psychology.* Boston: Allyn & Bacon.

Kazi, M., & Wilson, J. T. (1996). Applying single-case evaluation methodology in a British social work agency. *Research on Social Work Practice, 6*, 5–26.

Lucey, J. F. (1997). Editorial. *Pediatrics, 100*, A76–A77.

Mattaini, M. (1996). The abuse and neglect of single-case designs. *Research on Social Work Practice, 6*, 83–90.

Matyas, T. A., & Greenwood, K. M. (1997). Serial dependency in single-case time series. In R. D. Franklin, D. B. Allison, & B. S. Gorman (Eds.), *Design and analysis of single-case research* (pp. 215–243). Mahwah, NJ: Lawrence Erlbaum Associates.

Nelsen, J. (1994). Ethics, gender, and ethnicity in single-case research and evaluation. *Journal of Social Service Research, 18*, 139–152.

Nuehring, E. M., & Pascone, A. B. (1986). Single-subject evaluation: A tool for quality assurance. *Social Work, 31(5)*, 359–365.

Nugent, W. R. (2000). Single-case design visual analysis procedures for use in practice evaluation. *Journal of Social Service Research, 27(12)*, 39–75.

Pinkston, E. M., Howe, M. W., & Blackman, D. K. (1987). Medical social work management of urinary incontinence in the elderly. *Journal of Social Service Research, 10(2, 3, 4)*, 188.

Rubin, A., & Knox, K. S. (1996). Data and analysis problems in single-case evaluation: Issues for research on social work practice. *Research on Social Work Practice, 6*, 40–65.

Rymer, R. (1993). *Genie: An abused child's flight from silence.* New York: HarperCollins.

Steinschneider, A. (1972). Prolonged apnea and the sudden infant death syndrome: Clinical and laboratory observations. *Pediatrics, 50*, 646–654.

Sundel, M., & Sundel, S. S. (1993). *Behavior modification in the human services: A systematic introduction to concepts and applications.* Newbury Park, CA: Sage.

Thyer, B. A., and Thyer, K. B. (1992). Single-system designs in social work practice: A bibliography from 1965 to 1990. *Research on Social Work Practice, 2(1)*, 99–116.

Tripodi, T. (1994). *A primer on single-subject design for clinician social workers.* Washington, DC: NASW Press.

ASSIGNMENT 4.1: Preparing for a Single-System Design

Objective: *To learn how to operationalize a client's behavior for a single-system design.*

Think about a client, or if you are not in a practicum, then reflect back to people you know who have some kind of a problem that might lend itself to monitoring with a single-system design. Perhaps a client forgets to take his medicine on a regular basis? What about a teen who spends too much time watching television? You might want to create a fictitious client.

1. Briefly describe the client's problem.

2. Identify the context. What is the agency? What is your role as a social worker?

   The actual or likely agency:

   My role as social worker:

   The intervention is:

3. Operationalize a target behavior so that it can be easily measured:

ASSIGNMENT 4.2: Identifying All the Components for a Single-System Design

Objective: *To learn all of the parts that go into a single-system design.*

Before constructing a single-system design, identify the following important components:

1. What are the units of measurement for the operationalized target behavior?

2. What units will be used to measure increments of time (i.e., minutes, hours, days, weeks, months)?

3. How long will the baseline be?

4. What design will you be using?

5. Will your single-system design show that intervention on the client's problem was successful or unsuccessful? Who will be counting or measuring the target behavior?

6. Besides the effect of your intervention, what other factors might contribute to the client's success (or lack of success)?

Student's Name

ASSIGNMENT 4.3: Creating a Single-System Design

Objective: *To learn how to prepare the graph for a single-system design.*

In this space on the front of this page construct a graph for a single-system design. Use a ruler or straightedge to help you create a tidy and professional-looking presentation. Be sure to label both the vertical and horizontal axes so that a reader who has not seen your responses to Assignments 4.1 and 4.2 will be able to understand your effort. Also, give your graph a caption or title, being careful to disguise any real names of clients. Finally, show data both for the baseline and the intervention phase(s).

5

CHAPTER | # Research Designs for Group Comparisons

Single-system designs (SSDs) are impractical on a large scale. If you are the director of a community agency that provided a recreational program to 750 young people last summer, you probably would not want to look at more than 700 SSDs in order to evaluate the program's success. The problems of possible ambiguity and your staff's selection of diverse and wildly different target behaviors aside, single-subject designs in this instance would be the wrong research tool because the focus is no longer on a particular client but on the larger group. Did the majority of participants benefit from the program?

The research designs contained in this chapter are the quantitative approaches commonly used for program evaluation and basic research in the social sciences. The results they report are concerned with group averages, not with an individual client's success. In the stronger group designs, one group is provided with an intervention, and these results are compared to a control group that does not receive any treatment. As you'll see, most of these designs are based on the concept of *comparison* and usually employ statistical analysis to understand change. They are not designs typically used by qualitative researchers.

Few of us would want to hire a carpenter who is skilled only with the use of a hammer. While this knowledge is important, it is also essential for carpenters to know something about other tools. Similarly, single-system designs will not always be the right tool for every research occasion. Many times you need to aggregate data in order to understand to what extent a group, program, or community improved as a result of our services. Group research designs are particularly appropriate for those who work with various systems, agencies, and communities and are involved with administration of programs, community development, and social policy analysis. Direct service social workers often find that they need a knowledge of group research designs in order to develop evaluation procedures when they apply for grants or wish to test hypotheses about specific interventions used in their agencies.

CHOOSING THE RIGHT DESIGN

Numerous research designs can be used to guide research projects, and choosing the right one is somewhat analogous to picking out a new car. The primary consideration may be how much money you have or how big a monthly payment you can manage. Similarly, the researcher must also consider how much has been budgeted for the research. Design issues related to finances are the use of staff time for collecting data (for example, making follow-up contacts with clients in person or by phone); postage, telephone, or travel expenses; purchase of copyrighted instruments or scales; computer processing of the data; the use of consultants; release time to write the report, and so on. These and other variables contribute to the cost of the project.

While the car buyer considers what optional equipment is really necessary, the researcher decides which facets of the study are essential. For instance, the researcher may believe that the success of the intervention should be determined by expensive in-home personal interviews instead of mailed questionnaires.

Besides the issue of cost, car buyers and researchers must simultaneously consider other variables. Both car buyers and researchers are presented with decisions about no-frills, low-prestige models. The experimental designs that we will talk about are highly respected, but other less rigorous designs are often adequate. Sometimes automobiles are chosen because their styling or color will turn heads; researchers desire good response rates and instruments that produce reliable findings. And while the car buyer may consider how long a particular vehicle might be expected to last, the researcher must give thought to the amount of time that he wishes the study to run. Often, the more data that are collected, the stronger the study.

Various motives or considerations have a bearing on the choice of a research design. No one design will be applicable or correct in every situation. The design depends on the nature of the problem being investigated, the availability of clients or other data, monetary and staff resources, the amount of time one has to complete the project, and the purpose of the research.

In terms of evidence-based practice, group research designs with randomized assignment to the treatment condition (experiments), or with time-series designs with a good comparison group, provide the most credible evidence. Time-series designs without a comparison group provide a middle range of credibility. Before and after designs with no comparison group provide the least credible evidence of effectiveness—for reasons that will become more clear as you read this chapter.

Research strategies are most often developed from the specific objectives of the study and the nature of the presenting problem. Social work researchers generally move from interest in a problem to the selection of a design. One wouldn't choose a design and then look for a problem to investigate.

SELECTING SUBJECTS

Even before choosing a research design, most researchers have to give some thought to the individuals who will be asked to participate in their research project. Sometimes it is not possible to draw a sample from a larger population of potential subjects or clients. That is, the question being investigated or intervention being tested may involve only the 30 most chronic abusers of the agency's 24-hour crisis line. Or, the school social worker may be concerned with evaluating the progress of 18 children in two support groups who have bereavement issues. It is often the case that group research designs do not employ probability sampling procedures to constitute the study group of research subjects. Researchers can, and often do, however, randomly assign clients to either an experimental or control condition (more about this later) when the pool of clients or research subjects is large. Even with 30 chronic hotline abusers, half ($n = 15$) could be randomly assigned to participate in a new intervention to address the frequency and the other half could constitute the control group.

Sometimes researchers have the good fortune to be able to plan months in advance and can build a process for future recruitment (**proactive research**) of eligible clients. Sometimes current clients are the group of interest; they also may be compared to clients who previously completed a program or who have already dropped out (**retroactive research**). In retroactive research the investigator often draws upon existing data in agency records. As a practitioner in a social service agency, sometimes your access to research subjects is limited to only your clients or those in the program where you are assigned; often, you must take what you can get because random selection opportunities may be very limited.

Group research designs are classified as explanatory research and, more often than not, involve small samples of research subjects. (However, an exception to this is that many studies in the social sciences—psychology in particular—are conducted on college students because of their easy availability.) You probably recognize that college students or a small sample of children with bereavement issues from one school may not resemble the larger population of adults in the United States or school children in other cities or states. For example, how well would the sample represent all college students if the sample of 30 came from a liberal arts college of 1,500 students where the tuition alone was about $35,000 a year? What if the school children were all Native Americans?

Researchers conducting explanatory research are not as concerned with representativeness or generalizability in the same sense that survey researchers are. For survey researchers, if the sample doesn't represent the larger population then there may be little or no generalizability and the whole survey effort may fail to meet expectations. Investigators conducting explanatory research hope that their findings will be so solid that other researchers will want to come along and replicate the original study; and if the findings are repeated again, this begins to look like or approximate generalizability.

While the sample relative to the larger population is not a huge concern for those conducting group research designs, what is terribly important is that the control and intervention groups be created by random assignment in experiments; this creates the condition of maximum comparability. In the quasi-experimental designs, the more the control group resembles the experimental group, the better the study. Conversely, a weaker study results when the two groups are very dissimilar, and this could come about quite easily, or for example, if therapists are allowed to nominate clients for a special group, or whenever random selection is not possible.

EXPERIMENTAL RESEARCH

The classic experimental design is the "ideal," the "gold standard" or model to which all other research designs are compared. Even though the opportunities to conduct true experiments may not often come your way, the experimental design remains the standard when it is important to be as scientific as possible. Other designs in this chapter are discussed in terms of how close they come to the "ideal."

For many social workers, the notion of experimentation involving human subjects brings to mind misconceptions about unethical, painful, or presumably painful stimuli being inflicted on unsuspecting persons in a climate-controlled laboratory. These notions are best forgotten. Today there is much greater concern for and widespread protection of the rights of persons participating in research than in the past. The federal government requires institutional review boards to oversee research being funded with federal money and involving human subjects.

What is an **experiment?** Simply stated, it is a controlled study where clients or subjects are randomly assigned to a group (sometimes called a condition) where they will receive a new (or different) intervention from those designated to be in the control group. Data collection in these studies typically involves the use of standardized quantitative instruments. Individuals in the control condition may receive the customary or usual treatment for comparison with the new one. The notion of random assignment is crucial—it prevents a number of **extraneous** (unwanted, confounding) **variables** and biases from interfering with the researcher's ability to make a conclusion about the strength or weakness of the intervention.

It may be helpful at this point to briefly discuss an example of relevant experimental research. Barber and Gilbertson (1996) conducted a study examining the effectiveness of three different interventions for partners of heavy drinkers. The Pressures to Change approach coached partners in how to assist drinkers in changing their drinking behavior; some clients were assigned to receive this instruction by individual counseling and others by group instruction. A second group was involved with Al-Anon, which places primary emphasis on improving the quality of life for those living with the drinker. A third group, the control, was placed on a waiting list until the conclusion of the study.

Clients recruited through a newspaper were screened for eligibility. To be eligible, drinkers had to score above the threshold for dependence on the family form of the Short Michigan Alcoholism Screening Test. At the conclusion of the study, Barber and Gilbertson (1996) found that none of the drinkers whose partners had been assigned to Al-Anon or to the control group had sought help, cut down, or quit drinking. This outcome was in contrast with four partners each in the individual and group interventions who reported drinkers who sought help. The authors concluded the Pressures to Change approach was an effective intervention to help drinkers resistant.

The Classic Experimental Research Design

True experiments are the most rigorous of research designs and the ones that best permit causal inferences to be made. These designs have two main features that distinguish them from other designs. First clients (or subjects) who participate in the experiment are **randomly assigned.** That is, no favoritism or bias is shown in appointing them to one condition or the other. Second, besides the experimental group, some subjects must be assigned to a control (or comparison) group that does not get the new intervention.

The shorthand notation for the classic **pretest-posttest control group design** is often written as follows:

$$R \quad O_1 \quad X \quad O_2$$
$$R \quad O_3 \quad \quad O_4$$

The R in this notation scheme stands for the random assignment of clients to either the experimental or the control group; the X represents the intervention or stimulus. Observations, measurements, or assessments of each group are made twice. The first observation (O_1) is called the **pretest,** and the second observation (O_2) is called the **posttest.** This design provides information not only about changes in the group that receives the intervention, but also comparable information from the group that does not get the experimental intervention. What kind of changes would the true experiment pick up? This result depends entirely on the dependent variable or variables the researcher has chosen and the way they have been operationalized. Random assignment *must* occur prior to the intervention. One should never begin a treatment—and then if clients are not improving—assign them to the control group.

As an example of this design, suppose you are a medical social worker assigned to a dialysis clinic. Let's further assume that the management of anxiety is a major problem for patients in the clinic. You decide to start a support group for anxious patients because you believe it will help alleviate some of their health concerns. Because you are limited in the amount of time you can allocate for this project, you want to start small with about 25 patients. Since this is a large dialysis clinic with hundreds of patients, you have no problem finding willing participants. In keeping with the experimental pretest-posttest control group design, you randomly assign 25 dialysis patients to the support group and randomly assign an approximate number to the control group.

Next, you use a standardized measure like the Clinical Anxiety Scale to determine the anxiety level of both groups prior to the start of the intervention. The support group begins and runs its normal course (six to eight weeks). Afterwards, you administer the instrument a second time to both groups and make comparisons. Has the average level of anxiety in the experimental group decreased? Has the average amount of anxiety in the control group remained about the same or increased? Finally, is the level of anxiety in the experimental group less than in the control group? If so, then you have some evidence that the intervention was effective.

This is a strong design because the group that receives no intervention provides a "control" for possible alternative explanations affecting the experimental group. (Random selection of subjects makes the group equivalent before the intervention begins.) For instance, if clients tend to make better decisions because they grow wiser with the passage of time (maturation) and not because of the intervention, then the control group would also show similar improvement or outcome. (There would be little reason to believe that the intervention was responsible for any changes if the same changes were also found in the control group.)

Researchers sometimes choose to strengthen their studies even more (particularly in medical and pharmaceutical research) by using a **double-blind procedure.** In double-blind experiments, neither the researcher nor the research subjects know whether they are in the control or the experimental group. (Obviously, someone other than the experimenter has to know, but this information is not shared.) This procedure eliminates any experimental bias—for instance, in unintentionally giving those in the experimental group more attention or advantages because the experimenter so wants the intervention to work.

The Posttest-Only Control Group Design

A second true experiment design, the **posttest-only control group design,** is handy for those situations where a pretest might affect the posttest results or when it is not possible to conduct a pretest. This design is also useful in situations where anonymity is paramount—so it would not be possible to compare an individual's pretest and posttest scores.

Campbell and Stanley (1963) note that there is a common misconception that pretests are always needed in an experimental design. Not so, they say.

Early experimental designs in agriculture did not make much use of pretests. As with the previous design, random assignment of subjects establishes the initial equivalence between the experimental and control groups. Measurement of the control group (O_2) then serves as a pretest measure for comparison with the experimental group's posttest (O_1).

$$R \quad X \quad O_1$$
$$R \qquad\quad O_2$$

As an example of this design, consider the following problem. Counseling agencies often find that 30% or more of scheduled appointments result in "no-shows" or last-minute cancellations. Productive or "billable" time is lost, which can seriously affect the revenue needed to operate an agency. Suppose you have a hypothesis that the 30% no-show rate could be reduced by the agency's receptionist calling clients to remind them of their scheduled appointments. The group receiving the phone calls would constitute the experimental group. Those clients who do not receive a reminder constitute the control group. Membership in either the experimental or control group would be randomly determined. (For instance, even-numbered clients scheduled for an appointment during the first week of March would be assigned to the experimental group and would get a reminder. Odd-numbered clients would be assigned to the control group.) At the end of the study period, the cancellation rates for the two groups could be compared.

The Solomon Four-Group Design

The third true experiment design is called the **Solomon four-group design.** As you can see from the notation below, it is composed of the basic experimental design plus the posttest-only control group design. This is an elaborate, sophisticated design that social workers may not often have the opportunity to utilize because of the logistics involved with the creation and maintaining of four different groups.

$$R \quad O_1 \quad X \quad O_2$$
$$R \quad O_3 \qquad\quad O_4$$
$$R \qquad\quad X \quad O_5$$
$$R \qquad\qquad\quad O_6$$

This design provides two opportunities for the treatment effect to be demonstrated. The design's strong point, however, is that the investigator can maximally control for alternative explanations and thus increase the confidence that can be placed in the findings. While this is a rigorous design and provides greater confidence that the intervention produced any observed changes, the tradeoff for this certainty is greater difficulty in coordinating and implementing the design.

Reid and Finchilescu (1995) have reported an interesting application of a Solomon four-group design to measure the effects on women who viewed violence against women portrayed in film. Female college students in Group 1

Practice Note: Cancer Prevention

Colorectal cancer is a health concern for middle-aged and older adults and their loved ones. More than 50,000 Americans die from this disease each year although it is treatable. Screening with a fecal occult blood test detects the cancer in its early stages when treatment is most effective and is recommended for persons over the age of 50, those with a history of polyps or inflammatory bowel disease, those who have a close relative with the disease, a change in bowel habits, or weight loss. Historically, persons with low education and income, the elderly, and those with inadequate medical insurance have low participation rates in colorectal screening.

Plaskon and Fadden (1995) designed a posttest-only experiment to test if a combination of listening to a physician talking about the benefits of screening and being provided a free test kit would increase

participation in screening. In a rural area known for high rates of colorectal cancer, experimental and control group assignment were determined by the contents of an envelope given from the top of a stack left with the receptionist. Both the experimental and the control group received educational materials and a talk by the physician on the importance of screening. The control group was informed that they could pick up a test kit at the desk. The intervention group was given the test kit in their envelopes.

Within a week of their appointment, all subjects were called or mailed a questionnaire to ask whether they had used the fecal occult blood test. The findings: very few of the control group had asked for a test kit and none of them had actually used it, while 51% of the intervention group had utilized their screening kit.

completed a disempowerment scale, watched film clips from such films as *The Burning Bed* (which showed a woman being assaulted by her husband), and completed the disempowerment scale. Group 2 was the same as Group 1 except that they saw film clips of violence against men (from such movies as *Point Break*). Group 3 saw the violence against women clips and completed a posttest. Group 4 saw the violence against men clips and completed the disempowerment posttest scale.

The researchers found that completing the disempowerment scale before the viewing did not sensitize the group who were shown violence against women, and that the experimental group revealed significantly more feelings of disempowerment than did the group who watched clips of violence against men. In other words, female participants experienced an increase in feelings of disempowerment after viewing film depicting women as victims of violence. If this research is confirmed by additional studies, what implications do you see concerning the media's portrayal of violence?

INTERNAL AND EXTERNAL VALIDITY

Campbell and Stanley (1963) and Cook and Campbell (1979) are prominent in social science research because of their conceptualization of research designs. Their books are classic books on the topic, and few research methodology books have not cited their work. Besides identifying a host of experimental, quasi-experimental, and preexperimental research designs (more about these a little later), these authors contributed much to our understanding of internal and external validity.

■ Sidebar: Validity Unpacked

Validity is a concept that can have many nuances. Here is a quick review of what we've learned thus far:

- **Internal validity** relates to extraneous variables that can sneak into a study and rob the investigator from concluding that the intervention was the cause of the client's improvement. Researchers must consider threats to the internal validity to help understand the results that were achieved. For instance, did the intervention appear less effective than it really felt because clients dropped out of the study before its conclusion (a problem of mortality—sometimes clients drop out when they are doing better)? In order to assess whether the threat of mortality might have been undermining the findings, researchers can consider such information as the number of clients who began and finished the program.

- **External validity** is concerned with whether a study can generalize well to other populations, locations, and client groupings. Generally, random selection of individuals who compose the study sample is a good way to build external validity. Being able to demonstrate that a sample is, in fact, representative of a larger population adds to the credibility of a study and its external validity. Many studies are published each year that do not involve random sampling; the fact that they appear in print does not make their findings generalizable. If some wanted to make an argument that a study didn't generalize well, they would probably complain that the individuals in the study were somehow different, that the location was out of the ordinary, or that the timing of the study was unusual.

- **Measurement validity** is concerned with how well an assessment instrument measures the concept it was designed to capture. Investigators conduct small studies to learn if the empirical measure they've created or adapted successfully operationalize the abstract idea of it. In other words, they gather empirical data to assess the performance of the instrument. Various forms of this type of validity include criterion-related, face, construct, and content validity.

- Conversational uses of "validity" or "valid" when applied to a research project generally mean that a study was real, authentic, meaningful, relevant, or simply just a "good" study—probably meaning that it seemed to have used an appropriate methodology or that the findings support the speaker's ideas about the topic. However, this is an inexact and confusing way to refer to a study. A researcher will want to know, more specifically, if the speaker is talking about whether the study's instruments revealed strong measurement validity, whether the study's design anticipated threats to internal validity, and to what extent the study's design allowed for generalizability (external validity).

Threats to the **internal validity** of a study (that is, whether the intervention was truly responsible for the observed differences in the dependent variable) come from **extraneous variables** (those not purposely incorporated into the experiment). Studies with greater internal validity allow the researcher to rule out alternative explanations and rival hypotheses. Studies with less internal validity cannot control (account for) the effect of extraneous variables on the experimental group. As we learned in the single-system design chapter, unplanned and unexpected variables can affect the intervention's outcome. Group research designs also are susceptible to threats to their internal validity.

The following section is presented to help you think about the variables that can influence your study and make it difficult to determine if your intervention was effective. As you learn more about research, you will develop an appreciation for factors (not limited to those listed here) that can interfere with your study.

MAJOR THREATS TO INTERNAL VALIDITY

1. *Maturation.*   The aging of participants or different rates of physical growth or development within two comparison groups are examples of an influence that you should be cognizant of and attempt to control as much as possible. Certainly, there is a lot of difference between kindergarten students at the beginning of the school year and at its end. Why? Because they have grown older and been socialized into the culture of "student." Similarly, anyone who has been hurt when a relationship breaks up knows that there is a lot of truth to the adage, "Time heals all wounds." The simple passage of time is an alternative explanation that should not be discounted when gauging the effects of an intervention that runs over several weeks or months. The longer the intervention, the more likely that (client) maturation (the passage of time) may play a role. Another example: Sometimes our clients cease certain behaviors not because of any special intervention they received but because, for example, they become too old to engage in criminal behavior or they are not as fleet-footed and no longer have the athletic quickness to avoid arrest. Clients sometimes change for reasons independent of the intervention they've received.

2. *History.*   This refers to the specific events (for example, national crises, tragedies, or, on a local level, a large factory laying off hundreds of employees) that occur between the pretest and posttest that were not part of the researcher's design and that could influence the results. For instance, if you were trying to evaluate the impact of an AIDS prevention program, and a national celebrity made a public announcement about obtaining the disease through unsafe sex practices, this would constitute a threat to the internal validity. Similarly, events like the World Trade Center tragedy will impact such interventions as those involving clients struggling with anxiety disorders and post-traumatic stress.

Personal events in a client's life (e.g., a "history of abusive relationships") are not generally considered to threats to the internal validity of a study. However, significant events that occur in the world and within an agency or a group can become factors that influence the trajectory of an intervention. Consider a treatment group that is well established (there is a strong sense of "the group")—and one of the members commits suicide. This event becomes a threat to the internal validity of the study. Group members may be adversely affected and lose the progress they had made. Or, they might pull together in a way that was completely unexpected and make much greater strides than they would have made without the suicide. History is a threat to validity because once it occurs, the investigator doesn't know whether it was the intervention or the event that caused the improvement. If the group shows no improvement, was it because of the suicide or because the intervention was ineffective? There is no good way to know when a study has weak internal validity.

3. *Testing.*   Taking a test on more than one occasion can affect later test results. Repeated testing provides practice and in itself can improve test scores. If clients' scores improve over time, but they were measured six times with the

same scale, was the improvement because they figured out what you were measuring or because the intervention made a difference? The threat of testing is sometimes known as the *practice effect*. The influence of testing can also be a factor when pretests sensitize subjects to issues or attitudes and cause some reflection so that subjects' responses change as a result of measurement and not intervention. Instruments can also be too difficult or too lengthy; subjects can get bored (*test fatigue*) and may not pay careful attention to how they respond. If you anticipate that testing may be a problem, then you can choose designs to assess it (Solomon four-group) or eliminate the pretests altogether (i.e., posttest-only control group design).

4. *Instrumentation.*   This term refers to changes in: (a) the use of the measuring instrument, (b) the way the instrument is scored, (c) procedures used during the study, or (d) the way the dependent variable is counted or measured. Suppose you administer a timed test to some students, and because you are not paying attention, you give them five fewer minutes at the posttest than they had at the pretest. You have created a situation where the intervention will likely look less powerful than it really is. (Because they had fewer minutes to complete the test, double-check their answers, and so forth, their scores will be lower.) Conversely, if you accidentally give them too much time—maybe you were interrupted by a phone call—then you might conclude that the intervention was more effective than it actually is. Not administering the instruments the same way each time or not according to directions—and not training staff on how to collect the data—can result in inaccurate reporting. Another instrumentation problem would be to change instruments and use different ones at posttest than were used at pretest.

5. *Selection of subjects.*   This threat to internal validity stems from any bias that causes the experimental and control groups to be different from each other or to be different from those individuals in the larger population that they should represent. For instance, suppose you have come up with a new intervention for parents who are having difficulty getting along with their teenagers. You purchase an advertisement in the paper that says: "Having trouble communicating with your teenager? Call *321-6543* for information on a free parents' group at Shiloh Baptist Church on Wednesday evenings." How does the ad create a selection problem? First of all, some parents who are having trouble with their teens may not respond because they can't read, or don't subscribe to the newspaper. Other parents needing the intervention may not respond because they don't like the idea of discussing their problems in a group. So who would be most likely to respond to the ad? Possibly better-educated, more assertive people; individuals who may be somewhat outgoing or at least comfortable in social situations—certainly, *motivated* parents. A researcher who uses such an ad has to remain cognizant that the parents in his or her study may not represent all parents who are having trouble communicating with their teens. If the intervention works well, then the researcher may want to find a group of less motivated parents (for example, parents who were court-ordered to participate) to see if the intervention works equally well with them.

Selection is nearly always a concern in studies because of self-selection that occurs when clients choose one agency over another (i.e., public or private) or possibly one known for one type of treatment modality and not some other kind. This threat to the internal validity of a study is best handled by random sampling from the population of interest. However, this is not always possible, and researchers quite often have to admit that their studies have **limitations—** problems that may prevent the study from generalizing well to the larger population or other geographical areas—because of the way their subjects were chosen or selected.

6. Statistical regression.   This refers to the selection of subjects who were chosen because of extreme scores. There is a tendency for extreme scores to move toward the group average on a second testing. For instance, think about a situation where you scored a perfect 100% on your first test in research methods. Even though you may be a very bright individual, it will be a lot easier for you to do not as well on the second test than it will be to score 100 again. So even if you obtain a 95 on the second test, your score will have regressed. Similarly, if you score 15 on the first test, it is quite possible that you will improve on the second test and your score will move more in the direction of the class average. Statistical regression as an internal threat to the validity of a study means this: Subjects who were chosen because of extreme scores (either low or high) at pretest can be expected to have either higher or lower scores at posttest simply because of statistical regression. As a researcher, you can't prevent this occurrence, but you can measure it when there is random assignment and a control group. (Any improvement that the control group shows could be due to statistical regression. This amount can then be subtracted from the improvement shown by the experimental group in order to understand the impact of the intervention.)

7. Mortality.   Also known as attrition, this threat to internal validity refers to the loss of research subjects (for example, they terminate services, move out of town, get sick, or simply just drop out of the study). The loss of subjects may change the overall group complexion and may produce differences in the data at the posttest that have nothing to do with the intervention.

Think about a scenario where you are running a group for nine sixth-grade boys who have behavior problems in the classroom. The intervention is going well, but for one reason or another the group dwindles to four participants by the end of the school year. While all four showed definite improvement, what about the five who dropped out or moved to other school districts? Had they been present at the posttest, would you still have been able to conclude the intervention was a success? A major loss of subjects from a study can undermine whatever conclusion the researcher is prepared to make regarding the effectiveness of the intervention. Social work researchers have to be aware that individuals in the control group are at risk for dropping out of the study or may be unavailable at posttest. Because they are less involved with the study by nature of the fact that they are receiving no intervention, they may be less motivated to participate in posttesting. Especially when testing procedures are lengthy or demanding, incentives like coupons for a fast food restaurant or small gifts may be necessary to keep subject mortality from being a problem. Here's another tip that might help for long-term studies: Some researchers have discovered that mailing out birthday and holiday cards is a useful way to stay in contact with study participants when attrition might be a problem. Since the post office will forward mail for only one year, mailing twice a year keeps addresses current.

8. *Interaction effects.* This occurs when any of the extraneous variables interact with one another. In a selection and maturation interaction, the subjects in one group may mature at a faster rate than those in the comparison group. In a selection and mortality interaction, there could be differences in motivational level or severity of psychiatric illness between the groups, with resulting differential dropout rates. By the study's end, the groups could look vastly different—and not because of the intervention. Another example could be that the demands on subjects at pretest could force many to reconsider their participation—forcing a selection and mortality interaction. Many possible interactions with extraneous variables may complicate the investigator's ability to understand the true impact of the intervention.

Threats to the internal validity of a study are like viruses that can infect and weaken it. They sap the confidence that you as a researcher have in the finding that it was the intervention, and only the intervention, that was responsible for any improvement in clients' lives.

The use of experimental designs will help you gauge the extent of any of these threats to the internal validity of your study. The use of randomization and a control group allows the investigator to determine if any extraneous variable has exerted an unexpected influence. For instance, if you notice an unexpected improvement in the control group, you might suspect that an extraneous variable (such as history, maturation, or testing) had an effect on the study.

When you have considered these eight threats and ruled them out as having produced an effect, then you have established that your study has internal validity. You can now conclude with some confidence that the intervention was likely responsible for the observed changes. Then, if you want to ensure that the findings from your study can be generalized to different subjects or settings, you should consider the threats to the external validity of the study.

MAJOR THREATS TO EXTERNAL VALIDITY

Campbell and Stanley (1963) must also be given credit for identifying several ways in which the **external validity** (the generalizability or representativeness of the study) can be threatened. External validity is important if you want to convince others that your study or experiment has produced a major scientific discovery.

Note first, though, that in those situations where you are evaluating a local or specific program, it might *not* be important to you to demonstrate external validity. In such instances, you are concerned only with whether treatment worked in a specific program—you may not be interested in generalizing your results to their communities or subjects because your program is not like any others.

On the other hand, if you *are* concerned with generalization and obtaining maximum credibility, you'll want to use an experimental design and attempt to anticipate all the potential threats to the internal and external validity of your study. In particular, you will want to pay attention to these factors that could influence external validity:

1. *Reactive or interactive effect of testing.* This occurs when a pretest affects the respondent's sensitivity or awareness to important variables associated with the study. The pretest could make the subjects unrepresentative of the population from which they were drawn by raising their consciousness or by stimulating new learning, or simply because they realize that they are involved in a study. This threat should seem familiar to you because it is the same as the internal validity threat of testing.

2. *Interaction effects of selection biases and any research stimulus.* These occur when there are problems getting a random sample. If you are conducting a study that requires in-depth interviews of two or three hours in duration, the majority of persons you contact might turn you down and not participate. Those who agree to the interview may not be representative of the larger population—they have volunteered when most others have not. They may have some traits or characteristics (for example, they are lonely) that make them less representative and therefore affect the generalizability of the study. Selection bias is not a problem in experiments with random assignment; it is always a concern in quasi-experimental designs with nonequivalent comparison groups.

3. *Reactive effects of arrangements.* This has to do with the experiment being conducted in a setting that is different from the subject's usual experience. Subjects' behavior may change because of the different environment. Subjects may be more productive or more wary and nervous. They may behave in a way not indicative of their normal style. (Would your behavior change if you knew that you were being videotaped or observed through a two-way mirror?)

4. *Multiple-treatment interaction.* This becomes a problem when there is more than one intervention. The researcher needs to be sure that the same timing, sequence, or order is followed for each subject. Multiple treatments may have a cumulative effect, which could make reaching conclusions about a specific intervention difficult.

Researchers who want to generalize their findings beyond the setting in which they conducted the study need to be concerned that: (a) subjects in the study are representative of other clients with the problem or the population to which they are being compared; (b) the intervention is not vague but well defined and structured; and (c) staff are qualified, trained, and uniformly deliver the intervention in the same way using the same approaches, theoretical orientations, and emphases.

Those colleagues who will read your research and want to implement the intervention must be given sufficient detail to replicate the study. Without critical information about the characteristics of your clients (for example, are they first-time or multi-offenders?), your staff (were they MSWs with at least five years of experience or graduate students?), and the nature of your intervention (did the group meet twice a week for a total of three hours weekly or once a month?), those who attempt to replicate your study may not achieve the same results. This would be most unfortunate if you had a successful intervention, but because you failed to provide sufficient explanation about it, the staff, or the clients, assumptions were made that resulted in another researcher using a weaker or diluted version of the intervention or choosing a tougher client population and then encountering a lack of success.

In summary, there are always distinct threats to a study's internal and external validity. Experimental research designs use random assignment of subjects to comparison groups to help the researcher monitor and understand the threats to internal validity. As a rule, the more control you have over the situation or experiment, the greater the internal validity. However, there is a corresponding cost in terms of external validity.

As greater effort is made to control for possible influences on the subjects or in the experimental setting, the investigator runs the risk of creating a situation that is vastly different from the way most programs of a similar type would be run in real life. Sometimes it is comforting to realize that all studies have some limitations or weaknesses. Research with actual clients and in real social service agencies often means that compromises have to be made.

Not too long ago, I learned of an evaluation being conducted of a family preservation program. Families in crisis were randomly assigned to the special intensive intervention or to a control group that received the usual services provided by the agency. After the death of a child whose family was receiving the customary (not intensive) services, a decision was made to end the random assignment. Supervisors placed families that they were most concerned about into the intensive intervention condition. The control group from that point on no longer resembled the intensive intervention group because their problems had been judged to be less serious. The evaluation of the intensive intervention was seriously compromised due to differences between the two groups. These are the kinds of things that can happen when research is conducted not in the laboratory but in the "field."

PREEXPERIMENTAL DESIGNS

Suppose you are a counselor in an agency and are working with a group of shy individuals. You have developed an approach that, over the course of 10 meetings, significantly alleviates shyness. You administer a shyness inventory to the group on its first meeting, and the average score for the group is 135. From the scores and your clinical impressions, you know that this group is extremely shy. Your group meets 10 times, and you administer a posttest on the last session. You find that the group's average score has gone down to 62, which indicates major improvement.

This type of design does not have the complexity of an experiment. Since subjects are not randomly assigned to either a treatment or a control group, this design is popular and often used in evaluations of social service programs. This design (which is similar to the AB design) is called the **one-group pretest-posttest design** and can be designated with the notation:

$$O_1 \quad X \quad O_2$$

Here, again, the O_1 represents the pretest measurement or observation and the O_2 the posttest.

Even though you, as a clinician, have seen major improvement in the individuals of the group, this design cannot rule out alternative explanations for the changes. It cannot rule out the internal validity threats of history, maturation, testing, instrumentation, statistical regression, or the interaction of selection and maturation. Any of these extraneous variables may have produced the changes in the shyness scores. Without a control group, it is impossible to say that these threats did not have an effect. You, however, may be able to rule out some of these threats because of the particular situation or context within which the study occurred. Although this is a weak design, it serves a purpose when no control group is available for comparison.

If there were no pretest data associated with the earlier study of shy individuals, the resulting design would be the one-group posttest-only design.

$$X \quad O_1$$

With this design, an intervention is delivered, and later, observations are recorded in order to determine the intervention's outcome. This design stipulates only that you make an observation after the intervention. If you were working with the group of shy individuals described above, this design would require only a posttest after the intervention. Since there would have been no pretest for comparison, an average posttest score of 62 would not provide much information. With no data available for comparison, any perceptions of a reduction in shyness are unsubstantiated. Instead of the intervention having an effect on shyness, extraneous variables such as selection, history, maturation, or mortality may have contributed to any perceived effect after treatment.

With the one-group posttest-only design there is the presumption of an effect. Sometimes, however, you can see an effect more clearly—especially if you are conducting a study of a problem that is behavioral (for example, you have a group of clients who are trying to quit drinking). If the group reported after 10 weeks that they weren't drinking, you would be pleased and willing to take the credit. Indeed, your colleagues probably would have no difficulty attributing the cessation of drinking to the intervention. However, the "success" might have been due to spouses or mates threatening to leave if loved ones didn't stop drinking, bosses threatening to fire inebriated employees, court appearances for driving while intoxicated, or a combination of several factors. Again, without a control group, it is difficult to know the extent to which extraneous factors are influencing the outcome.

A third preexperimental design is called the **posttest-only design with nonequivalent groups.** It is expressed:

$$X \quad O_1$$
$$O_2$$

This design is an improvement over the previous two in that the control group functions as a pretest condition and can be compared with the group that receives the intervention. While it may seem logical to infer that any observed differences are due to the intervention, this is debatable, since we cannot assume that the two groups were similar prior to the intervention (there was no random assignment to the groups). As a consequence, differences between O_1 and O_2 may be due to their nonequivalence in the beginning and not to the effect of intervention.

By way of example, think of the population of women who have been battered by their partners. Assume we want to know if service programs connected with a shelter for battered women are instrumental in helping these women avoid returning to abusive situations. Of the battered women who contact the shelter, some request shelter services, while others request information about child custody, jobs, and police protection, and soon attempt to leave abusive situations on their own without spending time in the shelter. There are, then, two groups of women with the same basic problem. One group gets the intervention (the shelter) and its counseling services, while the other group does not. For the purpose of follow-up research to determine how many women were living in abusive situations one year later, would these two groups be equivalent? I think not. They may differ in the amount of financial resources at their disposal (those who don't stay at the shelter may have more money), in the extent of family or social support systems, and possibly with regard to the severity of the abuse experienced.

These two groups of women may be convenient groupings in terms of trying to determine the impact of a battered women's shelter, but if it were later found that a greater proportion of the women who used the shelter's services than of women who didn't were still in abusive situations, what does this say about the shelter's services? It would be risky to conclude that the shelter was in some way responsible for its clients returning to abusive situations. While it may appear that women who avoid the shelter are more successful in not returning to abusive situations, we must keep in mind that the two groups of women may not have been equivalent even though they shared a common problem. In fact, we might expect differences in the two groups even before our data are aggregated. Of course, the more similar (or homogeneous) the two groups are, the more comfortable everyone will be that the intervention did have an effect. The absence of randomization makes this design weak; we are unable to rule out such internal validity threats as those of selection, mortality, and interaction among variables (such as selection and client maturation).

These three preexperimental designs can be thought of as examples of *how not to do research* if there are alternatives. Fortunately, alternatives exist—they are known as quasi-experimental designs.

QUASI-EXPERIMENTAL DESIGNS

Quasi-experimental designs are those that fall a little short of the "ideal." Often in agency settings, it is not acceptable or possible to randomly assign clients to one of several treatment modalities (or to a control group receiving no intervention). When randomization cannot be done, the researcher should consider quasi-experimental designs.

The **nonequivalent control group design** is one of the most commonly used quasi-experimental designs because it is the most internally valid design that can be implemented in applied settings where random assignment is not possible. The notation for nonequivalent control group design is

$$O_1 \quad X \quad O_2$$
$$O_3 \qquad O_4$$

In this design, a control group is used, just as with the experimental design. However, there is no randomization. Usually a convenient natural group (for example, another class of fifth graders, another AA group, and another group of shy clients) is selected that is similar but may not be equivalent to the group receiving the intervention. Just as with the previous design, the control group consists of clients who have been chosen because they possess certain characteristics. The control group can come from those clients on a waiting list for service, clients receiving alternative services from the same agency or from another similar agency, or even from nonclients.

Researchers sometimes attempt to match the two groups on important variables (such as age, socioeconomic status, drug use history). As you can imagine, matching is difficult because of the number of variables that could be involved. A major problem with matching is that observed differences between the control and intervention groups at the end of the study may have been due to the influence of unmatched variables. When you must match, the best advice is to match the groups on as many of the relevant variables as possible. Equivalence is not guaranteed with matching, but it does serve to approximate equivalency. When random assignment is not possible, matching is a good alternative.

With this design, it is usually plausible to assume that the treatment produced the effect. Like the experiment, this design does provide the investigator with the ability to monitor internal validity threats such as those from testing, maturation, instrumentation, history, and mortality. The main threat to this design's internal validity comes from interaction of selection with maturation, with history, or with testing, since random assignment wasn't used (so there was no guarantee of equivalency). Still, this design is better than the preexperimental designs because of the use of a control group. The more similar

Practice Note: Group Work with Survivors of Child Sexual Abuse

Studies on adults who experienced childhood sexual abuse show that depression, low self-esteem, and a host of other problems (alcohol and drug abuse, relationship problems) are common. Therapeutic groups combat isolation and stigmatization by allowing survivors to safely share their histories in a milieu where what they say is valued and beneficial to others. Richter, Snider, and Gorey (1997) used a quasi-experimental design to evaluate the results of intervention. One hundred and fifteen women volunteered. Thirty-five of these went immediately to groups facilitated by an experienced MSW, which met weekly for 15 consecutive sessions of one-and-a-half to two hours. The other 80 women were placed on a waiting list and waited an average of four weeks to get service. These women served as a nonrandomized comparison group.

The authors found that survivors who completed the group work intervention were significantly less depressed as measured by the Beck Depression Inventory and Generalized Contentment Scale and had significantly improved self-esteem compared with their counterparts on the waiting list. At a six-month follow-up, more than 80% of the intervention group had lower levels of depression and higher self-esteem than the average for those on the waiting list.

the control and the experimental groups at pretest, the more confidence you can have in your findings.

As an example of this design, consider the problem of relapse among chronically mentally ill people. You want to know whether those patients who are served by your state-run hospital stay as long in the community and without relapse as those in a similar institution in a different part of the state. With the cooperation of both hospital administrators, you make comparisons of such variables as staff-to-patient ratios, percentage of first-time admissions, and average age of patients in order to establish that the patients and the facilities are roughly equivalent.

Suppose you find out that the patients from your hospital do seem to have longer stays in the community than patients of the other hospital. You might conclude that the programming or staff at your hospital is better. However, this design cannot unequivocally demonstrate this outcome. It could be that more of the clients in the other hospital return to rural areas, where there is not the same level of community support services (after-care) as is available to the patients from your hospital (who tend to remain in an urban area). There could be differences in staff morale at the two hospitals (which might affect the treatment received by patients) or in the ease of readmission or screening procedures. Could differences in the physical facilities be a factor? So, while you can be bolstered by your patients' success, the dissimilarities in the hospitals prevent you from *conclusively* determining that the intervention obtained there is the main reason for the patients' longer stays in the community.

Another quasi-experimental design is called **time-series** or **interrupted time-series**. This design is one of the older designs used in the natural sciences, but it has not been utilized extensively in the social sciences. The time-series design is an extension of the one-group pretest-posttest design, where a series of measurements are taken before and after an intervention. This step allows the researcher to understand trends and patterns in the data before the intervention is applied and then provides for continued monitoring for major changes. Notation for a time-series design is:

$$O_1 \quad O_2 \quad O_3 \quad X \quad O_4 \quad O_5 \quad O_6$$

With this design, the researcher is able to get a grasp on incremental changes (if any) in the study group's behavior prior to the intervention and then to determine if the change after intervention is greater or not. When possible, an equal number of measurements should be made before and after the intervention. Also, the period of time between the measurements should be comparable. Note that the researcher determines the period of time between intervals; it is not imposed from the design. The amount of time between O_1, O_2, and the other observations could be seven days, two weeks, or three months. This design is particularly well suited for research in social policy when historical or archival data are available. Each observation could then represent a year's data. For instance, you might monitor the number of suicides or homicides from handguns in a city three years before and three years after passage of a new ordinance requiring a five-day "cooling off" period before purchase of a handgun.

On a smaller scale, you might use the time-series design to look at staff productivity before and after the executive director implements a new 4-day, 40-hour workweek. When using the time-series design in this way, it is important to watch for seasonal variations. Would it be all right to compare January (O_1), February (O_2), and March (O_3) with June (O_4), July (O_5), and August (O_6)? This wouldn't be a fair comparison if productivity was lower in the summer months. To protect against making a conclusion influenced by seasonal or other natural fluctuations in data, include enough observation periods to get a stable baseline. This step may require getting more than just the three observation points suggested by the design.

When the data from time-series are graphed (recall the AB designs in the last chapter), the slope of the line is often of assistance in understanding whether the observed effect was caused by the intervention. On a graph, you can readily determine if the magnitude or frequency of a behavior is increasing prior to and after an intervention. Because the measurements are obtained over an extended period of time, history is the chief threat to the internal validity of this design. A threat from testing might also be apparent in some instances.

This time-series design provides even better information if a corresponding control group can be added:

$$O_1 \quad O_2 \quad O_3 \quad X \quad O_4 \quad O_5 \quad O_6$$
$$O_1 \quad O_2 \quad O_3 \quad \quad O_4 \quad O_5 \quad O_6$$

This new design with a control group is called the **multiple time-series design**. It resembles a stretched out nonequivalent control group design. Campbell and Stanley (1963) recommend this design for research in school settings. It is a strong quasi-experimental design with no serious internal validity threats. The investigator can use the control group to check for the influence of history and to understand the effects of testing, maturation, mortality, and instrumentation.

ADVANCED DESIGNS

Factorial Designs

There are even more sophisticated designs that the social work researcher may want to use. **Factorial designs** are often employed when Intervention A is being compared to Intervention B and both vary along some other dimension (for example, frequency, intensity, or duration). In the factorial design below, the researcher is able to determine not only whether Intervention A is more effective than Intervention B, but also whether the factor of meeting more frequently results in even greater improvement than the weekly sessions. Figure 5.1 shows two treatments and two levels of frequency, making this a 2×2 factorial design. If clients could have been randomly assigned to groups that met every day, five days a week, then this would have been a 2×3 design. Although it is not shown in Figure 5.1, random assignment is understood.

A major reason for using this design is so the investigator can look at the combined effect of two or more variables of interest (Kazdin, 1992). Within the same study, the investigator can assess the effects of separate factors (dependent variables) under different conditions—resulting in a savings of time and effort (compared to doing two different studies).

Crossover Designs

When clients are receiving more than one experimental treatment, the investigator may want to have the subjects switch places at a given point. In Figure 5.2, men who have been arrested for battering their partners are randomly assigned to participate in either Group 101 or Group 102. Those in Group 101 receive praise and encouragement for every comment, vocalization, or question they raise. After four weeks, their counselors begin to

Interventions

	Intervention A Once Weekly	Intervention B Once Weekly
Frequency	Intervention A Twice Weekly	Intervention B Twice Weekly

Figure 5.1   Factorial Design (2×2)

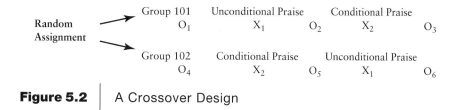

Figure 5.2 | A Crossover Design

reward with their verbal praise only those questions or comments where clients make an empathetic response regarding victims of abuse or express remorse. Facilitators in Group 102 start with the rewarding of empathetic and remorseful statements only, and after four weeks they "cross over" and begin giving verbal praise for any comment, question, or vocalization. Assuming the goal was to increase the level of empathy in these men and that the investigator would be using a standardized instrument for her observations, this design lets the researcher determine which sequence produces the best overall results.

You can see in Figure 5.2 that each group experiences three assessments. O_2 and O_5 do double duty, functioning both as posttests and as pretests at the beginning the second treatment.

There are many other variations of group research designs (such as a Latin square for randomly ordering the sequence of multiple interventions) that some day you may want to use as a social work researcher. If you are feeling overwhelmed—that there are too many different designs to learn—it might be helpful to sort them into the three broad categories of preexperimental, quasi-experimental, and experimental designs. And if that doesn't help, remember this: Having many designs to choose from is certainly a better situation than having fewer models that don't fit your particular application. By analogy, you wouldn't want to be preparing a pizza and have only a muffin tin to bake it on.

DESIGN AND VALIDITY CONSIDERATIONS

The main reason that researchers often choose experimental over preexperimental or quasi-experimental designs is that they make causal inference easier. Let's say that as a social work practitioner, you have a notion that an intervention employed by your agency is more effective with certain clients than others. To test this hypothesis, you would probably choose one of the experimental designs described in this chapter. Sometimes, however, social workers have questions like "Are parents of disabled children more likely to abuse their children than other parents?" Or, "What proportion of the homeless have a problem with substance abuse?" Questions as these do not require experimental research designs. Rather, they are more likely to be explored using secondary data analysis or a survey research design.

As previously discussed, preexperimental and quasi-experimental designs are susceptible to problems of internal validity. Yet, useful information and valuable studies can come from designs that are not truly experimental. For example, if you are hired as a school social worker in an alternative school providing group therapy and support groups for adolescents with chemical dependency problems, random assignment may not be possible. So, if you were interested in evaluating the success of your groups, the best design remaining might be the nonequivalent control group design. Even though experimental designs are the most rigorous, quasi-experimental designs should not be summarily dismissed, particularly when you are engaged in what might be called "salvage" research (when you're trying to rescue data that otherwise might be lost).

In order to make your study as strong as possible, careful planning is required. Some threats to the internal validity of your study can be eliminated or minimized by following the suggestions of Mitchell and Jolley (1988):

1. Keep the time between the start and the end of the study short. This helps minimize the threat of *history*. (Note that this suggestion does not apply to time-series designs.) Also, keeping the study period short can help minimize the threat of maturation (especially a problem when studying children and youth), as well as any interaction of maturation with selection.
2. Test subjects only once or use different versions of the same test at posttest to minimize the threat of *testing*.
3. Train your assistants and administer the instrument the same way every time. (This helps minimize the threat of *instrumentation*.)
4. Use innocuous or placebo treatments, brief treatments, or mild incentives so that control group subjects do not drop out of the study. Keep in touch with those in the control group when there is a long period between observations. (This helps minimize the threat of *mortality*.)
5. Be careful with choosing subjects on the basis of one extreme test score. (This helps minimize the threat of *statistical regression*.)
6. Randomly assign where possible. If you must match, match on as many key variables as is practical. (This helps minimize the threat of *selection*.)

Thinking about ways of preventing extraneous variables from influencing (or explaining away) the effect of your intervention will result in a stronger study. While the selection of a good research design is important, it is no substitute for good planning. Even a strong design can be poorly implemented and go awry when little attention is paid to details. If, for instance, you lose most of your control group through attrition, even an experimental design will be of little assistance in helping you infer that the intervention caused the observed changes in the treatment group.

Research designs are only guides to the research process. They structure a problem-solving process and provide an outline for how data will be collected. Choice of a particular design is a complex decision often hinging on feasibility considerations. Should you be faced with having to use a group research design sometime in the future, remember that numerous other designs (and multiple variations of the designs in this chapter) are available to you. Regardless of the design you choose, devote time to considering how extraneous variables may affect the internal and external validity of your study.

Finally, we need to address the concerns that some social workers have about experimental designs that randomly relegate clients to control groups. Denying clients needed services would be unethical—no disagreement there. However, most often programs are evaluated by comparing them against another program such that clients in the experimental group would be getting a new or more intense intervention, while those in the control group would still receive the traditional treatment. The experimental intervention may not, in fact, be any better than the usual and customary treatment. It might even be less effective. In other words, there doesn't have to be a definite disadvantage to being in the control group.

Another way to think about acquiring a control group is that many agencies have waiting lists, and these form natural control groups. Those on the waiting lists can be administered pretests at the point of application for service and posttests later when they arrive for their first appointment. That posttest, by the way, is actually a second pretest or observation (O_2). A third observation (the real posttest) would actually be taken toward the end of treatment to assess improvement. Additionally, persons on a waiting list might be given some mild form of intervention (such as educational pamphlets or videotapes) while they are waiting their turn for service. People naturally form themselves into control groups. Some men who batter would rather go to jail than attend a psycho-educational treatment program. Others are released with community service, fined, or put on probation. Even if random assignment is not possible, comparison to some of these other groups, such as those who drop out of treatment, can still reveal cogent and compelling information.

Social work researchers are no less ethical than their colleagues who provide direct services. And, as you learned earlier, a safeguard exists in that institutional review boards must approve human subject research if the agency or investigator has received federal funding. One of the key guidelines to which all approved researchers must abide is to cause no harm to those participating. In medical and pharmacological research, experiments are occasionally stopped when the early data convincingly show that the experimental approach is remarkably superior to the traditional method. When this happens, the control group is provided with the new intervention.

Randomization is not always possible even in the most research-friendly agencies. And when it is not feasible, comparison groups from other agencies or populations can be useful. Even the lowly preexperimental designs have a role. As exploratory or pilot studies, they attempt to expand our knowledge about the interventions we use and their effects on our clients. They may not be great studies, but they have the potential of providing new knowledge that can be explored later in greater depth and precision with a more powerful and rigorous design. In some instances, preexperimental designs provide all the evidence necessary to convince a funding source to underwrite a more extensive and scientific study.

KEY TERMS

proactive research

retroactive research

experiment

extraneous variables

randomly assigned

pretest-posttest control group design

pretest

posttest

double-blind procedure

posttest-only control group design

Solomon four-group design

internal validity

limitations

external validity

one-group pretest-posttest design

posttest-only design with nonequivalent groups

nonequivalent control group design

time-series

interrupted time-series

multiple time-series design

factorial design

SELF-REVIEW

(Answers at the end of the book)

1. Marsha has 80 clients meeting in grief counseling groups at a large hospice. At the end of each session she wants to administer a depression inventory. She's planning to evaluate these participants with 80 single-system designs (AB). Is this an appropriate design?

2. What two features must a true experiment contain?

3. _____ variables are those that confound the researcher's ability to interpret the data.

4. T or F. A posttest-only design with random assignment meets the requirements for an experiment.

5. T or F. Maturation is a possible threat to the interval validity of any study where the passage of time between pretest and subsequent observations is one or more years.

6. T or F. Instrumentation is the name of the threat to internal validity where subjects are administered the same instrument on six different occasions.

7. T or F. The use of volunteers, especially paid volunteers, should always suggest a possible threat to the internal validity of selection.

8. T or F. Statistical regression is where subjects at posttest score lower than they do at pretest *and* they were selected originally on the basis of their high pretest scores.

9. T or F. The following notation represents a true experiment:

$$O_1 \quad X \quad O_4$$
$$O_2 \qquad O_3$$

10. What design in this chapter was said to be well suited for social policy research?

11. T or F. Both the factorial and crossover designs require randomization.

12. What would be the major problem with using an O X O design?

13. Noah is interested in planning a study of patients who have dropped out of the agency over the past five years. What is a term for describing the type of research that looks at existing data?

14. T or F. Strong group research designs often employ small samples of clients or subjects.
15. T or F. With quasi-experimental designs it is terribly important that clients be randomly assigned to each group.
16. T or F. Measurement validity deals with how well the study approximates the size of the population being studied.

QUESTIONS FOR CLASS DISCUSSION

1. What are the different pretest-posttest comparisons that can be made with the Solomon four-group design?
2. What kinds of experimental research do you think are needed or would you like to see conducted? Make a list of these.
3. Consider the threats to internal validity as presented in this chapter and discuss how they also may pose threats to single-system designs.
4. Discuss how pragmatic considerations (the agency setting, its clientele) influence the choice of a research design. How do the possible implications or findings of the study affect the choice of a design?
5. Which two designs discussed in this chapter are identical except for the use of randomization?
6. How might the use of experimental designs in social service agencies involve ethical considerations?
7. Do you think practitioners who want to do research start with a specific research design that they want to use or start with an intervention they want to evaluate and then seek a research design that fits the situation?
8. Discuss the arguments for choosing an experimental design over a quasi-experimental design to evaluate an intervention.
9. Why is replication for researchers conducting explanatory research important?

RESOURCES AND REFERENCES

Barber, J. G., & Gilbertson, R. (1996). An experimental study of brief unilateral intervention for the partners of heavy drinkers. *Research on Social Work Practice, 6,* 325–336.

Campbell, D. T., & Stanley, J. C. (1963). *Experimental and quasi-experimental designs for research.* Skokie, IL: Rand McNally.

Cook, T. D., & Campbell, D. T. (1979). *Quasi-experimentation: Design and analysis issues for field settings.* Skokie, IL: Rand McNally.

Kazdin, A. E. (1992). *Research design in clinical psychology.* Boston: Allyn & Bacon.

Mitchell, M., & Jolley, J. (1988). *Research design explained.* New York: Holt, Rinehart, and Winston.

Plaskon, P. P., & Fadden, M. J. (1995). Cancer screening utilization: Is there a role for social work in cancer prevention? *Social Work in Health Care, 21,* 59–70.

Reid, P., & Finchilescu, G. (1995). The disempowering effects of media violence against women on college women. *Psychology of Women Quarterly, 19,* 397–411.

Richter, N. L., Snider, E., & Gorey, K. M. (1997). Group work intervention with female survivors of childhood sexual abuse. *Research on Social Work Practice, 7,* 53–69.

ASSIGNMENT 5.1: Creating a Group Research Design

Objective: *To gain firsthand experience in planning a group research design.*

Imagine that an agency director has asked you to come up with a research design to guide the evaluation of a pilot program that is scheduled to begin in a couple of months. You may be as creative as you wish, but you must build in a control group. There is no requirement that your control group receives no intervention; you may want to compare the innovative approach against the standard or typical treatment. Try to use an experimental design if possible. If you can't randomly assign, then use the quasi-experimental nonequivalent control group design.

1. Describe the intervention:

2. My hypothesis or research question is:

3. My operationalized dependent variable is:

4. I will need to collect data for the project for _____ (period of time).

5. I will recruit research subjects by:

6. I will randomly assign clients by:

7. The research design I will use is:

8. The control group will be obtained by: _____

ASSIGNMENT 5.2: Analyzing My Research Design

Objective: *To identify areas where my study may be vulnerable to possible internal validity threats.*

Once Assignment 5.1 is complete, evaluate it in terms of the threats to internal validity. Briefly explain your decisions in each instance. Alternatively, your instructor may want you to switch with another student and assess his or her Assignment 5.1 for threats to internal validity.

1. **Maturity** is a possible threat to the internal validity of the study. **Yes___ or No___ Why?**

2. **History** is a possible threat to the internal validity of the study. **Yes___ or No___ Why?**

3. **Testing** is a possible threat to the internal validity of the study. **Yes___ or No___ Why?**

4. **Instrumentation** is a possible threat to the internal validity of the study. **Yes___ or No___ Why?**

5. **Selection of respondents** is a possible threat to the internal validity of the study. **Yes___ or No___** Why?

6. **Statistical regression** is a possible threat to the internal validity of the study. **Yes___ or No___** Why?

7. **Mortality** is a possible threat to the internal validity of the study. **Yes___ or No___ Why?**

ASSIGNMENT 5.2: (*Continued*)

8. **Interaction effects** could be a possible threat to the internal validity of the study. **Yes___** or **No___** Why?

9. The number of "Yes" responses that I've checked in this assignment is _____.

10. What does your response to Question 9 tell you (and possibly others) about the confidence that could be placed in the proposed study's findings?

11. What one modification could you make to the study that would improve it by eliminating at least one threat to internal validity?

ASSIGNMENT 5.3: A Case Scenario for Assessing Threats to Internal Validity

Objective: *To obtain additional experience in identifying threats to internal validity.*

Instead of completing Assignment 5.1 and then doing Assignment 5.2, your instructor may direct you to read the case scenario presented on this page and then to use Assignment 5.2 to identify and discuss internal validity problems apparent in the vignette.

HOOKED ON VOWELS

Susie has begun a new job in a residential facility for adolescents who have been in trouble with the law on numerous occasions. Because the state agency which supplies the majority of the facility's funding requires an evaluation, Susie is asked to conduct a study showing that their programs make a difference. Susie wants to start with helping the teens to read and spell better. When their success in school improves, she believes that the teens will stay out of trouble with the law. The intervention that she plans to employ is a computer software program called "Hooked on Vowels." It comes highly recommended and is affordable. Here are some of the facts about the study:

There are about 150 boys who live in 15 different cottages; each cottage has three computer stations.

Boys can be randomly assigned to receive the Hooked on Vowels intervention.

About half of the boys will be designated to a control condition without the special intervention; about half will receive it.

Some boys stay in the facility three, four, or five years.

Some boys spend less than six months.

Her director has already informed Susie that once the boys leave the facility, it will be hard to keep track of them. In a previous study, only 10% of the boys who had left the facility responded to a questionnaire.

Susie wants to employ these dependent variables: number of new arrests, GPA after leaving the facility, highest grade level attained before quitting school, attitudes toward school, current reading level.

None of these boys like to study history; all of the boys have a history with the law.

The instrument that Susie was thinking of using to measure attitudes toward school is homemade. That is, she developed it herself and doesn't really know how well it will measure attitudes toward school. Susie has never developed an instrument before.

Susie was planning on learning about the boys' GPA by writing them and asking them to write her back with their grades after leaving the facility. That is, they would self-report their grades.

ASSIGNMENT 5.3: *(Continued)*

Susie's friend, Callie, recommends that instead of involving all the boys in the study, she test her intervention with a group of boys who volunteer to do the Hooked on Vowels program.

Six months into the study, the agency director—who was loved by all the staff and residents and who was constantly advocating that the boys stay in school—was exposed by a newspaper article that revealed he had misrepresented information on his résumé at the time he was hired. In fact, he had never finished college.

Susie believed strongly that the intervention would make the boys so much more enthusiastic about school. Because of that, she proposed to measure their attitudes weekly over a six-month period.

The assistant to the director recommended that Susie not base her study on all the boys in the facilities, but instead to target those who performed the worst on their last reading test.

Understanding and Using Research Instruments

As we learned in Chapter 2, quantitative social work researchers design and use special research instruments (scales) to measure concepts. For instance, take the problem of determining if a drug prevention program had the effect intended on its seventh-, eighth-, and ninth-grade target population. Assume that the intervention and curriculum are already established. The presenters are ready to go and the school administrators are eager for the program to start. What happens next?

Let's further assume that the goals of the intervention can be clearly established and all that is needed is some sort of instrument to measure any changes that occur from the pretest to the posttest. When I was presented with this problem several years ago, I immediately thought about going to the literature and trying to find an instrument to help me gauge the results of the intervention.

One of my first dilemmas was how to operationalize the success of the program. Ideally, the best test of the program's success would be if these middle school students didn't abuse drugs or alcohol as adults. Since we would be unable to lurk in the shadows and follow over 1,000 participants over that span of time, success had to be viewed a little differently.

We could have chosen to ask students about their current drug use prior to the intervention and then some time later (for example, six months after the program ended). However, school administrators tend not to be very comfortable with asking about current drug use. Plus, there was some concern that students might be prone to falsify statements about their drug use in order to appear "cool."

Perhaps improvement in knowledge about street drugs and their effects could have indicated whether the program was successful. However, the presenters would not be teaching that red pills do this and that blue pills have this other effect.

Having considered and rejected students' current *behavior* (drug usage) and *knowledge* about drugs and alcohol, we decided to measure changes in students' *attitudes* about drugs. (These are the three domains available to you as a researcher.) And as a first step, we quickly surveyed the literature. Not finding any instrument that excited us, we had to design our own.

Now, assuming that you were given this task, what would you do next? How would you know if the instrument you created is any good?

Measurement instruments are evaluated along two primary dimensions: reliability and validity. Let's discuss these terms.

RELIABILITY

Reliability is an easy term to understand because its usage by researchers is close to its use in everyday conversation. When a watch keeps time accurately, it is said to be reliable. If, on the other hand, your watch gained a half hour in one week, lost 17 minutes the second week, and gained three hours at the end of the third week, you would suspect that something is wrong with it—that it is not reliable. Similarly, a scale or instrument that consistently measures some phenomenon with accuracy is said to be **reliable.** When an instrument is reliable and has a certain amount of predictability, then administering it to similar groups under comparable conditions should yield similar measurements.

One of the ways we evaluate standardized instruments is by their reliability. Generally this information resembles a correlation coefficient and is reported in a journal article or in a manual describing the characteristics of the instrument. Reliability coefficients are numeric values between 0 and 1. Nunnally (1994) says that in the early stages of research one can work with instruments having modest reliability, by which he means .70 or higher; that .80 is needed for basic research; and that a reliability of .90 is the minimum when important decisions are going to be made with respect to specific test scores. If there is no reliability data on a scale and it is not well known, reliability cannot be assumed—the scale could have poor reliability. Data produced from a scale with poor or unknown reliability should always be suspect.

Researchers want their instruments to have a form of reliability known as **internal consistency.** This means that individual items correlate well with the full scale. If this doesn't happen, the items have very little in common. For example, say you construct a scale to measure assertiveness and you write the following items:

The Slap-Together Assertiveness Scale

Agree	Disagree	
_____	_____	1. I always speak my mind.
_____	_____	2. I am frank about my feelings.
_____	_____	3. I take care of myself.

After creating these three items, you develop writer's block. As you try to think of additional items to include, you recall your friend Henry, who is the most assertive individual you have ever known. You ponder Henry's distinctiveness and remember how fanatical he is about baseball. Maybe knowledge of baseball and assertiveness are somehow related, you think. So, you write a new item:

4. I believe professional baseball is superior to all other sports.

These four items complete the scale, and you administer the Slap-Together Assertiveness Scale to a large cross-section of adults. One of the ways to obtain information about the scale is by running the Reliability procedure available through the Statistical Package for the Social Sciences (SPSS). SPSS is computer software available at most universities.

After you've entered the way each individual responded to the items on the scale, the computer program will produce a reliability coefficient and indicate those items that do not correlate well with the rest. By dropping these items, it is often possible to improve a scale's internal consistency. For example, a simplified printout might show something like this:

	Item-Total Correlation	Alpha if Item Deleted
Item 1	.53	−.35
Item 2	.51	−.29
Item 3	.26	.12
Item 4	−.54	.72

The software program shows us how strong our items are individually and the contribution they make to the scale. In the first column, Item 1 has the highest correlation with the group of four items in the tentative scale, followed by Item 2. Item 3 has a weak correlation and Item 4 has a negative correlation suggesting that it is not measuring the same concept, but something different. The second column of information presents the coefficient alpha (the empirical representation of the concept of internal consistency). The "Alpha if Item Deleted" column shows the relative contribution of each item to the overall scale. The −.35 and −.29 alphas indicate that the scale's reliability

Other Terms for Instruments

- **Scale:** a collection of items that comprise a single concept
- **Index:** a set of items that produce a summated score—in effect, a scale
- **Questionnaire:** a group of questions or items used in survey research (internal consistency is not usually an issue for questionnaires)
- **Checklist:** a list of items related in some way to each other (e.g., the Child Behavior Checklist)
- **Self-Reporting Scale:** usually a brief instrument completed by the client or research subject

- **Inventory:** a collection of scales that are thematically related (e.g., used to assess the different dimensions representing psychological well-being or dysfunction)
- **Test:** generic term for any measurement procedure
- **Subscale:** one of several smaller scales contained within a larger index or inventory; to be useful, each subscale must be reliable and valid

suffers tremendously if either of these two items is deleted. In fact, the scale's internal consistency would be in the hole, and the scale would have worse than miserable reliability. If these two items were left in and Item 3 were deleted, the draft scale would have positive but inconsequential (terrible) reliability. What the second column shows is that all of the first three items are necessary for the scale to have acceptable reliability. We see this when it reports that by deleting Item 4 the overall scale's internal consistency improves to .72 (rounded). Dropping this item would be a good decision and would leave us with a three-item scale with an acceptable coefficient alpha of .72.

What if we wanted even higher reliability? Since internal consistency is based both on the number of items and their intercorrelations, it is reasonable to assume that writing a few more new items might increase our reliability. The Spearman-Brown Prophesy Formula indicates that by doubling the number of items, we could likely increase our reliability to .83. Tripling the number of items would likely produce a reliability of .88. Also, when a true/false response format has been used, another strategy for improving reliability is to modify it with a 5-point Likert scale (Strongly Agree, Agree, Undecided, Disagree, Strongly Disagree) so that greater variability in responding is allowed. If you create an instrument with several scales (e.g., Hudson and McMurtry's Multiproblem Screening Inventory), you will need to compute the internal consistency for each scale. A useful reference for those who want to learn more about coefficient alpha is Cortina (1993).

Sometimes researchers measure internal consistency by dividing their longer scales in half (either top versus bottom or even versus odd items) and examining how well the two halves correlate with each other. This method is known as the *split-half* technique. Another approach is to devise *parallel* or *alternate versions* of the scale and administer both forms to similar groups. The researcher hopes that both versions will correlate with each other—the higher the correlation coefficient, the stronger the reliability.

Once a scale has been shown to have internal consistency, researchers next want to demonstrate that its capability is not impaired by differences in space and time. Would those individuals who were identified as being assertive on the 15th of October still be assertive two weeks later? What about in January? To determine stability, researchers will often administer a scale to the same group on more than one occasion (*test-retest reliability*) to see, for example, if persons with high test scores at the first administration maintain high scores at the second administration.

Over short periods of time, scores (of assertiveness or other attitudes or characteristics) should remain fairly consistent when an instrument is reliable. While it is expected that some individuals will increase or decrease in assertiveness, possibly as a result of an intervention or some personal event that happened only to them, there would be no logical explanation for why the majority of a large group should experience extreme changes in their assertiveness scores. Should this happen, and if the researcher can find no other explanation, it is reasonable to assume that there is some problem with the instrument.

With the example of the Slap-Together Assertiveness Scale, there could be too few items to give it stability over time. Similarly, it would have reliability problems if it showed internal consistency with subjects from one part of the United States but not from another geographical area. What good would such an instrument be?

Internal consistency cannot be computed on a single item. As a general rule, fewer items usually equate to lower reliability. All else being equal, adding relevant items usually improves reliability, as does expanding the number of response choices—as in going from two to five.

Reliability of Procedures

Even if you don't use an instrument but depend on observation of some behavior (such as how many times a special education child pops out of his seat during class), you must make every effort to standardize your procedures for counting the phenomenon of interest. Similarly, procedures should be administrated uniformly whenever instruments are used and scored. An interviewer related an account recently that illustrates the importance of standardized conditions. She had been going into homes of rural families on welfare. Much of their housing was dilapidated with substandard fixtures. Many often had only one or two electrical outlets per room. In fact, sometimes she had to ask those she was interviewing to unplug the TV, fan, or air conditioner in order for her to use a tape recorder. It stands to reason that if the interviewees are hot and uncomfortable, they may abbreviate their responses, become impatient, or even terminate the interview quicker than if they were not forced to sit in stifling heat. In short, the quality of the data could be affected.

When more than one person is involved in rating clients' behavior, it is desirable to compute **interrater reliability** to determine the percentage of time the raters are in agreement. A correlation between their independent ratings may also be computed. If the correlation is low, then the criteria may not be

Cross-Cultural and Multicultural Assessment Considerations

Many of the older assessment instruments were largely tested and based on Euro-American populations and did not include persons of color. When you are examining an instrument for potential use with a cross-cultural or multicultural sample, it is important to check to make sure, at a bare minimum, that items will not result in different answers because of factors that are not caused or related to the concept being measured. For example, asking someone "Are you afraid when you walk alone on the street at night?" will very likely be responded to differently by people who feel that their neighborhoods are either safe or not—it will not be a good way to measure general anxiety level (de Vijver, 2000). This is known as differential item functioning.

Similarly, it is equally important to make sure that an instrument designed to use with persons of color is culturally relevant. Test items should have the same connotative and denotative meanings, for instance, with both African-Americans and Euro-Americans.

When instruments are reliable and valid on a cross-cultural and multicultural basis, they measure the same construct dependably for all groups, the test scores will relate well to other already established Afrocentric or Hispanic measures (concurrent validity), and they will have the same degree of predictive validity for persons of color as for Euro-Americans. Finally, the instrument should be developed from a sample of persons that are representative of a multicultural population (Morris, 2000).

well defined and subjective judgments could have a biasing effect. If the obtained correlation is high (.70 or above), then the researcher has evidence that her rating scale has succeeded in providing sufficiently reliable measurements.

Practice-Focused Reliability Overview

Although there may seem to be too many types of reliability to keep track of, here's a tip or two for what you ought to remember about reliability:

- Internal consistency is also known as coefficient alpha or Cronbach's alpha. Most researchers compute it with statistical software and it will always be less than 1. The closer it is to 1, the more reliable the scale, and the better all items work together to measure the same concept.
- The Spearman-Brown Prophesy Formula is available should you be developing your own scale and are trying to improve the coefficient alpha. If you are not developing a scale or trying to improve on an existing one, you may not need this formula.
- The split-half method of computing internal consistency is an old, time-tested method, but is not seen a great deal today because computer software like SPSS are so easy to use.
- Parallel or alternate versions of computing internal consistency is, again, an approach that you are not likely to use unless you are involved in creating standardized tests.
- Test-retest reliability is frequently reported in social science literature because the concern is that some human psychological states (e.g., depression or low self-esteem) might vary in a major way from week to week or month to month. Most researchers who are developing scales hope that their instruments capture stable personality tendencies or traits. For instance, if

one is inclined to be fatalistic about life in general, then a person with high fatalistic score in January should also be on the high end of the fatalism measure in March. You can see how this can get tricky—a person with high depression scores should improve with treatment, but might a person with depression improve over time even with no treatment? Researchers would generally expect that two administrations of the same instrument within a short period of time (e.g., two weeks) would yield a strong correlation. This would suggest that the instrument was measuring *the same thing* at the two different times. (The coefficient alpha does not, you'll remember, suggest what that concept is—that's a job for a validity study.)

- The reliability of data collection procedures is something that you need to be concerned with whenever you are doing research that involves agency data with multiple personnel, or more than one observer, or whenever instructions to clients or research subjects are unclear or confusing.

Reliability—Qualitative Perspective

Reliability in field research is concerned with whether content derived from interviews and observations fit together in a pattern that is logical and consistent with what is known about the phenomenon, activity, or group being studied. Internal consistency, then, has to do with the plausibility of the data; external consistency involves cross-checking one's data and verifying with other sources of information. In contrast to the reliability of standardized instruments, reliability from the qualitative perspective depends upon the researcher's own insight and ability to test suppositions about the data and sources of data by questioning and examining their credibility (Kreuger & Neuman, 2006). Thus, one might establish that a crack user's testimony about the amount of money spent per week on the drug is believable—if, that is, other drug users give approximately the same estimates—or if a police officer, parole officer, or social worker in a drug treatment agency were able to verify that the amount of money spent on crack seemed in line and not exaggerated.

VALIDITY

An instrument is said to be **valid** when it measures the construct it was designed to measure. For instance, an intelligence test should measure intelligence. An instrument designed to measure anxiety should provide an accurate assessment of anxiety but not social responsibility, dogmatism, or paranoia.

Validity research demonstrates how a scale performs—identifying its limitations and its strengths. Because the same instrument may be valid in one situation but not in another, validity research seeks to gather evidence to document that the instrument is a good method for assessing the construct in question. For instance, a self-esteem scale that you developed initially for use in a school system might be heavily influenced by what might be thought of as "academic self-esteem"—students' perceptions of their worth based on the grades they were making. Students who were having trouble with algebra or chemistry might score very low on such a scale. This result would be a rather limited way of thinking about self-esteem, which may not accurately assess a young person's "real" self-esteem when he or she is away from school or during the summer months. And, the use of your scale, even if it were valid for a school population, might not be the best tool for assessing the self-esteem of a different group of subjects—adults, or an incarcerated population, for example.

These are the situations when a researcher ought to conduct validity research:

- When an instrument is new and unproven
- When an instrument designed for one age group is going to be used with another
- When an instrument designed for one culture is going to be used in another
- When an instrument is being adopted for a different use than what it was intended for
- Whenever a researcher wants to improve the instrument

There are numerous ways to go about establishing the validity of an instrument. Demonstrating validity is more of an ongoing process than a single, one-time effort. Even though there is no absolute consensus or uniform taxonomy of terms used when discussing validity efforts (Koeske, 1994), when research books discuss the ways a scale's validity may be shown, they do it generally in terms of the following three major categories:

1. Content validity
2. Criterion validity
   a.   concurrent approaches
   b.   predictive approaches
3. Construct validity
   a.   convergent
   b.   discriminant
   c.   factorial (structural)

In order to have **content validity,** an instrument needs to sample from the entire range of the concept that it was designed to measure. For instance, it could be difficult for a scale measuring anger in children under the age of 8 to be valid if the scale did not consider pouting, hitting, or temper tantrums as manifestations of anger. Likewise, a scale measuring anxiety in adolescents might not have content validity if it did not include such behavior as nail biting, crying, stomachaches, and sleeplessness. To the extent that an instrument contains a representative sampling of the universe of behaviors, attitudes, or characteristics that are believed to be associated with the concept, then it is said to have content validity. Content validity is established when a panel of experts examines the scale and agrees that the items selected are representative of the range of items associated with the concept to be measured. However, there are no standardized procedures for assessing content validity and no computed coefficient of validity is produced.

While the terms *content* and *face validity* are sometimes used inter-changeably, they do not have the same meaning. An instrument is said to have **face validity** when it appears to measure the intended construct. Face validity has never been accepted as a legitimate form of validity because appearances can be deceptive. Neither face nor content validity is sufficient for establishing that a scale will allow generalizability.

Once the researcher is reasonably confident that the scale has content validity, then the next step is to plan a strategy to demonstrate that the collection of items possesses other, more substantial, forms of validity. **Criterion validity,** the second major category of validity research activities, is based on the scale's ability to correlate positively with some external criterion assumed to be an indicator of the attitude, trait, or behavior being measured. Criterion validity can be established in several ways. We will quickly discuss two approaches or subtypes of this form of validity.

Concurrent validity is demonstrated by administering your scale simultaneously along with another scale that has documented validity to the same subjects. If the two scales correlate well in the direction expected, then your scale has demonstrated one form of concurrent validity. As an example, suppose you had developed the Drug Attitude Questionnaire (Appendix B). How would you go about showing that it had concurrent validity? One way would be to administer it along with another "proven" instrument that also measures attitudes about drugs. In fact, this is what we did. We correlated the Drug Attitude Questionnaire (DAQ) with a similar but shorter (14-item) instrument. This meant that some students in our study had to complete both instruments.

We found that the DAQ correlated .76 with the shorter instrument at posttest using a sample of ninth-grade students, and correlated .79 using a sample of college students. These relatively high correlations show that low scores on one test correspond to low scores on the other and vice versa. When high correlations are obtained between two tests presumed to be measuring the same concept, then concurrent validity is demonstrated. When groups are selected because the researcher has a good notion of how they will respond, this is sometimes called known-groups validity.

Predictive validity is another subtype of criterion validity and is demonstrated when scores on a test or scale predict future behavior or attitudes. The Drug Attitude Questionnaire would have predictive validity if, years later, you find that within your study group of middle school students, those who had prodrug attitudes were suspended from school or arrested for drug possession, while those with antidrug attitudes were not suspended or arrested for drug possession.

The third major category in validity research is **construct validity.** Construct validity is an overarching or fundamental type of validity on which other types depend (Meier, 1994). Construct validity is not a specific procedure, but a collection of evidence that allows the researcher to see patterns in the way the instrument performs along expected theoretical lines. It is the ability of an instrument to distinguish among individuals who have a lot of, some of, or none of the characteristic being measured that makes the instrument useful.

The theory that gives rise to the instrument allows for various hypotheses to be tested about relationships among constructs. This may involve group differences or factor analysis or other methods as described below.

Convergent validation is obtained when theoretically relevant variables demonstrate a relationship with the measure. An instrument that you developed to measure children's self-report of fear of playground bullies could, for instance, be correlated with teachers' or parents' rankings of children's fear. If the different assessment approaches yield scores that are strongly correlated, the researcher can rule out alternative explanations for the validity findings because there was no variance attributable to using a shared method of measurement.

In **discriminant validity,** the researcher hopes to find no relationship between the instrument's measurements and variables that should not, in theory, be related to the construct. Self-report instruments of children who are fearful of playground bullies should not correlate with other self-reports indicating that these same children are best friends with the bullies.

Factor analysis is still another way of establishing construct validity. When a large number of items have been created or can be drawn on to compose a scale, factor analysis can be used to reduce the number of items to a smaller group that are statistically related. Factor analysis also helps researchers to explore inner structure, and reveals the number of dimensions that instruments may contain.

To illustrate, let's go back to our earlier example of developing a self-esteem scale. Let's say that we write 85 different items that seem to have face and content validity. After administering the instrument to 150 high school students, we then enter this data into a statistical software program and run the factor analysis program. In our hypothetical example, the computer printout reveals that instead of one simple scale, we have items that group together in four different areas: academic self-esteem, social competence, satisfaction with personal appearance, and assertiveness. We might decide that these four factors are "the essence" of self-esteem and keep all of them, or perhaps we would pare out a factor or items that don't conform. For instance, you might eliminate a group of items clustering together that seemed to measure selfishness or self-centeredness.

Depending on what we want from our instrument, we might choose to combine the original four subscales into a new summated index that provides a global measure of self-esteem. Many times researchers hope that factor analysis will produce only a single one-dimensional scale like the Rosenberg Self-Esteem Scale shown later in this chapter. Factor analysis is a fascinating but somewhat sophisticated procedure and beyond the level of this introductory text. You may encounter the term as you read professional journal articles about the development or refinement of scales. The term *loads* is used to indicate that a scale item correlates well with the collection of items that cluster together to form a factor—as in "Item 3 loads higher on assertiveness than on social competence." Factor loadings are interpreted the same way as correlation coefficients.

Establishing validity is not a one-time or a single-shot deal, but rather an ongoing process. Different uses of the instrument become opportunities to show its ability to discriminate among different populations, which adds to the

Examples of Articles Describing the Development of Instruments

O'Hare and Collins (1997) have developed an instrument designed to measure the frequency with which certain practice skills (such as making referrals, employing empathy, and providing emotional support) are employed with clients. They started off with a pool of 97 items that was reduced to 75; from that group, 33 of the strongest were kept that supported four factors: therapeutic, case management, supportive, and treatment planning/evaluation skills. Their article describes the theoretical framework for the Practice Skills Inventory, the sample of students, and the factor analysis procedures and results.

Hudson and McMurtry (1997) have reported on the procedures they used to gather psychometric information on the Multiproblem Screening Inventory (MSPI), a 334-item paper-and-pencil instrument with 27 different subscales measuring such client problems as depression, suicidal intent, physical abuse, self-esteem, personal stress, phobias, disturbing thoughts, aggression, guilt, sexual discord, and drug use. Their article contains a good description of

how they tested the MPSI for reliability, content, factorial, and construct validity. This article provides a "cookbook" example of how to go about demonstrating that a newly created instrument scale has good psychometrics.

More recent examples in the social work literature include:

- Emlet, C. A. (2005). Measuring stigma in older and younger adults with HIV/AIDS: An analysis of an HIV stigma scale and initial exploration of subscales. *Research on Social Work Practice*, 15(4), 291–300.
- O'Hare, T., & Sherrer, M. V. (2005). Assessment of youthful problem drinkers: Validating the Drinking Context Scale (DCS-9) with freshman first offenders. *Research on Social Work Practice*, 15(2), 110–117.
- Siebert, D. C. (2005). The Caregiver Role Identity Scale: A validation study. *Research on Social Work Practice*, 15(3), 204–212.

accumulative evidence of its validity. For example, even though the DAQ was designed for middle school students, it might be employed with inpatients or outpatients in drug treatment programs to determine if attitudes about drugs changed as a result of intervention. Instruments that have been around for a long time often have extensive bibliographies associated with them as various researchers report the results of their use of the instrument in different settings and with diverse populations.

For the purpose of instruction, reliability and validity are usually presented as separate concepts. However, these two concepts are interrelated in a complex fashion. On the one hand, when we can empirically demonstrate that an instrument is valid, it can generally be assumed to have adequate reliability. On the other hand, a reliable instrument may not be valid. That is, an instrument may provide dependable measurements but of some concept unrelated to what we thought we were measuring. Both reliability and validity ought to be demonstrated as evidence that an instrument is psychometrically strong.

As you come across various instruments in practice or in your reading, it is important to realize that if you know nothing about the reliability and validity of a scale, then any results you obtain from its use may have very little meaning. The scale may not provide consistent results (poor reliability) or it may measure something quite different from what you intended (poor validity). The importance of knowing a scale's reliability and validity cannot be emphasized enough.

VALIDITY FROM THE QUALITATIVE PERSPECTIVE

For the qualitative researcher validity is not focused on the data collection instrument because the researcher is, for all practical purposes, the instrument. Instead, validity has to do with the extent to which data can be corroborated and this is generally attempted by one of two ways. **Triangulation** involves the use of multiple sources or multiple approaches to see if the same pattern or conclusions would be drawn from the data. Thus, after interviewing high school dropouts, one might also want to interview teachers as well as the disciplinary principal or officer to see if the data dovetail or form a coherent whole. According to Neuman (2006), "A researcher's empirical claims gain validity when supported by numerous pieces of diverse empirical data ... Validity arises out of the cumulative impact of hundreds of small, diverse details that only together create a heavy weight of evidence" (p. 197).

Another approach is to employ **member checking** (or member validation) where the qualitative researcher provides preliminary results to some or all of the individuals the original data were collected from so that they have an opportunity to point out any inaccuracies or errors of interpretation.

Unlike the quantitative researcher who attempts to objectively measure or count, convincing others of the validity of the research by using a strong methodological design and instruments which yield precise and dependable results, the qualitative researcher is not always troubled when the data supplied by different informers provides a greater diversity of opinion or perspective than expected. What would trouble the qualitative researcher, for instance, would be little correspondence between her interpretations and the member doing the checking. In quantitative research, the researcher bears all of the responsibility for establishing the validity of a study. In contrast, the qualitative researcher largely leaves it to the reader: "Readers can decide for themselves whether the descriptions justify the claims." Lillian Rubin (1976) referred to this as the "aha" standard of validity (Preissle & Grant, 2004, p. 178).

LOCATING RESEARCH INSTRUMENTS

While complete scales are sometimes reproduced in journal articles, this is a fairly rare occurrence because of space limitations. Commonly, journal articles give examples of items from the scale and information about the scale's reliability and validity. This usually means that you will have to consult the bibliography and may have to search through several other articles to find the actual scale or more specific information about where to obtain it.

Some instruments are protected by copyright. To use these, you will have to purchase copies of these instruments from a commercial source or acquire permission from the author. Instruments that you find in journal articles are not likely to be protected by copyright. However, good research etiquette dictates that you contact the author anyway and request permission to use the instrument. It can be useful to make contact. Most authors want to keep informed of research conducted with their instruments. They'll be interested in yours. As you discuss with them your proposed research, they may be able to help in ways that you didn't expect. Sometimes they have prepared shorter or newer versions of old instruments or may share a bibliography of recent articles that have used the instrument.

Finding an appropriate instrument without immersing yourself completely in the literature can be a bit like chasing a rainbow. However, several good sources for scales may contain just the instrument you require. One place to start is with the *Test Link*, which is a computerized database accessible from the Internet (http://ets.org/testcoll/). Enter the topic or the name of the test that you are trying to locate in the search engine and it will return a set of abstracts about the corresponding scales or tests in its collection. By clicking on one or more of these links you can find a reference to the measure that you are seeking. It won't provide you with the instrument itself, but will help you to find it. When the test is commercial and must be purchased, contact information is provided.

Printed resources you may be able to obtain from your library are:

- Antony, M. M., Orsillo, S. M., & Roemer, L. (2001). *Practitioner's guide to empirically based measures of anxiety.* New York: Kluwer Academic / Plenum Publishers.
- Beere, C. A. (1990). *Sex and gender issues: A handbook of tests and measures.* Westport, CT: Greenwood Press.
- Beere, C. A. (1990). *Gender roles: A handbook of tests and measures.* Westport, CT: Greenwood Press.
- Corcoran, K., & Fischer, J. (2007). *Measures for clinical practice and research: A sourcebook for couples, families, and children* (3rd ed.). London: Oxford University Press.
- Davis, C. M., Yarber, W. L., Bauserman, R., & Schreer, G. (2004). *Handbook of sexuality-related measures.* Thousand Oaks, CA: Sage.
- Fayers, P. M., & Machin, D. (2000). *Quality of life: Assessment, analysis, and interpretation.* New York: John Wiley & Sons.
- Feindler, E., Rathus, J., & Silver, L. B. (2002). *Assessment of family violence: A handbook for researchers and practitioners.* Washington, DC: American Psychological Association.
- Frank-Stromborg, M., & Olson, S. (1997). *Instruments for clinical health care research.* Sudbury, MA: Jones and Bartlett.

- Goldman, B. A., & Busch, J. C. (1997). *Directory of unpublished experimental mental measures.* Washington, DC: American Psychological Association.
- Hamill, D. D. (1992). *A consumer's guide to tests in print.* Austin, TX: Pro-ED.
- Kelley, M. L. (2002). *Practitioner's guide to empirically based measures of school behavior.* New York: Kluwer Academic/Plenum Publishers.
- Keyser, D. J., & Sweetland, R. C. (1994). *Test critiques.* Austin, TX: Pro-ED.
- Maddox, T. (1997). *Tests: A comprehensive reference for assessments in psychology, education, and business.* Austin, TX: Pro-ED.
- McDowell, I., & Newell, C. (1996). *Measuring health: A guide to rating scales and questionnaires.* New York: Oxford University Press.
- Miller, D., & Salkind, N. J. (2002). *Handbook of research design and social measurement.* Thousand Oaks, CA: Sage.
- Murphy, L., Impara, J., & Plake, B. (1999). *Tests in Print V: An index to tests, test reviews, and literature on specific tests.* Lincoln, NE: University of Nebraska Press.
- Nezu, A. M., Ronan, G. F., Meadows, E. A., & McClure, K. S. (2000). *Practitioner's guide to*

(Continued)

(Continued)

empirically based measures of depression. New York: Kluwer Academic/Plenum Publishers.

- Plake, B., & Impara, J. (2001). *Mental measurements yearbook*. Lincoln, NE: Buros Institute for Mental Measurements.
- Peterson, D. J., & Alexander, G. R. (2001). *Needs assessment in public health*. New York: Kluwer Academic/Plenum Publishers.
- Robinson, J. P., Shaver, P., & Wrightsman, L. S. (1991). *Measures of personality and social psychological attitudes*. San Diego: Academic Press.
- Sajatovic, M., & Ramirez, L. F. (2001). *Rating scales in mental health*. Hudson, OH: Lexi-Comp Inc.
- Stamm, B. H. (1996). *Measurement of stress, trauma, and adaptation*. Lutherville, MD: Sidran.
- Touliatos, J., Perlmutter, B. F., & Straus, M. A. (2001). *Handbook of family measurement techniques*. Newbury Park, CA: Sage.

Other references, although somewhat dated, may provide a specific instrument:

- Chum, K., Cobb, S., & French, J. R., Jr. (1975). *Measures for psychological assessment: A guide to 3,000 original sources and their applications*. Ann Arbor, MI: Institute for Social Research.
- Fredman, N., & Sherman, R. (1987). *Handbook of measurements for marriage and family therapy*. New York: Brunner/Mazel.
- Keyser, D. J., & Sweetland, R. C. (1987). *Test critiques compendium: Reviews of major tests from the test critiques series*. Kansas City, MO: Test Corporation of America.
- Nurius, P. S., & Hudson, W. W. (1993). *Human services practice, evaluation, and computers*. Pacific Grove, CA: Brooks/Cole.

WHEN YOU CAN'T FIND THE INSTRUMENT YOU WANT

Most often when students complain that they can't find an instrument they need, they've had a problem narrowing down exactly what they want to measure. Not too long ago, a student told me she had spent hours in the library without finding the kind of instrument she was looking for. As we talked more, she revealed that she'd been searching under "children" and "families," when it would have been more profitable for her to look for literature on parenting programs. At times, a switch to a different database can also be beneficial.

Most often, a thorough search of the literature will produce either the instrument being sought or a literature review that discusses the pros and cons of several instruments measuring the same concept. For instance, in an article entitled "Twenty Suicide Assessment Instruments: Evaluation and Recommendations," Range and Knott (1997) reviewed the psychometric properties of the assessment instruments and then selected three scales as having more strengths and fewer weaknesses than the others.

Sometimes starting with one instrument that you know about can lead you to others. *The Web of Science* is a database available at many universities that allows one to enter an author of an article, the journal name, and year of publication; and then it will tell you (using the "Cited Reference" search button) which other authors/studies have cited that particular study in their own article. For instance, in trying to find additional information about the Child Abuse Trauma Scale, I typed in "Sanders, B" for author, the title of the journal in which her study was found (Child Abuse and Neglect), and the year

(1995). The search engine then found for me these two additional studies (among others) which list many other similar instruments for my (or your consideration):

- Hulme, P. A. (2004). Retrospective measurement of childhood sexual abuse: A review of instruments. *Child Maltreatment, 9(2)*, 201–217.
- Roy, C. A., & Perry, J. C. (2004). Instruments for the assessment of childhood trauma in adults. *Journal of Nervous and Mental Disease, 192(5)*, 343–351.

If you conduct an exhaustive literature search and even consult with knowledgeable people and still can't find the instrument you want, two avenues still lie before you. First, you can take an existing instrument and modify it to meet your needs. It is reasonable to take such drastic action if, for instance, you've found a potentially useful scale developed for adults that is too long to use with children.

In such a situation, write to the author of the instrument to ask if any short forms have been developed, and if they have not, if you may have permission to draw on the earlier version. Most authors, particularly if their scales have appeared in professional journals and are not copyrighted, will likely be interested in your research and grant you permission. The only caution here is that any time you modify an existing instrument, the burden is on you to prove that the resulting instrument is reliable and valid. Because the longer instrument was psychometrically sound does not guarantee that the shorter instrument will be.

It is not at all unusual for researchers to take a scale developed by someone else and to adapt it for a different purpose. A colleague and I once modified the Social Distance Scale created by E. S. Bogardus in 1925. To measure acceptance of different nationalities or races, Bogardus asked respondents if they would admit someone different from themselves into such situations as:

Kinship by marriage

Club membership

Neighbors

Employment in one's occupation

Citizenship in one's country

Visitors to one's country

Our Social Distance Scale asked some of these same questions, providing *Strongly Agree, Agree, Undecided, Disagree,* and *Strongly Disagree* as response choices:

SA **A** **U** **D** **SD**   I would be opposed to persons with AIDS living on the same street as me.

SA **A** **U** **D** **SD**   I would be uncomfortable if I had to work in the same department or office as persons with AIDS.

SA A U D SD   I would allow persons with AIDS to become
                         citizens of the United States.

SA A U D SD   I would exclude persons with AIDS from
                         visiting my country.

Even with just these four items, the reliability was quite strong (.82). Since this was an exploratory study, we didn't attempt to establish the validity of the instrument, but we did find that our Social Distance Scale correlated .67 with our Fear of Aids Scale and −.68 with our Empathy for AIDS Victims Scale, which at least suggests that our measure might have more than just face or content validity.

If you find no instruments you want to modify, a second option is to create your own scale. Once again, it will be your responsibility to establish that the instrument measures what you intended and does so reliably. Just because you think it has content or face validity does not make it a good instrument. Take, for example, Questions 7 through 15 of the *Attitudes about Research Courses Questionnaire* (from Appendix A):

7. T or F. I dread speaking before a large group of people more than taking a research course.
8. T or F. I would rather take a research course than ask a waitress to return an improperly cooked meal to the chef.
9. T or F. My fear of snakes is greater than my fear of taking a research course.
10. T or F. My fear of spiders is less than my fear of taking a research course.
11. T or F. I would rather take a research course than ask a total stranger to do a favor for me.
12. T or F. My fear of research is such that I would rather the university require an additional two courses of my choosing than require one research course.
13. T or F. I dread going to the dentist more than taking a research course.
14. T or F. I fear a statistics course more than a research methodology course.
15. T or F. I have always "hated math."

Can you guess what I was trying to measure with this scale? Although I had high hopes for it, the scale's reliability was so poor that I've never attempted any further research with it. What struck me as a clever way to measure fear of research simply didn't work. I suspect that individual responses to such things as spiders and dentists interfered with rather than facilitated the concept I was trying to measure. Oh, well, this is the way research moves forward. Sometimes there's considerable trial and error involved.

How do you go about constructing a scale? Normally, you begin by creating a pool of items that you think will measure different dimensions or degrees of the behavior, knowledge, or attitude that you have in mind. Sometimes you will invite experts in the field to contribute items. Then you weed out some items, and prepare a draft of the instrument. This version is then administered to a large group. From the data the group supplies, you use computer software to identify which items correlate well. The items that correlate most poorly are thrown out.

Depending on the reliability coefficient obtained, you might, at that point, decide that the refined list of items is adequate. If the reliability coefficient is lower than desired, you may add new items and administer the second version to another set of people, dropping and adding new items until you are is satisfied with the internal consistency of the instrument.

When would it be important to establish that a scale has validity? This would be something you would want to do if you were planning further research with the instrument or if you were thinking about getting a copyright in order to market it. Perhaps your scale could help social service employers screen out applicants who have no empathy for clients or who would be too fearful to work with AIDS patients. Or, if your responsibility with an organization is to provide in-service training, you might want a valid scale to help you evaluate what the participants acquired from the in-service training.

EVALUATING INSTRUMENTS FOR USE IN PRACTICE

Before adopting an assessment instrument for use in practice, social workers should consider several important questions:

PRACTICALITY—IS THE INSTRUMENT

- Affordable?
- Easy for clients to read and understand?
- Easy to administer?
- Easy to score and interpret?
- Not too long?

PSYCHOMETRICS—DOES THE INSTRUMENT HAVE

- Good reliability (.70 for research and at least .90 for clinical decision making)?
- The necessary sensitivity to detect small increments of improvement?
- Validity established through multiple studies and usages?

THEORETICAL APPLICATION—WILL THE INSTRUMENT

- Measure the concept that is the best indicator of client improvement in the particular population? Is the concept understandable to clients? Policy-makers? Funding sources?
- Allow you to make predictions consistent with the theory underlying your intervention?
- Allow you to compare your findings with other practitioners working with similar populations?
- Provide useful information to service providers?

If there are several instruments to choose from, then considering such questions as those identified above can help a researcher or committee to make better decisions about the assessment instruments under consideration.

Practice Note: Ethnicity and Measurement Issues

- Most standardized scales were not designed for use with ethnic populations. Many, if not most, of the measurement tools currently in existence have been developed by European Americans. Further, these tests are often interpreted based on scores obtained mostly from white subjects.

- The terms *race* and *ethnicity* are frequently confused and misleading. Many Hispanics, for instance, may identify their race as white. Persons who are biracial may not always be classified accurately.

- Socioeconomic status (SES) can be a confounding variable when investigators are looking at differences in their dependent variables by ethnicity.

- Instruments designed for one cultural group may contain substantial measurement bias when applied to another ethnic group. The ethnicity of the rater may affect those being rated.

- There has not been a great deal of study of bias or lack of it in cross-cultural studies pertaining to validity issues and psychological assessment.

- Instruments translated from one language into another then need to be back-translated by another independent party to make sure that the translation is accurate. In some cases, a literal translation is not as accurate as an idiomatic or conceptual equivalence.

Sources: Foster, S. L., & Martinez, C. R. (1995). Ethnicity: Conceptual and methodological issues in child clinical research. *Journal of Clinical Child Psychology, 24,* 214–226; Malgady, R. G. (1996). The question of cultural bias in assessment and diagnosis of ethnic minority clients: Let's reject the null hypothesis. *Professional Psychology, Research and Practice, 27,* 73–77; Land, H., & Hudson, S. (1997). Methodological considerations in surveying Latina AIDS caregivers: Issues in sampling and measurement. *Social Work Research, 21,* 233–246.

A SAMPLING OF INSTRUMENTS

This chapter has discussed instruments and scales from a technical standpoint. Now that you know how to evaluate them, it is useful to examine several examples more in-depth. For the section that follows, I've secured the permission of several authors to reproduce all or portions of their instruments. Even with this small sample, you'll see some of the great variety of instruments that have been created by social workers. Instruments contained in this section are:

- The Job Satisfaction Scale
- The Child Abuse and Trauma Scale
- The CES-D
- The Rosenberg Self-Esteem Scale

Job Satisfaction Scale (JSS)

Description The authors began using measures of job satisfaction in 1980 while exploring the antecedents and consequences of job stress and strain. The preliminary measure was a short 7-item scale, which has evolved over the years and is now made up of 14 items. Data from the Job Satisfaction Scale, in one form or another, has been obtained from more than 600 social service professionals in diverse human service settings. See Figure 6.1 for a sample Job Satisfaction Scale.

Psychometric Data Several studies reveal the JSS to have good internal consistency, ranging from .83 to .91. From factor analysis of the 14 job

Instructions: Please rate each of the aspects of your work listed below according to the degree of satisfaction or dissatisfaction it provides you. Circle a number between 1 (Very Dissatisfied) and 11 (Very Satisfied) for each aspect.

	Very Dissatisfied									Very Satisfied	
1. Working with your clients	1	2	3	4	5	6	7	8	9	10	11
2. The amount of authority you have been given to do your job	1	2	3	4	5	6	7	8	9	10	11
3. Your salary and benefits	1	2	3	4	5	6	7	8	9	10	11
4. Opportunities for promotion	1	2	3	4	5	6	7	8	9	10	11
5. The challenge your job provides you	1	2	3	4	5	6	7	8	9	10	11
6. The quality of supervision you receive	1	2	3	4	5	6	7	8	9	10	11
7. Chances for acquiring new skills	1	2	3	4	5	6	7	8	9	10	11
8. Amount of client contact	1	2	3	4	5	6	7	8	9	10	11
9. Opportunities for really helping people	1	2	3	4	5	6	7	8	9	10	11
10. Clarity of guidelines for doing your job	1	2	3	4	5	6	7	8	9	10	11
11. Opportunity for involvement in decision-making	1	2	3	4	5	6	7	8	9	10	11
12. The recognition given your work by your supervisor	1	2	3	4	5	6	7	8	9	10	11
13. Your feeling of success as a social worker	1	2	3	4	5	6	7	8	9	10	11
14. Field of specialization you are in	1	2	3	4	5	6	7	8	9	10	11

Figure 6.1 | Job Satisfaction Scale

Source: Courtesy of Gary F. Koeske: Koeske, G. F., Kirk, S. A., Koeske, R. D., & Rauktis, M. B. (1994). Measuring the Monday blues: Validation of a job satisfaction scale for the human services. *Social Work Research*, 29(4), 27–35.

satisfaction items, three different dimensions were found. The first was called Intrinsic Job Satisfaction and reflected intrinsic qualities of the work role. The second dimension was called Organizational Job Satisfaction and depicted satisfaction with supervision and other elements of agency operation. The third factor contained two extrinsic items dealing with salary and promotion. Internal consistency of these subscales ranges from .75 to .90. Test-retest reliabilities on the full scale ranged from .80 (9 months) to .64 (15 months).

In terms of predictive validity, a study of intensive case managers found that JSS scores were inversely related to later depression and emotional exhaustion scores, and were positively related to intention to quit the job. Supportive findings suggest convergent and construct validity. In one study, the Moos Work Environment Scale correlated .61 with the Job Satisfaction Scale, and the JSS correlated .76 with a global item that asked, "All things considered, how satisfied or dissatisfied are you with your job?" The authors found that this instrument was significantly correlated with each of the widely used Maslach Burnout Inventory dimensions (for example, .59 with emotional exhaustion). In a 1984 study the authors found that job satisfaction was inversely related to the percentage of "difficult" clients in one's active caseload. The JSS appears to be a short, reliable, and valid measure of job satisfaction in the human services.

Availability   The Job Satisfaction Scale is available for use without securing special permission. A description of the development of this scale can be found in Koeske, Kirk, Koeske, and Rauktis (1994). (Refer to the source note for Figure 6.1 for publishing information.) For additional information contact Gary Koeske, Ph.D., School of Social Work, University of Pittsburgh, 2217H, Pittsburgh, PA 15260.

Scoring   Overall and subscale scores are simple sums, corrected for missing and for any "not applicable" responses. The author has used 7- and 9-step response scales in the past with similar results for reliability and validity. He prefers 3.5 through 0 to 15 scaling, but notes that it complicates coding and probably introduces coding error. The numerical values used, however, do not affect reliability or validity.

Recent Use of the Instrument   Lambert, R. G., Abott-Shim, M., & Oxford-Wright, C. (2001). Staff perceptions of research in the context of specific strategies for collaboration with Head Start programs. *Early Child Research Quarterly, 16,* 19–34.

The Child Abuse and Trauma Scale

Description   The Child Abuse and Trauma Scale (CAT) is a 38-item rating scale designed for the retrospective assessment of negative childhood experiences so that researchers can examine the psychological effects of childhood maltreatment which may be understood as emotional abuse or psychological maltreatment. The scale is designed to reflect the extent of various forms of physical, sexual, and emotional maltreatment for research applications where group data would be obtained. However, the authors say that the CAT may be useful in clinical assessment as an initial screening instrument. See Figure 6.2 for the actual scale.

Psychometric Data   An initial version of the CAT was administered to 47 adolescents in a psychiatric hospital and their scores correlated significantly ($r = .44$) with Putnam's Dissociative Experiences Scale. Later the instrument was administered to two separate college samples ($n = 834$ and 301, respectively); sample means were .75 and .73. Three factors emerged: Negative Home Environment/Neglect (14 items), Sexual Abuse (6 items), and Punishment (6 items); separate mean scores were reported for these. Internal consistency for the overall scale was found to be .90; test-retest reliability for 67 subjects was found to be .89. With the second college sample the CAT scores correlated significantly with dissociation, depression, stressful life events, and the Object Relations Scale which is used to measure difficulty in interpersonal relationships. Additionally, the instrument was administered to 17 adults meeting the DSM-III-R criteria for MPD. The mean score for that group was 2.7.

Home Environment Questionnaire

This questionnaire seeks to determine the general atmosphere of your home when you were a child or teenager and how you felt you were treated by your parents or principal caretaker. (If you were not raised by one or both of your biological parents, please respond to the questions below in terms of the person or persons who had the primary responsibility for your upbringing as a child.) Where a question inquires about the behavior of both of your parents and your parents differed in their behavior, please respond in terms of the parent whose behavior was the more severe or worse.

In responding to these questions, simply circle the appropriate number according to the following definitions:

0 = never   1 = rarely   2 = sometimes   3 = very often   4 = always

To illustrate, here is a hypothetical question:

Did your parents criticize you when you were young?

If you were rarely criticized, you should circle number 1.

Please answer all questions.

1. Did your parents ridicule you?	0	1	2	3	4
2. Did you ever seek outside help or guidance because of problems in your home?	0	1	2	3	4
3. Did your parents verbally abuse each other?	0	1	2	3	4
4. Were you expected to follow a strict code of behavior in your home?	0	1	2	3	4
5. When you were punished as a child or teenager, did you understand the reason you were punished?	0	1	2	3	4
6. When you didn't follow the rules of the house, how often were you severely punished?	0	1	2	3	4
7. As a child did you feel unwanted or emotionally neglected?	0	1	2	3	4
8. Did your parents insult you or call you names?	0	1	2	3	4
9. Before you were 14, did you engage in any sexual activity with an adult?	0	1	2	3	4
10. Were your parents unhappy with each other?	0	1	2	3	4
11. Were your parents unwilling to attend any of your school-related activities?	0	1	2	3	4
12. As a child were you punished in unusual ways (e.g., being locked in a closet for a long time or being tied up?)	0	1	2	3	4
13. Were there traumatic or upsetting sexual experiences when you were a child or teenager that you couldn't speak to adults about?	0	1	2	3	4
14. Did you ever think you wanted to leave your family and live with another family?	0	1	2	3	4
15. Did you ever witness the sexual mistreatment of another family member?	0	1	2	3	4
16. Did you ever think seriously about running away from home?	0	1	2	3	4
17. Did you witness the physical mistreatment of another family member?	0	1	2	3	4
18. When you were punished as a child or teenager, did you feel the punishment was deserved?	0	1	2	3	4
19. As a child or teenager, did you feel disliked by either of your parents?	0	1	2	3	4
20. How often did your parents get really angry with you?	0	1	2	3	4

(Continued)

Figure 6.2 | Child Abuse and Trauma Scale

21. As a child did you feel that your home was charged with the possibility of unpredictable physical violence?	0	1	2	3	4
22. Did you feel comfortable bringing friends home to visit?	0	1	2	3	4
23. Did you feel safe living at home?	0	1	2	3	4
24. When you were punished as a child or teenager, did you feel the "punishment fit the crime?"	0	1	2	3	4
25. Did your parents ever verbally lash out at you when you did not expect it?	0	1	2	3	4
26. Did you have a traumatic sexual experiences as a child or teenager?	0	1	2	3	4
27. Were you lonely as a child?	0	1	2	3	4
28. Did your parents yell at you?	0	1	2	3	4
29. When either of your parents was intoxicated, were you ever afraid of being sexually mistreated?	0	1	2	3	4
30. Did you ever wish for a friend to share your life?	0	1	2	3	4
31. How often were you left at home alone as a child?	0	1	2	3	4
32. Did your parents blame you for things you didn't do?	0	1	2	3	4
33. To what extent did either of your parents drink heavily or abuse drugs?	0	1	2	3	4
34. Did your parents ever hit or beat you when you did not expect it?	0	1	2	3	4
35. Did your relationship with your parents ever involve a sexual experience?	0	1	2	3	4
36. As a child, did you have to take care of yourself before you were old enough?	0	1	2	3	4
37. Were you physically mistreated as a child or teenager?	0	1	2	3	4
38. Was your childhood stressful?	0	1	2	3	4

Figure 6.2 | *(Continued)*

Availability   The CAT scale is found in the article by Sanders, B., & Becker-Lausen, E. (1995). The measurement of psychological maltreatment: Early data on the Child Abuse and Trauma Scale. *Child Abuse & Neglect, 19*(3), 315–323.

CES-D Scale

Description   Developed by the staff at the Center for Epidemiologic Studies, National Institute of Mental Health, the CES-D is a brief self-report scale designed to measure depressive symptomatology in the general population (Radloff, 1977). It was developed from previously existing scales and was designed not to distinguish primary depressive disorders from secondary depression or subtypes of depression but to identify the presence and severity of depressive symptomatology for epidemiologic research, needs assessment, and screening (Radloff & Locke, 1986). See Figure 6.3 for an example of a CES-D Scale.

During the past week:	Rarely or None of the Time (Less Than 1 day)	Some or a Little of the Time (1–2 days)	Occasionally or Moderate Amount of the Time (3–4 days)	Most or All of the Time (5–7 days)
		(circle one number on each line)		
1. I was bothered by things that usually don't bother me.	0	1	2	3
2. I did not feel like eating; my appetite was poor.	0	1	2	3
3. I felt that I could not shake off the blues even with help from my family or friends.	0	1	2	3
4. I felt that I was just as good as other people.	0	1	2	3
5. I had trouble keeping my mind on what I was doing.	0	1	2	3
6. I felt depressed.	0	1	2	3
7. I felt that everything I did was an effort.	0	1	2	3
8. I felt hopeful about the future.	0	1	2	3
9. I thought my life had been a failure.	0	1	2	3
10. I felt fearful.	0	1	2	3
11. My sleep was restless.	0	1	2	3
12. I was happy.	0	1	2	3
13. I talked less than usual.	0	1	2	3
14. I felt lonely.	0	1	2	3
15. People were unfriendly.	0	1	2	3
16. I enjoyed life.	0	1	2	3
17. I had crying spells.	0	1	2	3
18. I felt sad.	0	1	2	3
19. I felt that people disliked me.	0	1	2	3
20. I could not get "going."	0	1	2	3

Figure 6.3 | The CES-D Scale

Source: Courtesy U.S. Department of Health and Human Services.

Psychometric Data   This depression scale has been found to have high internal consistency (.85 in the general population and .90 in the patient sample) and acceptable test-retest stability. The CES-D scores discriminate well between psychiatric inpatient and general population samples and moderately well among patient groups with varying levels of severity. The scale has excellent concurrent validity, and substantial evidence exists of its construct validity (Radloff, 1977).

Availability   The CES-D Scale is in the public domain and may be used without copyright permission. The Epidemiology and Psychopathology Research Branch of the National Institute of Mental Health is interested, however, in receiving copies of research reports that have utilized the instrument.

Scoring   Because the CES-D is a 20-item scale, it is easily scored. Responses are weighted 0 for "rarely or none of the time" to 3 for "most of the time." Items 4, 8, 12, and 16 are reverse-scored (given a 3 for "Rarely" and 0 for "Most"). The range of possible scores is 0 to 60. High scores indicate high levels of depression symptomatology, with scores of 17 or greater identified as "at-risk cases" and scores of 23 or above as "probable cases" of depression.

Recent Uses of the Instrument   (1) Bosworth, H. B., Bastian, L. A., Kuchibhatla, M. N., Steffens, D. C., McBride, C. M., Skinner, C. S., Rimer, B. K., & Siegler, L. C. (2001). Depressive symptoms, menopausal status, and climacteric symptoms in women at midlife. *Psychosomatic Medicine, 63,* 603–608. (2) Knowlton, A. R., Latkin, C. A., Schroeder, J. R., Hoover, D. R., Ensminger, M., & Celentano, D. D. (2001). Longitudinal predictors of depressive symptoms among low-income injection drug users. *AIDS Care, 13,* 549–559.

Rosenberg Self-Esteem Scale

Description   The Rosenberg Self-Esteem Scale was originally developed on a sample of over 5,000 high school juniors and seniors from ten randomly selected schools in New York state. *Social Science Citation Index* shows well over 1,000 citations for Rosenberg's instrument—making it the most popular measure of global self-esteem and prompting Blasovitch and Tomaka (1991) to observe that "it is the standard with which developers of other measures usually seek convergence" (p. 120). See Figure 6.4 for an example of the Rosenberg Self-Esteem Scale.

Psychometric Data   Fleming and Courtney (1984) have reported a Cronbach's alpha of .8 and test-retest correlations of .82 with a one-week interval. Rosenberg (1965) presented a great deal of data on the construct validity of this measure. Demo (1985) reported self-esteem scores correlating .55 with the Coopersmith SEI.

Availability   This scale is in the public domain and may be used without securing permission.

Instructions: Below is a list of statements dealing with your general feelings about yourself. If you agree with the statement, circle **A**. If you strongly agree, circle **SA**. If you disagree, circle **D**. If you strongly disagree, circle **SD**.

	Strongly Agree	Agree	Disagree	Strongly Disagree
1. On the whole, I am satisfied with myself.	SA	A	D	SD
2. At times I think I am no good at all.	SA	A	D	SD
3. I feel that I have a number of good qualities.	SA	A	D	SD
4. I am able to do things as well as most other people.	SA	A	D	SD
5. I feel I do not have much to be proud of.	SA	A	D	SD
6. I certainly feel useless at times.	SA	A	D	SD
7. I feel that I'm a person of worth, at least on an equal plane with others.	SA	A	D	SD
8. I wish I could have more respect for myself.	SA	A	D	SD
9. All in all, I am inclined to feel that I am a failure.	SA	A	D	SD
10. I take a positive attitude toward myself.	SA	A	D	SD

Figure 6.4 | Rosenberg Self-Esteem Scale

Source: Courtesy of Morris Rosenberg. Rosenberg, M. (1965). *Society and the adolescent self-image.* Princeton, NJ: Princeton University Press.

Scoring   Using the Likert procedure, responses are assigned a score ranging from 1 to 4. Items 1, 3, 4, 7, and 10 are reverse scored. (For example, item 1, "On the whole I am satisfied with myself," the "strongly agree" response is assigned a score of 4 and "strongly disagree" is assigned a score of 1.) This procedure yields possible total scores ranging from 10 to 40. The higher the score, the higher the self-esteem.

FINAL NOTES

Students occasionally ask about handling clients who deliberately misrepresent the truth on assessment instruments—especially when they may know of an actual incident (e.g., a beating by a partner that required medical attention) that is not reported on the scale. All self-report scales are based on the assumption that some error is involved but that respondents are usually honest. Further, an inaccurate response to any one item on a scale generally does not create a measurement problem. Thus, people who live with abusive partners would still likely have higher scores on a scale such as Hudson's Partner Abuse Scale than people who don't live with hurtful partners—even if they are dishonest on a few items. Of course, clients may be motivated to lie and this might not always be detected—particularly in shorter instruments that don't allow the researcher to check for inconsistencies.

These are some of the ways that subjects can bias their responses:

- **Social desirability**—putting the "best foot forward," not reporting behavior or attitudes that might meet with disapproval from one's friends or peers.
- **Faking good**—creating a false positive impression.
- **Faking bad**—creating a false negative impression.
- **End-aversion**—avoiding extreme categories like "never" and "always" and consistently choosing a middle response on a scale.
- **Acquiescence**—tending to agree with or give positive responses regardless of what is being asked.

On rating instruments, there's another response bias possibility. Because of a previously formed impression about someone (e.g., a chronic patient who is manipulative or an employee who is thought to be unethical), raters may find it difficult to assess *objectively* certain individuals. Thus, there may be a tendency to rate a client who is well-liked and personable as higher functioning than he or she really is, and, conversely, a client who has caused trouble or complained a great deal may be viewed as having made less progress. This is known as the *halo effect*. The use of behaviorally anchored scales may help to reduce this expectancy effect. (More on this topic in Chapter 7.)

KEY TERMS

reliable	content validity	concurrent validity	factor analysis
internal consistency	face validity	predictive validity	triangulation
interrater reliability	criterion validity	construct validity	member checking
valid			

SELF-REVIEW

(Answers at the end of the book)

1. Pam has created a scale and administered it to the same group of her chronically mentally ill clients on two occasions, a week apart. It is likely she is trying to determine:
   a. construct validity
   b. test-retest reliability
   c. a correlation coefficient with all the extraneous variables
   d. content validity
2. If an item correlates strongly with the other items on a scale, would Pam want to throw it out and create a new item, or keep it because it would add to the scale's internal consistency?

3. If you and another school social worker were observing children with suspected attention deficit disorder and each of you is using a rating scale, what would you call the effort to determine the correlation between your two ratings?

4. _____ is when an instrument measures the construct it was designed to measure.

5. T or F. Pam shares her newly created instrument with several coworkers and they agree it appears to possess face validity. Pam doesn't need to conduct any other validity studies before using her scale in a large project involving 300 clients over a two-year study period.

6. T or F. Factor analysis is the approved way of establishing concurrent validity.

7. T or F. Predictive validity is when the researcher finds no relationship between the scale's measurements and variables that should not be correlated with the construct.

8. T or F. A scale with an internal validity of .60 could be said to be "quite strong."

9. T or F. Once a scale is determined to be valid, say, with a group of clients with chronic mental illness, no additional validity studies would be needed if the scale was then used with a group of high school underachievers.

10. T or F. The problem with designing a new instrument each time you need one is that it always has unknown psychometrics until studies establish its reliability and validity.

11. Read the description on the Child Abuse and Trauma Scale and then identify which approach to establishing validity that the authors took.

QUESTIONS FOR CLASS DISCUSSION

1. Why would a researcher prefer to measure a concept like depression or self-esteem with an instrument rather than just by observation?

2. Does it make sense to debate whether reliability is more important than validity? Why or why not?

3. Do you think it is important to disguise from research subjects the title of the scale they are completing? Under what circumstances might it make sense to cloak the title or purpose of a study?

4. The term *discrimination* usually has a negative connotation, such as when it is associated with sexism or racism. However, does the term have a positive or negative connotation when we think about a scale with construct validity as being able to discriminate well?

RESOURCES AND REFERENCES

Abell, N. (1991). The index of clinical stress: A brief measure of subjective stress for practice and research. *Social Work Research and Abstracts, 27(2)*, 12–15.

Blascovitch, J., & Tomaka, J. (1991). Measures of self-esteem. In John P. Robinson, Phillip R. Shaver, & Lawrence S. Wrightsman (Eds.), *Measures of personality and social psychological attitudes* (pp. 115–160). New York: Harcourt Brace Jovanovich.

Camasso, M. J., & Geismar, L.L. (1992). A multivariate approach to construct reliability and validity assessment: The case of family functioning. *Social Work Research and Abstracts, 28(4)*, 16–26.

Combs-Orme, T. D., Orme, J. G., & Guidry, C. J. (1991). Reliability and validity of the Protective Services Questionnaire (PSQ). *Journal of Social Service Research, 14*, 1–20.

Comrey, A. L. (1988). Factor analytic methods in scale development in personality and clinical psychology. *Journal of Consulting and Clinical Psychology, 56*, 754–761.

Congdon, D. C., & Holland, T. P. (1988). Measuring the effectiveness of substance abuse treatment: Toward a theory-based index. *Journal of Social Service Research, 12*, 23–48.

Cortina, J. M. (1993). What is coefficient alpha? An examination of theory and applications. *Journal of Applied Psychology, 78(1)*, 98–104.

Cummings, S. M., Kelly, T. B., Holland, T. P., & Peterson-Hazan, X. (1997). Development and validation of the Needs Inventory for Caregivers of the Hospitalized Elderly. *Research on Social Work Practice, 8*, 120–132.

De Vijver, F. V. (2000). The nature of bias. In Richard H. Dana (Ed.), *Handbook of cross-cultural and multicultural personality assessment*. Mahwah, NJ: Lawrence Erlbaum Associates.

DeVellis, R. F. (1993). *Scale development: Theory and applications*. Newbury Park, CA: Sage.

Demo, D. H. (1985). The measurement of self-esteem: Refining our methods. *Journal of Personality and Social Psychology, 48*, 1490–1502.

Fleming, J. S., & Courtney, B. E. (1984). The dimensionality of self-esteem. Hierarchical facet model for revised measurement scales. *Journal of Personality and Social Psychology, 46*, 404–421.

Holden, G., Cuzzi, L., Rutter, S., Chernack, P., & Rosenberg, G. (1997). The Hospital Social Work Self-Efficacy Scale. *Research on Social Work Practice, 7*, 490–499.

Hudson, W. W., & McMurtry, S. L. (1997). Comprehensive assessment in social work practice. *Research on Social Work Practice, 7*, 78–98.

Koeske, G. F. (1994). Some recommendations for improving measurement validation in social work research. *Journal of Social Work Research, 18*, 43–72.

Koeske, G. F., & Koeske, R. D. (1992). Parenting locus of control: Measurement, construct validation, and a proposed conceptual model. *Social Work Research and Abstracts, 28(3)*, 376.

Koeske, G. F., Kirk, S. A., Koeske, R. D., & Rauktis, M. B. (1994). Measuring the Monday blues: Validation of a job satisfaction scale for the human services. *Social Work Research, 29(4)*, 27–35.

Kreuger, L., & Neuman, W. L. (2006). *Social work research methods: Qualitative and quantitative approaches*. Boston: Allyn & Bacon.

Meier, S. T. (1994). *The chronic crisis in psychological measurement and assessment: A historical survey*. New York: Academic Press.

Morris, E. F. (2000). Assessment practices with African-Americans: Combining standard assessment measures within an Afrocentric Orientation. In Richard H. Dana (Ed.), *Handbook of cross-cultural and multicultural personality assessment*. Mahwah, NJ: Lawrence Erlbaum Associates.

Neuman, W. L. (2006). *Social research methods: Qualitative and quantitative approaches*. Boston: Pearson Education.

Nugent, W. R., & Thomas, J. W. (1993). Validation of a clinical measure of self-esteem. *Research on Social Work Practice, 3(2)*, 191–207.

Nunnally, J. C. (1994). *Psychometric theory*. New York: McGraw-Hill.

O'Hare, T., & Collins, P. (1997). Development and validation of a scale for measuring social work practice skills. *Research on Social Work Practice, 7*, 228–238.

Preissle, J., & Grant, L. (2004). Fieldwork traditions: Ethnography and participant observation. In Kathleen DeMarrais and Stephen Lapan (Eds.), *Foundations for research: Methods of inquiry in education and the social sciences*. Mahwah, NJ: Lawrence Erlbaum Associates.

Radloff, L. S. (1977). The CES-D Scale: A self-report depression scale for research in the general population. *Applied Psychological Measurement, 3*, 385–401.

Radloff, L. S., & Locke, B. Z. (1986). The Community Mental Health Assessment Survey and the CES-D Scale. In Myra M. Weissman, Jerome K. Myers, & Catherine E. Ross (Eds.), *Community surveys of psychiatric disorders*. New Brunswick, NJ: Rutgers University Press.

Range, L. M., & Knott, E. C. (1997). Twenty suicide assessment instruments: Evaluation and recommendations. *Death Studies, 21,* 25–58.

Research on Social Work Practice, 12(1). (2002, January). Special issue on scale development and validation.

Rosenberg, M. (1965). *Society and the adolescent self-image.* Princeton, NJ: Princeton University Press.

Rubin, L. B. (1976). *Worlds of pain: Life in the working-class family.* New York: Basic Books.

Shields, J. J. (1992). Evaluating community organization projects: The development of an empirically based measure. *Social Work Research and Abstracts, 28(2),* 15–20.

Sector, E. E. (1992). *Summated rating scale construction: An introduction.* Newbury Park, CA: Sage.

Streiner, D. L., & Norman, G. R. (1995). *Health measurement scales: A practical guide to their development and use.* New York: Oxford University Press.

ASSIGNMENT 6.1: Creating a Scale

Objective: *To obtain practice in developing an instrument to be used to measure a single concept.*

We use many concepts every day in conversation and assume that others share our same definitions. In the space below, identify a single concept (i.e., honesty, impulse control, altruism, stress, depression, self-esteem) then attempt to develop at least 10 items that would measure that concept. Show the *response set* as well as the individual items. You may want to create your rough drafts on other sheets and then transfer your effort to this page. (*Note:* Since depression and self-esteem scales are provided as examples in this chapter, it will be your challenge to try to come up with different items than those shown.)

The concept I want to measure is:

The response set would consist of:

My scale is composed of the following 10 items:

ASSIGNMENT 6.2: The Psychometric Properties of a Scale

Objective: *To learn about the various evidence needed for reliability and validity, and ways to document it.*

The concept being measured in Assignment 6.1 is _____.

1. **Reliability:** To show that my scale is reliable I would need to:

2. **Known Groups Validity:**

   To find persons who would likely have high levels of this concept, I would need to collect data from:

   I anticipate finding low levels of this concept in the following persons:

3. **Concurrent Validity:** A good indication of concurrent validity would be if my scale correlated well with:

4. **Predictive Validity:** I would know my scale had predictive validity if it:

ASSIGNMENT 6.3: Finding a Measurement Instrument

Objective: *To become familiar with the literature and the resources that aid in locating research instruments.*

This chapter gave several suggestions for finding a measurement instrument that could be the primary dependent variable for a study that you design. For this assignment, try to find a scale that measures some concept of interest to you (or perhaps one that your instructor assigns). (*Note:* Commercial instruments will not likely be as available to you as those from the academic sector.)

Step 1. Attach a copy of the instrument that you have located.

Step 2. How did you find the instrument?

Step 3. Summarize what you have learned about the instrument's reliability.

Step 4. Summarize what you have learned about the instrument's validity.

Step 5. Conclusion: After having read at least one journal article about this instrument, what do you conclude about it? Is this a psychometrically strong instrument? Why or why not?

Developing Data Collection Instruments

CHAPTER 7

Scales, Questionnaires, and Interview Schedules

In the previous chapter we examined ways to evaluate our measurement instruments for reliability and validity. Often researchers can benefit from locating instruments that have already been designed and used in previous studies. If an instrument works consistently and dependably along expected lines, you are well-advised to adopt it rather than to spend valuable time developing a new one and testing its psychometric properties. However, on some occasions no instrument can be found exactly like what you need or when those that exist have problems or flaws that argue against their use. Sometimes it is necessary to create a new scale or questionnaire. To prepare you for such situations, this chapter will examine some of the finer details that go into the construction of data collection instruments.

Social workers are familiar with the use of questionnaires. In almost every social service agency, initial data collection is conducted before new clients are admitted for services. This process is called "intake," "screening," completing the "face sheet," or "taking the client's history." To collect data, social workers follow a set of previously determined questions in an established order and sequence. Although most agencies' admission forms may not have been designed for research purposes, they have enough in common with research questionnaires that we can use them to increase our knowledge about questionnaires.

Think for a moment about an agency's admission form (or any other questionnaire with which you are familiar). Someone (or perhaps a committee) may have spent considerable time deciding which questions were important to ask and which ones were not. One of the purposes of the questionnaire is to standardize the information gathering process so that the *same* set of questions is asked the *same* way each time. The prepared questionnaire also guarantees that the same set of questions will get asked, that no questions will be forgotten.

From the agency's perspective, this standard set of questions provides the minimal level of information required of each client. The social worker does not have to guess or anticipate what information the agency needs, because it has already been predetermined on the printed form. The social worker is also freed from worrying about wording the question the same way each time. If the social worker had to decide with each new client how to phrase the questions, these questions might not generate the same type of information each time. With a standard set of pretested questions in a carefully designed admission form, problems are minimized.

Similarly, research questionnaires collect data in a uniform way in order to produce the information desired. Carefully considered questions structure the respondents' responses (for example, instead of asking the respondent to state his or her age, the questionnaire may ask for year of birth). Through exact wording and attention to such matters as the sequence and order of questions, researchers attempt to minimize the collection of erroneous data.

Questionnaire design requires greater precision in statements and questions than we use in ordinary conversation. In casual conversation, one person may say to another, "I've noticed that Martha has a pretty low self-esteem." Seldom will the other party say, "How are you operationalizing self-esteem?" However, in the conduct of research, the concepts we use must be clearly operationalized. Ambiguities and vague terms in questionnaires can cause problems for respondent and researcher alike. Such problems can be discovered and eliminated during pretests of the questionnaire.

DeVaus (1986) articulates well the importance of specificity in developing useful items for questionnaires:

> It is not enough to say, "I'm interested in getting some answers about inequality." What answers to what questions? Do you want to know the extent of inequality, its distribution, its causes, its effects, or what? What sort of inequality are you interested in? Over what period? (p. 27)

Designing research questions that are clear and concise and that result in data that can be used by the researcher is not an easy task. Clients may find questions confusing that seem to be straightforward to agency staff. In an effort to become precise, it is possible to become too wordy so that the intent of the question is hard to comprehend. Questions may also inadvertently omit important response choices or contain overlapping response choices. And unconsciously biasing the responses simply by the way the questions are phrased is a potential problem.

Even professionals can slip. After the movie *Schindler's List* was released, a Roper poll seemed to suggest that 34% of Americans were uncertain about whether the Holocaust actually occurred. However, the Roper question was not worded as well as it might have been. It asked, "Does it seem possible or does it seem impossible to you that the Nazi extermination of the Jews never happened?" A subsequent Gallup poll used this wording: "In your opinion did the Holocaust definitely happen, probably happen, probably not happen, or definitely not happen?" When asked this way, 79% said it definitely happened and another 17% said it probably happened—for a total of 96% of Americans expressing belief that the Holocaust did occur (Moore & Gallup, 1994). This example shows how seriously we have to take item construction for our survey questionnaires, needs assessments, and scales.

THE IMPORTANCE OF APPEARANCE

The vast majority of this chapter discusses phrasing of items in the construction of questionnaires and scales. However, before moving to that discussion, here are a few thoughts about the appearance of the instruments you prepare.

In real estate, there is an expression about the three most important considerations when buying or selling a house. They are: location, location, location. In the preparation of data gathering instruments, a similar aphorism might guide us: appearance, appearance, appearance. Saying that the success of our research rests solely on the physical attractiveness of questionnaires and scales is, of course, putting it much too strongly. But remember, more times than not our research subjects are *voluntarily* providing us with data they may not be eager to share. *They don't have to cooperate!*

As a social work researcher, you are more likely to get a higher rate of completed forms if they are visually appealing—when they don't appear too long to complete or to be too difficult. They also should not look amateurish as do the two examples provided in Figure 7.1 and Figure 7.2. Questionnaires that look like they were quickly thrown together with misspelled words or poor grammar will not entice most people to respond unless the topic is one that they are passionate about. So, always revise several times, looking carefully for any potential ways that a question can be misinterpreted and eliminating any spelling or grammar problems. Then, if at all possible, run a pilot test to see if a small sample of research subjects understand the questions and are able to respond as you had intended.

What problems do you see with the example in Figure 7.1? What would be your reaction if you were asked to complete the questions? In Figure 7.2 there are too many choices. If there is no other way around that, then some verbiage could be eliminated by just listing the problem (such as housing, transportation, child care). That would result in a set of responses that could be read faster and require less effort. How important is a clear, easy to read font?

WHAT IS YOUR OPINION???
DO YOU AGREE OR DISAGREE WITH THESE COMMENT???

11. Peeple who ask for help should do as they're told and not complain.

   /__/ Strongly agree   /__/ Somewhat disagree

   /__/ Somewhat agree   /__/ Strongly disagree

   /__/ Don't know

12. The workee always knows what's best for the client.

   /__/ Strongly agree   /__/ Somewhat disagree

   /__/ Somewhat agree   /__/ Strongly disagree

   /__/ Don't know

13. Most workers don't know what it really like to need help.

   /__/ Strongly agree   /__/ Somewhat disagree

   /__/ Somewhat agree   /__/ Strongly disagree

   /__/ Don't know

14. When it comes to an agency for help, a person usual knows what he needs.

   /__/ Strongly agree   /__/ Somewhat disagree

   /__/ Somewhat agree   /__/ Strongly disagree

   /__/ Don't know

15. Most people can choose their own services if they know.

   /__/ Strongly agree   /__/ Somewhat disagree

   /__/ Somewhat agree   /__/ Strongly disagree

   /__/ Don't know

16. Most people who come to an agency don't really know what they need.

   /__/ Strongly agree   /__/ Somewhere disagree

   /__/ Somewhat agree   /__/ Strongly disagree

   /__/ Don't know

Figure 7.1 | Illustration of an Unattractive Questionnaire

DEVELOPING A DATA COLLECTION INSTRUMENT

First and foremost, you must have a clear idea of what data are needed. What is it that you want to find out? What are the specific content areas to be covered? If you are designing a questionnaire for a survey, then you must concurrently decide which survey modality will be used to present the questions to the respondents. Some formats (for example, questions requiring many response options) work better in mail surveys than in telephone surveys. In mail surveys, respondents can simultaneously view all of the response categories (such as "Strongly agree," "Agree," "Undecided," "Disagree," "Strongly disagree")

*Recently you went to*_____

They sent you to another agency. We want to know your feelings about what happened to you.

1. Why did you go to _____*?*

_____*Wanted to obtain food or clothing.*

_____*Wanted better housing.*

_____*Wanted to talk about money (Social Security, unemployment, emergency aid, etc.).*

_____*Wanted a job.*

_____*Wanted to know about going to school.*

_____*Wanted to know about medical or dental help.*

_____*Wanted to talk about family problems.*

_____*Wanted to know about day care or child care.*

_____*Wanted to get transportation.*

_____*Wanted to talk to a lawyer.*

_____*Wanted to know about budgeting or credit.*

_____*Wanted to work on a personal problem not listed above.*

_____*Other:*_____

Figure 7.2 | Illustration of an Uninviting Questionnaire

before choosing one. In telephone surveys, respondents may find it difficult to keep the question as well as all of the response options in mind. Even five categories can stretch a respondent's ability to keep a whole scale in mind at once. Consequently, respondents may remember some but not all of the responses, and their responses may have a narrower range of variation ("Agree" or "Disagree"). When recall and recognition questions are vital to the survey, interviews seem to work better than mail surveys.

The nature of the content, the intended survey approach, the targeted respondents, and their reading level affect the final form that the questionnaire takes. Only after consideration has been given to these areas should further conceptualizing of the questionnaire begin.

A review of the literature can provide questions or examples of ways that researchers have approached the topic of interest. It is not unethical, but rather good research practice, to use questions that have worked well for other researchers (Sudman & Bradburn, 1982). Do not, however, "borrow" items that are protected by copyright without the author's permission. Customarily, you write the author of the instrument for permission to use it and request any additional information that the author may have on the instrument.

Sometimes the author can refer you to other researchers who have recently modified or used the instrument with interesting results. Besides the possibility of saving time in questionnaire design, another advantage of using questions that have already been employed by other researchers is that you can then compare your findings to those from existing studies.

As you begin selecting and composing questions for the first draft of a questionnaire, you will have to give some thought to whether your research topic requires **closed-ended questions** (multiple-choice type responses) or **open-ended questions** (unstructured responses).

Closed-Ended Questions

Closed-ended questions are those that have their own predetermined response set. The major advantage of closed-ended questions is that a great deal of time is saved in the tabulation of the data and coding it for computer analysis. Since the response choices are supplied (for example, "Yes," "No," or "Strongly agree," "Agree," and so on), the person who is tabulating the responses does not have the problem of deciphering lengthy, illegible responses. Virtually no interpretation is required of what the respondent intended or whether a response is more like an existing set of responses or deserves a whole new category. Another advantage is that closed-ended questions with their response options communicate the same frame of reference to all respondents.

Closed-ended questions are used when you know how respondents might reply. If their responses are difficult to anticipate, you can use open-ended questions in a pilot study to find out what terms or language respondents tend to use in responding. It is then possible to identify frequent or common responses as well as the range of responses so that closed-ended questions can be developed.

Closed-ended questions can be used effectively in practically all areas of interest to social workers. For example, perhaps you are interested in residents' adjustment to nursing homes. One area that you feel is important is how the residents evaluate the food prepared by the nursing home. You might construct a closed-ended question that allows for ratings of "Excellent," "Good," "Fair," or "Poor." However, a "fair" rating does not provide a wealth of information about the food. It doesn't tell you, for instance, whether oatmeal is served every day for breakfast, whether it arrives cold or warm, or if there is a variety of breakfast foods available.

Open-Ended Questions

Open-ended questions have no prepared response choices. This form of question allows respondents to communicate without having to choose from a set of prepared response categories. Open-ended questions are best suited for those occasions when the researcher intends that direct interviewing be

Qualitative Researchers and Open-Ended Questions

Qualitative researchers may use open-ended questions in a number of ways. They might, for instance, conduct a group discussion or a group interview. Group discussions tend to allow the group members maximum freedom to range freely all over a topic. In group interviews the researcher is more active, if necessary, in keeping the group focused on a set of specific questions. Open-ended questions are also asked during structured individual interviews. During these interviews the qualitative researcher might use a technique called "free listing," which uses open-ended questions like this: "If you were the director of The Women's Clinic, what three changes do you think you would make right away?"

employed—either face-to-face or by telephone. Few respondents take the time to elaborate on their thoughts or feelings when they must write them out on paper, and as a result, mailed questionnaires that rely heavily on open-ended questions have a poorer response rate than those that use closed-ended questions. However, some evidence suggests open-ended questions, when asked by an interviewer, result in greater reporting of sensitive or socially disapproved behavior than when closed-ended questions on a self-reporting questionnaire are used. One possible explanation is that respondents will avoid placing themselves in categories that indicate high levels of socially unacceptable behavior when they can choose from categories that suggest a more acceptable level of behavior.

At times you may want greater detail than closed-ended questions typically provide. For example, if you wanted to know more about the quality of life in a nursing home as the residents experience it, closed-ended questions are not likely to provide you with much insight into their personal reflections. Open-ended questions can supply you with quotes from residents—their experiences in their own words. Because open-ended questions produce greater detail and depth, they are greatly favored by qualitative researchers.

One disadvantage to open-ended questions is that a respondent can ramble; it can require a skillful interviewer to bring a talkative respondent back on topic. Another is that it is impossible to assess the reliability of the single item.

In any given survey, it is possible to combine both closed-ended and open-ended questions. In the example of an evaluation of a nursing home, you could rely chiefly on closed-ended questions for rating various facets of the nursing home (for example, courteousness of the staff, noise level, social and recreational opportunities) and still employ an open-ended question such as: "Is there anything else you would like to tell us about how it feels to live in this skilled nursing facility?" Alternatively, you could use these open-ended questions: "What is the *best* thing about living in this skilled nursing facility?" and "What is the worst thing about living in this skilled nursing facility?"

Your use of open- or closed-ended questions depends on the goals of your research and the type of information you require. Keep in mind that open-ended questions are easier to develop than closed-ended ones, but they are harder to analyze. For instance, suppose you ask a group of volunteers

Brief Example of a Qualitative Structured Individual Interview

1. The Appalachian Cancer Survivors Network has been in existence about four years. What changes have you seen over that period of time?
2. How would you describe your level of involvement as a board member of the Network?
3. If you had a magic wand that could grant you any wish, what three wishes would you make regarding the Network?
4. Most of those who attend the weekly support group meetings are breast cancer survivors. How would you explain the fact that survivors of other types of cancer don't attend?
5. How do you think health care professionals in the community view the Network?
6. Agnes Smith has announced that she is stepping down as the Network director next year. What kind of skills do you think the next facilitator should have?
7. What difficulties do you think the next facilitator might experience?

this question: "What kinds of things did you do as a Big Brother or Big Sister?" You might get back a list of such activities as:

Went out to eat	Played Monopoly and board games
Played basketball	Worked on my car
Went to movies	Went fishing
Tutored	Watched television
Visited the mall	Went bicycling
Visited the zoo	Went to the library
Went shopping	Baked cookies
Built model planes	Took a walk
Talked on the phone	Visited friends

Now suppose you want to summarize these into a few categories to understand what kinds of activities Big Brothers and Big Sisters favored. Would you use categories of athletic and nonathletic activity? If so, is fishing athletic? Would you create categories for those activities that required spending money (such as going to a movie or to a restaurant) versus those that didn't (such as watching television)? But then, couldn't making cookies involve an expense (if you had to buy chocolate chips and sugar)? Does fishing involve an expense? A visit to the mall doesn't have to be expensive, but it could be if the Big Brother bought soft drinks and tacos.

Take my word for it, closed-ended questions are a great deal easier to analyze. The only problem is that with them you have to anticipate in advance how the respondents might answer. However, a small pilot test with open-ended questions can often suggest the categories or response set that you need in order for the same item to be converted to a closed-ended question.

Whether you adopt questions that have been used by other researchers or write your own, be sure to circulate a rough draft of the proposed questionnaire among your colleagues for comments and suggestions. Use their responses to revise the questionnaire before it goes out for a pilot test. After the pilot test, scrutinize the questionnaire again for questions that might have been

Practice Note: Open-Ended Questions

The best argument for why open-ended questions should be included in most questionnaires comes from a student who was interning in a state social service agency. Foster children were routinely given questionnaires on which they could evaluate their placement.

On one particular form completed by a female adolescent, the girl indicated that the placement was satisfactory on all the criteria used by the agency. The last question on the back of the form asked simply, "Is there anything about this placement you don't like?" The teen wrote in response, "One thing I didn't like was that Jim [the foster father] came into my bedroom every night about the time I started getting ready for bed."

Obviously, the foster father's behavior was inappropriate. He had no business trying to make conversation in the foster child's bedroom when she was changing into pajamas. As a result, this foster home was viewed as not being acceptable for future placements of young women.

misunderstood, biased items that suggest responses, insufficient response categories, typographical errors, and similar problems. Only after several revisions should the questionnaire be printed and distributed.

To assist you in developing good questionnaires, the next section will elaborate some important guidelines. These guides will help you recognize the ways in which item construction can affect the data you obtain. Poorly phrased or constructed questions appear in this chapter; consider each of the examples and try to decide why it is flawed before reading the discussion accompanying it.

PITFALLS IN WRITING GOOD QUESTIONS
Double-Barreled Questions

Example: Have you donated blood or gone to the dentist this month?

( ) Yes   ( ) No   ( ) Don't know

This question is poorly constructed because it asks about two different behaviors but is structured so that only one response is expected. A response of "Yes" could mean that the respondent had donated blood and been to the dentist. It is also possible that some respondents might respond "Yes" when they had visited the dentist but not donated blood, and vice versa. Some respondents will indicate "No" when they have done one but not the other, while other "No" responses will mean that the respondent has neither donated blood nor gone to the dentist. If it is impossible to interpret what any response means, then the item is not a good one.

As a rule, a question should ask about *one* issue, thought, or event at a time. If more information is desired, additional questions should be asked. In this example, two separate questions should be constructed—each one focusing on a single issue.

However, sometimes a single question might be used when there are two similar things to consider. For instance, if we were interviewing abuse victims to see if they were threatened with a weapon, it could be acceptable to ask, "Were you threatened with a gun or a knife?"

On the other hand, a question like "Have you ever been called names or threatened with harm?" is poorly constructed because being called names is a fairly common occurrence and doesn't imply the same order of danger as being threatened with harm.

Leading Questions

Example: Don't you agree with the president that the federal government should not overspend?

( ) Agree   ( ) Disagree   ( ) Don't know

This question clearly leads the respondent into thinking along certain lines. Most of us want to be agreeable and to get along with others. And most Americans believe it is important to respect the president and would generally want to support that office (by agreeing with the president when possible). This example is a leading question because it suggests the desired response.

The question "Don't you agree that the federal government should spend more on social services and less on biological warfare research?" is both leading and double-barreled. Besides begging for an "Agree" response, it also asks for information about two different things. First, it wants to know if the government should spend more money on social services. Second, it wants to know if the respondent thinks the government should spend less on biological warfare. Again, the respondent could agree with one of these two thoughts and disagree with the other and be confused about how to respond.

Unavailable Information

Example: How many hours of television did you watch last year?

Respondents should not be asked for information that would not normally be available to them. Since most of us do not keep records regarding how much television we watch, any response that we might give to a question like this one would be no more than a wild estimate. A much better way to get at this kind of information would be to ask about the average number of hours of television watched daily or weekly.

Possibly the best (worst?) example of a question asking for unavailable information was in a questionnaire actually used in an agency. The respondent was asked, "Describe your mother's pregnancy with you; for example, were there complications?" While it is true that a few individuals may have acquired this information because they were born prematurely, my hunch is that the vast majority of Americans would have no information at all about their mother's health status during pregnancy.

The recall of distant events is always problematic and increased error is associated with the passage of time. As a rule, it is better to ask about events and activities that have happened recently, say, within the past 30 days. However, sometimes it is necessary to ask what is known as "lifetime" questions, such as, "Have you ever been arrested?" or "How many times have you been in any kind of treatment program for alcohol or drug problems?"

Asking for information that might not be available to all respondents can present another problem. Consider the following question: "Do you agree or

Practice Note: Human Memory

Alcohol and drug use impair one's ability to accurately recall information. This includes prescription drugs such as Valium. Further, the more time that elapses after an event, the less accurate the recall of details associated with that event. In a study based on reports of traffic accidents where one or more persons were injured, when subjects were interviewed three months after their accident, 97% said they had reported the accident. Only 70% said they had filed a report when interviewed 9 to 12 months after their accident. In a study of concentration camp survivors, most of the people had forgotten the names of guards they had reported in earlier interviews. In a third study, professors were asked to recall the faces of former pupils. Their accuracy was only slightly above chance after four years. Human memory is affected not only by the passage of time, but also by our own internal motivations, so that our memories tend to take a self-advantageous direction—we're not all that objective in remembering our actions and contributions. Finally, our recollections can be reconstructed, supplemented, and even alerted by postevent information (Loftus & Doyle, 1992).

disagree with the philosophy of the state's Commission on Literacy?" This question is a poor one if the philosophy of the state's Commission on Literacy is not well known. If, on the other hand, the Commission has recently been in the news because of some unusual or controversial philosophy, then it would be quite reasonable to ask this question. However, it might be better to ask in one question if there is a Commission on Literacy; then ask those respondents who answer "Yes" to describe the Commission's philosophy. A third question in this series might ask if they agree or disagree with the Commission's philosophy. This approach involves the use of **contingency questions** (branching questions that can also be thought of as filter or screening questions). Those respondents who answer "Yes" to the first question are directed to the second and third subquestions. Those who respond "No" to the first question are guided to another set of questions. See Figure 7.3 for an example of a **contingency question**. Contingency questions might also be called **filter questions,** because the investigator may want to study a certain subgroup of subjects with particular characteristics.

Use of Jargon and Technical Terms

Example: Do you feel that Freud's structural hypothesis is an improvement over his topographic hypothesis?

Even those who are familiar with psychoanalytic theory may not know how to respond to this question. It is too technical, using jargon not known to most Americans. Your goal as a designer of questionnaire or scale items is to use familiar rather than unfamiliar language. Being cognizant of the reading level and vocabularies of your possible subjects, you would not want to use terms that might not be understood by everyone. For example, if you were surveying teens about their use of birth control methods, would you want to use the word prophylactic? Probably not. Would high school dropouts understand narcissism? Even terms that you think everyone should understand can be too

We have discussed several self-help groups found in our area. Now we would like to examine some additional services that may be available statewide.

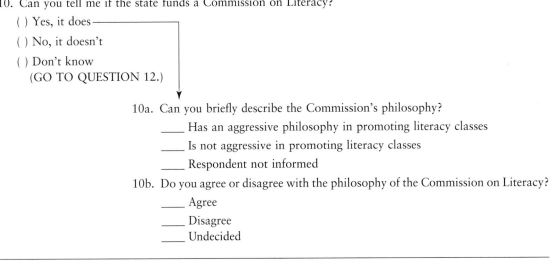

10. Can you tell me if the state funds a Commission on Literacy?

( ) Yes, it does

( ) No, it doesn't

( ) Don't know
   (GO TO QUESTION 12.)

   10a. Can you briefly describe the Commission's philosophy?

   ____ Has an aggressive philosophy in promoting literacy classes

   ____ Is not aggressive in promoting literacy classes

   ____ Respondent not informed

   10b. Do you agree or disagree with the philosophy of the Commission on Literacy?

   ____ Agree

   ____ Disagree

   ____ Undecided

Figure 7.3 | Illustration of a Contingency Question in a Personal or Telephone Interview Survey

sophisticated. A study of patients at the Primary Care Center of Yale New Haven Hospital found that one in four believed that "orally" referred to "how often" medication should be taken (Gibbs & Gibbs, 1987).

Use the simplest terms and vocabulary possible—in other words, the language that we use in everyday speech (sometimes called Standard English). Avoid colloquialisms, abbreviations (e.g., t.i.d., TIA), and foreign phrases. The general rule is to aim for a seventh- or eighth-grade comprehension level—unless, of course, you are dealing with younger children. Keep sentences short and simple. Avoid compound sentences if possible.

Insensitive Language

Example: How do *you* people feel about George Bush?

A question like this may make some people uneasy because it is suggestive of racial bias. It accentuates differences among respondents by saying, in effect, that the respondent is a member of a group that is dissimilar from others (possibly the majority of Americans). Instead of asking questions in the format of "How do *you blacks* [or *you Native Americans*] feel about . . . ?" simply ask "How do you feel about . . . ?" Or, present a statement and ask the respondent to choose a response that reflects his or her feelings about the subject. Later, when analyzing the data, you will be able to determine if racial groups differ in their attitudes—if you have collected data on the respondent's racial/ethnic identity as part of your questionnaire. Avoid using any language in a questionnaire that is insensitive.

Inflammatory or "Loaded" Terms

Example: Are you a religious fanatic?

As we learned earlier, **social desirability** is a term used to describe the tendency of people to want their behavior to be perceived as socially acceptable. It is a strong motivation, and response bias can easily occur as respondents avoid categories or labels that are stigmatizing. Few of us want to be labeled fanatic, zealot, or any other term that has socially undesirable connotations. Even though a respondent may have very strong convictions, he or she would likely deny having tendencies toward fanaticism. Examples of loaded terms that should be replaced with more neutral terms include *crisis, innocent, victim, forced,* and *coerced.*

Just as the word *fanatic* is loaded, few people would want to be labeled a drunk or alcoholic. Questions that get the information without labeling or stigmatization should be employed. A better way to explore the extent of problem drinking is to ask respondents about specific behaviors, for example, "How many times a week do you have a drink in the morning?" You want to provide a series of categories that give a respondent an opportunity to describe his or her pattern of drinking as objectively as possible.

Mutually Exclusive Response Choices

Examples: "Teetotaler," "Social Drinker," "I occasionally drink to excess," "I frequently drink to excess."

In our quest to avoid socially unacceptable labels, we might create another problem. Consider the two response choices of "social drinker" and "I occasionally drink to excess." Are they mutually exclusive? Is it possible to be a social drinker *and* to occasionally drink to excess? If you agree, then this response set will not provide "clean" data.

Some respondents will think of themselves as social drinkers even though they drink to excess. Being a social drinker is a more attractive response to some individuals than revealing how often they drink to excess. Measuring the number of times a person drinks in an average week is a more precise way of separating light drinkers from moderate or heavy drinkers. Behavioral measures such as these are much more useful than stigmatizing or labeling terms.

The problems of overlapping response categories and finding good behavioral measures are obvious examples of why you need to refer to the literature as part of the research process. It is very likely that other researchers have struggled with these problems and have developed response sets or categories (if not whole questionnaires) that you could use in your research.

We're not always aware of overlapping response choices. Can you detect any problems with the responses in the following example?

How often do you date?

a. almost every night

b. once or twice a week

c. a few times a month

d. three to four times a week

e. once every two weeks

f. a few times a year

Other examples of overlapping response options include:

What category best describes your income?

1. 0–$5,000

2. $5,000–10,000

3. $10,000–15,000

4. $15,000 or higher

What is your grade point average?

1. Below 2.00

2. 2.00 to 2.50

3. 2.50 to 3.00

4. 3.00 to 3.50

5. 3.50 to 4.00

Vague and Ambiguous Terms

Example: How many times in the past year have you seen a social worker?

The problem with this question is that it contains language that is vague. Is the intent of this question to find out how many social workers are observed (seen)? Or, is it to learn the number of appointments or sessions the respondent had with a social worker last year? To rephrase the question to "How many times in the past year have you talked with a social worker?" is not an improvement, since one can talk informally or socially with social workers. Would it be better to ask "How many appointments have you made with your social worker in the last 30 days?" Or, since it is possible to make appointments but not keep them, "How many sessions have you had with your social worker in the last 30 days?" Even these two questions could be refined since a session could last 10 minutes or an hour or even longer. Both of these questions overlook home visits. A more exact approach might ask, "In the past 30 days, about how many hours have you spent talking about your problems face-to-face with your social worker?"

The following question also uses a vague term that may cause problems: "Do you attend Alcoholics Anonymous (AA) meetings *regularly?*" The problem with this sentence is that "regularly" is one of those terms that means different things to different individuals. Some respondents may attend AA regularly three times a year. Other respondents may attend regularly the first Wednesday of the month. Some respondents may attend twice a day every day. A better way to ask for information of this type would be: "How many times a month do you attend Alcoholics Anonymous meetings?"

Another example of the use of vague terms is the question: "What is your income?" This question is problematic because the respondent must figure out whether the information sought has a yearly, monthly, or weekly referent. It also is unclear whether the respondent should report annual salary (gross income) or the amount after all the deductions have been made (net income). A further problem is that the question does not indicate whether combined family income is expected or whether the respondent should report only his or her personal income (even though others in the household may be working).

Similarly, "Are you employed?" may be difficult to answer because there are several responses that can be made in addition to "Yes" or "No." The status of being employed usually includes full-time and part-time workers. Also, respondents could be employed seasonally (for example, migrant workers or college students who work full time in the summer but not at all when school is in session). Finally, there are those who help with a family business (such as, a spouse who keeps the books) but who do not receive a paycheck.

Vague and ambiguous terms do not convey the same frame of reference to all respondents. For instance, some respondents will read "Has your child missed a lot of school?" and think in terms of the whole school year. Other parents may think only about absences in the past month or week. Parents may also respond to this question in terms of their own experience in missing school or compare one child to another so that even though Hugh has missed 14 days of school in the first grading period, that's not a "lot" compared to his sister Edna who missed six weeks due to illness. It is better practice to provide the same frame of reference for everyone—for example, by asking, "How many days of school did your child miss during the first grading period?"

Even when we think an item is not vague, pretesting or reliability scaling may show that respondents have different impressions of what it is asking. Agreeing to the item "I have difficulty getting up in the morning" may mean that the respondent needs assistance because of a physical disability or that the individual tends to oversleep.

All-Inclusive Terms

Example: Are you always in bed by 11:00 P.M.?

The use of such words as *always* and *never* creates problems for the respondent and for the researcher attempting to interpret the data. Does *always* allow for exceptions? For instance, what if you are in bed by 11:00 P.M. every night of the year except for New Year's Eve, when you stay up until 12:01 A.M.? Does that mean that you should respond with a "No" to the above question? *Always* and *never* imply that there are no exceptions. Researchers are more concerned with general patterns; for example, "On most weeknights, about what time do you usually go to bed?"

Negatively Constructed Items

> Example: Marijuana should not be decriminalized.

This item, borrowed from DeVaus (1986), is a good example of how the word *not* confuses the meaning of the statement. In this instance, it reverses the meaning of decriminalized so that a person agreeing to the statement is saying in effect that marijuana usage should be illegal. A respondent disagreeing with the statement is saying that marijuana use should be made legal. It is much more clear and straightforward to ask, "Should the private use of marijuana be made legal?" Where possible, the term *not* should be avoided in questionnaires.

Sequence of Questions

There is general agreement that the first questions to be asked should be of interest to the respondent. Respondents need to "warm up" to the survey process and establish a sense of trust or rapport with the researcher, the mailed questionnaire, or the researcher's representative. Accordingly, the first several questions should be applicable to all respondents. Respondents seem to prefer closed-ended questions at the start of mailed questionnaires but open-ended questions when interviewed in person or over the phone. Information about potentially sensitive areas such as age and income should occur at the end of the questionnaire. Such information, if asked at the beginning of the interview or questionnaire, may result in refusals to participate and a lower response rate. More important questions should be asked earlier than less important ones in case the respondent decides to terminate the interview or stop working on the questionnaire before all questions have been completed. *Respondent fatigue* can be a problem with especially long questionnaires. Experts agree that topically related questions should follow one another in some sort of recognizable sequence as opposed to being interposed and spread throughout the questionnaire. Usually, some sort of "funnel sequence" is used, in which general questions are followed by more narrowly focused questions. A problem may occur if an item has an effect on subsequent responses because it creates some sort of expectancy or "mind set." Some topics seem to be immune to this sort of problem, and others are sensitive to it. The best advice we can offer regarding order effects is to be alert to the possibility that earlier questions can affect later responses.

Acquiescence, a tendency some respondents have to agree with items regardless of their content, can be countered by constructing items so that the respondent must respond positively *and* negatively in roughly equal proportions. With a little creativity, items can be prepared so that the respondent does not know which response is the one desired by the researcher. Figure 7.4 provides an example of wording questions so that a respondent sympathetic to people who are HIV positive could not respond either "Strongly Agree" or "Agree" to all four questions. Nardi (2006) recommends in any listing of choices (e.g., books read in high school) that the researcher build in at least one "trap" (e.g., a nonexistent book) to expose any response bias.

	Strongly Agree	Agree	Undecided	Disagree	Strongly Disagree
1. Children who are HIV+ should be allowed to attend school.	( )	( )	( )	( )	( )
2. Persons who are HIV+ should be quarantined.	( )	( )	( )	( )	( )
3. Persons who are HIV+ should be allowed to eat in public restaurants.	( )	( )	( )	( )	( )
4. Persons who are HIV+ deserve what they get.	( )	( )	( )	( )	( )

Figure 7.4 | Phrasing Questions to Avoid Acquiescence

THINKING ABOUT GUIDELINES

The problem with guidelines is that sometimes it makes sense to violate them. At times you might use a loaded question to try to determine the extent of some socially undesirable behavior. For instance, the implication that "everyone does it" may be useful in reducing the threat of reporting some behaviors. This approach is illustrated in the following example:

"All parents get angry when their children misbehave. About how many times in the past month did you scream at your children?"

Besides the guidelines identified in this chapter, there are other concerns, too. For example, crowded, cluttered, or difficult-appearing questionnaires result in lower response rates than those that appear interesting, inviting, or simple to complete. Mailed questionnaires should be visually attractive. Blank or white space should be used to full advantage. The responses should appear in the same area of the questionnaire so that the respondent can easily locate them. Instructions, questions, and response categories should be kept brief, and diagrams should be used to visually direct the respondent where necessary. Numbering the questions is also useful to both respondents and those who must process the data. If you have multiple components or parts to the study, use a sentence or two to smooth the transition (for example, "Now we would like to change the subject just a bit and ask some health-related questions").

In Appendix B you'll find a shortened version of the Drug Attitude Questionnaire, an instrument designed to measure the effects of the drug education program. A longer version than I've shown had excellent reliability (.93 to .97). You might want to examine the Drug Attitude Questionnaire to review some of the items. If you look closely, you'll note that this reliability came despite some items that I would change if I were to write them again. For instance, what about Items 8, 9, and 17? Do they violate any guidelines that we have learned in this chapter?

SELF-ANCHORED SCALES

Another option available to you when developing a research instrument is to generate self-anchored or behaviorally-anchored single-item scales for measuring clients' problems. These types of scales are especially valuable when you need to estimate quickly the magnitude or severity of a problem. A chief advantage is that they can be used to assess thoughts and feelings (such as security in a relationship or anger) that may be expressed by a client when you don't have a standardized measurement tool nearby.

While many self-anchored scales are based on 10 equal intervals, it is not unusual to find scales based on 5, 7, 9, or even 100 points. The only thing tricky about designing these scales is keeping in mind that only one dimension of a concept should be presented. For instance, "angry" and "not angry" would be logical to place at opposite ends of a continuum. However, using "angry" at one end and "happy" at the other involves two concepts instead of one and may make the scale less accurate because of different feelings associated with anger and happiness.

Self-anchored scales can also be used in single-subject designs as a repeated measure to keep track of progress resulting from intervention. When self-anchored scales are designed for specific clients, their actions and feelings—described in their own words—can be used to anchor the ends of the continuum. To demonstrate what self-anchored scales look like, several examples are shown in Figure 7.5.

The Amount of Anger I Felt Today

| 0 | 1 | 2 | 3 | 4 | 5 | 6 | 7 | 8 | 9 | 10 |

None   *Moderate*   *Extreme*

Had pleasant   Slammed the door and   Shouted obscenities,
conversation   walked away   punched wall

How Satisfied I Am with My Life

| 0 | 1 | 2 | 3 | 4 | 5 | 6 | 7 | 8 | 9 | 10 |

No Satisfaction   *Average Satisfaction*   *Very Satisfied*

Community Involvement

| 0 | 1 | 2 | 3 | 4 | 5 | 6 | 7 | 8 | 9 | 10 |

Not Involved   *Medium Involvement*   *Very Involved*

Feelings of Emotional Intimacy with Loved One

| 0 | 1 | 2 | 3 | 4 | 5 | 6 | 7 | 8 | 9 | 10 |

Not at All Close (Unhappy;   *Very Close (Happy with*
not much sharing)   *relationship; lots of sharing)*

Figure 7.5 | Examples of Self-Anchored Scales

One problem with the use of single-item scales and even single questions, whether used in a large survey or in a qualitative interview, is that ordinarily it is not possible to compute their reliability or validity in the same way that is possible for a well-developed scale. An exception to this is that certain facts can sometimes be checked. For example, imagine you give a questionnaire to a class of high school students in a health class. You know ahead of time from the teacher that 20 are sophomores, 5 are juniors, and 3 are seniors. If you ask on the questionnaire for students to report their classification and if you then examine that item on the 28 surveys and find 20 sophomores, 5 juniors, and 3 seniors, then you know that at least that item captured reliable data. Do you think you would find the same kind of reliability if you asked high school students about their sexual experiences or experimentation with marijuana?

THE ROLE OF QUESTIONNAIRES IN GENERALIZING RESULTS

Even if you have a strong sampling design that would ordinarily allow for generalizing your results, a poorly constructed questionnaire or scale can ruin your study. Remember the term *instrument error* introduced in the last chapter? The expression "garbage in, garbage out" applies here. Minimize the inclusion of worthless items by ensuring that your target respondents can understand each and every item as you intended it. Don't be afraid to circulate your draft among colleagues whose opinion you respect, or to pilot-test the instrument. Good questionnaires do not result from a single draft.

The items you develop for your study are the foundation for any knowledge that will be acquired. If you do a good job with the design of your questionnaire, respondents will not find it burdensome. In fact, it just might be possible to make it so interesting that respondents *enjoy* participating; when they are cooperative and honest, you will have much better data. Poorly designed questionnaires can generate worthless data when interviewers or raters get confused and enter data on the wrong line or in the wrong box. A well-designed questionnaire will not only be easy to complete, but also easy for the investigator to interpret responses and record data.

Although this chapter has placed a lot of importance on the wording and phrasing of individual items, other elements can influence the responses you obtain. For instance, research subjects may need a line or two of directions on how to complete your questionnaire or scale. If the survey is being mailed, a cover letter is essential to provide a brief explanation of why the study is being conducted, who is being involved, and the extent to which confidentiality is afforded. It is also good practice to inform potential participants how much of their time the survey will take.

SURVEY QUESTIONNAIRE CHECKLIST

- Do you have a cover letter that invites participation?
- Do you have it printed on letterhead?

- Does the letterhead mention the support of a well-recognized organization or person?
- Is the questionnaire visually attractive? (Avoid printing on the back.)
- Does the questionnaire look like it can be easily completed? (Is it of reasonable length?)
- Are there simple directions on the questionnaire?
- Is there plenty of room for responses to be recorded?
- Is a postage-paid, self-addressed return envelope included?
- Is the mailing list accurate and free of duplication?

Finally, each question should give you some essential information, and all of the questions taken together should help you conclude something about the topic of your investigation.

Perhaps my relating an actual experience will serve to reinforce this point: A group of local citizens once asked for my assistance in conducting a mental health needs assessment of their community. "Okay," I said, "tell me more." Their spokesperson indicated that they had found a book about needs assessment that included, in its appendix, a complete set of questions that could be photocopied and used with very little modification. As I looked at the needs assessment instrument, I saw a question that asked the respondents to list three problems in their neighborhood and another that asked for a ranking of the most serious problems in the community. In my mind, I saw respondents being concerned with streetlights and potholes, police protection, and a great many other community concerns. I did not, however, believe the use of that particular questionnaire would produce much usable information about the mental health needs of the community. I asked the spokesperson, "What do you hope to learn from the community needs assessment?" "Well," she said, "we want to know about all the mental health needs in the community." Further questioning revealed that there wasn't anything more specific that they hoped to learn.

At that point I tactfully asked the group to meet together to determine what, exactly, they wanted to know about the mental health needs in the community. They met and discussed what they wanted to know, but to the best of my knowledge, that group never did conduct a community needs assessment. I strongly suspect that there was no agreement among them on what was important to learn about their community's mental health needs—or how the information would be used. As you can see, the point is not just to develop a set of questions—the questions we ask must have a clear focus and purpose. Each question should add another increment to that sum of information that we require. The well-designed questionnaire asks no less and no more than is needed for our research. Anyone can develop a questionnaire or conduct a survey. The "test" of a good survey is whether it produces useful data. Genuinely useful information seldom comes about just because someone happens to find a set of already prepared questions.

KEY TERMS

closed-ended questions	contingency questions	social desirability
open-ended questions	filter questions	acquiescence

SELF-REVIEW

(Answers at the end of the book)

1. T or F. Ideally, closed-ended questions should communicate the same frame of reference to all persons.
2. T or F. With large samples, it is easier to analyze the data obtained from open-ended questions than from closed-ended questions.
3. T or F. Double-barreled questions are useful to researchers because they allow the respondent to supply twice as much information in a single answer.
4. What is wrong with asking a child this question: "When did you last see the principal?"
   a. insensitive, inflammatory   c. uses jargon
   b. prevents contingency mock-up   d. vague
5. What is wrong with this question: "Do you agree or disagree that EMDR contributes to resiliency among victims of PTSD?"
   a. implies social desirability   c. is negatively constructed
   b. uses jargon   d. creates acquiescence
6. What is wrong with this question: "How many times did you argue with your mother last summer?"
   a. implies social desirability   c. unavailable information
   b. insensitive language   d. creates acquiescence
7. What is wrong with this question: "When you are punished by your parents, do you act like a jerk?"
   a. leading question   c. unavailable information
   b. insensitive language   d. uses loaded terms
8. What is wrong with this question: "Parents should not be so uncompromising and irrational."
   a. negatively constructed   c. leading question
   b. insensitive language   d. uses loaded terms
9. What is wrong with this question: "Do you always get your telephone privileges revoked when you don't clean up your room?"
   a. negatively constructed   c. leading question
   b. is all-inclusive   d. uses loaded terms
10. What is wrong with this question: "Do you regularly disagree with your parents' judgment on important issues?"
    a. uses loaded terms   c. leading question
    b. unavailable information   d. vague
11. What is wrong with this question: "Don't you think the city council should change the teen curfew to 2:00 A.M. on weekends?"
    a. uses loaded terms   c. leading question
    b. unavailable information   d. vague

12. Another name for a branching-type question would be a _____ _____ question.

13. Jack is interested in how adults in their twenties and thirties adjust in the first year after becoming divorced. He's particularly interested in identifying the range of coping strategies that these adults might use. In your opinion, would he be better advised to use open-ended or closed-ended questions?

QUESTIONS FOR CLASS DISCUSSION

1. Why is it important that the questionnaire communicate the same frame of reference to all respondents?
2. What would be a good way to check questionnaire and scale items to make sure that they do not contain jargon or some other problem?
3. To what extent do the items we construct reflect our view of the world and our values?
4. From a research perspective, what is the advantage of self-anchored scales over single-item scales that do not contain "anchors"?
5. What bothers you most when you are asked to complete a questionnaire or instrument?
6. Why is it important to decide on the survey methodology before designing the questionnaire to be used?
7. Do the advantages of open-ended questions outweigh their disadvantages?
8. What are the disadvantages of closed-ended questions?

RESOURCES AND REFERENCES

Bradburn, N., & Sudman, S. (1979). *Improving interview method and questionnaire design.* San Francisco: Jossey-Bass.

DeVaus, D. A. (1986). *Surveys in social research.* London: George Allen and Unwin.

Dillman, D. A. (2000). *Mail and internet surveys: The tailored design method.* New York: John Wiley & Sons.

Fink, A., & Kosecoff, J. (1998). How *to conduct surveys: A step-by-step guide.* Beverly Hills, CA: Sage.

Gibbs, R. D., & Gibbs, P. H. (1987). Patient understanding of commonly used medical vocabulary. *Journal of Family Practice, 25,* 176–178.

Loftus, E. F., & Doyle, J. M. (1992). *Eyewitness testimony: Civil and criminal.* Charlottesville, VA: Michie.

Moore, D. W., & Gallup, A. (1994). The Holocaust: It happened. *Gallup Poll Monthly, 340,* 25–27.

Nardi, P. M. (2006). *Doing survey research: A guide to quantitative methods.* Boston: Pearson Education.

Nugent, W. R. (1992). Psychometric characteristics of self-anchored scales in clinical application. *Journal of Social Service Research, 15(3/4),* 137–152.

Nugent, W. R. (1993). A validity study of a self-anchored scale for measuring self-esteem. *Research on Social Work Practice, 3(3),* 276–287.

Patten, M. L. (2001). *Questionnaire research: A practical guide.* Los Angeles, CA: Pyrczak.

Sudman, S., & Bradburn, N. M. (1982). *Asking questions.* San Francisco: Jossey-Bass.

Sudman, S., Bradburn, N. M., & Schwarz, N. (1995). *About answers: The application of cognitive processes to methodology.* San Francisco: Jossey-Bass.

ASSIGNMENT 7.1: Developing a Questionnaire

Objective: *To develop skills in designing questionnaires for survey research.*

Develop a set of questions to use in interviewing nursing home residents about the quality of their lives. Use a mixture of open- and closed-ended questions. It is assumed that sociodemographic information (i.e., age, sex, marital status, education, income, etc.) will be made available to you—it won't be necessary to ask about those items.

1. List your five open-ended questions:

    a.

    b.

    c.

    d.

    e.

2. List your five closed-ended questions along with their response set (in parentheses).

    a.

    b.

    c.

    d.

    e.

ASSIGNMENT 7.2: Critiquing a Peer's Questionnaire

Objective: *To obtain practice in evaluating items that compose a peer's questionnaire.*

Take the questions that you developed in Assignment 7.1 and swap with another student in your class. Read that student's questions carefully and check to see if there are any of the problems discussed in this chapter (i.e., double-barreled questions, jargon, insensitive language, etc.) Last, what is your subjective reaction to these questions? Will you be confident that they will give you good insight into nursing home life? Write the name of the student whose questionnaire you are reviewing here: _____

PROBLEMS DETECTED

Open-ended Q 1:

Open-ended Q 2:

Open-ended Q 3:

Open-ended Q 4:

Open-ended Q 5:

PROBLEMS DETECTED

Closed-ended Q1:

Closed-ended Q2:

Closed-ended Q3:

Closed-ended Q4:

Closed-ended Q5:

SUMMARY COMMENTS:

ASSIGNMENT 7.3: Critiquing a Questionnaire

Objective: *To obtain practice in objectively evaluating items that compose a questionnaire.*

Critically review the draft of a set of questions (below) designed for a client group of men charged with domestic violence. How many mistakes can you find? Some problems are major while others merely require that the item be revised to yield more useful information.

	Question	Problem
Example	Are you presently employed?	Can't determine if respondent is working part-time or full-time
Q1	Have you received any counseling since you left the program?	
Q2	Have you talked with anyone since you left the program?	
Q3	Are you getting along better with your spouse?	
Q4	Are you using more drugs than are good for you?	
Q5	Would you say that your behavior was motivated by feelings of anger and powerlessness?	
Q6	How many times have you hit, kicked, or otherwise injured a female partner?	
Q7	Could both overt and covert forms of narcissism be risk factors in the prediction of your interpersonal violence (IPV)?	

ASSIGNMENT 7.3 *(Continued)*

	Question	Problem
Q8	Wouldn't you agree that your IPV has improved since you've been with the agency?	
Q9	Do you tend to be friends with scum like yourself—people with rage problems?	

Quantitative and Qualitative Sampling

CHAPTER 8

SAMPLING THEORY

Virtually every day you are involved in sampling. On cold winter days you may stick your foot out from under the covers and decide that it is too cold to get up right then. Later on, you test your bath or shower water to see if the temperature is right. You might take a sip of coffee and decide it is too strong. You sometimes walk into a clothing store, glance at a few price tags, and decide the store has items more expensive than you can afford. When you donate blood, a tiny sample of your blood is tested to see if it has sufficient iron content.

In each of these instances sufficient information came from sampling. It was not necessary to experience the *whole* of the phenomenon. You didn't have to drink the whole cup of coffee to realize it was too strong. One sip served as a sample of the whole cup. You didn't have to examine every article of apparel in the clothing store to know that the store catered to an exclusive clientele. The phlebotomist at the blood center didn't have to draw a sample from every part of your body because your blood is pretty much the same regardless of whether it is in your arm or foot or ear.

The notion behind sampling theory is that a small set of **observations** (**sampling units**) can tell you something about the larger population. Let's say that you have been elected to a school board in a town with 50,000 registered voters. If there is a movement to raise taxes to build a new high school, you wouldn't have to talk to all 50,000 registered voters to get an accurate notion of whether the majority of the adults in the community were in favor of this tax. A telephone poll of several hundred randomly selected registered voters could provide you with an accurate assessment of support for a new tax. Polling 50,000 individuals is both impractical and unnecessary.

Sampling works because trends or tendencies within a large population can be discovered from a small number of individuals. For instance, if 90% of the registered voters in the above example were going to vote for an increase in their taxes, an indication of support for the tax issue should be apparent whether you sample 100 or 500 of the registered voters (if these voters were randomly selected). The larger sample merely allows for greater confidence and precision in estimating the "true" level of support or nonsupport for the tax issue. It is possible that if you sample only a handful of individuals, these few may not feel, act, or believe as the majority of the larger population. But if the sample is large enough, and there is no bias in the selection of the individual sampling units, then the pattern or characteristics found in the sample should match what you would find if you could contact everyone in the total population. This is great news for quantitative social scientists. Can you imagine how difficult it would be to conduct surveys in large cities like New York or Chicago if you couldn't sample? As you might guess, sampling saves money and time.

You can get a rough idea of how sampling works by imagining that friend has a bowl with 10 marbles in it. She holds it where you can't see into it and asks you to guess the colors of the marbles in the bowl. You may change your opinion each time, if you wish, after you have drawn a marble out. On your first draw you retrieve a blue marble, so you might think that most of the marbles are blue. On the second draw, you obtain a red marble so your best guess at this point is that there are 5 red and 5 blue marbles. The third draw produces another blue marble so you revise your estimate to two-thirds blue and one-third red. The fourth draw is a blue marble, as are the fifth, sixth, and seventh draws. At that point it is clear that the majority of marbles are blue. In fact, over 80% of those marbles selected have been blue. However, the remaining 3 could all be red and so the most conservative estimate would be that 60% of the marbles are blue (since 6 blue ones have already been selected). Alternatively, you might take a bit of a risk and guess that 70%, 80%, or 90% of the marbles will be blue when all 10 are examined.

What this brief example shows is that at some point in drawing a sample, it becomes clear if one viewpoint, opinion, candidate, or color of a marble is represented more often than some other viewpoint, opinion, candidate, or color. The portion found in the sample gives the researcher a "window" into the larger population and a good basis for estimating the actual occurrence in a larger population. If, that is—and this is a very important point—the sample derives from a random selection process.

Imagine your friend's bowl held 200 marbles instead of 10. Let's say that she carefully placed 190 red marbles in the bottom of the bowl and 10 blue ones on top of the red. If you chose a marble off the top each time without stirring the marbles up or moving them around, do you see why a sample of 6 blue marbles could have been obtained? If the marbles had been shaken up or stirred before you selected your first 6 or 7, do you think you would have made a different guess as to the true proportion of red and blue marbles?

Surveyors employing scientifically selected samples (known as **probability samples**) are meticulous about how their respondents are selected. Their attention to random selection and sample size gives these surveys a great deal of accuracy in their findings.

THE ACCURACY OF PROBABILITY SAMPLES

The Gallup organization is one of several nationally recognized professional survey research organizations. Even though the population of the United States is in excess of 300 million, Gallup is able to develop representative samples of the U.S. adult civilian population with interviews of approximately 1,500 respondents. That sample size allows them to be 95% confident that the results they obtain are accurate within plus or minus 3 percentage points. Their accuracy is impressive.

With probability sampling the investigator has a good idea of both the number of people or units in the target population and their characteristics. With these parameters the researcher can determine if a sample is representative. The term **cross-sectional survey design** is used to refer to probability sampling designs. The term indicates that a one-time survey is made with a randomly selected sample. The cross-sectional design allows a broad representation of the population and thus involves persons of all ages, incomes, and educational levels.

There are several probability sampling designs to consider. The first one we will examine is the **simple random sampling design,** where each sampling unit in the population has the same probability (an equal chance) of being chosen.

Suppose the president of your university is retiring, and the board of trustees is interested in selecting a former governor for the new president. You think it is a good idea, but you want to know what the rest of the student body thinks. You find out from the registrar that there are 19,787 students enrolled in the university. Knowing the population of university students, you can begin to make some decisions about how many to contact and which survey approach to use.

If the registrar provides you with a listing of all the enrolled students as well as their phone numbers and addresses, you could use a table of random numbers (see Appendix C) to find a starting place and randomly select a sample of students to contact. This listing would be known as the **sampling frame.** Let's say you decide to contact a sample of 100 students. If you have a good list and you randomly select from it, the names you draw for your sample should be representative of the population enrolled at the university. Your sample should be a microcosm of the population of university students. The proportion of males and females in the sample should reflect their proportion at the university, as should the proportion of freshmen, sophomores, juniors, and seniors. (For example, if you find that 42% of your sample are seniors and yet seniors make up only 18% of the student body as a whole, then you should suspect something is wrong with either your sampling procedure or your list of students.)

Sometimes researchers talk about **systematic sampling.** What they mean by this is best explained by way of example. Let's say that you plan to take a 10% sample of the 19,787 university students. However, a quick calculation shows that this would require almost 2,000 interviews. Since you plan to conduct the telephone survey in a week's time, you decide that this would be far too many students to attempt to contact. As you think about the realistic constraints on your time, you decide that 200 interviews is much more feasible. Dividing the proposed sample size of 200 by the university's population of 19,787, you get a **sampling ratio** of .01, which means that your sample will draw one name for every hundred students enrolled in the university.

In this example of systematic sampling, the next thing you need to do is to number all of the students on the listing you received from the registrar. Then you refer to the random number table (Appendix C) and get a random starting place (any number between 1 and 19,787).

Why is it important to get a random starting place? Because lists are often organized in some way. The list you get from the registrar might place seniors first and then juniors, or it might be organized by grade point average or by whether students are undergraduates or working on a graduate degree.

While probability sampling is the best insurance against a sample being unrepresentative, sometimes chance or some form of unexpected bias will produce a random sample that is not representative. For example, 48% of the university population may be female, but 54% of those drawn for your sample could be female. If you play cards, you understand how this could happen. Even though the deck is shuffled many times, luck plays a role in which cards you are dealt; it is possible to get all hearts or four aces. Similarly, any sample from a population is by definition only an approximation of the total population. Numerically large samples are the best guarantee against obtaining unrepresentative samples.

Some researchers try to guard against a freak or fluke sample by using **stratified random sampling.** When certain important characteristics of the population (for example, the percentage of men and women) are known, exact proportions are obtained by dividing the study population into subgroups or subsets called **strata** and sampling the appropriate proportion from each stratum.

For instance, suppose that instead of sampling from the whole student body, you want to interview only seniors and freshmen. You already know that there are twice as many freshmen as seniors and that you want to interview 200 students. You again approach the registrar and this time ask for two listings: one for the first-year students and another for seniors. Once again you number each of the freshmen and seniors, choose a random starting place, and begin selecting from each stratum. Since there are twice as many freshmen as seniors, you decide to select 65 seniors to interview and 130 freshmen. This keeps the proportion of seniors to freshmen in your sample the same as it is in the university, and you have retained the sample size that you think is manageable. This is not simple random sampling because sampling was done within each stratum.

At this point it would be good to note that single random, systematic random, and stratified random sampling techniques are often used in association with surveys. However, you can still use the same technique and way of thinking about sampling in other research projects. For example, if you were asked to evaluate a program in your agency and needed to randomly assign 60 clients to either the control condition where they would receive the usual intervention or to the experimental condition where they would get the new, hopefully improved intervention, you could decide which random sampling procedure would work the best. A Web site for generating random numbers to assist you in this process can be found at http://www.random.org/sform.html.

When it is not possible to obtain or feasible to construct a sample frame of all the individuals who make up a population (for example, the names and addresses of all social work majors in the United States), researchers sometimes employ a **cluster sampling design.**

Used primarily for convenience and economy, cluster sampling randomly selects individuals from natural groupings or clusters. Because human beings are social creatures, we tend to belong to groups like civic organizations, clubs, fraternities, sororities, and churches.

For example, if you want to know how the parents of children with emotional, mental, or learning problems view helping professionals, you might go to your local mental health center and ask for their cooperation. If you wanted a more geographically diverse sample, it might occur to you to contact such national organizations as the National Alliance for Mental Illness (NAMI), the Attention Deficit Disorder Association (ADDA), or the Learning Disabilities Association of America (LAD). Once you obtain a list of their chapters, you could then call, write, or e-mail for permission to survey their membership. Such organizations could be very supportive of your research and eager to assist.

An example of a **one-stage cluster sampling** is dividing the population of a town into households (households would be the clusters because they usually contain more than one individual) and then taking a sample of households and obtaining information from all the members of the household. **Two-stage cluster sampling** involves dividing the population into households or clusters and then taking a sample of members from each selected household.

A **multistage cluster sampling design** consists of several steps that must be taken prior to sampling the population of interest. For example, suppose you want to conduct a survey of hospital social workers who regularly are involved with crack babies and their mothers. You might start by identifying which states have the highest birth rates of crack babies. From that cluster of states you could identify those with cities having a population of a million or more, and from that cluster of cities list all hospitals with neonatal care units.

Example of a Stratified Multistage Area Probability Sampling Design

Shavers, Lynch, and Burmeister (2000) conducted a survey of African-American and white residents of Detroit to investigate knowledge about the Tuskegee syphilis study. They found that 81% of African-Americans but only 28% of whites had prior knowledge of the study. Seventy-six percent of the African Americans and 59% of the whites who claimed to be familiar with the study believed that the men obtained syphilis from an injection by researchers. Fifty-one percent of the African-American respondents and 17% of the white respondents indicated that their knowledge of the study resulted in their having less trust of medical researchers. The authors concluded that the study "confirms . . . that distrust arising from knowledge of the Tuskegee Study negatively impacts the willingness of African-Americans to participate in medical research activities" (p. 569).

Depending on the size of that list (since large cities can have many hospitals), you could randomly select hospitals or take all of them. The last stage could involve writing the directors of the hospitals' departments of social work and asking them to identify social workers who had worked with 10 or more crack babies in the past year. From this listing you could mail questionnaires to the social workers with the most experience with crack babies.

Professional survey organizations often use multistage cluster samples simply because there is no sample frame of all American citizens. Typically, they randomly draw from large geographic tracts. The next stage would involve drawing from cities, towns, and even smaller units, such as census tracts or blocks—and from those, clusters of dwellings from which respondents would be selected.

One of my students used a multistage cluster sampling design in connection with a research project. She had been reading about transracial adoption and found little information about black people's attitudes toward this topic. Since she was not interested in white people's attitudes, a random community survey would have been inefficient. Instead, she selected a multistage cluster sampling design.

She (with assistance from me and another colleague) first identified the nine census tracts in one city containing the highest concentrations of black people. From these nine tracts, three were randomly selected (since she was doing the interviewing all by herself, there was no need to walk her legs off). From these three tracts, 40 city blocks were randomly chosen. Finally, every sixth household was selected from these blocks (after getting a random starting place) until 150 interviews had been completed (Howard, Royse, & Skerl, 1977).

Because the individuals within a cluster tend to be more homogeneous than individuals in different clusters, the researcher typically should maximize the number of clusters for greater representativeness. Sampling error is reduced when researchers take fewer individuals from more clusters rather than more individuals from fewer clusters. This may mean that few individuals are selected from any one cluster. However, because of the efficiency permitted with random sampling, there is no obligation to sample from each cluster.

DETERMINING SAMPLE SIZE

How big a sample is necessary for a good survey? This is a major question in the minds of many would-be researchers. Unfortunately, there is no simple response to this question. Sample size is related to the researcher's objectives, monetary and personnel resources, and the amount of time available in which to conduct the research. A precise sample size cannot be determined until you are able to state your expectations in terms of the accuracy you need and the confidence that you would like to have in the data. Also, the accuracy of your survey is much more dependent on the size of the sample than on the population size.

Let's acquaint ourselves with several terms useful for discussing statistical probability statements associated with surveys. **Margin of error** refers to the precision needed by the researcher; that is, the amount of sampling error that can be tolerated. A margin of error of 5% means that the actual findings could vary by as much as five points either positively or negatively. A consumer satisfaction survey, for instance, with a 5% margin of error associated with a finding of 65% of clients being "highly satisfied" with services—would mean that the true value in the population could be as low as 60% (65 − 5 = 60) or as high as 70% (65 + 5 = 70). If you believe that greater precision is needed (for example, plus or minus two points), then you must plan on obtaining a larger sample to support that precision. This can be seen in Table 8.1 if you compare the sample sizes in the .05 column with those in the .02 column.

The other term that is important to understand is **confidence level.** A confidence level (or level of confidence) is a statement of how often you could expect to find similar results if the survey were to be repeated. Since every survey varies slightly (depending on who is selected to be in the sample), the confidence level informs about how often the findings will fall outside the margin of error. For example, in a sample developed to have a 95% confidence level with a 5% margin of error, the findings could be expected to miss the actual values in the population by more than 5% only 5 times in 100 surveys. (In the example above, findings that less than 60% or more than 70% of the clients were "highly satisfied" would be expected to occur no more than 5 times in 100 surveys.) The use of a 95% confidence level and 5% margin of error is a common standard in the social sciences.

Table 8.1 will help you decide how large a sample to select in your own surveys. This table is used when you don't know how those surveyed will respond but you want to be reasonably confident in the findings (95%). Both level of confidence and margin of error can be adjusted (by you) up or down in the planning stages of your survey. Each adjustment has implications for sample size. In order to be confident that the same findings would have occurred in 95 surveys out of 100, and to be accurate to within plus or minus 5 percentage points, you would need to interview 79 persons in a population of 100. However, in a population of 1 million, you would have to interview only 384 persons. The greater the precision you require, the larger your sample must be. Note that for a permissible error of 1% with the same population of 1 million, you would need a sample of 9,513.

Table 8.1 | Appropriate Sizes of Simple Random Samples for Specific Permissible Errors Expressed as Absolute Proportions When the True Proportion in the Population Is 0.50 and the Confidence Level Is 95%

Population Size	Sample Size for Permissible Error (Proportion)				
	0.05	0.04	0.03	0.02	0.01
100	79	86	91	96	99
200	132	150	168	185	196
300	168	200	234	267	291
400	196	240	291	343	384
500	217	273	340	414	475
600	234	300	384	480	565
700	248	323	423	542	652
800	260	343	457	600	738
900	269	360	488	655	823
1,000	278	375	516	706	906
2,000	322	462	696	1,091	1,655
3,000	341	500	787	1,334	2,286
4,000	350	522	842	1,500	2,824
5,000	357	536	879	1,622	3,288
6,000	361	546	906	1,715	3,693
7,000	364	553	926	1,788	4,049
8,000	367	558	942	1,847	4,364
9,000	368	563	954	1,895	4,646
10,000	370	566	964	1,936	4,899
15,000	375	577	996	2,070	5,855
20,000	377	583	1,013	2,144	6,488
25,000	378	586	1,023	2,191	6,938
30,000	379	588	1,030	2,223	7,275
40,000	381	591	1,039	2,265	7,745
50,000	381	593	1,045	2,291	8,056
75,000	382	595	1,052	2,327	8,514
100,000	383	597	1,056	2,345	8,762
500,000	384	600	1,065	2,390	9,423
1,000,000	384	600	1,066	2,395	9,513
2,000,000	384	600	1,067	2,398	9,558

Source: Sampling and statistics handbook for research in education. (1980). Washington, DC: National Education Association. Courtesy of Chester McCall. McCall, C. Reprinted with permission.

There are numerous other tables that can be consulted or computed, too. If you had conducted prior studies and had a good idea of what proportions the survey would likely reveal (for example, 90% opposed to a tax increase), then there are tables that will allow you to get by with smaller sample sizes. In the example of a 90/10 split, then you could get by with a sample of approximately 150 individuals (95% level of confidence, 5% margin of error). With an expected 80/20 split, a sample of 256 would be needed (95% level of confidence, 5% margin of error). Because a pattern is more easily detected as the proportions move away from a 50/50 mix, smaller samples can be used.

Sample size is obviously much more of a concern if you are planning a probability sampling design than if you are planning a sample of convenience. With a probability design, you very likely will need to consult a table to arrive at the appropriate sample size. Besides the margin of error and level of confidence considerations, the research must also anticipate how many respondents might be captured, or in a more elaborate study where there might be follow-up and posttests, how many might be lost to attrition. Also, the quantitatively oriented researcher needs to give some thought to analysis of the data and whether there will be subgroup analysis by gender, ethnicity, age group, and so forth. If the beginning sample is too small, then it may not produce a sufficient number of respondents in the desired subgroups for analysis. So for the quantitatively minded, more subjects are almost always better.

NONPROBABILITY SAMPLING DESIGNS

Nonprobability sampling designs are an alternative to probability sampling designs. Qualitative researchers aren't nearly as concerned about sample size as the quantitatively oriented researchers. For qualitative investigators, sample size is a matter of judgment or intuition; there is not a set rule or pattern that they have to conform to. One way to understand the difference in orientation is to think about quantitatively oriented researchers focusing on *breadth* of data (e.g., a wide exposure to people and their different experiences as represented in the larger population) while qualitatively oriented researchers are more focused on *depth* of their data (Patton, 2002). Thus, a decision can be made about contacting fewer individuals in greater depth or contacting a larger number of people at less depth.

This is not to say that qualitative researchers care nothing at all about sample sizes, it is just that their approach is different. Instead of following the rule that "more research subjects is better," the qualitative researcher is more likely to sample to the point when they don't feel that they are learning anything new about the problem or issue. When they encounter redundancy in responses, then they know that their sample has been large enough. In other words, size of the sample doesn't matter. What's important is feeling that one has a good handle on understanding the issue at hand.

To the quantitative researcher, the qualitative approach to sampling is less rigorous because there's not the ability to state margin of error and level of confidence and they don't know how representative the sample is. However, it is not uncommon for even these researchers to occasionally conduct a study with a small qualitative sample. When there's not a lot of money for large samples, convenience samples might be utilized as straw polls—unofficial estimates of opinions or concerns about issues. It is likely that social workers in their practice employ more of the nonprobability designs than probability ones because they are generally cheaper, faster, and more easily conducted. Let's take an example.

Assume you are concerned about some issue—maybe it is the number of homeless on the street in your city and it appears to you that the community leaders are ignoring this problem. You want to see if others agreed with you, that it wasn't your imagination, so you decide to poll 10 friends. That would be easier to do than randomly selecting a sample from the 50,000 registered voters in your town. Your nonprobability approach would be called taking a **sample of convenience.** When you draw a convenience sample, you do so because it is easy or quick, and you want *some* information—you're willing to settle for less than the best data in order to take the pulse or get a quick reading. But this type of sampling can be prone to error. Your friends, for example, knowing how strongly you feel about an issue such as the homeless may not be completely honest in telling you how they would vote. Furthermore, the reasons they are your friends (common interests and values; perhaps they are also social workers) will likely influence how they would vote. In other words, your 10 friends may not be representative of the other 49,990 voters in your town.

If you were to skim a wide variety of professional journals, you would find that many surveys of college students are conducted each year. Why do you think that is? Could it have anything to do with the convenience with which researchers might access them? At the same time, how well do college students represent the other adults in our population? Could they be younger, more educated, and more liberal in their views? Although college students may not be representative of the adult population, often researchers are interested in using such convenience samples before they commit to a larger-scale investigation.

Nonprobability sampling is often done when the extent of the population is not known. For instance, in my exploratory research to find out how much money trash pickers make each day from gathering and selling aluminum beverage cans (Royse, 1987), I did not know the actual number of can pickers in the area, so I arbitrarily chose a nonprobability sample of 50. This group may have been somewhat unrepresentative of the larger population of all trash pickers, but I had no way of knowing this. (I tried, however, to make the study a little more representative by interviewing can pickers in two different cities.) This type of sampling is also known as **purposive sampling,** because the respondents had to have certain characteristics in common in order to be selected for an interview (in my study, they all had to be trash pickers). Another way to think about purposive sampling is to envision the extreme or deviant cases. If one is trying to figure out why some children remained the longest in foster care, for example, a representative sample isn't needed, just those children who have been in much longer than the others.

Another variation of purposive or extreme case sampling would be to identify those cases or clients that are widely or vastly different. **Maximum variation sampling** might involve not only the children who were in foster care the longest, but also those who were in foster care the shortest period of time. This allows the qualitative research to look for themes or characteristics that distinguish the two groups as well as those which might be shared in spite of the wide variation.

There is a good reason that samples of convenience are also known as **accidental** and **available samples.** I once watched a television camera crew approach different individuals for "person-in-the-street" interviews. What was of interest to me was the number (perhaps the majority) of individuals who, seeing the camera, crossed to the other side of the street to avoid it. While the process of indiscriminately stopping people and asking for their opinions seemed random, actually there was a noticeable bias in those who constituted the sample. Did the more vocal individuals represent the views of the shy ones? This cannot be determined in a sample of convenience.

Similarly, if you stand outside of a supermarket at 4:00 A.M. on Friday your respondents may be quite different from those who show up at 10:00 A.M. or even 8:00 P.M. Might there be a difference between the supermarket shoppers at 11:00 A.M. on Sunday and those at 3:00 P.M. on the same day?

With nonprobability convenience samples, the consumer of the information is often left to his or her own to figure out if the group of persons who were interviewed or surveyed is a fair representation of the larger population. What may appear to be a random process (e.g., choosing every other shopper going into the grocery store) can have severe limitations imposed upon the data because of such factors as the time of day and the location (was it an upscale or inner-city neighborhood?).

Snowball Sampling

When one respondent leads you to another, and that one refers you to another, the approach is known as **snowball sampling.** Suppose as a school social worker you encounter a high school student who, for all practical purposes, is homeless. He stays first with this friend and then that one, sometimes sleeping in his car or in an abandoned building. When you talk with him, he indicates that he has several friends in the same predicament. If he leads you to them and they lead you to others, then you have created a snowball sampling design. This type of nonprobability sampling design grows by referrals to other potential responders. Remember, just because you don't know the respondents does not mean that you are selecting them randomly—you are not. They are all linked, in some way, to the one or two individuals you started with. They could be expected to be more homogeneous than if a sample frame of all the persons in that population could be selected and then a sample drawn. This approach is used when it is difficult to locate respondents by any other means.

Quota Samples

Quota sampling involves knowing certain characteristics of a population (for example, the proportion of an agency's clientele who are under 30, middle aged, and 65 or older) and then striving to obtain the same proportions in the selected sample. With this approach, screening is often done early in the interview so that interviewers will not have to continue with those who do not have the desired characteristics. Although the final sample may match the population in terms of the proportions of respondents having certain characteristics, the sample may be unrepresentative in other areas because of characteristics for which they were not screened. That is, a quota sample may resemble the population by containing an identical proportion of those who are over the age of 65, yet because they aren't probability surveys, the results possibly may not accurately reflect "the real picture"—depending on how the respondents were chosen. In quota samples, interviewers and data gatherers have a great deal of freedom in finding respondents any way they can. To take a ludicrous example, one could get his or her quota of persons over the age of 65 fairly easily by going to the nearest nursing home or respite care center for senior citizens. If the survey were to report later that all of those 65 and older were impaired in some way, that finding could be entirely true but not at all representative of the population of persons 65 and older who lived on their own in the community. Quota samples are convenience samples with specifications regarding a certain number or proportion of respondents.

The problem with all nonprobability sampling designs is not knowing how representative the sample is or how closely it resembles the "true" population. Quantitatively oriented researchers and qualitatively oriented researchers view this issue somewhat differently. While the quantitative researcher tends to think of the nonprobability sample as less rigorous because it is difficult for the investigator to know how well it estimates the attitude or behavior as it actually exists within the larger population, the qualitative researcher views the nonprobability approach as a way to learn more detail about a problem or issue. The qualitative researcher is less concerned with generalization from any survey but puts more emphasis on its value for elucidating or illuminating the topic better.

Additional Survey Designs

Longitudinal surveys may not be representative of the population. These surveys are conducted on multiple occasions over an extended period of time. There are three types of longitudinal surveys: **trend surveys, cohort surveys,** and **panel surveys.** Trend surveys require multiple samples from the same population over months or years in order to monitor changes or trends. The same individuals are not repeatedly interviewed.

A **cohort** is a group of persons who have some critical or significant experience in common (for example, Iraq war veterans). Cohort studies involve only persons who fit into these subgroups. Persons who have some event in

Table 8.2 | Comparison Trend, Cohort, and Panel Longitudinal Surveys

Type	Subjects' Ages in 2007	Subjects' Ages in 2012	Subjects' Ages in 2017
Trend	15 years old	15 years old	15 years old
Cohort	15 years old	20 years old	25 years old
Panel	15 years old	20 years old	25 years old

common (e.g., are married or graduate from high school in a given year) could be used to form cohorts by marriage or graduation, respectively. Cohort studies involve multiple samples from the cohorts of interest. Comparisons of cohorts are most commonly found in sociological studies of the population.

Panel studies are studies of the *same* group of persons over an extended period (for example, the survivors of Hiroshima or Hurricane Katrina). Panel studies are used to detect changes in individuals over time.

Table 8.2 shows the three types of longitudinal surveys. Each study began with interviewing 15-year-old runaways in San Francisco. In a trend survey, the investigator is interested in differences in 15-year-old runaways over time. Do their characteristics change? Do the reasons they run away change? An investigator using a cohort survey would want to interview *any* person who was 15 years old and a runaway in a specific year (e.g., 2007). The panel surveyor would go back to his or her sample of runaways in 2007 and follow up with them as adults in the years 2012 and 2017. Although Table 8.2 shows five-year increments, longitudinal follow-ups could be on an every-year or every-other-year basis; the researcher decides the schedule.

NOTES ABOUT BIAS AND ERRORS

Even if you plan a probability design instead of a nonprobability sampling design, be alert to any limitations that could result in your sampling frame being less inclusive than you had planned. Be particularly alert to sample selection bias that could occur because of the order in which the sample units are listed. For instance, a list of students' names from the university registrar might be arrayed by hours completed, GPA, or residential students only. If you were to select only the first 100 names thinking that the listing was random, you would very likely not have a full representation of all the students at the university. In other words, you could have a biased sample. One always needs to be alert for incomplete listings (for example, part-time students or graduate students might not be in the listing provided by the registrar unless you were very clear about what students the sample frame should contain).

Another possible problem occurs when respondents self-select. Ideally, every person asked to complete an interview or survey form would comply. In reality, people make decisions based on how much time they have, the topic, what their children or pets are doing, and the presentation made by the interviewer. Many people don't want to be stopped on the street and interviewed even if it is presumably for a reputable organization because they fear there is some "catch" such as being asked to donate money.

Other factors that can affect your samples and ultimately the findings of your surveys include:

Interviewer bias—The often unconscious biases and stereotypes that lead people to approach people like themselves, to avoid those they fear or dislike, and to attribute positive or negative attributes based on such traits as gender, race, or age—is a serious concern when interviewers and telephone callers have few guidelines regarding whom to include or exclude for a survey.

Interviewer error—To try and minimize mistakes, inconsistencies, and interviewer bias when interviews are being employed, one needs to train interviewers well to prevent careless errors in the field or in the recording of responses. Sometimes with telephone surveys a small portion of respondents are contacted again to validate their answers. Knowing this might help to keep the interviewers more objective, honest, and accurate. Of course, that shouldn't be a problem but a sociologist once told me that as a student he sat in a coffee shop and made up information for a community directory when he should have been going door-to-door to actually obtain data.

Respondent error—Clients of an agency may distort their satisfaction with agency services because they might fear losing the services that they currently have. They may also refuse to respond out of fear and this could affect the sample size.

Instrument error—Questionnaires that are difficult to read or comprehend can result in flawed, unreliable data. Instruments that look like they will take a long time to complete will produce samples that may have fewer respondents and a lower response rate. Also, persons with lower levels of education may be less likely to complete complicated mailed surveys than persons with higher levels of education.

Whenever you conduct a survey, allow sufficient time to follow up on nonrespondents. Sending reminder postcards and mailing second and third questionnaires to nonrespondents greatly increase response rates. In telephone and face-to-face interviewing, unless you follow up on those who are not home when you call, you run the risk of having a bias against those who work during the hours that you attempt to reach them.

For the quantitatively oriented researcher, a low response rate is just as problematic as too small a sample. If less than a majority of the respondents reply, you are left wondering about the attitudes or characteristics of those who chose not to respond. Are the data biased when only 20% respond? Would a different pattern of findings emerge if the response rate could be raised to 60% by following up on the nonresponders? There is no way of knowing. A terribly low response rate (such as 20% or 30%) brings to mind an analogy that

Practice Note: Creating an Asian-American Sampling Frame

Although some Asian-Americans live in areas known by such names as "Chinatown" and "Little Saigon," most do not. Because of their geographical dispersal, it is not easy to obtain a representative sample of Asian-Americans using random methodologies such as random digit dialing. As a result, much of the research from this population has come from convenience samples. However, in order to obtain prevalence estimates regarding health and mental health issues, survey methodologies with greater external validity have been sought. Sasao (1994) reports an effort that created lists of persons with unequivocally Asian surnames from telephone directories—a process that was more cost-efficient than "true" random sampling and that seemed to produce reliable data when compared to focus group interviews in three different cities.

concerns the old story of three blind men who encounter an elephant for the first time. One fellow standing beside a massive leg says, "An elephant is like a tree trunk."

"No," the second one says, feeling the elephant's trunk, "it is more like a boa constrictor."

The third man touches the elephant's tail and says, "It has a tail like a pig."

Low response rates don't enable you to get the whole picture—you may hear from the most satisfied or the most dissatisfied clients, the most compulsive or educated, but you can't be sure of what you've got until you have 55% or more of the responses. The more you have, the better you can understand your "elephant."

KEY TERMS

observations (sampling units)

probability samples

cross-sectional survey designs

simple random sampling designs

sampling frame

systematic sampling

sampling ratio

stratified random sampling

strata

cluster sampling design

one-stage cluster sampling

two-stage cluster sampling

multistage cluster sampling designs

margin of error

confidence level

nonprobability sampling designs

sample of convenience

purposive sampling

maximum variation sampling

accidental and available samples

snowball sampling

quota sampling

longitudinal surveys

trend surveys

cohort surveys

panel surveys

cohort

panel studies

SELF-REVIEW

(Answers at the end of the book)

1. T or F. The notion on which sampling is based is that a much smaller randomly selected sample can yield approximately the same findings as one would obtain with interviewing every person in that population.

2. _____ surveys are not noted for their generalizability.
3. _____ is the list of every person or unit eligible to be contacted in a survey.
4. T or F. Systematic random sampling is recognized by the ratio of the sample to the population—as in contacting every fourth client.
5. If you were implementing a probability sampling design and wanted to make sure that the exact proportions of BSWs, MSWs, and PhD social workers were represented in the sample, the type of design would be _____.
6. T or F. Margin of error and confidence interval are independent. One could select, for example, a 90% confidence level and a 3% margin of error.
7. T or F. The relation of sample size to population is this: generally, greater accuracy requires larger samples.
8. T or F. Sample size is more of a consideration with samples of convenience than with probability surveys.
9. Other terms for convenience samples are _____ and _____ samples.
10. T or F. A quota sample is a type of probability sampling.
11. T or F. Panel surveys are different from cohort and trend surveys in that the same individuals are contacted at different points in time.
12. T or F. Longitudinal studies are always based on probability samples.
13. T or F. Once one has a randomly selected sample of about 385 persons, that sample can adequately represent a population of 100,000 or 1 million—assuming a 95% level of confidence, 5% margin of error, and a 50/50 split in response proportions.
14. The type of sampling where one respondent leads the researcher to another possible participant is called _____ sampling.
15. _____ bias is the tendency of an interviewer to shy away from people who do not resemble the interviewer.
16. T or F. When it comes to sample size, both qualitative and quantitative researchers take the position that "more is better."

QUESTIONS FOR CLASS DISCUSSION

1. You want to conduct a national survey of social workers. What are three ways in which you might stratify the sample? Why might you want to stratify the sample?
2. Give an example of a topic that might best be explored with the following:
   a. snowball sampling
   b. cluster sampling
   c. a longitudinal design
3. Your agency has asked you to conduct a random sampling of clients to determine how satisfied they are with the agency's services. After some

discussion, it is decided that a telephone survey is the most sensible approach. If the agency closed approximately 3,000 cases last year, how big a sample would be needed in order to have 95% confidence in the findings, plus or minus 5%? If the agency decides to use a mail approach, how many persons would you have to contact in order to get the same level of confidence and accuracy? (Keep in mind that about 30% of the respondents in a mail survey respond on the first mailing.)

4. Let's pretend that *Money* magazine prints a questionnaire in a recent issue mailed to subscribers. One of the questions asked is "What do you think about most—money or sex?" Can the findings from this study be considered to represent the thinking of most American adults? If you wanted to investigate that question, what would be a better way to do it? Would you expect the findings from the *Money* magazine survey to be different from findings from the same questionnaire in an issue of *Playboy*?

5. In his book *The Superpollsters*, David Moore (1992) discusses criticisms of books written by Shere Hite. He mentions that for one book she distributed approximately 100,000 questionnaires through women's organizations and got back approximately 3%. Further, she instructed respondents that they didn't have to answer every single question but only those that interested them. And she didn't standardize her questionnaire, but used multiple versions. Could she claim a representative sample? Did her methodology deserve criticism?

6. Nelson Flake constructs a sample of 200 African-American, 200 Hispanic, 200 Asian-American, and 200 white students at a large state university. What type of sample design is this? After Nelson Flake conducts his study can he generalize his findings to all college students in America? Why or why not?

RESOURCES AND REFERENCES

Harkness, J. A., van de Vijver, F. J. R., & Mohler, P. (2003). *Cross-cultural survey methods*. Hoboken, NJ: John Wiley & Sons.

Howard, A., Royse, D., & Skerl, J. A. (1977). Transracial adoption: The black community perspective. *Social Work, 22(3)*, 184–189.

Moore, D. W. (1992). *The superpollsters: How they measure and manipulate public opinion in America*. New York: Four Walls Eight Windows.

Patton, M. Q. (2002). *Qualitative research and evaluation methods* (3rd ed.). Thousand Oaks, CA: Sage.

Royse, D. (1987). Homelessness among trash pickers. *Psychological Reports, 60*, 808–810.

Sasao, T. (1994). Using surname-based telephone survey methodology in Asian-American communities: Practical issues and caveats. *Journal of Community Psychology, 22*, 283–295.

Shavers, V. L., Lynch, C. F., & Burmeister, L. F. (2000). Knowledge of the Tuskegee study and its impact on the willingness to participate in medical research studies. *Journal of the National Medical Association, 92(12)*, 563–572.

ASSIGNMENT 8.1: Locating and Critically Reading a Survey Study

Objective: *To be able to identify studies involving surveys and to be able discuss the strengths and weaknesses of survey efforts.*

For this assignment, you should browse one of the social work journals and locate a research article where the methodology involves the use of a survey.

1. Give the full APA citation of the article that you read.

2. Was a probability or nonprobability sampling design employed? Was a margin of error reported? What was it? Give the more specific name for the sampling design.

3. What was the sample size?

4. Does the sample appear to be adequate? Does its size and construction give you a sense of confidence in the study's findings? Explain.

5. Did the author devise a questionnaire or scale just for this study, or did he or she use one already developed? (*Note:* Your instructor may want you to append the copy of the article you read to this assignment.)

6. List three major findings of the study.

ASSIGNMENT 8.2: Creating a Random Sample

Objective: *To obtain practice in producing random numbers and creating a random sample.*

Assume that you are a social worker in an agency that closed 750 cases last year. Your supervisor asks you to draw a random sample of 50 clients for a utilization chart review that she wants done.

Go to the Web site http://www.random.org/sform.html for a random number generator. Enter the highest and lowest numbers that will be in the sample (e.g., 1 and 750). Then answer the following questions:

1. How do you go about selecting a sample of 50 from the list produced? List the steps that you would need to take.

2. Would it be equally permissible to take the first 50 numbers as well as the last 50?

3. If you repeated the request on the random number generator, would you expect to get a list the second time that looked identical to the list you obtained the first time? Why or why not?

4. If you wanted to do a systematic random sample by taking every fifth client from the pool of 750, how many clients would be in your sample?

9 CHAPTER | Survey Research Methods

If the topic of experimental design seemed foreign to you, survey research should be more familiar. We see results of surveys in newspapers and magazines almost every day. Social work literature abounds with surveys. Surveys are the research methodology most commonly used by social workers. Surveys have been conducted to explore such issues as job burnout, values and ethical dilemmas, client satisfaction with services, and drug use among high school students. Pick up any social work journal and you are likely to find some type of a survey. Surveys have been called "the single most important information gathering invention of the social sciences" (Adams, Smelser, & Treiman, 1985), and it is essential that social workers, both as consumers and producers of research, understand them well.

Surveys can be thought of as snapshots of attitudes, beliefs, or behaviors at one point in time. Using a predetermined set of questions or issues, surveys reveal what a group of respondents is thinking, feeling, or doing. Social workers might use surveys to uncover special needs within their communities or within special populations of clients. Often called **needs assessments,** these surveys might try to determine the prenatal care needs of low-income clients, understand transportation barriers, or help agencies plan how to improve services. These surveys provide information about what the targeted population knows or perceives about the availability and accessibility of services and can also identify unmet needs or gaps in services. Needs assessments may consist of prepared questionnaires or personal interviews and may solicit information from clients, their caseworkers, other professionals such as parole officers, physicians, or citizens randomly selected from the community. Needs assessments are sometimes used to provide evaluative information, such as when a program director wants to know if the clients or community view the agency as providing acceptable service.

Social service agencies can also use these surveys internally to identify areas where staff members feel that they need additional training or continuing education. Following a situation where an intoxicated client punched the receptionist and broke her jaw, the administration might conduct a needs assessment of staff to identify ideas about how to provide greater security.

Needs assessments may involve surveys of key informants—individuals in the community who are likely to know about special needs as a result of their positions. They may be physicians, social service providers, clergy, public officials, and so on.

Another type of needs assessment involves **community forums**—public meetings or hearings where members of a community state their preferences or present their demands. These meetings can be loud and boisterous or poorly attended. For the most part, clients typically seen by social workers seldom attend such meetings. A conceptual weakness with this approach is that those who attend and express their views may not be representative of the community or even familiar with its needs.

Possibly the most popular form of needs assessment would involve some sort of community survey. These surveys can range from those hastily conceived and executed to those based on scientifically selected samples that provide the researchers with a good deal of confidence in the findings. Surveys of clients are also quite common and given in conjunction with program evaluation efforts. In short, there are many, many uses for surveys.

Surveys are appealing because they are rooted in the democratic process of asking people about their opinions. People like to know how their attitudes compare with those of others—to learn whether they are in the mainstream or not. But also, surveys invite participation. Designing a questionnaire can be great fun, almost like a game. If a committee is designing a survey, practically everyone can participate either by suggesting items or by pointing out ways specific items might be misinterpreted or could be improved. Other reasons for the popularity of surveys are that they are quickly implemented and convenient to administer. Once the survey instrument has been chosen or designed and a sample identified, the survey (for instance, a mail survey) can often be handled by a clerical person, thus freeing the researcher to attend to other matters until a sufficient number of survey questionnaires have come in for analysis. Sometimes, the investigator can coordinate the collection of data from personal or telephone interviews. Each of these approaches has its own set of advantages and disadvantages that we'll discuss later in the chapter.

Surveys come in many different varieties. It is common in social work literature for authors to note that they have conducted an **exploratory survey**. These surveys are generally recognized by their small samples. Exploratory or pilot studies are sometimes conducted prior to applying for federal grant dollars and allow investigators to test out hypotheses or instruments on a small scale. Since science is built by small, incremental steps, exploratory surveys are legitimate even though the knowledge they produce is often seriously limited.

When investigators are ready to define a phenomenon definitively, they must increase their sample sizes and address the problems of acquiring representative samples. While an exploratory survey of teens involved in Satan worship may consist only of six individuals, a **descriptive survey** must be concerned with obtaining a representative sample. As you might imagine, getting a representative sample can be difficult to do, and so descriptive surveys often try to compensate by constructing very large samples. These surveys may involve 400, 2,500, or even more research subjects. To give another example, a descriptive survey of the homeless in Illinois might involve having every shelter in the state collect data each night for a week during a winter month. Even though you may gather information on 5,000 different homeless persons, many would still be missed because they don't stay in shelters even in cold weather. However, the large sample size probably does accurately reflect the characteristics of most of the homeless and would allow the researcher to create a profile of the homeless and to generalize about the homeless population in Illinois that frequents shelters.

When conducting a survey, four different methods may be used to collect data:

- Mail surveys
- E-mail surveys
- Telephone surveys
- Personal interviews

Each of these approaches will be discussed in turn.

THE MAIL QUESTIONNAIRE

The *advantages* of the mail questionnaire have been noted by Mangione (1995):

- Relatively inexpensive
- Large numbers of respondents can be surveyed in a relatively short period
- Respondents can look up information if they need to
- Privacy is maximized
- Visual presentation
- Can be completed when convenient for the respondent
- Respondents can see the context of a series of questions
- Insulates respondents from the expectations of the researcher

A final advantage of the mail questionnaire is that it reduces errors that might occur in the process of interviewing. Not all interviewers are equally skilled, and some may have traits that annoy, offend, or cause those being interviewed to be less than honest.

On the other hand, there are a number of specific *disadvantages* to the mail questionnaire. First of all, unlike with personal or telephone interviews, researchers experience some loss of control over the survey process once the questionnaire has been mailed. Although the questionnaire may be delivered to the proper address, there is no guarantee that the intended recipient will be the one who completes the questionnaire. An 11-year-old child could respond for his or her mother or father even though the researcher intended the survey form to go to adults. A related problem is that the survey could be completed under less than optimal conditions (for example, when the respondent is ill or intoxicated, or completes the questionnaire while the television is blaring or a party is going on in the living room).

Second, investigators cannot assume that all recipients of the survey will be literate or will be able to comprehend complex issues. While college students are accustomed to questionnaires and multiple-choice response sets, individuals with lower levels of educational attainment may find structured response sets (such as "Strongly agree," "Agree," "Undecided," "Disagree," "Strongly disagree") confusing or too confining for the responses they want to give. A potential response bias exists if questionnaires are mailed to groups who may have high rates of illiteracy. In such a situation it would be very likely that those who couldn't read wouldn't respond. Some client groups you may encounter are either frequent movers who don't always leave forwarding addresses or don't have addresses at all (e.g., the homeless).

Third, mail questionnaires tend to be highly structured and relatively short. These questionnaires may not provide the detail that could emerge from a face-to-face contact. In personal interview situations, the interviewer is able to ask for additional information (to **probe**) if the respondent says something exceptionally interesting or if the interviewer is not sure of the response or thinks the respondent did not understand the question.

Mail questionnaires have become a popular gimmick with some businesses (for example, an official-looking survey form arrives asking for information about how much you travel or take vacations, but its real purpose is to sell real estate or vacation time-sharing plans). Consequently, some Americans see surveys as a form of solicitation or junk mail. Even if a survey form arrives in an envelope carrying first-class postage, it can be seen as an invasion of privacy and thrown away. Individuals with good intentions can put the survey form aside until "later" with the result that questionnaires get lost, thrown out, or put in the parakeet's cage.

Another problem is that Americans are a highly mobile population and are constantly changing addresses, last names, and places of employment. Your survey will be seriously disadvantaged if your mailing list is inaccurate or out of date.

All these factors have a direct affect on the number of people who complete and return survey questionnaires. Commonly only 25% to 35% of those who are mailed a questionnaire return it. The response rates for mail surveys are often as low as 5% to 10%, and response rates over 30% are rare. Of course, if your addresses are recent and the topic is one that interests the respondents, response rates will improve, but will seldom reach response rates of telephone or face-to-face interviews. However, these rates apply only to those who receive one mailing. With a reminder postcard and the mailing of a second questionnaire to those who did not initially respond, these rates can be improved quite a bit—up to 50% or more. This is discussed in the next section.

Getting a Good Response Rate

Designing a mail questionnaire is not as simple as it may first appear. Extensive research exists on all aspects of the mail survey. It is known, for instance, that using first-class postage results in better response rates. Similarly, increasing the perceived personalization of each letter seems to pay dividends. In addition to the use of first-class stamps (versus meter or bulk mail), Ransdell (1996) recommends handwritten addresses and signatures. Personalized notes at the bottom of cover letters also seem to increase the response rate. Other successful tactics include prenotifying the potential participants that they will be asked to participate in a survey, having a university or "official" sponsorship, and sending reminder postcards or making phone call follow-ups to those who have forgotten to return their surveys.

Dillman (1983) has provided an overview of steps that contribute to what he calls the "Total Design Method." He suggests that long questionnaires be photo reduced and designed as a booklet to make them more appealing and less imposing (preferable size is 6.5 inches by 8.25 inches). The first page is designed as a cover with an interesting title and illustration; the back page is left blank for additional comments. The booklet should be printed on white paper (preferably 16-pound weight) and arranged so that the most interesting questions appear first. The whole questionnaire should be designed so that lowercase letters are used for questions and uppercase letters for the preprinted response categories. Visual clues (arrows, indentations, and spacing) are used to their fullest advantage to help respondents answer in a straight vertical line rather than going back and forth across the page (see Figure 9.1).

Considerable thought and research have also gone into the implementation of survey procedures. Dillman (1983) suggests a one-page cover letter on letterhead stationery explaining that a socially useful study is being conducted and why each respondent is important. Individual names and addresses are typed on the cover letter and the envelope. One week after the first mail-out, a reminder postcard is sent to all recipients. Three weeks after the first mail-out, a second cover letter, questionnaire, and return envelope are sent to all those who have not responded. Seven weeks after the first mail-out, another cover letter and questionnaire are sent by certified mail to all those who have not responded.

The total design method greatly improves the response rates ordinarily found with mail surveys. Dillman (1978) states that the average response rate for 48 surveys using his procedures was 74%, with no survey receiving less than a 50% response.

Child Abuse Survey

1. How serious a problem is child abuse and neglect in our community?

_____ VERY SERIOUS

_____ SOMEWHAT SERIOUS

_____ NOT VERY SERIOUS

_____ NOT A PROBLEM AT ALL

2. Have you ever had reason to suspect that a child living in your neighborhood has been emotionally abused?

_____ NO

_____ YES

    2a. Have you ever reported a case of suspected emotional abuse?

        _____ YES

        _____ NO

3. Compared to 10 years ago, do you think there is now more, less, or about the same amount of child abuse?

_____ MORE

_____ LESS

_____ ABOUT THE SAME

Figure 9.1 | An Example of Items from a Questionnaire

Incentives are sometimes necessary to increase response rates. The good news, however, is that monetary inducements don't have to be very large. One study (James & Bolstein, 1992) found that a prepaid incentive of $1 almost doubled the response rate. Further, a $5 check produced almost the same response rate (52%) as a $40 check (54%). Too large of an incentive can actually work against the researcher (possibly because potential respondents think there is a hidden "catch"). Promising even as much as $50 did not improve response rates over providing no incentive at all. Wilk (1993) reported a systematic random survey of 400 names chosen from the NASW *Register of Clinical Social Workers*. She found that a $1 incentive improved her response rate from 43% to 63%. Lotteries are another way to reward participation.

Nonmonetary incentives such as pens, refrigerator magnets, bookmarks, and the like can also be effectively used. I once bought a large 500-piece jigsaw puzzle and taped a piece of it to each questionnaire being sent a second time to nonresponders. My cover letter started off, "I'm puzzled. About two weeks ago, I mailed you a questionnaire, but I've not heard from you. . . ." While the puzzle pieces weren't exactly an incentive, the novelty of the idea was effective and a number of respondents actually mailed the pieces back.

Occasionally, I've seen companies use bright new pennies ("A penny for your thoughts . . .") to engage the reader's interest. A penny isn't enough compensation to function as a monetary incentive, but the point here is just to be creative in your thinking. Remember, respondents don't *have* to cooperate; each one who does so is doing you a favor!

When designing a survey questionnaire, follow these steps:

- Make it interesting and easy to read.
- Keep the questionnaire as short as possible (response rates and length of questionnaires are inversely related).
- Pilot-test it (to make sure the questions provide you with the information you seek).

No matter which approach you select to conduct your survey, it is important to **pilot-test** (or pretest) your procedures and instrument. Generally, pilot testing is informal and can involve giving the survey instrument to a few friends or coworkers to see if they understand the questions and respond in the ways you anticipate. Even better, administer the survey instrument to a group of persons as similar as possible to the population that you will be surveying. The major purpose of the pilot test is to determine if the type of information you want is supplied by the respondents. Pilot testing need not involve more than 20 persons if the respondents have no problems understanding the questions or recording their responses. Pilot testing also provides estimates of the time required for completing the questionnaire and, in the case of telephone and face-to-face interviews, provides useful data for estimating the cost of the survey.

Unless a new scale is being developed, designers of surveys don't often worry about calculating the internal consistency of their questionnaires. But they do worry about response rates because response rates are good indicators of how much faith can be put in the resulting data. With less than 50% responding, you have to estimate the size of the iceberg based on what you see sticking above the water rather than what's below.

Take the time to ensure that the mailing list is current and as accurate as possible. Also, plan on mailing at least a second letter and questionnaire to all nonrespondents. You may want to include a toll-free number for respondents to use if they have questions about the survey, how they were selected, and that sort of thing. Some institutional review boards require that researchers routinely provide such a phone number for potential respondents to inquire about their rights as research subjects. (Clients of an agency, for instance, might worry that they could be in jeopardy of losing their services if they refuse to participate.)

E-MAIL AND WEB-BASED SURVEYS

The popularity of the Internet and e-mail has made it possible for researchers to gather information at less cost than mailed surveys and with less obtrusiveness than a telephone call or personal interview. Researchers have the option of sending out surveys attached to e-mails or subscribing to a commercial company which will allow for custom designed Web pages and instant tabulation of the survey data. Companies such as SurveyMonkey.com keep the electronic returns from cluttering up the researcher's inbox and provide the anonymity that is often desired by respondents. (Lack of anonymity to an e-mailed survey may affect response rates.) The commercial survey sites are secure and, unlike completed paper surveys that could sit around on someone's desk and possibly be read by an unauthorized person, only those people with the correct password are allowed to view the responses collected on the commercial survey sites.

Online commercial companies make it easy for the researcher to create questionnaires without having to learn or purchase special software. Those being surveyed can be directed to a Web page from either electronic or printed media (e.g., a letter requesting participation). Advantages are that there is no return postage or bulky envelopes to deal with, electronic questions can be presented one question at a time and respondents can be automatically directed to different sections of the questionnaire depending upon their responses or gender or age. The software can employ filter questions to steer respondents to questions that can be skipped because of a previous response without confusing the respondent, or to instructions or a range of responses that are available from drop-down boxes. Another difference between mailed surveys and Web-based ones is that respondents are not able to see how long or lengthy an online questionnaire is. This may work to the advantage of the researcher if the questionnaire is long, but on the other hand, some respondents may be hesitant to open an attachment or begin responding to an electronic survey if the researcher or host site is not known to them, because they may fear acquiring a virus.

Although computers are standard equipment at most places of business, those who send and receive e-mail from home are not a cross-section of Americans but a slice of the more affluent segment of the population. Therefore, the generalizability of findings from Web-based surveys may be problematic if one is attempting to understand the "average" American. However, there is much less of a problem if the population to be sampled can be assumed to have easy access to computers (e.g., university students).

Mehta and Sivadas (1995) have noted these advantages of electronic mail surveys: (1) speed of delivery, (2) virtually no cost, (3) greater control over who may read the e-mail, and (4) convenience of sending and receiving responses. Mehta and Sivadas' experiment compared response content and response rates when mail and e-mail surveys were used. They found that e-mail respondents wrote more comments than the mail respondents and that the best response rates (83%) were obtained when they used prenotification of the mailed survey along with an incentive of $1. Roughly two-thirds of the e-mailed groups with prenotification responded. However, 40% of the e-mail sample without prenotification responded, which was roughly comparable to the 45% return rate from those receiving their questionnaire from the U.S. Postal Service without prenotification or incentive.

Sending out long, unsolicited e-mail surveys may result in complaints from those who may view them as spam. Given the higher response rates that were obtained by using prenotification of the impending survey, it makes good sense to give potential respondents some information about the questionnaire (such as the topic, the number of items, how long it might take to complete it, and, if possible, the benefit or value of the study). Both Web surveys and e-mail surveys work best when the populations to be surveyed are discrete and easily identified (e.g., university students, a specific group of government workers) as well as computer literate.

THE TELEPHONE SURVEY

More expensive than mail and e-mail surveys but less expensive than face-to-face interviews is the telephone survey. Telephone surveys avoid the expenses associated with traveling to the respondent, allow the interviewer to have control over the choice of respondent, and give the interviewer the ability to probe when questions or responses are not understood.

Telephone surveys also allow interviewers access to individuals who will not open their doors to strangers and those who are not ambulatory. Another advantage is that when timeliness is important, special issues can be explored and data gathered almost overnight. A final advantage is that telephone interviewers can be closely monitored and the quality of their work frequently evaluated to ensure that they ask questions correctly and code responses satisfactorily.

A disadvantage of the telephone survey is that the interviewer cannot see the respondent. This means that some items such as the person's race or the condition of the house cannot be observed. When the phone is used, the interviewer misses facial expressions, which can indicate confusion or the beginning of an emotion like anger or sadness. Not everyone can be a successful telephone interviewer; he or she must be articulate, personable, and a good conversationalist. The quality of the interviewer's voice is also important. An interviewer must quickly interest the potential respondent in cooperating and establish rapport before the respondent loses interest. If open-ended questions are used, the interviewer must be able to record the responses quickly and accurately.

Another disadvantage of telephone surveys is that they must be kept short. Telephone interviews should be under 20 minutes long, and the shorter the better. There are exceptions—much longer surveys have been successfully completed by phone, but respondent fatigue can cause hang-ups and incompletions. As a general rule, the more interesting the topic is for the respondent, the greater the probability that the respondent will complete the interview even if it is lengthy.

Some believe that interviewing by telephone is unacceptable because of built-in bias associated with the inability to interview persons who do not have telephones. While it is true that telephone surveys will underrepresent the poorest of the poor, it is estimated that about 80% of households with annual incomes of less than $10,000 in central cities have telephones (Gwiasda, Taluc, & Popkin, 1997). Nationally, about 94% of all American households have telephones (U.S. Department of Commerce, 1997). Except when the most economically disadvantaged are being targeted, telephone surveys are generally thought to be adequate and representative of "most" Americans. Professional market survey and polling organizations do not simply accept the responses of just anyone who answers the phone, rather they often go to great lengths to find individuals who fit a specific category (for example, African-American males with incomes over $30,000). They may reject some households where they already have too many respondents (for example, white females 30 to 45 years of age) in their quest to make their samples representative of the larger population.

The use of a telephone directory to produce samples for telephone surveys can lead to biased data. Police officers, celebrities, single and divorced women, mental health professionals, and public officials often do not have listed phone numbers. And the number of unlisted phones varies markedly by geographical area. To compensate for unlisted numbers, most large-scale telephone surveys use *random-digit* or *added-digit dialing procedures*. With random-digit dialing, the researcher intentionally selects the first three digits for the desired local exchanges, and a computer randomly generates the last four digits. In added-digit dialing, a legitimate "seed number" is provided for those local exchanges from which the samples are to be drawn, and then consecutive digits are added to the last digit or to the last two or three digits. While these procedures result in some phone calls to businesses or others who are not target respondents, it provides a good way of accessing households with unlisted numbers and thus getting a representative sample of all households with phones.

Although telephone response rates are often much better than those obtained from mailed surveys, recent advances in electronic technology have expanded the use of computers in telephone solicitation, resulting in many more "nuisance" calls to households with phones. As a defensive measure, many Americans have resorted to screening their calls with answering machines or with Caller ID services. As many as two-thirds or more of Americans may own telephone answering machines. The use of these technologies and new products still being developed is going to create interesting challenges for those who use telephone surveying techniques. Already the Gallup organization, one of the better-known survey companies in the United States, has noted a decline in response rates from 80% when they first began interviewing by phone in the 1970s to approximately 60% (Farhi, 1992).

Getting the Most from Telephone Surveys

Interviewers need to be trained in the conduct of the survey. This training should include role-plays and interviewing other trainees to ensure that the purpose of each question is well understood. All interviewers should be given

Practice Note: The Reliability of Drug Use Reporting Obtained from Telephone Interviewers

Students and investigators often are concerned about the reliability of sensitive information obtained from telephone interviewers. Aktan, Calkins, Ribisl, Kroliczak, and Kasim (1997) have reported that when 100 respondents, 55 of whom were receiving alcohol and other drug treatment and 45 of whom were randomly selected, were interviewed a second time one week later, the test-retest reliability for all categories of lifetime dependence (for example, alcohol, cocaine, marijuana) exceeded 93%. They concluded that psychoactive substance abuse diagnoses can be obtained reliably over the phone by trained lay interviewers.

standardized introductory statements that move quickly to the survey questions. A brief introduction might go something like this:

> Hello. My name is _____. I'm calling from the Survey Research Center. We're conducting a survey this month of people randomly selected from across the state. The survey will take 15 minutes. We have only a phone number and not any names, so all of your responses will be anonymous. If I have your permission, let me begin by asking how many years you have lived in this state. . . .

It is strongly recommended that the questionnaire and interview procedures be pilot-tested with a small sample ahead of time to determine if there are any unforeseen problems.

PERSONAL INTERVIEWS

The personal interview provides the interviewer with more control than either mail or telephone surveys. The interviewer can read facial expressions and moods, monitor environmental distractions, and determine if the interview should move to a quieter room or be continued at a later date. See, for example, the following report from an interviewer:

> It was a three-ring circus—the respondent had five children ranging from 1 to 8 years and they all had a great time climbing all over the furniture. One child stood on her head on the couch next to me. I managed to hang onto my pencil, the questionnaire, my purse—but it wasn't easy! (Converse & Schuman, 1974, p. 3)

Observational data (e.g., affect, interest in the topic) can also be determined from the personal interview without requiring questions to be asked of the respondent. Further, visual aids can be used to help a respondent. This is particularly advantageous if there is a need for a complex response set. In such situations, the respondent can be handed a card from which to choose a response. Another advantage is that the personal interview usually achieves a higher response rate than either mail or telephone surveys.

The prime disadvantage of the interview is that it is much more expensive than the two other approaches. While interviewers can be paid either by the

■ Practice Note: Interviewing Children

Interviewing young children presents special problems for researchers. They are, for instance, assumed to be highly suggestible. Particularly when children are being interviewed in connection with sexual or physical abuse, the interviewer needs to be extremely cautious about using any leading questions. However, if the interviewer suspects the child's responding indicates a susceptibility to suggestion, several leading questions might be used as a test. In such a situation, the interviewer may want to ask questions that he or she knows to be false such as: "You came here by taxi, didn't you?" (Yuille, Hunter, Joffe, & Zaparniuk, 1993). Having detailed information about some past event (such as a shopping trip, a prior interview) allows the interviewer to assess the accuracy of the child's recall.

While it is important to establish rapport with children before beginning and this may lengthen the

investigatory or research process, most experts feel that children should be interviewed as few times as possible. Yuille et al. (1993) note one study where the average number of interviews of child victims by police was seven per child.

Here are several guidelines for interviewing young children suggested by Boat and Everson (1988):

1. Limit the number of words used in sentences.
2. To check for a child's understanding, do not say "Do you understand what I said?" but ask the child to repeat what was said.
3. When children do not understand a question, rephrase it rather than repeat it.
4. Interviewers should avoid asking questions involving a time sequence (for example, "When was the first time this happened?").
5. Repeat a person's name instead of using pronouns.

hour or by the number of interviews completed, expenses include allowances for travel time to the respondents' homes. Occasionally, multiple trips must be made when appointments are broken (because they have been forgotten or minor emergencies arise). Interviewers can get lost, find it difficult to locate the respondent's residence, or have car trouble. Further, comments hurriedly scrawled in the margin of the questionnaire can become difficult to discern hours later in the office. The safety of interviewers can also be a major concern, and sometimes interviewers must be assigned in teams of two. Supervision and quality control of the interview process can be more difficult to assure than with the telephone survey.

In order to avoid the great expense of selecting a random sample of households, going door-to-door, and then personally interviewing those selected, another approach is called **intercept surveying.** Typically, these surveyors position themselves in malls or on busy streets and attempt to interview those who are willing to stop and talk to them.

Intercept surveys are convenience samples where surveyors seek to fulfill certain quotas or to capture information from persons with certain apparent characteristics (for example, executives carrying briefcases). Even if they strive to reach a cross-section of persons, there's always a problem with self-selection (some people don't like to be stopped on the street). These surveys are limited by the location and times chosen to do the interviewing.

Because they draw nonprobability samples, there is no way to tell whether the data they obtain is representative of the larger population. On the other hand, interviewing convenience samples can be accomplished a lot faster and cheaper than going door to door.

◼ | **Practice Note: Safety Concerns**

On occasion, researchers need to conduct interviews in high-crime neighborhoods. Gwiasda, Taluc, and Popkin (1997) have reported on their experiences in surveying for the Chicago Housing Authority's anti-drug and crime prevention program.

Among the steps they took were to hire residents of the projects as interviewers because they had familiarity with other residents and the neighborhoods; and they avoided interviewing during evenings and weekends. Similarly, they interviewed during months when school was in session. Further, they worked in teams of two and were instructed to complete the interviews in the hallway and to never enter an apartment or building alone.

Surveyors going into risky neighborhoods need to inform residents by letter or newsletters, or even by TV or radio announcements; in other words, by using existing formal and informal networks so that residents can "be on the lookout" for surveyors and reduce possible perils. Certainly, advising the police of the surveyors' presence in the neighborhood is important, and it may be necessary to request additional patrols or to postpone the survey altogether when conditions are too threatening (such as the presence of warring gangs). Giving each interviewer a cell phone might also afford a measure of safety.

Getting the Most from Personal Interviews

The Survey Research Center at the University of Michigan is one of several well-known institutions that have many years of experience in conducting surveys. Another is the National Opinion Research Center at the University of Chicago. Anyone seriously considering conducting a large number of personal interviews for research purposes should start by reading the Survey Research Center's *Interviewer's Manual,* Revised Edition (1976). This very practical publication outlines, in a step-by-step format, what the interviewer should and should not do. Suggestions are provided for such concerns as securing the interview and responding to questions such as "How did you pick me?" and "What good will all this do?" With regard to the first question, the interviewer briefly explains the sampling process. To answer the second question, it is helpful to pull out newspaper or periodical clippings to show the respondent how information from surveys is used.

The Survey Research Center also recommends that the interviewer ask questions exactly as they are worded and in the order in which they appear on the questionnaire. Interviewers are not to assume that they know the respondent's position or response. Every question should be asked, even if a preface is needed ("I know that we have already touched on this, but . . ."). The Center recommends that the interviewer repeat questions that are misunderstood or misinterpreted, and probe when necessary. (You can probe by repeating the question, by being silent for a few seconds and giving the respondent time to expand on his or her thoughts, by repeating the respondent's reply, by making a neutral comment such as "Can you tell me a little more?" or "Anything else?" or by simply stating that you do not understand.)

Internet Resources

The Gallup Organization (http://www.gallup.com) maintains an informative Web site that features in-depth articles on recent surveys that they have conducted as well as other articles on social issues. These change regularly. Depending on the topic, data may be presented that goes back 30 years or more—allowing you to observe trends in American public opinion. Unfortunately, full access to their archives comes only with a paid subscription. An alternative Web site (http://www.pollingreport.com) provides selected data from many polling organizations and is a resource that is free. On these Web sites readers can view the exact wording of questions employed and often can see the sample size and margin of error.

Training should assist interviewers in becoming familiar with the survey instrument so that they don't stumble over words or questions. Taking turns interviewing each other is a good way to achieve a degree of comfort and knowledge of the procedures as well as to identify possible problems with the recording of responses. How to dress should also be covered—interviewers need to look neat and professional but should not dress in a way that calls attention to themselves. If you are a supervisor of interviewers, it is a good idea to review closely the first several completed interviews and then randomly sample the interviews later to ensure that all interviewers are capturing the same type of information.

COMPARISON OF THE APPROACHES

All of the approaches discussed have something to recommend them. Lengthy surveys and complicated questions are sometimes more easily handled by a personal interview. Mailed responses allow the respondent to feel anonymity is protected. E-mail and telephone surveys can be implemented quickly when results are needed fast. Which is the best method? Researchers have to weigh such variables as costs, response rates, the type of questions being asked, the need for confidentiality, the length of the questionnaire, the characteristics of the targeted population in making a decision, how fast the data are needed, and issues as to who the technique includes or excludes. Given all the considerations and limitations, however, surveying via the U.S. mail is likely to remain a favorite method employed by quantitative social scientists for the foreseeable future.

INTERPRETING SURVEYS: POINTS TO REMEMBER

Surveys are versatile and powerful sources of information about the world. However, they can also be flawed—that is to say, in error, even though there was no intent to deceive. In this chapter, as well as in the previous chapter on sampling, we have discussed many of the ways that surveys can be misleading if certain key elements are ignored. Whenever you are reading the results of a survey or preparing to conduct one, certain considerations will help you to evaluate its worth. Knowledge of these factors can help you understand how seemingly similar survey efforts can produce dissimilar conclusions. Here's a checklist to review when evaluating surveys:

✓ *How the sample was drawn:*
  Does the survey employ a probability or a nonprobability design?
  If the sample is a probability sample, are the margin of error and level of confidence adequate?
  Does the sample appear to be reasonable, to have been constructed without bias?
✓ *Sample size:*
  Is the sample adequate for the level of generalization the authors want to make?
✓ *Response rate:*
  Is the response rate greater than 50%?
✓ *Recency:*
  When was the survey conducted?
✓ *Item construction:*
  Are the questions straightforward and clear? Vague? Leading?

Surveys, particularly political polls, may appear to be at odds with one another when in fact they were conducted at different times or used different questions or sampling procedures. Attitudes can and do change over time—sometimes on a national level almost overnight when a president or other important person does something decisive or unpopular.

You shouldn't necessarily be persuaded by a large sample size. I recently read an article in the newspaper about a survey that had been mailed to 5,000 families. "Interesting," I thought to myself. "I wonder how they arrived at that number? Don't they know about random sampling?" As I read further into the article, I became convinced that the researchers didn't know much at all about survey methodology. What were the clues? Here's two: 78% of the respondents were women (what happened to the men?), and they used telephone books to construct their sample frame (we already know what bias that interjects into a study).

Remember our discussion in Chapter 5 of the internal validity threat of testing? The designer of surveys also has to worry about how attitudes are measured. Questions can be too complex or too long, resulting in respondents forgetting the response choices available to them or prematurely terminating the survey. We'll discuss in more detail in the next chapter the effect that wording can have on obtained responses, but you might already have some ideas about how the very act of raising a question can influence a respondent.

One last thing: sometime you may encounter a study in which the authors survey all of a population. For instance, Vissing and Diament (1997) wanted to know how many teenagers were homeless or at risk of homelessness in the seacoast area of New Hampshire and southwestern Maine.

They distributed surveys to 100% of those in attendance at nine high schools and 3,676 students responded. Since the whole population was surveyed, there is no statement about margin of error or level of confidence. Unlike the situation when one draws small samples from a large population, the results obtained from contacting the whole population represent "reality." There is no need to try and estimate **sampling error** (another way of saying margin of error) because no sampling was done.

Don't assume that large numbers of responders always make for a credible survey. For instance, CNN carries a disclaimer on its QuickVote Web page polls that the results are not scientific and reflect only those Internet users who have chosen to participate. Thus, the results cannot be assumed to represent the public in general. (See http://www.cnn.com.)

KEY TERMS

needs assessment	exploratory survey	probe	intercept surveying
community forum	descriptive survey	pilot-test	sampling error

SELF-REVIEW

(Answers at the end of the book)

1. Which approach would be the most labor-intensive?
   a. telephone interview
   b. personal interview
   c. e-mail survey
   d. mail survey
2. T or F. Incentives seem to increase response rates.
3. T or F. It is not uncommon for mail surveys to have response rates of less than 30%.
4. T or F. The use of a telephone directory produces biased samples.
5. The accuracy of the Gallup poll in predicting the results in the last 30 national elections is
   a. extremely accurate (less than 3% error)
   b. somewhat accurate (7%–12% error)
   c. slightly accurate (15%–20% error)
   d. not accurate (more than 25% error)
6. One major advantage of a personal interview over a mailed survey is _____.
7. Exploratory surveys are generally noted by their _____.
8. List three advantages to using the mail questionnaire.
9. T or F. With mail questionnaires a researcher can expect about a 55% response rate.

10. _____ is a pretest of a survey instrument to make sure that potential respondents understand the questions as intended.

11. T or F. Those who send and receive e-mail from home are a cross-section of all Americans.

12. T or F. It is estimated that less than 75% of Americans have phones.

13. T or F. The use of a telephone directory to produce a sample leads to biased data.

14. Lengthy surveys and complicated questions are most easily handled by which method?
    a. telephone
    b. mail
    c. personal interview
    d. email

QUESTIONS FOR CLASS DISCUSSION

1. Assume that you have a budget of $3,500 (exclusive of your own time) with which to conduct a national survey of social workers. What survey approach would you use? Why?

2. How have surveys advanced our understanding of human nature or improved our lives? Cite examples if possible.

3. Cite examples of surveys in which you have participated or experiences you have personally had with surveys.

4. Without referring back to the book, list the advantages and disadvantages of the various survey methods discussed in this chapter.

RESOURCES AND REFERENCES

Adams R. M., Smelser, N. J., & Treiman, D. (Eds.). (1982). Behavioral and social science research: A national resource, Part I. Washington, DC: National Academy Press. In S. E. Fienberg, E. F. Loftus, & J. M. Tanur. (1985). Cognitive aspects of health survey methodology: An overview. *Milbank Memorial Fund Quarterly/Health and Society, 63(3),* 547–564.

Aktan, G. B., Calkins, R. F., Ribisl, K. M., Kroliczak, A., & Kasim, R. M. (1997). Test-retest reliability of psychoactive substance abuse and dependence diagnoses in telephone interviews using a modified Diagnostic Interview Schedule Substance Abuse Module. *American Journal of Drug and Alcohol Abuse, 23,* 229–248.

Boat, B. W., & Everson, M. D. (1988). Interviewing young children with anatomical dolls. *Child Welfare, 67,* 337–352.

Bradburn, N. M., & Sudman, S. (1988). *Polls and surveys: Understanding what they tell us.* San Francisco: Jossey-Bass.

Converse, J. M., & Schuman, H. (1974). *Conversations at random: Survey research as interviewers see it.* New York: John Wiley & Sons.

Corwin, D., & Faller, K. (1995). Children's interview statements and behaviors: Role in identifying sexually abused children. *Child Abuse and Neglect, 19,* 71–80.

Dillman, D. A. (1978). *Mail and telephone surveys: The total design method.* New York: John Wiley & Sons.

Dillman, D. A. (1983). Mail and other self-administered questionnaires. In P. H. Rossi, J. D. Wright, & A. B. Anderson (Eds.), *Handbook of survey research*. New York: Academic Press.

Dillman, D. A. (2000). *Mail and internet surveys: The tailored design method*. New York: John Wiley & Sons.

Farhi, P. (1992). Pollsters looking at who's not talking. *Lexington Herald Leader*, April 15, A3.

Gwiasda, V., Taluc, N., & Popkin, S. J. (1997). Data collection in dangerous neighborhoods: Lessons from a survey of public housing residents in Chicago. *Evaluation Review, 21*, 77–93.

Institute for Social Research, Survey Research Center. (1976). *Interviewer's manual*. (Rev. ed.). Ann Arbor: University of Michigan Press.

James, J. M., & Bolstein, R. (1992). Large monetary incentives and their effect on mail survey response rates. *Public Opinion Quarterly, 56(4)*, 442–453.

Lavrakas, P. J. (1993). *Telephone survey methods: Sampling, selection, and supervision*. Newbury Park, CA: Sage.

Mangione, T. W. (1995). *Mail surveys: Improving the quality*. Thousand Oaks, CA: Sage.

Mehta, R., & Sivadas, E. (1995). Comparing response rates and response content in mail versus electronic mail surveys. *Journal of the Market Research Society, 37*, 429–439.

Moore, D. W. (1992). *The superpollsters: How they measure and manipulate public opinion in America*. New York: Four Walls Eight Windows.

Ransdell, L. B. (1996). Maximizing response rates in questionnaire research. *American Journal of Health Behavior, 20*, 50–56.

Sasao, T. (1994). Using surname-based telephone survey methodology in Asian-American communities: Practical issues and caveats. *Journal of Community Psychology, 22*, 283–295.

Schwarz, N., & Sudman, S. (1995). *Answering questions: Methodology for determining cognitive and communicative processes in survey research*. San Francisco: Jossey-Bass.

Sudman, S., Bradburn, N. M., & Schwarz, N. (1995). *Thinking about answers: The application of cognitive processes to survey methodology*. San Francisco: Jossey-Bass.

U.S. Department of Commerce, Bureau of the Census. (1997). *Statistical abstract of the United States: 1997*. Washington, DC: U.S. Government Printing Office.

Vissing, V. M., & Diament, J. (1997). Housing distress among high school students. *Social Work, 42*, 310.

Warren, K. F. (2001). *In defense of public opinion polling*. Boulder, CO: Westview.

Wilk, R. (1993). Research note: The use of monetary incentives to increase survey response rates. *Social Work Research and Abstracts, 29(1)*, 33–34.

Yuille, J. C., Hunter, R., Joffe, R., & Zaparniuk, J. (1993). Interviewing children in sexual abuse cases. In Gail Goodman and Bette Bottoms (Eds.), *Child victims, child witnesses: Understanding and improving testimony*. New York: Guilford.

ASSIGNMENT 9.1: Locating and Critically Reading a Survey Study

Objective: *To be able to identify studies involving surveys and to be able discuss the strengths and weaknesses of survey efforts.*

For this assignment, you should browse one of the social work journals and locate a research article where the methodology involves the use of a survey.

1. Give the full APA citation of the article that you read:

2. Was a probability or nonprobability sampling design employed?

    a. Was a margin of error reported? What was it?

    b. Give the more specific name for the sampling design.

3. What was the sample size?

4. Does the sample appear to be adequate? That is, does its size and construction give you a sense of confidence in the study's findings? Explain.

5. Did the author devise a questionnaire or scale just for this study or use one already developed? (*Note*: Your instructor may want you to append a copy of the article you read to this assignment.)

6. List three major findings of the study.

ASSIGNMENT 9.2: Creating a Survey

Objective: *To obtain practice in constructing a sampling design.*

In this assignment, think about a community issue or question that could be answered by a random survey of residents. You may use any of the probability designs. Your population might consist of clients of a single agency, students in a university, members of an organization, or citizens in a given community.

1. List at least five questions that you would like answered:

   a.

   b.

   c.

   d.

   e.

2. What is your population?

3. What is your sampling frame and how would you acquire it?

4. What is the name of your sampling design?

ASSIGNMENT 9.2 (*Continued*)

5. What is your margin of error and confidence interval?

6. What sample size would you need?

7. Describe your methodology for obtaining the data you desire.

Unobtrusive Approaches to Data Collection

Secondary Data and Content Analysis

The research approaches we have discussed thus far have one thing in common—they involve interaction with respondents in order to collect the needed data. Unfortunately, any time interviewers interact with respondents there is the potential for producing unintended changes in their attitudes and responses. For example, imagine that you are involved in presenting a workshop to your coworkers on the avoidance of sexist language. A week before the workshop you send each participant a small questionnaire that asks if he or she uses certain terms or phrases in conversation. Suppose Robert Doe reads the questionnaire, briefly considers how he will respond, and then indicates on the form that he does not use any of those terms in his normal conversation. However, driving home from work that night, he reflects back on the questionnaire and realizes that there are several other ways in which his choice of words or phrasing might be considered sexist. As a result of thinking about the pretest, he resolves to eliminate these terms and phrases from his speech and writing.

Your workshop is conducted as scheduled, and you administer the posttest. An examination of the data reveals a decrease in the use of sexist language at the time of the posttest. But if others in the agency had the same experience as Robert Doe, how would you know which had the most impact, the workshop or the pretest? Perhaps any reduction in sexist language was merely the result of respondents' reactions to the questionnaire. It is conceivable that as mild an

243

interaction as testing can bring about changes in attitudes, behavior, or knowledge.

Even if we are considerate and polite about it, asking respondents to give us information about themselves can be experienced as an invasion of privacy. Researchers can roughly gauge this sense of violation by the number of respondents who refuse to cooperate with interviewers or to complete survey forms. And although people may agree to participate, there is still the possibility that merely asking certain questions may have an inadvertent effect on the respondents.

In physics there is a principle, known as the Heisenberg Principle, which states that it is impossible to measure with a great deal of precision both the position and velocity of an electron in motion; the very act of trying to measure the position of an electron may change its velocity. Shouldn't those of us concerned with measurement in the social sciences be equally concerned that our tests and scales might somehow alter the very phenomena we are trying to understand?

One of the more famous examples of an unanticipated effect on research subjects has come to be known as the **Hawthorne Effect.** Prior to World War II, researchers at a Western Electric plant in Chicago found that employees in the study raised their production output possibly because they realized they were being studied. Productivity increased no matter what physical changes were made in their work environment (for example, the lighting was both increased and decreased). What researchers learned is that subjects may be significantly influenced by the knowledge that they are taking part in a research study. In fact, knowing that they have been chosen to participate in a research project had more influence on them than the independent variables.

One way to avoid problems with measurements affecting that which we wish to study is to utilize data that already exist instead of collecting new data from respondents. The use of existing data that does not involve interaction with research subjects fits into the category called **unobtrusive research.** The classic work in this area is that of Webb, Campbell, Schwartz, and Sechrest (1966), *Unobtrusive Measures: Nonreactive Research in the Social Sciences.*

Whether they are aware of it or not, social workers in performing their routine tasks help collect mountains of data each year. The vast majority of these data come from the ordinary processing of clients in and out of service delivery systems. Each use of an admission form, evaluation form, progress note, or social history generates valuable information. These data are not usually collected with research purposes in mind. However, collections of such data represent a wealth of research opportunities for interested social workers.

Researchers who rely on public documents, reports, and historical data are said to be engaged in a type of unobtrusive research called **archival research** or **secondary data analysis.** This type of research involves the analysis of an existing data set that results in knowledge, interpretations, and conclusions beyond those stated in the original study. The intent is not to find fault with another's study, but rather to test new hypotheses or explore questions not examined in the original report. While the original study may have collected data on the attitudes of a cross section of Americans, a secondary analysis might examine only the attitudes of a minority subgroup. Secondary analysis extends or goes beyond what the initial investigators reported. Secondary data analysis has a certain flexibility in that new hypotheses can be easily spun off and tested without a great deal of extra work. Investigators are not limited to a single data set or source document and may utilize several data sets from different sponsors or agencies.

In a fascinating article on the history of child protection efforts, Lindsey (1994) used multiple sources of data to show that reports of child abuse in the United States have risen from approximately 6,000 in 1963 to almost 3 million by 1992. During approximately the same period of time, child murder victims 15 to 19 years of age have increased from under 500 per year in 1962 to more than 2,500 by 1991. Increased reporting of abuse has not reduced child fatalities, and Lindsey speculates as to why this might be. One possibility could be that child welfare professionals are using inadequate technology to assess the risks children face. Another possibility is inadequate funding of child protective services. What other explanations might this secondary trend data suggest to you?

A good use of secondary data is to identify trends. For example, a student once approached me with some concern because she had heard from a relative that her home county had the highest suicide rate in the state. I was somewhat skeptical about this, but when I had the opportunity, I examined several of the Department of Health's Vital Statistics annual reports and found that in the most recent year, the county in question, with a population of slightly more than 12,000, had 7 suicides. This gave it a rate of 52.5 suicides per 100,000 population. (This is a standard basis of comparison; it is used so that urban counties can be compared with rural counties.) This was in fact one of the highest suicide rates in the state, as the overall average for the state was 14.3 suicides per 100,000 population.

This is the information the student had originally obtained for a specific county—it is easy to see why she was concerned:

Number of Suicides	County Suicide Rate	State Suicide Rate
7	52.5	14.3

Had the student gone to the library and looked at the previous year's data, this is what she would have found:

	Number of Suicides	County Suicide Rate	State Suicide Rate
Previous Year	0	0	13.2
Current Year	7	52.5	14.3

Thus, the span of two years, the county had one of the lowest and one of the highest rates in the state. This kind of fluctuation is not uncommon when the actual number of events (such as suicides) is relatively small. This example shows the inherent danger in selectively drawing a single year's statistic instead of examining a longer span of time. Depending on the year she chose for representing the county's problem with suicide, she might have come away with completely different impressions about the need for a suicide prevention program there.

When the secondary data are available, the good researcher wants to examine trends to have confidence that there is a real pattern one way or the other. And so, if you look at the period of time 1980 to 2003, you discover that Tobacco County's suicide rate exceeded the state's average in 17 of 24 years, or about 71% of the time. These data are much stronger than any one year in which something quite strange and out of character might have occurred. As you can tell by looking at Table 10.1, this one rural county has a noticeable tendency to have higher suicide rates than expected. Despite four years when there were no suicides, over the span of time in the study period its average rate was 19.28 per 100,000 population compared to the state average of 13.3%. If you were associated with a suicide prevention program, would you be concerned about this county?

ADVANTAGES AND DISADVANTAGES OF UNOBTRUSIVE APPROACHES

Right away, some exciting advantages of unobtrusive research are apparent. First, if you discover that someone else has already collected data that you can use for a study, you can save considerable time and effort in your data collection phase. Once you identify an interesting database, it is often possible to move rapidly into data analysis. Secondary data sources may already be held by the library or university, or you may be able to purchase them for a nominal fee.

Second, any bias associated with the collection of the data may be generally known and accepted. It may be known, for instance, that the data tend to underestimate the true incidence of a social problem (as in the case of suicide data). Other data sets may overestimate the incidence of a problem. For example, data on psychiatric hospital admissions that didn't differentiate new patients from those patients with previous admissions could overestimate incidence of the most severe form of mental illness. (Epidemiologists use the term **incidence** to refer to the number of *new* cases or events during a given period of time while **prevalence** is the total number of cases present in a population at a given time.) Since all studies have some limitations, the secondary data analyst may choose to use a data set even though it has several known problems. Problems with the data set are not a reflection on the researcher using secondary data analysis. After all, the secondary data analyst is only borrowing the data set.

Third, since you are not interviewing clients or patients or interacting with them in any way, you need not worry that your inquiries will put them at risk or have any harmful effects.

The final but best reason for conducting secondary data analysis is that it both provides an opportunity to study social problems in terms of long-term change and enables comparative study. Secondary data analysts can make

Table 10.1 | Suicide Rate in One Rural County

	Number of Suicides	County Rate	State Rate
1980	1	8.1	13.3
1981	2	15.7	12.1
1982	2	15.4	13.5
1983	4	31.0	13.2
1984	2	15.2	13.7
1985	0	0	13.2
1986	7	52.5	14.3
1987	5	38.1	13.8
1988	2	15.1	13.0
1989	3	22.4	13.2
1990	6	46.4	15.2
1991	1	7.8	13.9
1992	2	15.1	13.8
1993	4	29.7	14.1
1994	3	21.6	13.7
1995	0	0	12.5
1996	3	20.6	12.8
1997	9	61.2	13.0
1998	2	13.6	13.3
1999	2	13.3	11.9
2000	3	19.9	12.6
2001	0	0	12.5
2002	0	0	13.1
2003	1	6.4	13.7

comparisons across localities, states, and nations (presuming, of course, that the data are available).

On the other hand, some disadvantages are associated with relying on secondary or archival data. Sometimes the important historical records you need have been destroyed by fire, flood, tornadoes, or rodents. Occasionally researchers, well into their projects, find gaps in the data because of changes in procedures or policies that affected the data collection. With the passage of time, it is quite possible for variables to change; categories can become more or less inclusive.

I once discovered that a set of child abuse archival data I wanted to explore was compartmentalized. The data were recorded in two different computers in two different formats because the data collection forms had been redesigned. There was no way to combine the data sets into one large file without going to the expense of hiring computer programmers to prepare the data in a more usable form. As a result, I did no research with that data.

If the data were reported more or less voluntarily (there was no penalty for not reporting), it may not be as reliable as when 100% of the units were required to report. Several years ago I was examining one state's outpatient admissions to community mental health centers and found that not all centers were fully cooperating in returning their monthly reports. While the vast majority of these centers did, perhaps 5% didn't. These tended to be small, rural centers without a lot of staff. While their failure to report on a timely basis didn't have a huge effect in terms of the total number of admissions in the state, it did raise questions about the reliability of the data set. Could there have been other, larger agencies that failed to report their admissions on occasion? Did anyone monitor the data to make sure there were 12 reports from each agency at the end of each year? Researchers using secondary data have to be concerned about the reliability of the data that they intend to analyze.

Occasionally agencies alter their reporting practices in ways that adversely affect reliability of the data for future policymakers and analysts. Journalists Matza, Faziollah, and McCoy writing for the *Philadelphia Inquirer* (November 22, 1998) reported in a story entitled "The Victims Suffer Again by Rewrites of Crime Logs: No Record, No Victim, No Financial Help" that Philadelphia police were discovered downgrading assaults so that the statistical profile of crime in the city would be distorted to present a better image.

One estimate was that as many as 10% of all major crimes might have been reduced to minor offenses or wiped off the books altogether. Victims of violent crime, in some instances, did not have their uninsured hospital bills paid because the police did not maintain incident reports. Since the correct numbers of these assaults were not reported, the reliability of the FBI's Uniform Crime Report is called into question.

Finally, recent data may not be available as soon as the researcher may desire it. It is not unusual for some agencies or departments to take 6 to 12 months (or longer) to produce their most "current" annual report of the previous year's data.

In summary, while many advantages are associated with secondary data analysis, you should be alert to changes in data items in terms of completeness, accuracy, or definition.

STATE-MAINTAINED DATA SETS AND SECONDARY ANALYSIS

Secondary analyses can be conducted in both private and public agencies. However, private agencies tend to be more protective of their data. Even though researchers agree not to divulge personal data, private agencies often feel that any research within their agencies may endanger the privacy of individual clients. Another argument often heard from private agencies is that the proposed research will require too much clerical support for locating archival records or selected cases. Unlike private agencies, the data from public agencies and departments are often viewed as public information and available to all. While public agencies are not always as cooperative as many researchers would like, they generally do provide some form of aggregated data each year in the form of annual reports.

Table 10.2 contains examples of variables or **social indicators** (they tell us something about trends within social problems) that are commonly collected by all states. Generally these data are reported by county. Public and university libraries often will be designated as state depositories and will receive reports from governmental agencies.

Table 10.2 | Examples of Variables for Secondary Research

Indicator	Source
Marriages	Department of Health
Divorces	Department of Health
Suicides	Department of Health
Live births	Department of Health
Infant deaths	Department of Health
Deaths (all ages)	Department of Health
Deaths from cirrhosis of the liver	Department of Health
Inpatient admissions	Department of Mental Health
Outpatient admissions	Department of Mental Health
Temporary Assistance for Needy Families cases	Department of Public Welfare
Motor vehicle injury accidents	Department of Highway Safety
Motor vehicle deaths	Department of Highway Safety
Motor vehicle accidents	Department of Highway Safety
Dependency and neglect cases	Department of Child Welfare
Delinquency cases	Juvenile Court Statistics
Arraignments	Supreme Court Statistics
School dropouts	Department of Education
School enrollment	Department of Education
Unemployment	Bureau of Employment
Average weekly earnings	Bureau of Employment
Retail alcohol sales	Department of Liquor Control

APPLICATIONS OF SECONDARY DATA ANALYSIS

If information is power (Francis Bacon noted that "knowledge itself is power"), then the possibilities of being able to effect change are enormous when one has access to secondary data.

Example 1: Suppose you are a school social worker, and a number of children have been injured because there is no traffic light at a busy intersection they cross to get to school. Let's further suppose that "officials" are dragging their feet, saying that a traffic light is not needed. You obtain a list of all the locations where vehicular and pedestrian-injury accidents have occurred in your city in the past year. What if the intersection that you feel needs a light was the site of more injury accidents than any other location in the city for the past three years? Isn't that powerful information that you could use to help advocate for a traffic light?

Example 2: You are a state employee, the supervisor of a child abuse investigation team. You are painfully aware that your unit is understaffed. In talking with others, you sense that your unit may investigate more reported cases of abuse and neglect than any other unit in the state. Yet, when you talk to the agency director about this problem, she is not sympathetic about your need for additional staff. The director indicates that cases of abuse are increasing over the whole state—that it isn't just a problem in your county.

However, because you occasionally have the opportunity to talk to other social workers from across the state, you learn that some investigation units are adding staff, while your unit has added no new staff in three years. A research question forms in your mind. Which county has the highest incidence of child abuse/neglect cases in the state? When you look at the data you discover that while the more populous counties have significantly more cases of abuse and neglect, your county has more cases of child abuse and neglect *per thousand population* than any other county in the state. Would this information be enough to use for leverage to get some additional staff? If not, a next step might be to gather data on how many staff the other investigation units have and which units have the lowest ratio of cases to staff. If your county has the highest ratio (the most cases but fewest staff), this would be compelling objective information that could influence the decision to allocate additional staff to your unit.

This example could be carried further. What if you were to examine the ratio of cases to child protective services staff in your state to those of surrounding states? This type of information might be used to influence your legislators to increase appropriations at the state level. You could also compare salaries of child protective workers in your state with those in other states. If workers in your state are paid below the average, this information could be used for lobbying for increased pay.

Example 3: You become concerned about adolescents' use of illegal drugs in your community. You suspect that a new street drug is the cause of a rash of fatal overdoses, but you have no "hard" data to support this assumption. Since you want to conduct a drug education campaign for adolescents, you feel that local data are needed. You learn that the data are not obtainable from the state

Internet Resources

One Web site (http://www.fedstats.gov) can link you to over 100 federal government agencies that produce statistics, documents, and reports. Some of these agencies are Bureau of Labor Statistics, Bureau of Justice Statistics, Bureau of the Census, National Center for Health Statistics, Administration for Children and Families, Administration on Aging, Centers for Disease Control and Prevention, National Institute on Alcohol Abuse and Alcoholism, National Institute on Drug Abuse, Federal Bureau of Prisons, and Indian Health Service. Another database being maintained by the Urban Institute hosts state data on income security and social services at http://newfederalism.urban.org/nfdb/index.htm.

The Substance Abuse Mental Health Services Administration maintains a Web site with both mental health and drug abuse statistics. There is an Online Database Archive at http://www.samhsa.gov/statistics/statistics.html that not only will let you examine the National Household Survey on Drug Abuse data (as well as other surveys), but will also let you conduct your own data analyses.

The Kaiser Family Foundation (http://www.kff.org) is concerned with major health care issues, particularly those that most affect low-income and vulnerable populations. Statistics and 50 state comparisons are available in such categories as health coverage and the uninsured, health costs, women's health, minority health, Medicaid, and Medicare. The

Children's Defense Fund profiles states on a number of different criteria at http://www.childrensdefense.org.

The United Nations supplies social indicators on the various countries around the world in such areas as childbearing, education, health, housing, literacy, unemployment, and youth and elderly populations at http://www.un.org/Depts/unsd.

Other Web resources you might want to consult include the following:

U.S. Census

    (http://www.census.gov)

Tiger Map Service

    (http://tiger.census.gov)

National Clearinghouse for Alcohol and Drug Information

    (http://www.nida.nih.gov)

National Criminal Justice Reference Service

    (http://www.ncjrs.org)

Child Welfare Information Gateway

    (http://childwelfare.gov/)

National Center for Juvenile Justice

    (http://www.ncjj.org)

Cancer Data

    (http://cancercontrolplanet.cancer.gov/)

---

health department or from the police department. You find, however, that the hospital emergency room keeps this sort of data. Even if the hospital does not make these records available, you may find that the county's ambulance service keeps this data and would be happy to share it.

There is no shortage of ways that secondary data can be used. You could investigate whether the high school dropout rate has decreased within your community over the past five years. Has the dropout prevention program had an impact? Most school systems have good records on the number of dropouts. It would be relatively easy to determine if the dropout rate has changed dramatically. Other uses of social indicators include examining how your state compares with other states in terms of unemployment, teen pregnancies, or some other social problem.

Additionally, you might want to test hypotheses formally. You might want to conduct correlational studies to see if increases in unemployment are associated with increases in mental hospital admissions or if high school dropout rates are associated with juvenile delinquency rates. You could be interested, as Guyer, Miller, and Garfinkel (1996) were, in examining the state-by-state data on child support enforcement in order to understand the limitations of reporting measures employed by public officials, and to design a better index of performance.

Social indicators can also be used to make national comparisons. How does the United States compare with other industrialized countries on such indicators as infant deaths or literacy rates? Have we made advances in the last five years, or have these indicators remained at about the same level?

Scanlon and Harding (2005) used secondary data, along with interviews and existing documents, to examine historical and contemporary alliances between unions and social workers. Bryan (2005) used existing data from drug courts for her secondary data analysis in a dissertation that examined the role that individual and community factors played in drug court outcomes.

There is virtually no end to social indicators that may be gleaned from state and federal departments, bureaus, agencies, and offices. And thousands of organizations collect information on their membership and the services provided to members. Social service agencies across this nation have fascinating questions they would like explored—if only someone with the right combination of research skills and interest would come along.

As you have seen from these illustrations, secondary data analysis is versatile and can be used with problems that vary from those with a macro focus to those with a micro concern. One of the main strengths of secondary data analysis is that there are generally multiple sources of data relevant to the topic in which you are interested.

SECONDARY ANALYSIS OF SURVEY DATA

With the advent of computer processing has come a proliferation of large-scale surveys. These surveys, often with thousands of respondents, are generally available to a broad range of researchers because of the ease with which the data can be shared from one computer to another. These surveys differ in several ways from the occasional surveys social workers conduct.

First of all, these surveys are designed so that they can be easily manipulated by computer processing. This greatly facilitates their use by researchers other than the original investigators. In fact, some of the surveys (for example, the General Social Survey) were designed particularly for secondary analysis.

Second, these surveys tend to use large, national, cross-sectional samples. Some of these surveys (or at least portions of their questions) are repeated at regular intervals, so that trends can be observed over time.

Finally, these surveys often are indexed, and usually even the entire data set can be purchased at nominal cost. Through the Internet, researchers can get a good idea of the data available before purchasing it.

The federal government funds and conducts hundreds of surveys every year. Perhaps the best known of these is the decennial Census of Population and

Public Opinion of the Death Penalty over Time

The public has been polled about capital punishment since the1950s. The following survey data shows how polling organizations track important social issues. Also, this example furnishes a quick glance at the kind of data that already exists from randomly selected national samples of adults, data that could be used with a secondary survey analysis to test hypotheses or research questions. What events or factors do you think might affect the public's attitudes either for or against the death penalty? Do all groups in this country view the issue the same way? In what years were adults most and least in favor of the death penalty?

"Are you in favor of the death penalty for a person convicted of murder?"

Survey Date	Percent For	Percent Against	Percent No Opinion
October 2005	64	30	6
October 2004	64	31	5
October 2003	64	32	4
October 2002	70	25	5
February 2001	67	25	8
February 2000	66	28	6
February 1999	71	22	7
May 1995	77	13	10
September 1994	80	16	4
June 1991	76	18	6
January 1986	70	22	8
January 1981	66	25	9
April 1976	66	26	8
March 1972	50	41	9
May 1966	42	47	11
March 1960	53	36	11
November 1953	68	25	7

Source: This data comes from http://www.brain.gallup.com/poll/ (Retrieval date 9/20/2006).

Housing, but the various agencies of the government also provide for special purpose surveys that supply statistical information on different facets of our national character.

Many of these surveys provide researchers interested in secondary data analysis with exceptional opportunities to explore topics that might have been much more difficult to investigate without the availability of the large data sets. For instance, Maschi (2006) has reported on a secondary data analysis that examined individual and cumulative effects of trauma on male delinquency using a national sample of over 2,000 from a survey conducted in 1995.

Internet Survey Depositories and Databases

The Inter-University Consortium for Political and Social Research (http://www.icpsr.umich.edu/index.html) contains more than 50 data collections on health and medical care, aging, criminal justice, and substance abuse/mental health where the user can perform statistical procedures on the data and create custom subsets without downloading the whole collection and importing the data into a statistical software package. The National Archive of Criminal Justice Data alone contains over 700 data collections relating to criminal justice. Another collection of surveys can be found at http://www.pollingreport.com.

Limb and Organista (2003) examined a statewide sample of over 7,000 MSW students entering California universities between 1991 and 1999 in order to discover whether students of color were more or less motivated than Caucasian students to work with the poor. They concluded that MSW students of color and Caucasian students were more alike than different in professional philosophy—but students of color and American Indian students were somewhat more likely to express views consistent with social work's traditional mission.

These few examples show how secondary data sources can be tapped as resources to support a wide range of research interests.

CONTENT ANALYSIS

Content analysis is another unobtrusive research process that examines the content of communications using quantification. Accordingly, content analysis involves searching for and counting key words, phrases, or concepts in communications. Key words and phrases may be counted (frequencies of occurrence), measured (for example, the size of a newspaper article in column inches or the amount of time allocated to a specific topic in a speech), or otherwise categorized in a manner that others could replicate. Content analysis can be used either retrospectively (to examine materials already in existence) or prospectively (to analyze impending events or narratives). However, the major use of content analysis is to provide a framework so that a quantitative approach can be used to analyze communications after they have been spoken or printed.

Examples of materials that can be content analyzed include newspapers, magazines, journals, books, television programs, audio and videotapes, minutes from agency board meetings, congressional records, presidential addresses, and historical documents such as letters, diaries, and so on.

While the first dictionary definition of content analysis appeared in 1961, its intellectual roots go back considerably further. In 1910, Max Weber proposed a large-scale content analysis of newspapers at the first meeting of the German Sociological Society. Also, around the turn of the century in this country, quantitative newspaper analyses (measuring the column inches devoted to specific subjects) were conducted because of concern that newspapers were not providing as much factual content as they were gossip, sports, and scandals (Krippendorff, 1980).

During World War II, content analysis was used to analyze propaganda. After the war, the value of content analysis as a research tool was widely recognized, and interest in it spread beyond the field of communications to the disciplines of political science, psychology, history, sociology, and literature.

Several interesting applications of content analysis can be found in the literature beyond the field of communications to other social science disciplines. Kramer, Pacourek, and Hovland-Scafe (2003) examined a sample of 50 social work textbooks to see to what extent they dealt with end-of-life content. With three reviewers and using a simple scale (0 = content absent, 1 = content present, and 2 = content is helpful or commendable), they found that only 3.35% of the total content in these textbooks concerned end-of-life issues. The authors found that "the lack of attention to assessment issues at the end of life was a striking feature" (p. 308), and that "the content provided on near-death awareness and near-death experiences was dated and superficial, with no discussion of the implications for practice" (p. 310).

Voorhis and Wagner (2002) conducted a content analysis of content on lesbian and gay people that was published in four social work journals between 1988 and 1997. The authors found that out of 1,974 articles published during the study period, only 77 or 3.9% addressed homosexuality and that the "overwhelming majority of these addressed HIV/AIDS" (p. 347). Only 4 of the 77 articles had a macro emphasis. Interestingly enough, their article closely paralleled a content analysis published 10 years earlier that examined published content in social work journals on persons of color (McMahon & Allen-Meares, 1992). Duran and Brown (2004) have more recently looked at content on elderly racial and ethnic groups that was published in mainstream social work journals between 1995 and 2002.

Santhiveeran (2005) conducted a content analysis of 73 e-therapy Web sites to examine how they conduct therapy, the communication tools they use, and the fee structure. Craig, Cook, and Fraser (2004) examined five years of articles nominated for outstanding research awards by the Society for Social Work and Research. Of 300 articles nominated, 11.5% employed solely qualitative methods, and 25% of these studies employed computer software to analyze the data. Another 11% were of mixed designs (containing both quantitative and qualitative data collection methods). Survey methods (50% of the articles) were the most widely used of the methodologies employed. Of the 16 studies that won awards, 13 or 81% were quantitative in design and the balance used mixed methods. None used only qualitative methods. Two-thirds of all the studies used nonprobability sampling. Slightly more than a quarter of the nominated articles was categorized as intervention research.

Bentley, Walsh, and Farmer (2005) took the findings of a 2001 national survey of social workers' practice roles and activities and conducted a content analysis of two open-ended questions. Bullock (2005) used content analysis to explore the experiences of grandfathers raising grandchildren. Zimmerman, Holm, and Starrels (2001) examined self-help books on relationships appearing on the *New York Times* bestseller list over a 10-year period to determine which books supported a feminist approach to therapy.

Dekel (2004) used content analysis to examine what 11 Israeli mothers revealed in a focus group, and Luquis and Villaneueva (2006) employed content analysis to help summarize the results of eight focus groups conducted with Hispanic women to investigate how cultural factors might influence both knowledge about breast cancer and the importance given to screening for breast cancer. These are just a few examples of content analyses that can be found in the literature. They also show that content analysis is frequently employed in qualitative studies and is very compatible with focus groups, interviews, and open-ended questions.

ADVANTAGES AND DISADVANTAGES OF CONTENT ANALYSIS

Like secondary data analysis, content analysis has the advantages of

- Being unobtrusive
- Being generally inexpensive to conduct
- Allowing the investigator to "mine" existing agency documents and databases
- Being able to deal with large volumes of data

No special training or expertise is required to conduct a content analysis—all that is needed is a research question or hypothesis and a set of communications or a body of materials from which to begin developing categories.

Probably the greatest disadvantage of content analysis is directly related to the methodology of counting individual words, expressions, or events commonly known as the **manifest content.** As you know, often the actual choice of words we use is less important than how we say something. For instance, Wanda asks Renetta if she likes her new apartment, and Renetta responds sarcastically, "I *love* it, the tiny kitchen is especially appealing." Wanda realizes her friend is really *not* impressed with the apartment. As we read this dialogue, we could count the words *love* and *appealing* and conclude that *twice* something good was said about the apartment. Not being there, we miss Renetta's wry smile, the way she rolls her eyes to the ceiling. The context in which something is said or done is often very important. In one study of TV violence, the finding was that 73% of the time the perpetrators went unpunished. However, critics quickly argued that counting incidents of violence without looking at the context means very little. Thus, a police sniper could save a family held hostage by shooting a terrorist and become one of the "perpetrators" who got away (Gunther, 1996).

Besides the countable elements in the source material being analyzed, interpretative readings can be made of the **latent content.** While manifest content is comparable to the surface structure in a message, latent content refers to the deep structural meaning (Berg, 1998). Researchers concerned with latent content need to develop techniques that allow independent coders to corroborate the findings. Identifying three or more detailed excerpts to support each coder's interpretations is recommended (Berg, 1998).

A second disadvantage of content analysis is that it is like archival research in that it relies on material that already exists and therefore prevents the researcher from controlling influential extraneous variables. Unlike experiments, content analysis cannot be used to demonstrate cause and effect.

STEPS IN CONDUCTING CONTENT ANALYSIS

Step 1: Framing a Research Question

Content analysis starts with a research question or hypothesis. Perhaps you have a notion that the newspaper you most frequently read has a negative opinion of social workers or some other definite bias that you want to document. Or you may want to test the hypothesis that fewer articles on community development have been written in social work journals during the past five years than on the topic of managed care. Whatever your interest, some question or assumption that can be tested through an examination of written or spoken communications must be stated.

Step 2: Deciding on Source Materials

From that hypothesis or research question, you begin to think about what materials would provide the best source of communications for the content analysis. Will you use a local newspaper, the *New York Times, Social Work, Social Service Review, Families in Society,* or some combination of journals or papers? Naturally, you have pragmatic decisions to face. The materials should be relatively easy to obtain. You need familiarity with the source materials; some journals or newsletters may be less relevant to your topic than you originally thought.

Step 3: Deciding on Units of Analysis

You will need to decide what will constitute the **units of the analysis,** or the recording units. You may choose to examine words or terms, entire paragraphs, or the whole item itself (for example, an entire article or speech).

The most common units of analysis are individual words or terms. However, if you search for selected key words, you may miss other terms that could also refer to the concept you are studying. Thus, if you instruct reviewers to search for the number of times "clinical social worker" is used in the newspaper, they might overlook references to "family services worker" or "mental health therapist"—both of which could require clinical social work skills. This problem is more likely to occur when computers are used to conduct the content analysis without the investigator pretesting categories on a sample of source materials. A good operational definition of categories or events to be counted is crucial.

Thinking about what you intend to count or quantify generally leads to conceptualizing what categories will be needed. These categories should not be developed apart from the material being reviewed; your familiarity with the material will assist you in devising definitions and categories. As with questionnaire development, the use of a pilot test will assist you in refining the operational definitions of categories. Written rules, especially if more than one person is going to be involved in the content analysis, assist with the classifying and categorizing of data. It is important that categories be exhaustive and mutually exclusive.

The examination of themes from whole items can involve some complex decision rules. Take, for instance, the situation where you want to determine what newspaper editorials reveal about the president. Searching for a set of specific words or phrases (such as "the president is doing a good job in office") may not be of much help because there are so many ways to characterize the president's actions positively or negatively. Then there's the issue of balance—the editorial writers might like some of the president's policies but not others.

Step 4: Deciding on Sampling Design

You also need to decide how much of the source material you can practically review. This is not a problem when the universe of materials is small enough that it is feasible to review all of it. However, if there are hundreds or thousands of items to be examined, then sampling is a logical decision. As discussed in the chapter on survey research, there are several ways to draw a sample. With regard to content analysis, it makes the most sense to think of a random or systematic random design. Convenience samples yield less valuable data.

Step 5: Conducting Reliability Checks

As with other methods discussed in this book, you will need to make sure your results meet the test of replication, especially with regard to reliability in the classification of content categories. Of chief concern is intercoder reliability. If those who code the content don't agree with each other very often, the coding system will not be reliable. Particularly if multiple coders are used, it will be important to compute the reliability (consistency) of the categorization process. Reliability is strengthened when there is practice session training for the raters and clear coding instructions and rules. If one person is doing all of the coding, reliability can still be tested by giving an independent rater the criteria and a sample of the source materials already reviewed. A simple approach would be to select 10 samples and then see what percent of the time Rater A agreed with Rater B.

A PRACTICAL APPLICATION OF CONTENT ANALYSIS

A potential problem for mental health and social service agencies is poor public image. Bad publicity may affect agency admissions or the community's perception of the quality of care provided by an agency. What follows is an account of how content analysis was used as a research tool to bring about needed change.

At one point in my career I was employed by a mental health system that was (so the administrators thought) too often in the local news. A newspaper reporter covered every board meeting, and much of the coverage had a negative slant to it. For instance, one editorial stated that the mental health system had "axed practically all hope of renewing the [mental health] levy with the construction of a $2.2 million building." Since the vote on the mental health levy was more than two years away, such a statement by the newspaper seemed to indicate a stance that was not supportive of the community mental health system's need for the county's property tax levy.

Our fear was that the newspaper had a powerful potential for influencing citizens of the community to vote against the renewal of the mental health levy. Since more than half of the revenue to operate the mental health system came from the tax levy, it became clear that effort should begin right away to counter negative perceptions held by the newspaper staff. Our strategy was to demonstrate objectively how the content of their articles and headlines was not balanced and could have a detrimental effect on public opinion.

Every morning the director's secretary clipped articles from the local newspapers that referred to the mental health system. These clippings were kept in a historical file. Clippings had been kept for about 10 years and constituted an obvious source of material for a content analysis. Since reading 10 years of newspaper clippings was a sizable task, we decided that reading headlines was much more manageable. A listing of all the headlines and captions above the news articles was made, and this constituted our units of analysis.

While our interest was in identifying the amount of negative coverage by the newspaper, this quickly became problematic. It was not difficult to identify those headlines we regarded as negative ("Hostility Erupts at Mental Health Board Meeting," "Mental Health Board in Dispute," "Mental Health Officials Squabble"). In addition, we might have viewed a headline as positive, but the article below it might have been negative. And some headlines were difficult to interpret ("Crisis Center May Resume Services" or "Judge Promises Fast Ruling") without reading the whole article. Consequently, we decided to conduct the content analysis on selected key words.

It was not possible to anticipate every term or key word that indicated a negative reflection on the mental health system. Even clusters of negative words or phrases would have been very difficult to specify. Therefore, we decided to search for those key words that had something to do with the delivery of services or administrative issues.

Among our findings were 37 headlines that, over the 10-year period, contained the key word *facility*. This number of appearances was larger than that of any problem-specific key word, such as *divorce, alcohol, stress, depression, addiction, domestic violence, incest, runaways, death,* and so on. It also occurred more times than population-specific terms, such as *aging, elderly, stepparent, families, teenagers, juveniles, children,* and *students*. Clearly, the newspaper was much more concerned with administrative issues (such as building a new facility) than with service delivery issues.

The number of square inches of newspaper coverage associated with each headline was also included in the study. We found that over 40% of all the coverage dealt with the mental health system's administrative board. The balance of the coverage was spread over the five local mental health agencies that actually delivered services to consumers. We also found that of the three local newspapers, the one perceived to be the most negative was providing about a third more coverage on the mental health system in terms of square inches of the articles than either of the two other papers.

When the study was finished, it was nicely typed and presented during a meeting of the agency and editorial staff of the most negative newspaper. When confronted with the results of the study and examples of how the public could be interpreting their coverage, the editorial staff agreed to review their policies and coverage of the mental health system. Subsequent coverage was much more balanced and presented no opposition to the renewal of the mental health levy.

FINAL THOUGHTS ON UNOBTRUSIVE APPROACHES

This chapter provides only a few examples of secondary data sources and content analyses and illustrations of how they might be used. Unobtrusive methods provide a needed alternative for those situations where resources are lacking for conducting large-scale surveys or other more rigorous forms of investigation, or where the nature of the question or problem does not lend itself to firsthand data collection. Even if we could collect the data ourselves, often there is no need to because someone else has already compiled it.

Given the considerable wealth of information available just for the asking in this society, consider first, before planning a whole new original research project, whether secondary data might provide sufficient needed information. Since unobtrusive methods do not require a lot of research expertise, even social workers who don't think of themselves as researchers can apply them. Finally, informed social workers need to be familiar with the social indicators available in the special fields in which they work.

KEY TERMS

Hawthorne Effect	secondary data analysis	social indicators	latent content
unobtrusive research	incidence	content analysis	unit of analysis
archival research	prevalence	manifest content	

SELF-REVIEW

(Answers at the end of the book)

1. T or F. Mailed surveys can be considered unobtrusive research.
2. How is a researcher who wants to conduct only secondary data analysis limited?
3. T or F. The identification of trends is often an important focus of secondary data analysis.
4. Comparing social service expenditures in Sweden, Ireland, and South Africa with the United States and Canada would be an example of:
   a. content analysis
   b. deconstructionism
   c. secondary data analysis
   d. systematic random sampling
5. T or F. In order to do secondary data analysis, the existing data set you examine must have been developed for a purpose identical to your own research interest.
6. T or F. Content analysis can be used with any set of communications, whether they are written, spoken, or performed.
7. Besides being unobtrusive, what is another major advantage common to both secondary data analysis and content analysis?
8. What is a disadvantage common to both secondary data analysis and content analysis?
9. What is the term associated with content analysis that describes context, subtle meanings, or nuances?
10. T or F. Course syllabi from major universities could be content analyzed to determine if term papers are more common than exams or tests for evaluating students' performance.

QUESTIONS FOR CLASS DISCUSSION

1. On the chalkboard, list the social service agencies where students have worked or been placed in a practicum. In a separate column, list the types of social problems these agencies deal with. Next, make a list of the social indicators that social workers could use to determine if their programs are having an impact on the social problems.
2. Using the social indicators listed in Table 10.2, discuss potential bias in terms of how each might under- or overestimate the extent of a social problem.
3. Among the social service agencies with which you are familiar, what local information do they report to the state capital each year? What should they report?
4. Identify a local issue or controversy in your community or on your campus. Discuss how content analysis might be used to provide some insight into how important this issue is compared to others.

5. Discuss ways that secondary data or content analyses could be used to advocate for clients or for the profession of social work. Suggest studies that need to be conducted.

RESOURCES AND REFERENCES

Berg, B. L. (1998). *Qualitative research methods for the social sciences*. Needham Heights, MA: Allyn & Bacon.

Bentley, K. J., Walsh, J., & Farmer, R. L. (2005). Social work roles and activities regarding psychiatric medication: Results of a national survey. *Social Work, 50(4)*, 295–303.

Bryan, V. (2005). Individual and community-level socioeconomic factors and drug court outcomes: Analysis and implications. (Unpublished doctoral dissertation, University of Kentucky, Lexington.)

Bullock, K. (2005). Grandfathers and the impact of raising grandchildren. *Journal of Sociology and Social Welfare, 32(1)*, 43–59.

Craig, C. D., Cook, P. G., & Fraser, M. W. (2004). Research awards in the Society for Social Work and Research, 1996–2000. *Research on Social Work Practice, 14(1)*, 51–56.

Dekel, R. (2004). Motherhood in a time of terror: Subjective experiences and responses of Israeli mothers. *Affilia, 19(1)*, 24–38.

Duran, A. G., & Brown, S. M. (2004). Elderly racial and ethnic groups: A content analysis of mainstream social work journals, 1995–2002. *The Journal of Baccalaureate Social Work, 10(1)*, 118–135.

Gunther, M. (1996). Latest TV violence study seen as flawed, misread, distorted. *Lexington Herald-Leader*, February 16, A3.

Guyer, J., Miller, C., & Garfinkel, I. (1996). Ranking states using child support data: A cautionary note. *Social Service Review, 70*, 635–652.

Kramer, B. J., Pacourek, L., & Hovland-Scafe, C. (2003). Analysis of end-of-life content in social work textbooks. *Journal of Social Work Education, 39(2)*, 319–299.

Krippendorff, K. (1980). *Content analysis: An introduction to its methodology*. Beverly Hills, CA: Sage.

Limb, G. E., & Organista, K. C. (2003). Comparisons between Caucasian students, students of color, and American Indian students on their views on social work's traditional mission, career motivations,

and practice preferences. *Journal of Social Work Education, 39(1)*, 91–110.

Lindsey, D. (1994). Mandated reporting and child abuse fatalities: Requirements for a system to protect children. *Social Work Research, 18(1)*, 41–54.

Luquis, R. R., & Villaneuva-Cruz, I. J. (2006). Knowledge, attitudes, and perceptions about breast cancer and breast cancer screening among Hispanic women residing in south central Pennsylvania. *Journal of Community Health, 31(1)*, 25–42.

Maschi, T. (2006). Unraveling the link between trauma and male delinquency: The cumulative versus differential risk perspectives. *Social Work, 51(1)*, 59–70.

Matza, M., Faziollah, M., McCoy, C. R. (1998). No record, no victim, no financial help. *Philadelphia Inquirer*, November 22, p. A01.

McMahon, A., & Allen-Meares, P. (1992). Is social work racist? A content analysis of recent literature. *Social Work, 37*, 533–539.

Neuendorf, K. A. (2002). *The content analysis guidebook*. Thousand Oaks, CA: Sage.

Santhiveeran, J. (2005). Use of communication tools and fee-setting in e-therapy: A web site survey. *Social Work in Mental Health, 4(2)*, 31–45.

Scanlon, E., & Harding, S. (2005). Social work and labor unions: Historical and contemporary alliances. *Journal of Community Practice, 13(1)*, 9–30.

Voorhis, R. V., & Wagner, M. (2002). Among the missing: Content on lesbian and gay people in social work journals. *Social Work, 47(4)*, 345–354.

Webb, E., Campbell, D. T., Schwartz, R., & Sechrest, L. (1966). *Unobtrusive measures: Nonreactive research in the social sciences*. Chicago: Rand McNally.

Zimmerman, T. S., Holm, K. E., & Starrels, M. E. (2001). A feminist analysis of self-help bestsellers for improving relationships: A decade review. *Journal of Marital and Family Therapy, 27(2)*, 165–175.

ASSIGNMENT 10.1: Conducting a Content Analysis

Objective: *To identify the key decisions required for a content analysis and to provide experience in conducting one.*

Three different ideas are presented for content analyses. These can be done individually, with a partner, or in a small group. On a continuum that has scientific merit on the right end of the spectrum, the first two projects would be way to the left. These two will yield results that are more fun than academically rigorous. The third idea, however, provides the basis for a project that could, if properly conducted, conceivably result in publication in one or more professional journals. Your instructor will tell you which project to choose and advise you to print out your responses using the following boldfaced terms for the headings in your paper.

Idea 1: Select a popular magazine generally available in drugstores and supermarkets. Select two different issues of the same magazine and skim through them, paying particular attention to the advertisements.

1. State a **hypothesis** that you could test using the advertisements as the source material. (For instance, are there more products being marketed for men than for women? Do the ads appear to target certain income or age groups?)

2. Define your **units of analysis**. (Will you be looking at only ads with pictures or graphics? Do they have to be a certain size? Do personal or classified ads qualify?)

3. Since any one issue (e.g., the December issue) may not be representative of typical issues, state a **sampling design**. How many issues should you review to be confident of your findings?

4. How will you conduct a **reliability check**?

5. Conduct your content analysis. What were your **results**? State the evidence that supports or doesn't support your hypothesis.

ASSIGNMENT 10.1 *(Continued)*

Idea 2: Before watching a movie, identify several behaviors that would not be examples of healthy role modeling for adolescents (e.g., smoking, cursing, violence, etc.).

1. State a **hypothesis** that you could test using the movie as the source material.

2. Define your **units of analysis** (e.g., what behaviors constitute an act of violence? Is kissing or hand-holding a sexual act?). Write down your definitions before watching the movie.

3. For a **reliability check,** get at least one other person (two others would be great!) to count the behaviors that you have identified as the units of analysis to be tallied. Each of you should keep notes independent of the others. (No fair calling out, "There's one!")

4. Compare the findings from the different observers. What were the **results**? Does the evidence support your hypothesis?

Idea 3: Choose a social problem (e.g., poverty, homelessness, drug abuse, mental illness, elder abuse, etc.) or topic that you are passionate about. The purpose of this exercise is to see how much coverage it is receiving in one or more of the major social work journals.

1. Identify the **source materials** (the professional journal or journals that are appropriate for your investigation and the time frame covered).

2. State a **hypothesis** or research question that you could test using the journal as the source material.

ASSIGNMENT 10.1 *(Continued)*

3. For this exercise the **units of analysis** can either be the number of articles on a particular topic or the number of pages devoted to a particular subject. Both of these can be easily determined from reviewing the journal's table of contents.

4. Since many social work journals have been in existence for decades, what **sampling design** will you use? How many tables of content will you review? How many years will you survey?

5. What would be a good plan for a **reliability check**?

6. Conduct your content analysis. What were your **results**? State the evidence that supports or doesn't support your hypothesis.

ASSIGNMENT 10.2: Conducting a Secondary Data Analysis

Objective: *To identify the key decisions required for a secondary data analysis and to provide experience in conducting one.*

Three different ideas are presented for content analyses. These can be done individually, with a partner, or in a small group. Your instructor may allow you choose from the three or may direct you to a particular one. Be sure to describe your project clearly and then use the following boldfaced terms for headings in your paper.

Idea 1: County Comparisons within a State. This chapter contains a table listing social indicators (e.g., births, deaths, suicides, school dropouts, etc.) that generally can be found in state-maintained data sets. You may want to go back and skim that table. Then, choose one of the indicators and try, by going to the Internet, to find relevant data from your state for the past 5 to 10 years. Once you are sure the data are easily accessible, follow the steps below. Before getting started, though, you might want to think about other variables that might help you to interpret your findings. For instance, would you want to consider the population of each county in terms of children under 18 if you are examining school dropout rates? Some databases may provide rates and ratios; others may provide only raw numbers. Rather than compare raw numbers county by county, it would make sense to look at rates or ratios (i.e., dropout rate per 1,000 students enrolled, suicide rate per 100,000 population).

1. State a **hypothesis.** For example, might urban counties have proportionately more of this problem than rural counties? Might a different problem (e.g., suicides) be more of a problem for older adults than younger adults?

2. Identify your **source materials** (e.g., the department that maintains the data) and the number of years you intend to survey (go back five years unless your instructor tells you differently).

3. Identify your **social indicator.** Is it a ratio or rate? If so, explain.

4. Define **other key variables.** For instance, what is a rural county? An urban county?

ASSIGNMENT 10.2 *(Continued)*

5. What are your **findings**?

6. **Why** do you think you found the results that you did?

Idea 2: State Comparisons. This chapter contains several suggestions for Internet resources that provide data sets that allow for state-by-state comparisons. Explore a few Web sites until you find an interesting variable. Then, choose one of the indicators and compare your state with one that is similar to it in population (e.g., Montana and Idaho or Nevada and New Mexico). Once you are sure the data are easily accessible, then follow the steps below. Before getting started, though, you might want to think about other variables that will help you to interpret your findings. If the database supplies only raw numbers, you might want to convert those numbers to rates or ratios based on population or some other variable.

1. State a **hypothesis.** Do you expect both states to have similar rates of the indicator?

2. Identify your **source materials** (e.g., the agency that maintains the data) and the number of years you intend to survey (go back five years unless your instructor tells you differently).

3. Identify your **social indicator.** Is it a ratio or rate? If so, explain.

4. Define any **other key variables.**

5. What are your **findings**?

6. **Why** do you think you found the results that you did?

ASSIGNMENT 10.2 *(Continued)*

Idea 3: National Comparisons. Choose a social problem like infant mortality or illiteracy, and find a database from the United Nations (http://unstats.un.org/unsd/) that will allow you to compare one nation with another. You might want to examine the social indicator in terms of other variables—such as the amount of money spent on military expenditures. You might want to compare countries which have similar geography in common—for instance, choose two countries in Africa or two in South America.

1. State a **hypothesis.** Do you expect both nations to have similar rates of the indicator?

2. Identify your **source materials** (e.g., the agency that maintains the data) and the number of years you intend to survey (go back five years unless your instructor tells you differently).

3. Identify your **social indicator.** Is it a ratio or rate? If so, explain.

4. Define any **other key variables.**

5. What are your **findings?**

6. **Why** do you think you found the results that you did?

Qualitative Research

One summer day I was driving through a rural part of Appalachia where years before the chief source of income had been coal mining. As the deep, rich veins of underground coal had been depleted, high rates of unemployment caused many families to live in abject poverty in the midst of the lush greenery of Daniel Boone National Forest. As I slowed to pass through one small town, I casually looked off to the side and immediately noticed a young man who was unlike any others I had ever seen. The right side of his face hung loose and sagged like a large deflated balloon, the skin hanging four or five inches below his chin. At first, I thought my eyes were playing tricks on me and that he was wearing a Halloween mask. But he wasn't. The left side of his face, as best I could determine, appeared ordinary. He was engaged in a conversation with two other fellows who, by their mannerisms, seemed to suggest that everything was quite normal.

I didn't stop the car and talk to the young man, although I burned with curiosity about him. Had he been told there was nothing medical science could do for him? Indeed, had he even sought medical attention, or had he merely assumed that nothing could be done?

Had he led a sheltered life, kept from school where children would have made fun? Or was he "mainstreamed"? Did he finish high school, did he work? Did he have many friends? What psychological defense mechanisms had he developed to protect him from the stares of strangers? Did he have an intimate partner? What was the quality of his life? What were his hobbies and how did he pass his time? What did he look forward to? What were his goals and aspirations?

Was he "normal" in intelligence? What was his personality like? Was he bitter and angry? Did he have a sense of humor? In short, who was this man? What was his world like?

If you find yourself reading these questions and almost automatically thinking that you, too, would like to have interviewed this young man in depth, then you may be thinking like a qualitative researcher. As Deborah Padgett (1998b) notes,

> Qualitative methods are inherently *inductive;* they seek to discover, not test explanatory theories. They are *naturalistic,* favoring *in vivo* observation and interviewing of respondents over the decontextualizing approach of scientific inquiry. As such, they imply a degree of *closeness* and *absence of controlled conditions* that stand in contrast to the distance and control of scientific studies. (p. 2)

WHY CONDUCT QUALITATIVE RESEARCH?

There are several reasons why an investigator might choose to examine a problem or phenomenon qualitatively rather than quantitatively. For instance, you might select a qualitative approach if you can't find a quantitative instrument that meets your needs, if the one you find is not appropriate for the population, if you want to investigate a "hidden" or "hard-to-reach" population (Neale, Allen, & Coombes, 2005), or if you want to study a phenomenon in its natural setting. Additionally, Padgett (1998b) has suggested these reasons:

1. When little or no literature or previous studies are available on the phenomenon.
2. When the topic requires great sensitivity to explore it.
3. When the investigator wishes to obtain the perspective of participants in their own words and actions and wishes to write a "rich description" of it. (The term **emic** is used to describe studies from the participant's perspective.)
4. When the focus is on the process and not the outcome of a program or activity (e.g., what happens during an intervention).
5. When the quantitative findings don't go far enough or need more explanation.

A qualitative approach might be chosen any time detailed, in-depth information is desired. It is *not* the appropriate approach if one wants answers to factual questions involving quantifiable variables. A quantitative approach would be needed to answer such questions as: what percent of my clients are over the age of 25? How many have been previously diagnosed with an anxiety disorder? Or, what is the proportion of female to male clients?

However, if you wanted to understand on a deeper level what the lives are like for those college students with clinical anxiety who are struggling to go to school and work, then you would probably want to approach this topic qualitatively.

Qualitative researchers can begin their investigations and examine the phenomenon or problem of interest through a variety of methodological approaches—there is not a single qualitative approach or single formalized process. Qualitative research is more of a generic term than a precise description of a methodology. What qualitative designs tend to have in common is that the researcher is, foremost and above all, considerably *involved* with the collection and analysis of data from individuals. This normally requires a sustained contact with the study participants in their natural settings (as opposed to the brief or minimal exchange of a survey). The focus is always on the individuals' lived experience of their world and the meanings they attach to it. And last, qualitative research is characterized by a narrative or descriptive report of the findings. The steps that one would follow in a qualitative study depend upon which methodology the researcher thinks would best provide the information that he or she desires. There are numerous methods that qualitative researchers use—too many, really, to be covered in this chapter. One effort at listing them might include these methodologies:

Action research	Memory work	Life-world analysis
Analytic Induction	Field Research	Mixed methods
Biographical research	Framework analysis	Narrative analysis
Conversation Analysis	Grounded theory	Objective hermeneutics
Constructionism	Hermeneutics	Phenomenography
Comparative analysis	Interpretative Phenomenological Analysis (IPA)	Phenomenology
Discourse analysis		Symbolic interactionism
Ethnography	Life History	Template analysis
Ethnomethodology		

A brief description of each of these can found at the following Web site connected with MAXqda (a special software program for qualitative data). If you are interested in qualitative methods, http://onlineqda.hud.ac.uk/resources.php is a rich Web site with suggested readings and links for various methodologies.

Despite the array of approaches shown above, there are commonalities shared by all the qualitative methods; the purpose of this chapter is *not* to provide you with in-depth information about each of these methods, but to provide a general overview to introduce you to qualitative research.

We'll start with the qualitative approach known as the case study.

THE CASE STUDY

The young man in the previous description can be thought of as an example of persons with severe facial deformities. Looking into his situation could shed light on the problems and difficulties he experienced as well as ways of coping that he had learned. The value of focusing on this one individual is in the possibility that examining his situation will shed some light on the phenomenon of social adjustment of those with facial deformities. Even though no two cases will ever be exactly alike, there are things that can be learned from this example that might help social workers, doctors, nurses, and rehabilitation specialists when they work with other patients of this type. It is usually the uniqueness of the case that makes it worthy of study; for the qualitative researcher there is no interest in generalizability.

These are typically the steps followed in a case study:

1. Selecting the case (one must decide whether the unit of analysis will be an individual, a social service program, a neighborhood, a school, a community, an incident [e.g., a plane crash], or organization of some sort [e.g., a social service agency or even a street gang, etc.]).
2. Determining the issues and questions to be focused upon.
3. Selecting the sources of data to draw upon. For example:
   • interviews with neighbors, school officials, etc.
   • available documents and records
   • visits with and direct observation of the case
4. Collecting the data. Gaining entry to and the trust of those capable of providing useful information about the case is always a major consideration and sometimes challenge for the qualitative investigator.
5. Interpreting and analyzing the data.
6. Writing the report.

Qualitative researchers seek to understand the life experiences of those who may not be visible or well-known to "mainstream" society. For example, Marc Sherrod (2005) has written about understanding the Appalachian way of death and his challenges in accepting the folk practices of some inhabitants of western North Carolina who kept "memory pictures" of deceased loved ones in their caskets. They may also seek to describe the social worlds of drug addicts, prostitutes, the chronically mentally ill, illegal immigrants, persons dying of terminal illness, victims of abuse, or mothers who have put children up for adoption. Qualitative researchers want to understand the experiences of selected individuals—not to test hypotheses so much as to examine a culture or way of life through the perspective of those living it.

Problems framed by large numbers (for example, nationally more than 500,000 children are in substitute care) can be difficult to understand on a personal level. This is the value of qualitative research—its ability to help us translate social problems by examining closely the lives of a few.

A qualitative researcher conducting a case study would likely use as many sources of information as is feasible and the strength of that approach is that the same patterns or themes can emerge from different informants, a review of documents, etc. However, the qualitative researcher may devise a study that only involves interviewing.

Examples of Case Studies in Social Work Literature

Macro Focus Case Study Examples:

Balaswamy, S, & Dabelko, H. I. (2002). Using a stakeholder participatory model in a community-wide service needs assessment of elderly residents: A case study. *Journal of Community Practice, 10(1)*, 55–70.

Kotval, Z. (2006). The link between community development practice and theory: Intuitive or irrelevant? A case study of New Britain, Connecticut. *Community Development Journal, 41(1)*, 75–88.

Malks, B., Schmidt, C. M., & Austin, M. J. (2002). Elder abuse prevention: A case study of the Santa Clara County Financial Abuse Specialist Team (FAST). *Journal of Gerontological Social Work, 39(3)*, 23–40.

Spath, R., & Pine, B. A. (2004). Using the case study approach for improved program evaluations. *Child and Family Social Work, 9*, 57–63.

Micro Focus Case Study Examples:

Bergeron, L. R. (2001). An elder abuse case study: Caregiver stress or domestic violence? You decide. *Journal of Gerontological Social Work, 34(4)*, 47–63.

Charles, L. L., Thomas, D., & Thornton, M. L. (2005). Overcoming bias towards same-sex couples: A case study from inside an MFT ethics classroom. *Journal of Marital and Family Therapy, 31(3)*, 239–249.

Lemieux, C. (2001). The challenge of empowerment in child protective services: A case study of a mother with mental retardation. *Families in Society, 82(2)*, 175–186.

Poindexter, C. C. (2003). Sex, drugs, and love among the middle-aged: A case study of a serodiscordant heterosexual couple coping with HIV. *Journal of Social Work Practice in the Addictions, 3(2)*, 57–83.

Rogers, P., Gray, N. S., Williams, T., & Kitchiner, K. (2000). Behavioral treatment of PTSD in a perpetrator of manslaughter: A single case study. *Journal of Traumatic Stress, 13(3)*, 511–519.

THE QUALITATIVE INTERVIEW

The qualitative interview is like an in-depth or planned conversation where there are a set of initial or guiding questions. Typically, these are few in number but very broad in nature so that they elicit a narrative from the individual being interviewed. Questions which can be answered with a short "yes" or "no" and those with multiple-choice response formats are not employed very often. The researcher's role is to ask for more information by probing content further. The researcher may capture more details by saying something like, "Tell me more about that." Or, "What were your friends doing while you were doing this?"

From responses received from questions, interviewers frame new questions that may not have been planned and may actually lead into new areas of inquiry. Qualitative interviewers have more flexibility and are less structured than survey interviewers. The emphasis for qualitative interviewers is on fully exploring the phenomenon—examining it in depth. Qualitative interviewers are free to share their own personal experiences and share their own narratives with the individual being interviewed as a way of building trust and rapport.

Because it is difficult to write down everything, and because the researcher doesn't want to lose important material, key interviews might be taped so that they can be listened to again and transcribed. Stories, jokes, and even digressions can be important for what they may reveal about the worldview or culture of the informant being interviewed. The interviewer often takes the position of one who is a learner and ignorant of the informant's daily life—this frees the informant to become a "teacher" who can explain the nuances or details that might otherwise not be explained or mentioned.

According to deMarrais and Laplan (2004), the qualitative interviewer needs to avoid

- Long, complicated questions
- Yes-or-no questions
- Vague questions that don't bring out specific details
- Leading questions based on the researcher's pet theories or assumptions
- *Not* paying close enough attention to subtle signs that the individual might have more information to share if asked

As we discussed in a previous chapter, qualitative interviewers do not prepare detailed questionnaires as a quantitative investigator might. However, they may use structured or standardized interview schedules—which are particularly useful if more than one interviewer is involved.

The person being interviewed is acknowledged as the insider, the teacher, the expert concerning his or her world, and the qualitative researcher seeks to enter into that subjective reality, to discover that unique world. Unlike diagnostic or investigatory interviews that social workers may conduct, the qualitative interviewer does not try to maintain a formal distance or "objective" stance. The interview is conversational and the goal is to form a dialogue to facilitate the investigator's journey (Franklin & Jordan, 1995).

PARTICIPANT OBSERVATION

Researchers in the qualitative tradition might observe only, but on occasion they may choose participant observation—meaning that the investigator would try, as much as possible, to become fully immersed in the culture of those being observed by living alongside them and sharing their activities (without violating personal or professional ethics, of course). Even though we will discuss participant observation and observation separately in this section, they are best thought of being on a continuum with some qualitative studies involving observation only, some projects completely involving the observer as a participant, and other studies employing both interviewing and observation.

Although the research is quite dated now, some of the best (and most fascinating participant observation) was done by Rosenhan (1973). Eight sane "pseudo-patients" sought admission at a variety of psychiatric hospitals. All were admitted when they complained of hearing voices and were kept an average of 19 days (the range was from 7 to 52 days), although they ceased simulating any symptoms once they were admitted. None of them were detected as being sane, and most were discharged with a diagnosis of schizophrenia "in remission." Try to find the time to read his article, "Being Sane in Insane Places."

Other "classic" examples of participant-observer research might interest you as well. See, for example, Caudill, Redlich, Gilmore, and Brody (1952); Deane (1961); Ishiyama, Batman, and Hewitt (1967); Goldman, Bohr, and Steinberg (1970); and Estroff (1981).

For an extra-credit assignment one semester, an MSW student at my university attempted to find out how the public would view her if she were morbidly obese. She went to a thrift store and bought the largest sweater and the largest pants she could find and then used foam stuffing to make herself appear to weigh about 400 pounds. Once her disguise was in place, she went to a local mall and visited stores like Victoria's Secret. She said she was surprised that no clerks even asked if they could be of help when she was "fat," but they were eager to assist her when she went back without the padding.

Contrast that participant-observer study with an observational study where a social work student goes into a classroom of second graders where three or more pupils are known to have Attention Deficit Hyperactivity Disorder (ADHD). As a quantitative researcher, the social work student might have constructed hypotheses to test, and might have prepared a standardized observational form that could count, for instance, the number of times that the ADHD kids walked away from their desks during instruction, or recorded the duration of specific activities (like not paying attention by looking around the room). However, qualitative researchers don't go into a study with hypotheses, as a rule, and would be unlikely to use standardized forms in their observations.

Observation for the qualitative researcher involves capturing full visual details as well as auditory and sensory aspects of a classroom or other environment. Qualitative researchers would very likely note that the wall between the two second-grade classes was very flimsy and that it was very distracting to hear the students from the other class talking loudly with their teacher while having to sit in a different classroom with a soft-spoken and demure teacher. The qualitative researcher would *definitely* note the hamster in the blue plastic ball rolling about the classroom and colliding with students' desks, and the street noise from trucks and traffic coming in the open window. In other words, quantitative researchers tend to not pay a great deal of attention to the context from which their data are drawn while good qualitative researchers record as many details as possible.

What exactly does one observe during an observation? Gall, Borg, and Gall (1996) suggest some possible facets:

POSSIBLE OBSERVATIONAL FACETS IN A QUALITATIVE STUDY

- The physical environment and context (where is the observation taking place and what is the occasion?)
- The participants (who is in the setting?)
- Interactions/behaviors (what are the participants doing? What behaviors are allowed, discouraged, punished, encouraged? What activities are planned? Are the activities planned or spontaneous? Are there routines?)
- Nonverbal communication (how do participants communicate nonverbally?)

- Appearance (is there a special way of dressing to indicate rank or status?)
- Organization (how are the participants organized? Is there a hierarchy?)
- Speech patterns (is there a special vocabulary or way of speaking?)

In addition to these elements, the qualitative researcher usually records his or her own interpretations (the meanings the researcher intuited), and may note any of the participants' reactions to the observer, as well as how any behaviors affected the observer. (For instance, a qualitative researcher might grow so frustrated with a second-grade teacher who talked too softly that the researcher might make a personal resolution to talk louder in group situations to ensure that she is always heard.)

Observation may be either overt, where it is clear to the participants that they are being observed, or covert when it is conducted surreptitiously. When observation is overt, it is important that the observer's presence not change the nature of the activities normally occurring. Good qualitative researchers take the time both to allow the participants to get to know the investigator and to establish rapport and trust.

When Has Enough Data Been Collected?

There are several different indicators that can be helpful to the qualitative investigator for identifying when enough data have been collected.

- When the investigator has interviewed or collected data from all of the available key informants
- When there are no new findings or discoveries
- When there is enough consistency in the data that the investigator reaches "theoretical saturation"—the point at which new data replicate earlier findings

Padgett (1998b) suggests that there is no good answer to the question of how many participants are needed in a qualitative study: "Because the emphasis is on quality rather than quantity, qualitative researchers sample not to maximize numbers, but to become 'saturated' with information about a specific topic" (p. 52).

What Does Qualitative Data Analysis Involve?

Unlike quantitative data analysis which involves statistical analysis, qualitative data analysis entails coding data into constructs and looking for themes or patterns that can describe the phenomenon. Qualitative investigators often have tens if not a hundred or more pages of text which have come from their field notes or from transcribed interviews or observations. While the search for themes and patterns can be done manually if the data set is small, qualitative investigators frequently employ computer software to manage the data and organize the findings. There are many qualitative software products available for turning documents into searchable databases.

Some allow the user to index and retrieve, in addition to written text, images, as well as audio and video material. A partial list of computer software programs includes: NVivo, Nud*ist, Metamorph, Ethnograph, Kwalitan, askSam, Folio VIEWS, HyperRESEARCH, MAXqda, and Qualrus. Go to their Web sites to learn more about them. Several allow you to download free demos. The exact type of software one needs is dependent upon the type of qualitative research one is doing.

Note that the software do not "process" or "analyze" the data. They simply facilitate the sorting and ordering of passages that the investigator identifies. Documents are imported into the computer software and a database is created. These data are unstructured ("free text")—unlike the variables in quantitative research. In quantitative data analysis the researcher knows before data collection begins which variables will be examined and even what statistical procedures will be used. In qualitative data analysis the researcher doesn't know what themes or patterns might emerge from the data and very seldom are statistical procedures used.

Once the data are entered into a database, the investigator reads the text and identifies meaningful units of information. This step can be thought of as breaking the data into digestible chunks. When an observation or quotation is found that might be illustrative outside of the passage or the context in which it is imbedded, it can be highlighted or coded so that it can be found later and grouped into a category or theme. These chunks can be a phrase or sentence, one or more paragraphs—the researcher is not limited to length. Another way of thinking about this process is that the investigator is identifying *meaningful* units of information from the data. These units or decontexualized segments are grouped into constructs or categories. This coding process is known as "**open coding.**"

Identifying units of information that may reveal something about the phenomenon being studied relies entirely upon the researcher's reading of the material and his or her construction of what might make sense to group into categories—and even what categories exist within the data. A frustrating thing for quantitative investigators is that two different qualitative researchers can read the same passages but group the chunks into different categories or themes depending upon their life experiences, knowledge, intuition about the data, etc. It would be wrong to think that there is only one set of "true" themes or categories that lie within a data set just waiting to be discovered by the "right" qualitative researcher. It may be possible in some instances, however, to start with categories defined by other researchers, but this is not mandatory. Most qualitative investigators develop their own categories and allow them to emerge from the data collected rather than from studies or theories. This is known as **grounded theory** because the themes are "grounded" in the original data collected by the investigator and his or her careful line-by-line reading of the material. This is an inductive approach because theory may arise from the data.

The qualitative researcher will usually read all of the collected material multiple times to ensure that all the meaningful segments are identified and coded. As a next step, all of the segments composing each of the categories will be read or printed out so that the investigator can check to make sure that they have meaning within each category as well as that the categories are unique and not overlapping. During this step the investigator may read the passages composing each of the categories or themes multiple times. This is called **constant comparative analysis** and is an iterative process that involves checking for the best fit for coded passages.

Farber (2006) provides a good example for understanding this process using a closet full of clothes. Imagine on your first entrance into the closet you notice all of the jeans that are folded on a top shelf. This might represent a category by itself or they might be included in a category that included pants and slacks. After you have identified all of those items, you might turn your attention to shirts. Shirts might be coded as a single category initially and then on a subsequent visit might be conceptualized as those that are short-sleeved and those that are long-sleeved. You might even choose to develop separate categories for "dress" shirts or blouses and casual shirts. If you are female, there may be skirts in your closet that deserve a separate category as would shoes, and so on. As you think about the items in each category, different facets might emerge. For instance, you might decide to code the items by color. Or by whether it had sentimental value or not, or by whether it was worn only on "special" occasions, or by its quality. What might you learn by examining the clothes in someone's closet?

When sorting written excerpts into categories, the same passage might be coded or shared in two or more categories. For instance, in an interview with a street gang, this passage: "I couldn't live without my gun. It is like, the main thing. No respect without a gun" might be coded to show that the gun is needed (a) for self-protection, and (b) because it places a gang member a rung higher in the gang's pecking order because it forces respect. There's the possibility that it could be coded in some other way (e.g., as part of the standard "uniform" that conveys membership in a particular group, along with a certain kind of jacket or tattoo).

Qualitative research must present the lives of others and convey these perspectives in a convincing way. Drisko (2005) cautions against using a single, brief quotation to illustrate an entire category or class of findings—what he calls the "sound bite" approach. Instead, he says, "[The] key is to provide the reader with ample raw data—the words and views of participants in their own voices. Use lots of direct quotes . . . let participants' views come alive to the reader" (p. 592).

Here's an example of how Swanberg and Logan (2005) used the stories of women who were trying to remain employed though they had abusive partners. They write,

> Among respondents who suffered beatings prior to work, the majority of them attempted to go to work. One participant reported:
>
> > [H]alf the time I wouldn't even want to go [to work] . . . I feared what he'd do [to me] before I went to work. One time he had beat me so bad I had to walk to work and I don't even know how I made it. Since then I'm cautious before leaving for work.

Characteristics of Qualitative Research

No experimental studies: There is no control group, no experimental design or manipulation of the variables associated with the phenomenon under study. However, there can be qualitative evaluations of programs.

Naturalistic: Unlike quantitative research, qualitative research (sometimes called field research because of its emphasis on conducting the study in the subjects' natural environment) is not as structured in the sense of knowing exactly what questions will be asked of whom and in what order. In fact, field researchers are quite comfortable with letting the study evolve and flow in unknown directions. Before going into the field, they may not have identified all of the persons they hope to interview or even all the questions they want to ask. Many rely on a snowball methodology where one informant may lead them to another and so on.

Participant observation: Researchers in the qualitative tradition rely primarily on in-depth interviewing and observations. They try, as much as possible, to "walk in the shoes" of the participant, to seek to understand the meanings associated with the participant's world.

Small sample size: Qualitative researchers do not worry about obtaining large, representative sample sizes. For example, Davidson (1997) conducted a qualitative needs assessment of relatives providing care for children who might otherwise have gone into foster care. Although she randomly drew names from a list of 420 relative caregivers, Davidson's goal was to obtain 10 interviews. She actually completed 9.

Little use of measurements: Unlike quantitative research, which deals with measurements and numerical values almost exclusively, qualitative research may use scales or questionnaires, but most don't. The investigator is the research tool; all data are filtered through his or her eyes and ears.

Journalistic narrative: The analyses produced by qualitative researchers most often are narratives and are based on the words used by informants to describe their life experiences. Jill Berrick (1995), for instance, learned enough as a participant-observer of five impoverished families to write a book entitled *Faces of Poverty: Portraits of Women and Children on Welfare*. Again, the emphasis is not on the quantity of subjects but on the rich details, the subtleties and interactions that may be overlooked by others.

Exploratory: Qualitative researchers explore problems and phenomena about which little is known. Unlike quantitative research, seldom is there any interest in testing a hypothesis or theory. While quantitative researchers tend to be *deductive* (using a specific theory to make predictions about a particular situation), qualitative research is basically *inductive*—generating new theory from the observation of a special phenomenon or situation.

Value-free: The researcher's position is that of learner, not expert or specialist; he or she wants to know "What's going on here?" Assumptions and prior knowledge are held in abeyance until the latter stages of the analysis when they may then be compared to the findings. (Morse & Field, 1995)

Another woman noted a particularly difficult situation:

> I was about seven months pregnant. . . . he started kicking me in the sides; I had a boot print on my side for months. . . . I went to work, I did not know what else to do.

Another woman who shared a car with her then boyfriend described missing work or reported to her job as a waitress late because she "wait [ed] for him to return from work with the car from his shift. He was always late, or he would not show up at all sometimes." (pp. 6–7)

Qualitative researchers are flexible; their research goals or questions may be altered even while data are being collected. While they usually have a

Books with Ethnographic Perspectives

Ethnography is a type of qualitative research closely allied with cultural anthropologists. The goal of this type of research is to describe a culture or society from the perspective of the insiders—those living in it. The following books not only are interesting to read but also illustrate the necessity for a prolonged engagement approach that is characteristic of this type of qualitative research.

Conover, T. (2000). *Newjack: Guarding at Sing Sing*. New York: Random House.

Griffin, J. H. (1961, 1996). *Black like me*. New York: NAL/Dutton.

Kotlowitz, A. (1991). *There are no children here: The story of two boys growing up in the other America*. New York: Doubleday.

Liebow, E. (1993). *Tell them who I am: The lives of homeless women*. New York: Penguin.

Seccombe, K. (1999). *So you think I drive a Cadillac? Welfare recipients' perspectives on the system and its reform*. Boston: Allyn & Bacon.

Shavelson, L. (2001). *Hooked: Five addicts challenge our misguided drug rehab system*. New York: New Press.

Sikes, G. (1997). *8 Ball chicks: A year in the violent world of girl gangsters*. New York: Anchor.

Simon, D. (1997). *The corner: A year in the life of an inner-city neighborhood*. New York: Broadway.

---

methodology in mind prior to starting their project, they do not require that the research design and methodology be rigidly and unalterably stated before they begin to collect data. There is nothing "wrong" with this fluidity, since many researchers feel that the purpose of qualitative research is to generate hypotheses for later testing. In this sense, qualitative research is commonly regarded as being exploratory.

RELIABILITY AND VALIDITY IN QUALITATIVE STUDIES

Qualitative researchers approach the issues of reliability and validity of their findings somewhat differently than quantitative investigators. According to Neuman (2006), "Most qualitative researchers accept the basic principles of reliability and validity, but rarely use the terms because of their association with quantitative measurement" (p. 194). Belcher (1994) notes that three different strategies are used to establish trustworthiness or credibility, which "is analogous to establishing validity and reliability" (p. 128). These efforts can involve:

1. *Prolonged engagement*—investing sufficient time to not only learn about the culture but also test one's understanding of it.
2. *Persistent observation*—to observe daily and keep records of the observations.
3. *Triangulation*—utilizing multiple sources of information, methods, or observers to cross-check for inconsistencies or misinformation.

Evaluating the Quality of Qualitative Studies

A recent article (Shek, Tang, & Han, 2005) involved a literature search of qualitative evaluation studies indexed in Social Work Abstracts. Drawing upon criteria identified by previous qualitative investigators and writers, the authors developed 12 criteria to use for assessing the quality of the studies. What they found is instructive for those who aspire to create and present the best possible qualitative study. Here are some of their findings and conclusions:

- The number of and nature of participants were often not clearly stated.
- The data collection procedures were not usually presented clearly and the ability to audit the process of the study was missing—undermining the external validity of the study.
- Honest reflection and discussion of biases or how biases might have been dealt with were not commonly found.
- Triangulation across researchers in studies with multiple researchers fell short, resulting in the conclusion that "social work evaluators adopting qualitative methods do not appear to be very enthusiastic about the issue of reliability" (p. 190).
- **Peer checking** was generally not mentioned as a way to check the interpretations of the researcher. (Peer checking involves having a colleague review one's coding of the data to confirm the categories and themes identified by the qualitative researcher.)
- Few studies mentioned alternative explanations, or looked for negative cases to disconfirm the findings, or limitations of the study.

While this list of frequent shortcomings found in the qualitative evaluation studies do not provide very convincing evidence that the quality of the published studies is satisfactory, the authors identified several reasons for this situation. First, member and peer checking involves additional cost and money; second, "journals rarely provide guidelines and standards" for the reporting of qualitative research, and third, space limitations in journals may force authors to abbreviate their work.

To this list Padgett (1998b) has added:

4. *Member checking*—going back into the field after data collection to verify with one or more participants regarding an interpretation or finding. Guba and Lincoln (1989) claimed that member checks were the "single most critical technique for establishing credibility" (p. 293).
5. Leaving an audit trail so that findings can be confirmed by others. This involves documenting steps taken in data collection and analysis.
6. *Negative case analysis*—looking in the data for any evidence that might disconfirm your finding or conclusion. Obviously, if you don't find any exceptions, then you can have more confidence in your findings.

Qualitative researchers have numerous ways of checking for reliability. For instance, if an informant were to reveal something that the investigator didn't think was true, he or she may want to ask other informants, get confirmation from the police or other officials, or view records or reports, newspaper accounts, or other forms of evidence. The importance of certain observations can be verified with different respondents within the same culture or confirmed again at a later time with the initial informant. Because qualitative researchers do not rely on a single source of information (such as a survey questionnaire or scale) but have "been there" themselves, they feel that qualitative research has greater validity than quantitative research.

It should not be overlooked that the differences in the way that quantitative and qualitative investigators view reliability and validity arises largely from the basic assumptions about the notion of reality. For qualitative investigators, there is no single reality but multiple ways of experiencing or viewing reality and thus notions like reliability or repetition of results that might hugely concern quantitative researchers is not always sought after with the same amount of ambition by their counterparts. Rolfe (2006) has argued, "We should not expect either expert researchers or respondents to arrive at the same themes and categories as the researcher" (p. 305). This view is in marked contrast to the quantitative position.

THE PROBLEM WITH QUALITATIVE RESEARCH

Qualitative researchers are at a disadvantage when it comes to having their research funded and published. This is a serious problem for the social work student or new professional who may be working toward either of those two goals. Here's a couple of excerpts from qualitative researchers who make these same points. "Quantitative research has become the normative mode of inquiry taught in universities, and quantitative researchers have tended to dominate review panels of funding agencies and the editorial boards of prestigious research journals" (Morse & Field, 1995, p. 3). Padgett (1998b) has acknowledged that there are many sound reasons for conducting qualitative research but also has written "if you are concerned with scientific utility and with procuring research funding from government or private foundations, proposing a qualitative study will probably reduce your chances of success. It is better to think of qualitative research as a labor of love than as the fast track to the researcher's hall of fame" (p. 11).

The very characteristics of qualitative research (for example, little structure, few guidelines) that make it exciting and innovative may also make it difficult for the qualitative investigator to compete against the quantitatively oriented project for resources. This is not to say that this situation is right or fair, but simply to inform you that qualitative research might not always be viewed with the same amount of respect as quantitative research. Because it does not produce generalizable knowledge, many academics in the positivist tradition question its value.

As we've discussed previously, in some situations qualitative methods are superior to quantitative approaches. However, the decision to use qualitative methods should not be made quickly. Certainly, the wrong reasons to choose qualitative approaches include because they seem easier, because they don't require knowledge of statistical procedures and sampling designs, or because one doesn't have to be overly concerned with reviewing all the relevant literature. Like anything else, there is good qualitative research and there is bad. Despite fewer funding and publication opportunities for qualitative studies, these approaches remain very popular.

FOCUS GROUPS

More and more social workers are using focus groups to obtain preliminary data about services and programs as well as evaluative information about its progress. Unlike personal interviews, focus groups generate interaction among participants, which may then result in valuable suggestions or recommendations as different perspectives are exchanged. Nonprofit agencies are increasingly adopting focus groups because they are relatively inexpensive and do not require a large investment of time for development or analysis of findings. This qualitative methodology is so popular that it is very likely that some time in your career as a social worker you may be called on to develop or lead a focus group. Focus groups tap the thinking of participants and elicit their ideas, attitudes, reactions, advice, and insights. Market research firms often use special rooms with one-way mirrors so that observers can watch and record the process when certain stimulus questions are presented. However, such facilities for focus groups are not deemed necessary by most social workers.

Here's a brief summary of several studies using focus groups: McMillen, Rideout, Fisher, and Tucker (1997) conducted focus groups with young adults who were former consumers of an independent-living program designed for youth in out-of-home care. The consumers were asked such questions as "What services helped you learn to live on your own?" and "What did you find helpful in the programs?" The audiotaped focus group sessions were transcribed and then themes were identified from a reading of the transcripts. The former consumers found that, among the nine themes that were identified, instruction in managing a budget was particularly valuable. The most dominant theme, however, was that participants appreciated the opportunity that the independent-living program provided for meeting other young people who were in a similar situation. This helped to reduce their feelings of isolation and stigmatization.

Linda Crowell (2001) developed a set of 23 open-ended questions to evoke responses from participants in a JOBS Program regarding their ideas, perceptions, concerns, and experiences being on welfare and receiving services from the program. Five separate focus groups were conducted involving 24 persons. One theme that emerged was that participants felt that they were discriminated against because they were welfare recipients; another was that looking for work was "difficult" and "frustrating." Respondents also felt that "no one cared about them as persons."

Prior to developing a training model to help child welfare workers deal with job stress and vicarious traumatization, Barbara Dane (2000) asked workers these and other questions: "What was it like for you when you first started working with abused children? When the work becomes difficult how have you managed to cope? Are there particular cases that affect you more than others?" Ten workers participated in a focus group that lasted over three hours. All workers reported changes in their coping responses over time to avoid further stress. These changes included detachment, setting limits, and staying busy. Respondents were unanimous in that a child's death from maltreatment or neglect was traumatic for everyone and that they tended to blame themselves even though they were not responsible.

Example of Focus Group Research

Corbie-Smith, G., Thomas, S. B., Williams, M. V., Moody-Ayers, S. (1999). Attitudes and beliefs of African-Americans toward participation in medical research. *Journal of General Internal Medicine, 14*, 537–546.

Seeking to understand African-Americans' attitudes toward participation in medical research, four researchers used focus group interviews.

Purpose: The research objectives were to identify barriers to participation in research, participants' attitudes and beliefs about informed consent, knowledge about the Tuskegee Syphilis Study, and perceived benefits and risks of participation in medical research.

Method: Focus group interviews were conducted at Grady Memorial Hospital in Atlanta. African Americans were recruited from outpatient medical and oncology clinics. An instrument was used to screen patients while they were waiting for their scheduled appointments. They were then assigned to groups based on the clinic where they were receiving care. Five focus group interviews were conducted from consecutive patients approached by a research assistant. These patients were asked to participate in a discussion about their attitudes and beliefs about medical care and medical research.

Data Collection: A moderator conducted all the groups using a written discussion guide. Some of the questions asked were: What comes to mind when you hear the term medical research? What are your general feelings about medical research? What are reasons why you would not or might not participate in medical research? Are you aware of legal protections for participants in medical research? Can you describe the protections you know? How many of you are familiar with the Tuskegee Syphilis Study?

The focus group sessions were audiotaped and then transcribed. An assistant also made notes to supplement the tapes. Participants received $25 honorariums at the conclusion of the group.

Data Analysis: The data were analyzed using grounded theory in which theory is generated from the data. Two investigators reviewed the transcripts in order to identify emerging themes and concepts. Research team meetings refined the meaning of the content areas and discussed alternative interpretations and representative quotations. Participant comments were sorted into five content areas: (1) reasons for not participating in medical research, (2) perceived benefits of participating, (3) informed consent, (4) Tuskegee Syphilis Study knowledge, and (5) strategies for increasing the involvement of African-Americans in research.

Results: Thirty-three patients participated in focus groups. A brief summary of the findings regarding reasons for not participating in medical research include: a majority of the participants were in favor of medical research as long as they were not involved themselves. Expressed concerns were: inconvenience, too much risk, fear of injection and needles, concerns that physicians might not be totally honest, and failure to see the benefit of participation.

With regard to the Tuskegee Syphilis Study, participants were misinformed and knew few specific details about it. When the group moderator interjected correct information about the study, "many participants aggressively challenged her, questioning the information source and the historical accuracy of details" (p. 541).

Discussion: "This qualitative study gives voice to African-American mistrust of the medical community in general and medical research in particular. . . . In particular, the informed consent process seems to hinge on the presence or absence of interpersonal trust, rather than the intended careful deliberation of benefits and risks" (p. 544).

Steps in Planning and Conducting a Focus Group

Step 1: Decide on the problem to be solved or the specific questions that need to be answered. For the most part, these will be open-ended questions like "What do you think about the new program?" or sentence completions like: "What I like best about the new program is . . ." It would be a good idea to list ahead of time all of the questions to be raised in the session. (*Note:* This is called preparing a discussion guide.)

Step 2: Decide on the group of clients or participants to be invited. The reason underlying your study will suggest who ought to be asked to attend. (*Note:* Insofar as is possible, participants should be randomly selected so as to get a good representation of the clientele or target group.) Once details are finalized, mail invitations and follow up with telephone reminders.

Step 3: Locate a facility large and quiet enough to accommodate approximately 12 participants. (*Note:* The recommended size for a focus group is 6 to 12 people; however, anticipate that you will lose about 2 participants to attrition for every 12 you invite.)

Step 4: Decide who will be the moderator, the person who presents questions to the group. (*Note:* The moderator does *not* join the discussion but should ask probing questions when additional information is needed to clarify participants' comments.)

Step 5: Consider whether you want to audio- or videotape the session; if you do, then make arrangements for the equipment. (*Note:* You may want to use a typed transcript when writing your report.) If taping seems too intrusive, the facilitator should have an assistant take good notes. Other process issues to think about are whether you will provide light refreshments, name tags, or incentives for participation. You may also want consider the possibility of conducting more than one focus group.

Step 6: Explain the ground rules. You may want to have some sort of "icebreaker" exercise so that participants will feel comfortable with each other. After introductions, you will want to explain the general purpose of the session and what is expected of the participants (e.g., the necessity for candor and honesty). Then you will want to make sure that they understand that there are no right or wrong answers, that you are interested in each and every person's own thoughts and experiences. It would also be helpful to provide each person with paper and a pen. You might want to have them jot down the first two or three words that jump into their minds when a question is asked. (This will help the group from being swayed by someone holding a strong position on a given issue.) If there is a possibility that sensitive information might be revealed, then the group should be urged to respect confidential information.

Step 7: Analyze the data. Prior to writing the report, you may want to prepare a transcript of the proceedings so that a typed copy is available that

Selected Studies Involving Focus Groups

Brandwein, R. A., & Filiano, D. M. (2000). Toward real welfare reform: The voices of battered women. *Affilia, 15(2),* 224–243.

Crowell, L. F. (2001). Welfare reform: Reforming welfare or reforming families? *Families in Society, 82,* 157–164.

Dane, B. (2000). Child welfare workers: An innovative approach for interacting with secondary trauma. *Journal of Social Work Education, 36,* 27–38.

Lehr, R., & MacMillan, P. (2001). The psychological and emotional impact of divorce: The noncustodial fathers' perspective. *Families in Society, 82(4),* 373–382.

McMillen, J. C., Rideout, G. B., Fisher, R. H., & Tucker, J. (1997). Independent-living services: The views of former foster youth. *Families in Society, 78(5),* 471–479.

Perlmutter, S., & Bartle, E. E. (2000). Supporting the move from welfare to work: What women say. *Affilia, 15(2),* 153–172.

Tolliver, D. E. (2001). African-American female caregivers of family members living with HIV/AIDS. *Families in Society, 82(2),* 144–156.

Williams, J. H., Pierce, R., Young, N. S., & Van Dorn, R. A. (2001). Service utilization in high-crime communities: Consumer views on supports and barriers. *Families in Society, 82(4),* 409–417.

highlights the key themes that emerged. A somewhat more rigorous approach would be to give the transcript to three different individuals to read in order to protect against bias seeping in. At a minimum, the report should identify the key points and major themes arising from the group's discussion.

Points to Keep in Mind About Focus Groups

Focus groups provide qualitative data because they do not yield statistically significant results. Rather than establishing definitive "proof" or evidence, it is best to remember that the data represent nothing more than the thinking of 8 or 10 or 12 individuals who were present on a given day. Another group might have a completely different set of opinions. In this sense, a focus group is like having a conversation with several people—if one is asking the right questions, listening, and observing (i.e., body language and facial expressions), then there is an opportunity to learn something that otherwise might not be known. To make up for the fact that small sample sizes are always a limitation of focus groups, two, three, or four focus groups might be conducted with different groups of individuals to ensure that the responses being obtained are fairly widely held. When focus groups work well, it is because the facilitator is able to keep the participants on task, the group members feel that they can respond freely, and questions are asked without suggesting a desired response.

THE GREAT DEBATE

In the 1950s and 1960s, a debate began in professional journals regarding the relative virtues of quantitative and qualitative methodology. A continuation of this debate over appropriate research methods for social work flares up from time to time in social work journals. In essence, advocates for the use of quantitative methods believe that qualitative methods will not produce the knowledge needed to document effectiveness and to guide practice.

On the other hand, those who advocate for greater use of qualitative approaches argue that the trend toward empiricism results in research that is too restrictive and superficial, because of the tendency to investigate only those aspects that can be operationally defined and measured and for which data can be collected. They say that instead of looking at the whole situation, empiricists fragment a situation and focus on what they can easily count. In the empiricists' quest for "objectivity," important interactions between participants and other details are often overlooked.

Which viewpoint is right? What is the most appropriate research method for social work? Actually, the debate should not be about which side is right. There are limitations associated with both quantitative and qualitative approaches to learning about a phenomenon. As a researcher-in-training, you should learn how to use both approaches. Social workers can use both methodologies profitably in their practice and each approach can be used to enrich the findings of the other. In fact, it has become common for social work researchers and evaluators to use **mixed methods** of research—for instance, employing both quantitative surveys and interviews with a few participants or focus groups—to ensure that they have an understanding that encompasses both breadth and depth. Qualitative and quantitative approaches can complement each other and certainly improve the researcher's ability to comprehend the phenomenon or program in question.

It is more important to recognize the strengths and advantages that each perspective brings to the understanding of a problem or phenomenon than it is to insist on the superiority of one approach over another.

The nature of the study and the questions you want to ask should suggest the most relevant strategy. Under some circumstances, investigators ought to employ qualitative approaches and under others, quantitative. The methodology must fit the questions that one wants to explore.

A group of health educators has proposed four models to help us think about ways in which qualitative and quantitative methods might be integrated (Steckler et al., 1992).

Model 1: Qualitative methods are used at the initiation of a project to help develop quantitative measures and instruments.

Model 2: A quantitative study is conducted but a qualitative study is also implemented to help explain the results of the quantitative investigation.

Model 3: A qualitative investigation is conducted and then quantitative methods are used to help interpret the qualitative findings.

Model 4: Qualitative and quantitative methods are both used equally and in a parallel fashion to cross-validate the findings.

It is shortsighted to dismiss qualitative research (or quantitative, for that matter) prematurely. Each of these approaches has its place, and the

Examples of Qualitative Studies in the Literature

Boyd, R. C., Diamond, G. S., & Bourjolly, J. N. (2006). Developing a family-based depression prevention program in urban community mental health clinics: A qualitative investigation. *Family Process, 45(2)*, 187–203.

Iliffe, S., Wilcock, J., & Haworth, D. (2006). Obstacles to shared care for patients with dementia: A qualitative study. *Family Practice, 23(3)*, 353–362.

Matthews, C. R., Lorah, P., & Fenton, J. (2006). Treatment experiences of gays and lesbians in recovery from addiction: A qualitative inquiry. *Journal of Mental Health Counseling, 28(2)*, 110–132.

McPhee, D. M., & Bronstein, L. R. (2003). The journey from welfare to work: Learning from women living in poverty. *Affilia, 18(1)*, 34–48.

Swanberg, J. E., & Logan, T. K. (2005). Domestic violence and employment: A qualitative study. *Journal of Occupational Health Psychology, 10(1)*, 3–17.

Woodring, L. A., Cancelli, A. A., Ponterotto, J. G., & Keitel, M. A. (2005). A qualitative investigation of adolescents' experiences with parental HIV/AIDS. *American Journal of Orthopsychiatry, 75(4)*, 658–675.

contributions of both have been highlighted in a way that is succinct and profound:

> The methods are analogous to zooming in and zooming out with a lens. To the extent that they are reproduced objectively, wide-angle, telephoto, and microscopic views must be simultaneously valid, and zooming from different directions merely focuses attention on different facets of the same phenomenon. . . . There are no grounds, logical or otherwise, for calling any view simple. We can start anywhere and zoom in to infinite detail or zoom out to indefinite scope. (Madey, 1982, pp. 83–83)

Qualitative approaches are valuable tools for helping social workers to understand their clients and the world in which they live. As you encounter social problems that need investigation, consider the method—whether qualitatively or quantitatively oriented—that will help to answer the questions that you have.

KEY TERMS

emic

open coding

grounded theory

constant comparative analysis

member checking

negative case analysis

peer checking

mixed methods

SELF-REVIEW

(Answers at the end of the book)
1. Which group believes the world can be objectively determined?
   a. quantitatively oriented researchers
   b. qualitatively oriented researchers
   c. ethnomethodologists

2. Which of these characteristics does not describe qualitative research?
   a. no intervention   c. large sample sizes
   b. use of participant observation   d. journalistic narrative
3. Which of these characteristics does not describe qualitative research?
   a. diminished importance of literature review
   b. in-depth interviewing
   c. exploratory
   d. concern with instruments and measurement
4. For each of the research questions below, indicate the most appropriate research approach:
   a. You want to know how much time the average felon spends in prison.
   b. You want to know how prisoners experience the power wielded by their prison guards. You convince the warden to let you go "under-cover" as a prisoner for two weeks.
   c. To understand the influences that shaped criminal behavior, you develop a survey and administer it to 500 prisoners in one maximum security prison.
   d. To understand the influences that shaped their criminal behavior, you interview in depth five prisoners awaiting execution on death row.
   e. After advocating for college classes to be offered at a nearby prison, you follow the first 60 prisoners until they complete one class and leave prison. You want to know if they are less likely to be rearrested than other prisoners.
5. List three reasons why an investigator might want to employ qualitative research methods.
6. T or F. Qualitative interviewers need to avoid "yes" and "no" questions.
7. T or F. Qualitative interviewers prepare very detailed questionnaires.
8. T or F. In a qualitative observational study, the observer probably wouldn't attend to body language or nonverbal communication.
9. What is theoretical saturation?
10. What is member checking?
11. T or F. For qualitative investigators there is no single reality.
12. Explain the Madey (1982) quote in terms of its implied reference to quantitative and qualitative methodologies.

QUESTIONS FOR CLASS DISCUSSION

1. Suppose you want to know what it is like to live in poverty, so you interview an impoverished person in depth one Saturday afternoon. Compare and contrast a lengthy interview with an ethnographic study of impoverished persons. In what ways would they be similar? How would they differ?
2. Which research approach has the greatest potential for advancing social work practice? (List arguments for and against qualitative and quantitative approaches.)

3. What are the pros and cons associated with not doing a thorough literature search before beginning an ethnographic study?

4. Discuss any books, movies, or plays that recently may have helped you better understand the life of a unique group of persons.

5. Share your life experiences that have given you insight into other cultures. What special world views or vocabularies were discovered?

6. Into what situations or settings would you like to go in disguise? What would you learn that you couldn't learn without a disguise?

7. Discuss how qualitative research is different from research employing a single-system design.

8. Describe a study where you might employ a mixed-methods approach.

9. Think about the participant-observation study continuum and briefly describe a study that might be appropriate at three different points on the continuum.

RESOURCES AND REFERENCES

Becker, D. G., Blumenfield, S., & Gordon, N. (1984). Voices from the eighties and beyond: Reminiscences of nursing home residents. *Journal of Gerontological Social Work, 8(1,2)*, 83–100.

Belcher, J. R. (1994). Understanding the process of social drift among the homeless: A qualitative analysis. In Edmund Sherman and William J. Reid (Eds.), *Qualitative research in social work*. New York: Columbia University Press.

Berrick, J. D. (1995). *Faces of poverty: Portraits of women and children on welfare*. Cary, NC: Oxford University Press.

Caudill, W., Redlich, F. C., Gilmore, H. R., & Brody, E. B. (1952). Social structure and interaction processes on a psychiatric ward. *American Journal of Orthopsychiatry, 22*, 314–334.

Crowell, L. F. (2001). Welfare reform: Reforming welfare or reforming families? *Families in Society, 82(2)*, 157–164.

Dane, B. (2000). Child welfare workers: An innovative approach for interacting with secondary trauma. *Journal of Social Work Education, 36(1)*, 27–38.

Davidson, B. (1997). Service needs of relative care givers: A qualitative analysis. *Families in Society, 78*, 502–510.

Deane, W. N. (1961). The reactions of a nonpatient to a stay on a mental hospital ward. *Psychiatry, 24*, 61–68.

deMarrais, K. B., & Lapan, S. D. (2004). *Foundations for research: Methods of inquiry in education and*

the social sciences. Mahwah, NJ: Lawrence Erlbaum Associates.

Drisco, J. W. (1998). Using qualitative data analysis software. *Computers in Human Services, 15(1)*, 1–19.

Drisco, J. W. (2005). Writing up qualitative research. *Families in Society, 86(4)*, 589–593.

Estroff, S. (1981). *Making it crazy: An ethnography of psychiatric clients in an American community*. Berkeley: University of California Press.

Farber, N. K. (2006). Conducting qualitative research: A practical guide for school counselors. *Professional School Counseling, 9(5)*, 367–375.

Floersch, J. H. (2000). Reading the case record: The oral and written narratives of social workers. *Social Service Review, 74(2)*, 169–192.

Franklin, C., & Jordan, C. (1995). Qualitative assessment: A methodological review. *Families in Society, 76*, 281–295.

Gall, M. D., Borg, W. R., & Gall, J. P. (1996). *Educational research: An introduction*. White Plains, NY: Longman.

Goldman, A. R., Bohr, R. H., & Steinberg, T. A. (1970). On posing as mental patients: Reminiscences and recommendations. *Professional Psychology, 1(5)*, 427–434.

Guba, E. G., & Lincoln, Y. S. (1989). *Fourth generation evaluation*. Thousand Oaks, CA: Sage.

Ishiyama, T., Batmann, R., & Hewitt, E. (1967). Let's be patients. *American Journal of Nursing, 67*, 569–571.

Keigher, S. M. (1992). Rediscovering the asylum. *Journal of Sociology and Social Welfare, 19(4)*, 177–197.

Krueger, R. A., & Casey, M. A. (2000). *Focus groups: A practical guide for applied research*. Thousand Oaks, CA: Sage.

Madey, D. L. (1982). Some benefits of integrating qualitative and quantitative methods in program evaluation, with illustrations. *Educational Evaluation, 4(2)*, 223–236.

McMillen, J. C., Rideout, G. B., Fisher, R. H., & Tucker, J. (1997). Independent-living services: The views of former foster youth. *Families in Society, 78*, 471–479.

Morgan, D. L. (1997). *Focus groups as qualitative research*. Thousand Oaks, CA: Sage.

Morse, J. M., & Field, P. A. (1995). *Qualitative research methods for health professionals*. Thousand Oaks, CA: Sage.

Neale, J., Allen, D., & Coombes, L. (2005). Qualitative research methods within the addictions. *Addiction, 100*, 1584–1593.

Neuman, W. L. (2006). Social research methods: Qualitative and quantitative approaches. Boston: Allyn & Bacon.

Padgett, D. K. (1998a). Does the glove really fit? Qualitative research and clinical social work practice. *Social Work, 43(4)*, 373–381.

Padgett, D. K. (1998b). *Qualitative methods in social work research*. Thousand Oaks, CA: Sage.

Rolfe, G. (2006). Validity, trustworthiness, and rigour: Quality and the idea of qualitative research. *Journal of Advanced Nursing, 53(3)*, 304–310.

Rosenhan, D. L. (1973). Being sane in insane places. *Science, 179* (Jan.), 250–258.

Royse, D. (1994). *How do I know it's abuse? Identifying and countering emotional mistreatment*. Springfield, IL: Charles C. Thomas.

Sherrod, M. (2005). Remembering the dead, comforting the living: Adapting Christian ministry to Appalachian death practices. In Susan E. Keefe (Ed.), *Appalachian cultural competency*. Knoxville, TN: University of Tennessee Press.

Shek, D. T. L., Tang, V. M. Y., & Han, X. Y. (2005). Evaluation of evaluation studies using qualitative research methods in the social work literature (1990–2003): Evidence that constitutes a wake-up call. *Research on Social Work Practice, 15(3)*, 180–194.

Steckler, A., McLeroy, K. R., Goodman, R. M., Bird, S. T., McCormick, L. (1992). Toward integrating qualitative and quantitative methods: An introduction. *Health Education Quarterly, 19(1)*, 1–8.

Swanberg, J., & Logan, T. K. (2005). Domestic violence and employment: A qualitative study. *Journal of Occupational Health Psychology, 10(1)*, 3–17.

Weiss, R. S. (1995). *Learning from strangers: The art and method of qualitative interview studies*. New York: Free Press.

Yin, R. K. (2003). *Case study research: Design and methods*. Thousand Oaks, CA: Sage.

ASSIGNMENT 11.1: Designing a Qualitative Research Project

Objective: *To gain firsthand experience with participant observation.*

Before attempting this assignment it will be important for you to get *prior approval* from your instructor for your idea. The directions are simple: Spend a minimum of four hours (eight is preferable) observing a group of people, a way of life, or situation that you would like to know more about. For instance, to learn more about the stresses that police officers are under, contact the community relations officer of your local police department and see if you can arrange to spend a shift riding with a patrol officer or observing intake at the jail. To learn more about life in a nursing home, contact the social service department and ask to spend a day observing the residents. (*Note:* This is not about shadowing the social worker and her daily activities, but trying to understand what life must be like for the residents.) To understand what it might be like to be a stroke victim or to be physically disabled, rent or borrow a wheelchair and spend a day in it going about your usual activities. To get a little perspective on the life of a homeless person, spend one night in a homeless shelter. You must use good judgment for this assignment and not attempt anything that might be dangerous. When contacting social service agencies, homeless shelters, and so forth, always identify yourself as a student and ask permission to observe.

1. Who do you plan to observe?

2. What agency or department do you need to secure permission from? Have you already obtained permission?

3. What is your plan for participant observation?

4. What did you learn from your observation?

5. What did you learn about yourself in this participant observation?

ASSIGNMENT 11.2: Obtaining an Oral History

Objective: *To gain firsthand experience with in-depth interviewing.*

For this assignment you will need to think not only about a topic, but a person who would be most likely to have information about that topic. For instance, you might want to interview someone who lived through World War II to ask about how life was different then than it is now. You could interview an international student or a recent immigrant to this country to ask about their life experiences. Recovered alcoholics or drug addicts might also make good informants about life on the streets. You may want to use a tape recorder. Get prior approval from your instructor before beginning your interview.

1. What topic is being explored?

2. Give a brief background on the person interviewed:

3. List all of the questions you asked:

4. Discuss the most important things you learned from this oral history:

12 CHAPTER | **Program Evaluation**

Most often, program evaluation starts with a specific problem or question to be answered, such as: "Is our outpatient treatment program effective?" Or, "Are we as successful with our group counseling program as with our individual counseling?" Administrators, board members, and others may want to know if the program is a "good" program. If they decide that the program is not effective, then corrective action may be taken or funding may be cut off. Program evaluation, then, is an aid to program managers. It can improve program effectiveness and aid in decision making.

Program evaluation is used to decide whether a program has worth or merit. Although it uses the research methodologies already covered in this text, its focus is not on generating basic science or new generalizable knowledge, but on concluding or reaching a decision about the value of a program. In fact, program evaluations are sometimes referred to as "summative" evaluations—a reflection of their interest in "boiling down" information to make a determination about the effectiveness of a program and from there to decide its fate. Because programs vary tremendously, there is no one "recipe" or cookbook approach to designing program evaluations. Instead, each evaluation tends to be individually tailored to address the unique concerns or characteristics of the program. This chapter will give you an overview of several ways that program evaluation can be approached.

Program evaluation attempts to answer such general questions as:

- Are clients being helped?
- Is there a better (cheaper, faster) way of doing this?
- How does this effort or level of activity compare with what was produced or accomplished last year? (Did we achieve our objectives?)
- How does our success rate compare with those of other agencies?
- Should this program be continued?
- How can we improve our program?

Why do we need to conduct program evaluation? The best argument for evaluating social service programs comes from an analogy suggested by Martin Bloom: Running a program without evaluating it is like driving a car blindfolded. You certainly are going places, but you don't know where you are or who you've endangered along the way. Program evaluation provides accountability. It can be used to assure the public, the funding sources of programs, and even the clients themselves that a particular program works and that it deserves further financial support. Program evaluation can be used to ensure that certain expectations are met, that efforts are appropriately applied to the identified needs, and that the community is better off because the program is having a positive effect.

There are many other reasons for evaluating a program. In addition to providing a reassuring level of accountability to clients and the public, program evaluation may be used to meet accreditation standards, and provide information for managing programs and monitoring their effects. Ultimately, program evaluation benefits clients by informing whether they are being helped.

Program evaluation is an important phase in the development of a program. Ideally, every program should be examined, and what is learned from these efforts should go back to the managers and service providers to enable them to continually improve the effectiveness and efficiency of their activities.

THINKING ABOUT CONDUCTING A PROGRAM EVALUATION

Think about a social service program with which you have been associated. Perhaps it was an agency where you volunteered or were employed. Maybe you are currently there in a field practicum. Suppose that one day the agency director calls you into her office and says, "I've just got a letter from our major funding source informing us that we must provide them with results of a program evaluation within the next 90 days or risk losing our funding. There's nobody here with that kind of expertise, but since you are taking that research course at the university, I'm hoping you'll agree to be the team leader on this. Let's meet again tomorrow and toss around some ideas about how to proceed. Can you sketch out a rough plan for us?"

Although this scenario may seem a bit unlikely to you now, over the years, I've had a number of phone calls from students who have described being in a similar situation and frantically have asked, "What do I do now?" What kind of an evaluation plan would you recommend if you were put in such a spot?

CONSIDERATIONS BEFORE BEGINNING A PROGRAM EVALUATION

Before you can realistically begin planning a program evaluation, you must address a few questions:

How much time do you have to complete the evaluation?

What resources (staff, money, etc.) are at your disposal?

Who is the **audience** who will be reading the evaluation report? (Will they be consumers, lay individuals, or researchers?)

What is the **purpose** of the evaluation? (Are there certain questions that must be answered? How rigorous does it have to be?)

In this scenario, the expectation of a completed project within 90 days would certainly impose some limitations on the type of evaluation that could be conducted. There probably wouldn't be time to do a **prospective** (going forward into the future) **study** (for example, starting a new group or intervention and then capturing posttest data). You'd be more likely to do a **retrospective study** looking back over already collected, existing data. Generally, the more time that is available for planning, the more control and the more sophisticated the design can be.

Resources are a major consideration. If you are informed that no funds are available for the evaluation, that situation will likely result in a simpler effort than one where standardized, copyrighted instruments might be purchased or consultants employed. If clerical help is offered, or if an evaluation committee can be formed, then more might be proposed than if you have no assistance.

It is important to know the audience when writing the evaluation report. A report being prepared for consumers and laypeople could be less complex and use a different writing style than a report going to the research staff of the funding source. Consumers may not want to read about *t*-tests and chi-squares—or at least would need help interpreting them; professionals with PhDs may have different expectations and may expect you to address sampling design, sample size, the psychometrics of instruments, and so on. How you write the report is also closely associated with the purpose of the evaluation.

In the selection of an evaluation design, the factors of time, resources, audience, and purpose must be weighed simultaneously, insofar as that is possible. However, the purpose of the evaluation has an overarching influence for this reason: The results of an evaluation can be used to promote or to denigrate programs. If the required evaluation is viewed by your agency management as so much "busy work," then the effort and energy put into it will be minimal. On the other hand, if there is a perception that the principal funding source is looking for reasons to eliminate programs, your agency will want to do the best job possible given the constraints of time and resources. Sometimes agencies can, by demonstrating empirically the superior job they do, position themselves to receive more funding for continuing or special projects. And, of course, the more competition there is for scarce funds, the more attention that will be given to the program evaluation.

TYPES OF PROGRAM EVALUATIONS

Program evaluation is not a single methodology, but instead refers to a broad category of approaches that vary considerably and supply a wide range of different kinds of information. This next section describes some of the more common types of evaluation ranging from the fairly basic to outcome and cost-effectiveness studies.

1. Patterns of Use

- Answers the question, "Whom are we serving?"
- Focuses on the characteristics of clients.
- Is descriptive.
- Allows for the monitoring of specific objectives.
- Allows agencies to target services precisely where needed.
- Helps to identify new patterns and trends.

Patterns of use (also known as client utilization) data is the most basic information that every agency and program should be able to report; it is a prerequisite before designing more elaborate evaluations. Every director of a program needs to have access to such descriptive data as: How many clients were served in the past 12 months? How many were low income? How many were males? How many were over the age of 55? Who referred these clients? Where do they live? What are their problems? How many have dropped out? What is the average length of their stay with us?

As indicated in Table 12.1, this type of data inform only about those clients who have expressed a need for the program by appearing at the agency. It does not say anything about those who could have benefited from the program but who did not request it. It does not allow you to conclude that the program is good, effective, or efficient. While the data inform you about the number of clients served and allows you to establish who the recipients of the services were, they tell you nothing about the quality of care clients were provided. Even though many social service agencies report descriptive client utilization data in their annual reports, such information by itself should not be considered to be an evaluation of the agencies' activities or programs.

Patterns of use data are best used for indicating pockets of clients who are within the agency's target group for services but who are not being adequately served for some reason. For instance, in Table 12.1 it is apparent that the Happy Healthy Thinking Project is serving women predominantly. Now, it

Table 12.1 | Client Utilization Data from the Happy Healthy Thinking Project

	Clients Served	Census Representation
Number of clients served this year	523	
Female clients	361 (69%)	31%
Minority admissions	115 (20%)	26%
Clients under 18	26 (5%)	13%
Clients 55 and older	209 (40%)	27%
Low-income households	99 (15%)	27%
Median household income	$27,985	$25,221
Prior mental health services	89 (17%)	
Dual diagnosis	63 (12%)	
Self-referrals	507 (97%)	
Average number of treatment episodes: 2.3		

may have been designed to serve this population, but if it was conceived for both genders then it is obviously underserving men. Similarly, the program is serving fewer minorities than their representation in the community would warrant and proportionately fewer children than might be expected. Depending on the nature of the program, the small percentage of children being admitted may or may not be a problem. Also, the program seems to be doing a great job of reaching older adults but not doing very well in bringing in low-income clients. In fact, the clients' median household income is higher than the average for the community.

Other possible areas of concern are the extremely low number of referrals that come from other professionals and organizations in the community and the fact that clients appear to drop out after only a few sessions. Such data should concern program managers.

Directors and managers of programs study patterns of use data for **program monitoring**—that is, measuring the extent to which a program reaches its target population with the intended intervention. Despite bright, capable staff, programs without guidance from management can wander aimlessly, like ships without rudders.

With the data from Table 12.1, it would be possible to develop concrete, measurable **objectives.** For example:

1. To increase minority admissions by 25% by December 31, 2009.
2. To increase admission of low-income clients by 30% by December 31, 2008.
3. To decrease self-referrals to 75% by December 31, 2007.
4. To reduce the number of clients who don't return to 40% by June 30, 2009.

Notice that these objectives are:

- Specific—they state a desired result.
- Measurable—they are easily verified.
- Referenced to a date—they indicate when results can be expected.

Objectives are different from **goals,** which are broad, general statements of direction. For instance, the Happy Healthy Thinking Project might state any or all of the following goals: (a) to diminish loneliness and isolation and increase well-being, (b) to improve the quality of life for those who have lost a loved one to suicide, and (c) to eradicate suicide from the community. Note that goals may be idealistic and not easily obtainable—but that doesn't mean that they aren't worthwhile. Goals state what the program and its associated activities should be about, while objectives provide for pragmatic accountability. Once program objectives have been developed, program monitoring takes on a new importance.

The problem with relying on the program's own objectives as a way to determine how the program is doing—is that whoever developed the objectives may have made them so easy to accomplish that they are essentially worthless. For instance, if a program objective stated that 500 new clients would be served within the year, but for the past two years the agency has been serving 550 new clients, the objective will be met, but we would still have no idea about how "good" or effective the program was. Ideally, a program should have to stretch a bit in order to meet its objectives. Objectives should be attainable, but not be so easy to reach that no special effort is required.

If the agency thinks that the principal funding source would be happy with the kind of data provided in Table 12.1, then there may be no need to go further. But if the agency has a management information system in place and someone is already responsible for program monitoring, another type of program evaluation might be needed.

2. Formative Evaluation

- Answers the question, "What would make this a better program?"
- Is primarily narrative.
- Is most often used with new programs still being developed.

Like program monitoring, **formative evaluation** is not specifically concerned with the worth of a program. As its name suggests, it focuses on improving programs and can often be accomplished quickly and cheaply. Formative evaluations are used to modify or shape programs that are still in development. They tend not to rely on statistics or analysis of numerical data. In this sense, they are much more qualitative than quantitative and usually don't conclude whether a program is successful or not. However, they may describe the experiences of clients and staff.

There are several ways to conduct a formative evaluation. One avenue might be to *obtain expert consultation.* This could be a person with a national reputation in the field in which the program is based; it could be someone with a statewide or regional reputation. You could even use a social worker or agency director from a similar agency in the same town as long as his or her program had a "good" reputation. The person would visit the agency to review operating policies and procedures, interview clients and staff, tour the facility, and maybe even meet with board members and reflect on aspects of the program. Maybe the person will notice that staff have to share offices, that there aren't enough computers, that the agency is not in a location that is accessible to clients who have to rely on public transportation. Depending on the expert, his or her interest, and your instructions, the intervention might be closely scrutinized—or perhaps the staff caseloads, or turnover rates. The best that could come from this approach would be a list of specific things that the agency needs to address immediately and in the long term in order to improve the program.

If money is not available for experts and no one can be found to do a formative evaluation for free, there are still two other avenues. A second idea would be to *locate model standards* from national accrediting or advocacy organizations. For instance, the Child Welfare League of America has prepared standards for those who are in the child care business. These standards are quite specific and address everything from the facility itself to the number of staff. Also, don't overlook the possibility of finding a relevant program evaluation from a literature search. Such studies might provide rough guidelines for what your program might expect in terms of clients who drop out or relapse. You can be somewhat reassured if your rates match those reported in the journal articles and if they don't, then you have a strong argument that more evaluation is needed and, possibly, more resources to support the program.

A third approach to formative evaluation would be to *form an ad hoc committee*—sometimes known as a blue-ribbon committee. This task force could be composed of staff, clients, interested persons from the community, board members, and even university staff. The group could decide to establish one or more focus groups composed of clients to learn how, from their perspective, the program could be improved. Or, the group might ask for the evaluator to interview a sample of clients or to develop a questionnaire that could obtain clients' and even the staff's input. It would be important to use open-ended questions and to allow the respondents to be anonymous. The evaluation committee might want to visit other similar agencies to view their operations—maybe even talk with their current consumers. When a blue-ribbon task force is carefully chosen, a richness of ideas can emerge as participants share their thinking, experiences, and hopes for the program.

A fourth approach would be for the organization to hire an evaluator to make recommendations about what kinds of evaluation data ought to be collected, and then to go out and to actually collect it.

Formative evaluation can also be known as **process evaluation**; however, not all process evaluations are formative. Sometimes, process evaluations are done at the conclusion of a project in order to get some idea of why the program did or did not work the way it was intended.

Like formative evaluation, process evaluations are also primarily narrative. They often describe the decisions and key events in the development of a new program. The federal government likes process evaluation—especially with research and demonstration projects—because this type of information is valuable to those who are interested in implementing or replicating a similar program in a different community. It makes sense: Why reinvent the wheel? Unlike formative evaluation, process evaluation ought to address what has been learned in the launching and operating of a program, consider what mistakes should not be repeated, and provide advice for the next team.

Once again, note that the focus of process evaluation is not so much on the number of client successes that were experienced (although this can be a part of the evaluation report) but rather on what happened and why. In this sense, a process evaluator has a role not unlike that of a journalist. However, the process evaluation can also include client utilization data, consumer feedback data, even client outcome data. You can see why it is important to have a clear understanding of the purpose of the evaluation.

3. Consumer Satisfaction

- Answers the question, "Are clients pleased with our services?"
- Is easy to interpret.
- Is inexpensive.
- Allows trends to be monitored.
- Is client centered.
- Can be implemented quickly.

When asked to plan a program evaluation, many students have a tendency to think first of client satisfaction surveys, and for good reason. They are among the simplest and most frequently used of evaluation methodologies. These approaches do not require a lot of research expertise, expense, or planning, and once developed, the same instrument can be used over many years. What's more, obtaining client feedback is a democratic grassroots approach that values input from those receiving the services. There is no assumption that staff or the administration know best. Every client is given the opportunity to comment negatively or positively about his or her experience within the agency.

With these points in its favor, what is the argument against making consumer satisfaction the principal component of an agency program evaluation effort? Just this: In practically every study clients say that they are satisfied with services. The vast majority of published consumer satisfaction studies show that clients almost invariably report high levels of satisfaction. As Lebow (1982) noted, these high satisfaction rates come from clients who "have little choice of facility, type of treatment, or practitioner" (p. 250).

Questions and Data Sources Useful in Process Evaluation

GENERAL QUESTIONS

Why was the program started? By whom?

What needs was the program designed to address?

Who (people and organizations) were involved in starting the program?

Will/should other organizations be involved?

How well have various agencies and organizations worked together?

What key decisions were made as the program was developing?

How did implementation differ from plans presented in the proposal?

What theory or principles is the program based on?

What is the program? What are its major components?

How has the program changed over time?

What changes are planned for the immediate future? Why?

What are the characteristics of the clients using the program?

Is the program serving the intended population? If not, why not?

How are clients being recruited?

How satisfied are clients with the program?

POTENTIAL DATA SOURCES

Local, state, or national data from the census or needs assessments or professional literature; specific legislation or policy changes—interview key informants in the community, board members, administrators, clients.

Program documentation, agency agreements, correspondence and relevant memos, minutes from board and committee meetings—interview clients, staff, program directors, board members, key community leaders, and administrators and staff of collaborating agencies.

Treatment manuals or protocols, client literature or agency brochures—interview administrators, staff, clients, board members; observe the program; conduct a focus group of clients.

Case record reviews, annual reports, program documentation, client interviews or surveys, new needs assessments, focus groups—interview staff, administrators, clients, key informants in the community.

High satisfaction rates are not found just in the United States. Deane (1993) has reported that 95% of a sample of psychotherapy outpatients in New Zealand indicated that they would return to the program if they needed help and would recommend the program to friends. Gaston and Sabourin (1992) found no differences in client satisfaction among Canadian patients receiving dynamic, eclectic, or cognitive/behavioral therapy in private psychotherapy. Perreault and Leichner (1993) found that satisfaction rates varied between 87.5% and 98% with French-speaking psychiatric outpatients in Montreal.

Satisfaction rates have remained high whether clients with persistent mental illness were interviewed by staff or by other clients (Polowczyk et al., 1993). This is not to suggest that every client will give rave reviews. Most surveys will have a few unhappy and disgruntled clients, but usually there will be many more who indicate satisfaction.

There can be several reasons why this type of program evaluation tends to reveal positive findings. First of all, client feedback instruments are often "homemade," and nothing is known about their reliability or validity. Second, they tend to have a selection bias—clients who are dissatisfied with services often drop out early and may not receive or participate in these

Examples of Client Satisfaction Studies in the Social Work Literature

Brooks, F., & Brown, E. (2005). A program evaluation of Los Angeles ACORN's welfare case advocacy. *Journal of Human Behavior in the Social Environment, 12(2/3)*, 185–203.

Kapp, S. A., & Vela, R. H. (2004). The unheard client: Assessing the satisfaction of parents of children in foster care. *Child and Family Social Work, 9(2)*, 197–206.

Lowe, T. J., Lucas, J. A., Castle, N. G., Robinson, J. P., & Crystal, S. (2003). Consumer satisfaction in long-term care: State initiatives in nursing homes and assisted living facilities. *The Gerontologist, 43(6)*, 883–896.

Martin, J. S., Petr, C. G., & Kapp, S. A. (2003). Consumer satisfaction with children's mental health services. *Child and Adolescent Social Work Journal, 20(3)*, 211–225.

Moran, L., White, E., Eales, J., Fast, J., & Keating, N. (2002). Evaluating consumer satisfaction in residential continuing care settings. *Journal of Aging and Social Policy, 14(2)*, 85–102.

studies. Further, clients are in a vulnerable position and may not want to risk saying something negative for fear that they might lose their social worker or therapist—or even services at a future point in time. This vulnerability can sometimes be experienced even when those being surveyed are not clients. I once conducted a survey of high school principals and guidance counselors and found that they were very hesitant to give negative feedback about an agency. They feared that too much criticism might result in the funding agency "pulling the plug," and then this group of school administrators and guidance counselors would have one less resource in the rural community where they could refer students who needed services.

A problem with mailing client satisfaction forms is that often clients move frequently and do not leave a forwarding address. Also, clients with lower levels of educational achievement will not be as responsive to mailed questionnaires as those with higher levels of education. LaSala (1997) reported a response rate of less than 20% to a mail survey and a 53% response rate on samples that were telephoned. From a research perspective, you need to be very cautious when interpreting data from surveys when response rates are under 50%. Just imagine that 85% of respondents say that they are "very satisfied" with a certain program, but only 30% of those eligible return their survey forms. Wouldn't you wonder about the experiences of the 70% who did not respond?

Despite the generally positive bias and the problems associated with collecting representative samples of clients, there is much to recommend client satisfaction studies as one means of evaluating a program. Because professionals do not experience the agency in the same way as the clients, it is important to ask clients to share their experiences. The receptionist may be rude; a coworker may be insensitive, inattentive, or engaged in questionable practices. You need to know if clients have been mistreated, if their problems have not been addressed, and if they feel they have received a benefit from the intervention at the agency. If you don't ask questions like those listed in

1. How would you rate the quality of the services you have received?

   Poor   *Fair*   *Good*   *Excellent*

2. How satisfied are you with the help you receive?

   Very satisfied   *Mostly satisfied*   *Mildly dissatisfied*   *Quite dissatisfied*

3. If a friend needed similar help, would you recommend our program?

   Yes, definitely   *Not sure*   *No, definitely not*

4. Did the staff treat you with courtesy and consideration?

   Always   *Most of the time*   *Not very often*   *Not at all*

5. Have the services you received helped you to deal more effectively with your problems?

   Yes, they helped a great deal.   *No, they really didn't help.*

   Yes, they helped somewhat.   *No, they seemed to make things worse.*

6. How could our agency's services be improved?

7. What did you like best about this program?

8. What did you like least about this program?

Figure 12.1 | Examples of Client Satisfaction Questions

Figure 12.1, then you'll never know how clients might respond. Notice the use of both open-ended and closed-ended questions.

Client satisfaction studies should be used within agencies as *one* component of a comprehensive evaluation strategy. It is not recommended as the only means of evaluating a program, but as one way to gather supplemental information from the client's perspective. If you and the agency decide to conduct a client satisfaction study, here are a few recommendations:

- Use a scale that has known reliability and validity. One example would be the Client Satisfaction Questionnaire developed by Larsen and his colleagues (1979); another would be the Client Satisfaction Inventory (McMurtry & Hudson, 2000). The use of a scale that is known to have good psychometrics will eliminate many of the problems found in hastily designed questionnaires.

- Use the same instrument on repeated occasions so that you will have a baseline and trend data from which periods of uncharacteristically low satisfaction can be noted. "Low" client satisfaction rates may differ somewhat from agency to agency, but rates where only 65% to 70% of clients are satisfied probably means the program needs close inspection.

- Encourage client satisfaction surveys to be conducted regularly to minimize "bugs" in the system and to routinize the evaluation process.

- To reduce the problem of selection bias, consider using a "ballot box" approach where one week every quarter or every six months each client coming into the agency is given a brief questionnaire and asked to complete it.

- Use at least one open-ended question to give consumers the opportunity to inform you about problems you did not suspect and could not anticipate.

4. Outcome Evaluation (or Summative Evaluation)

- Answers the question, "Are clients being helped?"
- Is often based on group research designs.
- Is the type of evaluation every program should conduct.
- Requires that indicators of "success" or "failure" are well conceptualized.

Outcome evaluation, also known as impact or effectiveness evaluation, often makes use of quantitative group research designs. Typically, this approach will use a control group, random assignment of clients, and involve pre- and posttesting as a way to obtain hard objective data on the performance of a program. Outcome evaluation attempts to demonstrate that a program did make a difference, that clients were helped and did improve. The successful outcomes of a program should not be confused with "output." That is, an agency could "graduate" or "process" any number of clients during a year but outcome evaluation is concerned with the extent to which these clients are changed or improve.

Beutler (1993) has listed principles and Peterson and Bell-Dolan (1995) have listed some "commandments" that not only make a good review of what we already have covered, but also suggest key considerations for when an outcome study is being planned.

1. *Employ a control or comparison group whenever possible.* The essence of program evaluation is comparison. How well did the program do? The comparison group provides the basis for answering this question by furnishing the contrast that allows the evaluator to observe for threats to the internal validity such as maturation, history, and effects of testing.
2. *Client samples should be representative.* Invalid conclusions can arise from convenience samples and those where the sampling procedures produce a selection bias.
3. *Random assignment for controlling treatment groups is strongly recommended.* If random assignment is not possible, check pretreatment data to determine if there is group equivalence. Also, take steps to keep subjects from dropping out of the study (minimize the threat of mortality) because this can change the equivalence between groups. Start with a sufficient group size to support the statistical analyses you want to conduct and to protect against loss of subjects in the final stages of the evaluation.
4. *Outcome measures should have demonstrated reliability and validity.* If instruments are needed, it is recommended that only those with adequate reliability and validity be employed. Additionally, multimodal measurement (using multiple instruments and measuring more than one domain) is more likely to detect an intervention's effects than a single instrument.

5. *Interventions need to be standardized and applied as evenly and uniformly as possible.* Therapists, even of the same theoretical persuasion, are notorious for improvising and deviating from the planned intervention. Developing treatment protocols is useful for ensuring that clients with the same problems consistently receive the same treatment. To the extent that those providing treatment emphasize different themes or have different goals for their clients, the intervention will not be uniform and may produce inconsistent results.

6. *Samples of therapists providing the intervention need to be large enough to be representative.* While researchers often worry about whether they have large enough samples of clients, too few worry about whether they have an adequate sample of therapists who are providing the treatment being evaluated. Small, inadequate samples of therapists also limit the evaluator's ability to understand whether the intervention worked in the intended way.

7. *Assessment of clinical meaningfulness should accompany computations of statistical significance.* It is entirely possible to obtain mean differences in scores that are statistically significant, but that have no real meaning clinically. In other words, clients' scores may improve but not so much that it would be noticeable to the client, to his or her family, or to the therapist.

5. Cost-Effectiveness and Cost Analysis

- Answers the question, "What does it cost to help a client?"
- Focuses on desired program outcome (success) indicators.
- Allows policymakers to look simultaneously at the expense of running a program (efficiency) and its success (effectiveness).

A recent issue of *Research on Social Work Practice* (Vol. 16, January, 2006) was a special issue devoted to the topic of cost-benefit analyses in social work. In the first article, Rizzo and Fortune (2006) point out three of the main problems in attempting to conduct this type of study. The first problem is that of collecting uniform cost data (charges and payments) from private insurers and Medicare and Medicaid when some entities report billable charges and others the amount actually paid. These amounts may vary by region or state and be calculated with different formulas. Another problem is that simply gaining access to the data may be difficult. And finally:

> [A] problem with cost data is what to include in the cost of an intervention and the uniformity of this costing across studies using similar interventions. Does one include in the cost of the intervention staff time, materials, office space, and equipment? Does one include the cost of transportation and time lost or gained at work for the person receiving the intervention? Also, how does one calculate the cost of informal care, such as caregivers' and volunteers' time in transporting and providing care outside the intervention for consumers of the intervention?

How does one calculate the cost of improving the quality of life of caregivers as well as consumers beyond productive work hours? These are questions not easily answered, and there are no uniform guidelines for costing interventions. (p. 6)

Despite these problems, Rizzo and Rowe (2006), in a review of 40 articles on the cost-effectiveness of social work services in aging, concluded, "[T]he current body of outcome studies . . . provides convincing empirical evidence that social work services can have a positive and significant impact on quality of life and health care costs and use for aging individuals" (p. 72).

Cheaper is not always better. Some programs are inexpensive to operate but also, unfortunately, not very effective. More expensive programs may, in the long run, prove to be cheaper. For instance, Meltzer and colleagues (1993) demonstrated that there was a significant savings in hospitalization costs for psychiatric patients on the drug clozapine. It is very expensive and requires periodic blood testing to make sure the dosage is correct and not toxic. But those who remained on the drug for two years resulted in a cost savings to the hospital of $17,404 per patient, while those who discontinued its use experienced more hospitalizations and expense. Similiarly, Buescher and colleagues (1993) have reported that the Special Supplemental Food Program for Women, Infants, and Children (WIC) saved Medicaid $2.91 for every dollar spent on WIC. Women receiving Medicaid but not WIC benefits were 1.45 times more likely to have a low-weight infant. Costs to Medicaid for newborn services beginning in the first 60 days of life were lower for infants born to women who participated in WIC during their pregnancies. Clearly, providing good nutrition to pregnant mothers is a good value and ultimately results in savings for taxpayers.

Other examples of real-world cost-effectiveness studies: Toseland and Smith (2006) have reported on a health education program (HEP) designed for spouse caregivers of frail older adults with chronic illnesses. This study was designed to learn if the social work intervention would result in reductions in outpatient, inpatient, and total health care charges at a participating HMO. The study found that overall the intervention saved the HMO $309,461 on caregivers and care recipients during the study period. Care recipients whose spouses participated in HEP cost the HMO an average of $1,418 per person versus an average of $5,760 for those receiving the usual care (the control group).

A smoke alarm giveaway program in Oklahoma City cost $531,000 but over a five-year period it is estimated that 20 fatal and 24 nonfatal fires were prevented—resulting in a savings of $1.5 million in medical costs and over $14 million in productivity losses (Haddix, Mallonee, Waxweiler, & Douglas, 2001).

Cost-effectiveness and cost-analysis studies allow the evaluator not only to compare the success rates of different programs but also to examine these rates in terms of their costs. These studies could be classified as a type of outcome evaluation but have been given their own category in this book to highlight their distinctive quality of factoring in program costs.

STEPS IN CONDUCTING A COST-EFFECTIVENESS STUDY

1. *Operationalizing program success.* Think, for example, of a program designed to provide supported employment for persons with severe disabilities due to mental illness. What would success be? Being employed at least 20 hours a week and at least 40 weeks a year? Or would you have a more stringent requirement?
2. *Preparing to gather program outcome data.* In a retrospective evaluation, this step involves identifying the clients to be included in the evaluation and deciding how many years to examine. If there are many clients, a random sampling strategy may be developed.
3. *Gathering client outcome data.* This step typically involves contacting former "graduates" of the program in order to determine how many meet the criteria for success.
4. *Computing the program costs.* The total costs for operating the program need to be computed. Costs include such items as personnel salaries and benefits, facility rent, and maintenance (heating, air conditioning, electricity, water, insurance, painting, office equipment repair, travel, publicity, telephones, and so on).
5. *Computing the cost-effectiveness ratio.* The cost-effectiveness of a program is computed by dividing its total cost by the number of client successes. For instance, a program that expended $400,000 and had 125 "successes" costs $3,200 for each successful client.

As you can see, this type of evaluation supplies superior information for decision makers and enables them to choose the best programs. Those programs with substantial costs that produce few positive effects can be discontinued, and the resulting cost savings can be applied to more effective interventions.

OTHER MODELS

Cost analysis is not limited to cost-effectiveness studies. There are cost-benefit analyses, cost-utility analyses, and cost-feasibility analyses, to name a few. Unlike cost-effectiveness studies, in cost-benefit analyses effort is made to measure both costs and benefits in monetary units. However, sometimes it is difficult to measure the absolute benefit of interventions. Since many benefits are intangible and cannot be easily converted to a dollar value (for example, improved self-esteem, or the value of a new park), often these studies make estimates that you may not feel are defendable. Such findings should be viewed cautiously until you check their assumptions and methodology.

As social workers, we need to examine our interventions in terms of their cost-effectiveness. The profession of social work will be enhanced to the extent to which we can show a skeptical public that costs to society are far greater when social services are inadequately funded than when sufficient funds are provided for prevention and remediation programs. Important programmatic decisions should not be made without evaluation data to guide us. To the extent that we can successfully identify the most efficient *and* effective programs, the prestige of the social work profession will be enhanced by a grateful and appreciative society.

There are numerous models from which to pattern a program evaluation. Some of the differences among these approaches are subtle, others are not. In planning an evaluation, you need to select a model that makes sense to you, one that will answer the questions that provided the catalyst for the study. In this chapter, the goal has been to familiarize you with just a few of many designs. For example, a mixed-methods or qualitative evaluation might be undertaken either with focus groups or participant interviews.

PROGRAM EVALUATION WITH QUALITATIVE APPROACHES

Sometimes a qualitative approach is exactly what is needed to diagnose problems within a program or agency. Reflect on these questions: "How do clients experience your agency? Is the receptionist pleasant and courteous? Do staff treat clients with respect? What would it be like to be a client at your agency?" Funding sources often request the recipients of their monies to supply **process evaluations** which tend to be primarily narrative descriptions and may provide information about what it took to start up a new intervention, problems encountered along the way, the staff and clients' experiences with it, and so forth.

We've all experienced staff who were rude or not helpful—secretaries who wouldn't answer the phone because they were on a break, receptionists who said hurtful things to clients. I've personally observed counselors who would not see their clients early even if they were available; and I've been in buildings where the walls were so thin that voices from the next office traveled through the walls, buildings where there wasn't enough parking, and buildings where there were no handicapped-accessible facilities. Qualitative researchers posing as clients could provide information about an agency that administrators might otherwise never receive.

Qualitative investigators conducting a program evaluation of an agency or program would not be counting successful clients or documenting how much clients had improved. Their interests would be in how clients' lives have changed as a result of the intervention they've received. The qualitative program evaluator would be looking for the values and benefits that the intervention provided for clients (Ruckdeschel, Earnshaw, & Firrek, 1994). As Goldstein (1997) has noted, "It is not how to count but what counts in peoples' lives that will begin to enlighten and shape the course and nature of our inquiries" (p. 452). And along this line, the qualitative investigator would address the program or agency's adequacy by examining the clients' experiences as they reported them in their own words.

In a qualitative program evaluation, there is no formal model for the investigator to follow. The approach to be followed and the data to be gathered depend upon what it is that the investigator wishes to learn.

Qualitative Evaluation of a Prostitution Diversion Project

Commercial sex workers in Salt Lake City arrested for prostitution offenses had the opportunity to be diverted from jail by participating in a 16-week, three-phase program that involved individual and group counseling. A review panel assessed attendance and progress every 2 weeks.

All participants were paid $20 an hour and interviews lasted between one and two hours. At the time of the study 24 sex workers had been enrolled in the program and 12 consented to the semi-structured qualitative interviews. The sample also consisted of 19 service providers. A professional transcriber transcribed the audiotaped interviews which were then coded with open-coding and in-vivo techniques (where codes are conceptual names or phrases taken from participants' comments).

The sex workers made a number of recommendations about the program. One of the more interesting was one about the interventions they received—interventions which sometimes came across as being not well structured or coherent (e.g., there was no treatment manual or standard approach). As one sex worker observed,

> Even walking in, the counselors, they just kind of "winged" it, you know. They did the group like they were supposed to, but they really "winged" it. And any materials that they brought in, it was their own. . . . It was things that they found that they thought would help us. (p. 212)

Sex workers also identified a problem in that some of the participants who attended sessions were "high" but were not asked to leave and there appeared to be no consequences for their actions. These two observations were made:

> You know, they got to sit there . . . and it was kind of a distraction, and . . . it gives you the urge to use watching somebody else . . . that's that way. . . . And I think [it] was a really big distraction for me. . . . And that's what I think they need to change when somebody comes in there like that. (p. 215)

> I have a lot of treatment under my belt. . . . And to go share my stuff with clean and sober people that I know are clean and sober is one thing. But to just go give all this to people who are unpracticed and using is pretty unusual. (p. 215)

Another telling finding was that none of the service providers or sex workers was able to refer to written documents or explicit verbal instructions regarding the intended objectives of the program. It is apparent from reading even this small a portion of Wahab's article that the qualitative evaluation contained important information that could improve the diversion program. Did you read anything here that might concern you as a service provider or administrator?

Source: Wahab, S. (2005). Navigating mixed-theory programs: Lessons learned from a prostitution-diversion project. *Affilia,* *20(2)*, 203–221.

Qualitative research approaches are superior to quantitative methods in some instances. For example, to test whether an antidiscrimination ordinance is effective, an excellent way is to have a person of color make application and then, an hour or so later, a white person make application. If the first person was informed there were no vacancies, but the second person was shown a vacant apartment, then there is good evidence of discrimination—much better information (and evidence) than would be obtained by conducting a survey of apartment managers and asking if they discriminate.

Although this chapter has focused primarily on quantitative approaches, it is a good idea to read Wahab's (2005) qualitative evaluation of a Prostitution Diversion Project to get an idea of how a qualitatively oriented investigator might conduct an investigation.

PRACTICAL CONSIDERATIONS FOR MAKING THE EVALUATION PROCESS SMOOTH

While the conceptualization of the evaluation design often seems like the most difficult part, any number of factors can influence the choice of a design—even the political climate within the agency. Ideally, it is helpful to know something about a program's history and its personnel before being asked to evaluate it. As a new staff person, student intern, or contract evaluator, however, you may not have the opportunity to gain "inside" information. So, what can you do?

First and foremost, you need to keep in mind that all evaluation is inherently threatening. Practically everyone feels uncomfortable when they are being evaluated—especially when the evaluator is someone unknown. People are even more threatened when they think that person doesn't like them or might want to eliminate their jobs. Therefore, you need to be sensitive to the feelings of those who may be affected by the findings of the program evaluation. Try not to create anxiety within the staff. Communicate frequently with involved personnel. Avoid surprises. If at all possible, involve staff in the planning of the evaluation. Ask for their ideas. Remember that evaluations are a political activity. Someone may have a vested interest in making one program look good at the expense of another. Some policymakers may hope to use the program evaluation to justify firing staff or cutting a particular program's budget.

Second, expect that obstacles and objections to the evaluation effort will arise. Even staff members who should be supportive may have strongly held but erroneous beliefs about the evaluation. There may be weird political alliances and defenders of the status quo who view the evaluation as terrifying because it will bring about change from the way things have "always been done." As a result, some staff may overtly not cooperate and others may conveniently "forget" to complete assignments or forms. Other staff will be too afraid to reply honestly for fear of being recognized.

Third, it is recommended that you develop a contract or, if that seems too formal, then a detailed memo describing your understanding of the following:

1. The *purpose* of the evaluation, including questions to be answered or hypotheses to be tested. You may also want to list the evaluation design to be used.
2. The *audience* for whom you will be writing the evaluation report. (Will it go only to the program director, the whole staff, the board of directors, the public?)
3. The *amount of time* you have to conduct the evaluation and write the final report.
4. The terms of your *reimbursement* or the amount of time that you will be released from your regular duties to conduct the evaluation.
5. The *budget* or amount that you can spend purchasing standardized instruments, visiting other programs, photocopying, and so on.

Don't be afraid to negotiate if you feel that you need more time or funds to do the job right. Put it all in writing, even the issue of who will have access to the data for purposes of publication. You may want to state that you will have first opportunity to use the data or ask for something like six months of exclusive use if you want to write a manuscript for publication.

Meta-Analysis

A term that you may be hearing more about as a result of the growing interest in evidence-based practice is meta-analysis. A **meta-analysis** is a study whose purpose is the synthesis or integration of findings from other studies. A metric (the effect size) is created that allows for the comparison of treatment effectiveness across the individual studies. The **effect size** is typically created by subtracting the mean of the control subjects from the mean of the subjects receiving the intervention. That difference is divided by the standard deviation of the controls. Effect sizes from 0 to .32 are considered small, those between .33 and .55 are moderate, and those .56 or greater are classified as large effect sizes (Lipsey & Wilson, 1993).

Meta-analytic studies start with a thorough review of the literature to identify all of the pertinent research about an intervention. From the large pool, studies are culled out if they don't meet the inclusion criteria. Generally, only the most scientifically rigorous of studies are included and these would have such characteristics as random assignment to either the control or experimental condition, detailed description of the intervention, pretest and posttest data from a standardized measure, and so on.

Here are two examples of meta-analytic studies: Bohlmeijer, Smit, and Cuijpers (2003) found 20 studies meeting inclusion criteria where life review and reminiscence were applied as interventions with depressed elderly. After eliminating one study with methodological problems, the overall mean effect size for all studies was .67, a large effect, and the authors concluded that "... the results of this meta-analysis indicate that reminiscence and life review may very well be effective treatments of depressive symptoms in older adults. The mean effect sizes found, are comparable to the effect sizes found for well-established treatments, such as antidepressives and cognitive behavior therapy" (p. 1093).

Walker, McGovern, Poey, & Otis (2004) looked at the treatment effectiveness of interventions for male adolescent sexual offenders. In 10 studies they found an overall weighted average of .37; however, two studies where cognitive behavioral therapy was employed had the largest effect sizes (.66 and .77).

In summary, meta-analysis is still another conceptual "tool," like with the others discussed in this chapter, that can assist you as a researcher or program evaluator. As discussed earlier and throughout this text, it is becoming increasingly important that service providers be able to demonstrate that our interventions actually work. It is not enough to claim that we helped a given number of clients in need of services; we must be able to show with data that they improved. If we refuse to assume this responsibility, not only social work jobs but the very profession will be imperiled by governmental and funding sources who demand accountability.

KEY TERMS

audience	retrospective study	goals	meta-analysis
purpose	program monitoring	formative evaluation	effect size
prospective study	objectives	process evaluation	

SELF-REVIEW

(Answers at the end of the book)

1. Which type of evaluation design answers the question: "Whom are we serving?"
2. Which type of evaluation design answers the question: "What would make this a better program?"
3. Process evaluations are primarily:
   a. narrative
   b. statistical
   c. hypothetical
4. Which type of evaluation design answers the question: "How pleased are clients with our services?"
5. Which type of evaluation design answers the question: "Are clients being helped?"
6. Which type of evaluation design answers the question: "What does it cost to help a client?"
7. T or F. The focus of process evaluation is not so much on the number of client successes as on what happened during the intervention and why.
8. The main reason client satisfaction data can't be considered "proof" that a program is effective is _____.
9. Another name for an evaluation type that examines client utilization data is _____.
10. List four considerations to keep in mind when planning a program evaluation.
11. What is a meta-analysis?
12. In meta-analysis, what would be considered a large effect size?

QUESTIONS FOR CLASS DISCUSSION

1. The following could be called "Exemplars of Poor Evaluation Designs." What is wrong with each of the following plans for evaluating programs?
   a. The agency is a halfway house run by the Department of Corrections. Residents are all young men who have been in prison for the first time and are now on parole in a prerelease program. In this program evaluation, three new residents who have outward signs of depression

will be selected and compared with two other residents who are not depressed. The Zung Self-Rating Depression Inventory will be the instrument used to determine if a caring attitude by the program staff and conjugal visits can help with adjustment from prison to the larger community. A pretest-posttest design will be employed.

b. A school has developed a latchkey program for students in the elementary grades. Parents who want to participate must contribute $50 a week for the program for each child enrolled. A preexperimental (posttest-only with nonequivalent groups) design will be used to compare students enrolled in the program with other students who could benefit from it but whose parents can't pay the fee. At the end of the school year comparisons will be made on the variable of academic achievement. In order to show that the program is effective, the principal handpicks the students who will be in the control group based on low reading and math scores.

c. A family preservation program wants to perform an outcome evaluation. A student intern is given the names and phone numbers for the last 50 closed cases. Success is defined as "no subsequent abuse." The student is instructed to call the 50 former clients and, after introducing herself, to ask if there has been any subsequent abuse in the families since the cases were closed. If she receives an affirmative response, there is another set of questions she is supposed to ask.

2. What conditions present in an agency would make it "ripe" for evaluation?

3. What conditions present in an agency would make it difficult to conduct an evaluation there?

4. Does evaluation always have to be threatening? When would it not be?

RESOURCES AND REFERENCES

Beutler, L. E. (1993). Designing outcome studies: Treatment of adult victims of childhood sexual abuse. *Journal of Interpersonal Violence, 8*, 402–414.

Bohlmeijer, E., Smit, F., & Cuijpers, P. (2003). Effects of reminiscence and life review on late-life depression: A meta-analysis. *International Journal of Geriatric Psychiatry, 18*, 1088–1094.

Buescher, P. A., Larson, L. C., Nelson, M. D., & Lenihan, A. J. (1993). Prenatal WIC participation can reduce low birthweight and newborn medical costs: A cost benefit analysis of WIC participation in North Carolina. *Journal of the American Dietetic Association, 93*, 163–166.

Deane, F. P. (1993). Client satisfaction with psychotherapy in two outpatient clinics in New Zealand. *Evaluation and Program Planning, 16*, 87–94.

Gaston, L., & Sabourin, S. (1992). Client satisfaction and social desirability in psychotherapy. *Evaluation and Program Planning, 15*, 227–231.

Goldstein, H. (1997). Shaping our inquiries into foster and kinship care: Editorial note. *Families in Society, 78*, 451–452.

Haddix, A. C., Mallonee, S., Waxweiler, R., & Douglas, M. R. (2001). Cost-effectiveness analysis of a smoke alarm giveaway program in Oklahoma City, Oklahoma. *Injury Prevention, 7(4)*, 276–281.

Larsen, D. L., Attkisson, C. C., Hargreaves, W. A., & Nguyen, T. D. (1979). Assessment of client/patient satisfaction: Development of a general scale. *Evaluation and Program Planning, 2*, 197–207.

LaSala, M. C. (1997). Client satisfaction: Consideration of correlates and response bias. *Families in Society, 78*, 54–64.

Lebow, J. (1982). Consumer satisfaction with mental health treatment. *Psychological Bulletin, 91(2)*, 244–259.

Lipsey, M. W., & Wilson, D. B. (1993). The efficacy of psychological, educational, and behavioral treatment. *American Psychologist, 48*, 1181–1209.

McMurtry, S. L., & Hudson, W. W. (2000). The Client Satisfaction Inventory: Results of an initial validation study. *Research on Social Work Practice, 10(5)*, 644–663.

Meltzer, H. Y., Cola, P., Way, L., Thompson, P. A., Basteni, B., Davies, M. A., & Snitz, B. (1993). Cost-effectiveness of clozapine in neurolepticresistant schizophrenia. *American Journal of Psychiatry, 150(11)*, 1630–1638.

O'Farrell, T. J., Choquette, K. A., Cutter, H. S., & Brown, E. (1996). Cost-benefit and cost-effectiveness analyses of behavioral marital therapy with and without relapse prevention sessions for alcoholics and their spouses. *Behavior Therapy, 27*, 7–24.

Perreault, M., & Leichner, P. (1993). Patient satisfaction with outpatient psychiatric services: Qualitative and quantitative assessments. *Evaluation and Program Planning, 16*, 109–118.

Peterson, L., & Bell-Dolan, D. (1995). Treatment outcome research in child psychology: Realistic coping with the "Ten Commandments of Methodology." *Journal of Clinical Child Psychology, 24*, 149–162.

Polowczyk, D., Brutus, M., Orvieto, A. A., Vidal, J., & Cipriana, D. (1993). Comparison of patient and staff surveys of consumer satisfaction. *Hospital and Community Psychiatry, 44*, 589–591.

Rizzo, V. M., & Fortune, A. E. (2006). Cost outcomes and social work practice. *Research on Social Work Practice, 16(1)*, 5–19.

Rizzo, V. M., & Rowe, J. M. (2006). Studies of the cost-effectiveness of social work services in aging: A review of the literature. *Research on Social Work Practice, 16(1)*, 67–73.

Rogers, E. S. (1997). Cost-benefit studies in vocational services. *Psychiatric Rehabilitation Journal, 20*, 25–33.

Ruckdeschel, R. A., Earnshaw, P., & Firrek, A. (1994). The qualitative case study and evaluation: Issues, methods, and examples. In Edmund Sherman and William J. Reid (Eds.), *Qualitative research in social work*. New York: Columbia University Press.

Toseland, R. W., & Smith, T. L. (2006). The impact of a caregiver health education program on health care costs. *Research on Social Work Practice, 16(1)*, 9–19.

Walker, D. F., McGovern, S. K., Poey, E. L., & Otis, K. E. (2004). Treatment effectiveness for male adolescent sexual offenders: A meta-analysis and review. *Journal of Child Sexual Abuse, 13(3/4)*, 281–293.

Winegar, N., Bistline, J. L., & Sheridan, S. (1992). Implementing a group therapy program in a managed-care setting: Combining cost-effectiveness and quality care. *Families in Society, 73(1)*, 56–58.

ASSIGNMENT 12.1: Designing a Program Evaluation

Objective: *To gain experience considering the critical elements that go into a program evaluation.*

For this exercise you have the choice of five different programs that could benefit from an objective outcome evaluation. While you may wish to employ a scale or standardized instrument, all of these programs may also be evaluated by changes in clients' actual behaviors. (*Note:* Your instructor will inform you if he or she wants you to find an instrument.) Choose one of the topics below and then answer the listed questions:

PROGRAM EXAMPLES

- A peer educator–led eating disorders education and prevention program.
- A token economy system in a state psychiatric hospital.
- A program to prevent juvenile firesetters from recidivating.
- An alternative education program for expelled youth.
- A divorce adjustment group for young children.

1. List at least two questions that you would think would be important to answer about this program.

2. Operationally define your dependent variables(s).

3. Describe a program evaluation design and methodology for collecting your data.

4. What statistical procedure(s) will you use to analyze your data?

5. What limitations might your study have?

ASSIGNMENT 12.2: Reading a Program Evaluation

Objective: *To gain experience reading a program evaluation and critically thinking about it.*

This is a two-part assignment. The first step requires that you search the literature for an article in one of the professional journals that evaluates a program. Be careful to choose a piece that contains data (i.e., tables) and doesn't just talk about the need for program evaluation. Then, you will need to closely read the article in order to answer the questions listed below. (Your instructor may want the whole class to read the same article; if that is not the case, he or she may want you to append a photocopy of the article you read to this assignment.)

1. Which article did you read? (Use the whole citation.)

2. What is the major question that this program evaluation seeks to answer?

3. How was the dependent variable(s) operationalized?

4. Briefly describe the methodology used to determine if the program was successful.

5. Did the study involve a sample of clients? If yes, how many were in the sample? Was the sample size adequate?

6. What did you learn about evaluating a program of this type? (Be as specific as possible.)

7. What possible limitations does this study have?

13 CHAPTER | Data Analysis

Most researchers enjoy data analysis. It is at this stage that the data begin to "come alive." Patterns emerge, trends are detected, and support either is or is not found for our pet hypotheses. We may come away with the smug feeling that we were right in our predictions all along and now have the data to prove it! Or, perhaps we did not learn as much as we had hoped but ideas and questions were generated that we can test in our next project.

In quantitative data analysis, the focus of this chapter, the purpose of the data analysis is to take the **raw data** (the completed survey forms, scales, or questionnaires) produced in the data collection stage and summarize it. In a sense, the researcher is involved in a translation process. From a heap of raw data, the researcher hopes to wring something meaningful—patterns, trends, or relationships.

Simply reporting the individual responses to a specific question or questionnaire is not analysis. The researcher seeks patterns within the data and tests hypotheses that have "driven" the research.

There is no single way to go about analyzing a data set. The way you analyze your data will depend on what you want to know. However some basic techniques are frequently used by all quantitative researchers. These techniques will not only introduce you to the topic of data analysis but also assist you in understanding your data.

STEPS IN DATA ANALYSIS

We start with the assumption that you have already collected a sample of data. Perhaps you have administered an instrument to a sample of clients and are now in possession of the forms they have completed.

Even if you don't have a very large data set, there is virtually no argument for not entering the data into a personal computer for processing. Statistical software like SPSS are widely available on college campuses and are so user friendly with "help" features and statistical "coaches" that they make data processing almost painless. If you have a large data set (anything over 50 cases), it is essential that you use the power of the computer to look at your data.

The good news is that there are available a number of very sophisticated and easy to use interactive statistical Web sites to assist students with data analysis, and the free links work just as well as software that can be purchased. There are, of course, differences between the commercial products and the free ones. The commercial products allow you to save data and modify variables at different stages and provide paper printouts of your analyses. Additionally, the commercial products like SPSS and SAS have built in tutorial programs, and college bookstores often sell books providing additional information and instruction. But for many of the data analyses discussed in this chapter, you can go to the Web site http://statpages.org and find that you can perform the same operations without purchasing any product. You'll find that this Web page contains over 600 links and 380 calculating (interactive) pages.

Step 1: Cleaning and Editing the Data

Before data analysis can begin and before you enter the data into the computer, you need to examine the raw data for errors and missing data. You'll find that some individuals will have checked two responses for the same item because they forgot to erase one response, and that there will be a few cryptic markings where you'll wonder if the client had intended a 1 or a 7. Frequently, you find that a few individuals accidentally overlooked some items, and others purposely provided no information (especially if you are asking about sensitive information like income, age, number of arrests). Most researchers want their data fields to be as complete as possible and may attempt to complete the missing items if it is convenient and feasible to do so. For instance, a client may have failed to give his age on the questionnaire at posttest but recorded it six weeks earlier on the pretest form. In other instances, it may be important to contact respondents again. Data are also edited for common mistakes, as when an interviewer transposes two numbers, like 94 instead of 49. When too much information is missing and cannot be reconstructed or obtained because clients contributed the data anonymously, certain items or even whole questionnaires may have to be discarded. A set of responses, whether from a person randomly selected from the phone book or a client in a treatment group, is usually referred to as a **case**. All the cases together form the data set.

Step 2: Data Entry

There's not a great deal you have to know before plugging your data into the computer. When you open up SPSS for the personal computer, you will see a screen already set up and waiting for you to define your variables. It would be logical to number each respondent or client and, consequently, your first variable might be "client identifier." A second variable might be "marital status." With this variable you could enter the data from Joe Client as "single" or you could decide to **code** the various attributes of the variable "marital status." Coding simply means assigning a numeric value to the category as in the following example:

Coding Scheme for Marital Status

Category	Value
Single	1
Married	2
Divorced	3
Widowed	4

The coding scheme you use should be easy to remember. In the example, single is another way of saying 1; it takes 2 to be married. However, you could have started with widowed persons being 1, married persons as 2, and single persons as 3. If you wanted to start with 5 and go through 8, that would work too, as long as you were consistent. The rule here is to make it as easy to remember as possible. Thus, having a certain status (like being employed) would usually be coded 1 and the absence of that same status (being unemployed) would be coded 0. Similarly, it is much easier to remember a rule such as: "yes is always coded 1; no is always coded 0" than to try to remember exceptions.

Below, Var 003 and Var 004 (you can also think of these as variable #3 and variable #4) are coded so that the numeric values are associated with recognition of the problems caused by guns.

Coding Scheme for Var 003: Guns Are a Problem

Category	Value
Strongly agree	5
Agree	4
Undecided	3
Disagree	2
Strongly disagree	1

Coding Scheme for Var 004: Guns Are Easily Available

Category	Value
Strongly agree	5
Agree	4
Undecided	3
Disagree	2
Strongly disagree	1

The argument for coding rather than typing in the client's marital status is that you can punch in a 1 faster than you can type "single." And, if you have 200 or 300 questionnaires to enter, you'll soon realize the benefit of coding. In SPSS, you need to define each variable, which means you have to identify it as a numeric value or a "string"—describing categories using the alphabet instead of numbers (for example, "married").

If you employ coding, it is important that you write down your coding scheme on a reference sheet called a **codebook.** This will help you later if you get a printout of Var 017 and you can't remember whether the third category in Var 017 represented "10–12 years of employment" or "13–15 years of employment." Sometimes in data analysis it becomes necessary to merge categories, and the codebook can keep track of the various way you transform your variables.

As you enter data into the computer and discover missing items (such as "age") that cannot be reconstructed, it is often useful to define a value (such as "99") as the missing value. When you are editing your data for completeness, this lets you know, unlike leaving it blank, that nothing was missed. Blanks can also represent missing data that you know are missing, but unfortunately, blanks could also mean that someone was careless when entering the data. That's why it is a better practice to assign a unique number that informs the computer that data are missing.

If you employed one or more open-ended questions in your survey, it is highly likely you will want to code the responses. Take, for instance, individual answers to the question, "Why did you quit school?"

Had no money.

Couldn't pay my bills.

Parents couldn't afford to send me.

Loan didn't go through.

Couldn't borrow any more.

Didn't like it.

Hated school.

Reading the first five responses suggests that one possible motive for quitting school and, therefore, one category that ought to be represented in the data analysis is "financial reasons." The last two responses suggest that respondents were disinterested in school. So, "financial reasons" could be coded "1" (since it was the first category you identified) and "disinterest" could be coded "2." Computers are not yet so powerful that they can read these six different replies and form discrete categories for you. But once you indicate which responses are similar, then the computer will be quick to allow you to count them by category.

I find it helpful to read through 20 to 25 of the open-ended responses to look for similarities in the kinds of things that are being reported. Sometimes it is easy to come up with four or five categories, and then place the remaining responses in a category called "other." Later on, I might subdivide the "other" explanations into different categories. I don't like "other" to represent much more than 10% of the data. If it grows to 25% or 30% of all your categorized responses, then this is good reason to examine the "other" responses more closely and possibly create new categories from them.

Step 3: Univariate Analysis

Univariate analysis is looking closely at one variable at a time. Even though you have checked the data prior to entering it into the computer, as a conscientious researcher you should still search for possible data entry error by asking the computer to create a **frequency distribution** for each variable. A frequency distribution is a count or listing of all the categories of numeric values associated with one variable. In Table 13.1 these values are arranged from low to high.

Sometimes a little data cleaning is necessary. When entering a large amount of data into the computer, it is easy to lose one's place and make errors. But if you were careful, a quick look at the frequency distribution is often all that is needed to reassure you that the data are ready for analysis.

For instance, Table 13.1 shows four individuals 23 years of age and six who were 27. There were no teenagers. Had there been, the researcher would have known there was a problem because the sample consisted only of graduate students. Ages, quite appropriately, ranged from 23 to 55. Further, there was only one 55-year-old, but there were four persons 23 years of age. Note, too, that the 99 does not indicate the age of elderly persons but stands for missing data—two individuals did not report their age.

Reading down the third column, you see that these two individuals represent 3.8% of all those surveyed. There's nothing remarkable about that, but had it been 38%, then we might wonder if there was something about the way the information was elicited that generated such a large amount of missing data. Researchers don't like missing data.

The valid percent column removes the missing data from the calculations. These figures are computed by dividing each of the frequencies by a denominator of 50 (the number of cases with no missing data).

Table 13.1 | Frequency Distribution of AGE V0003

Value	Frequency	Percent	Valid Percent	Cumulative Percent
23	4	7.7	8.0	8.0
24	4	7.7	8.0	16.0
25	3	5.8	6.0	22.0
26	5	9.6	10.0	32.0
27	6	11.5	12.0	44.0
28	2	3.8	4.0	48.0
29	3	5.8	6.0	54.0
30	1	1.9	2.0	56.0
31	1	1.9	2.0	58.0
32	5	9.6	10.0	68.0
33	2	3.8	4.0	72.0
34	1	1.9	2.0	74.0
35	1	1.9	2.0	76.0
37	1	1.9	2.0	78.0
39	1	1.9	2.0	80.0
40	1	1.9	2.0	82.0
41	1	1.9	2.0	84.0
43	1	1.9	2.0	86.0
44	1	1.9	2.0	88.0
45	1	1.9	2.0	90.0
46	1	1.9	2.0	92.0
47	1	1.9	2.0	94.0
48	1	1.9	2.0	96.0
51	1	1.9	2.0	98.0
55	1	1.9	2.0	100.0
99	2	3.8	Missing	
Total	52	100.0	100.0	

You can use the cumulative percent column to partition the data into thirds, fourths, fifths, and so on. For instance, one-third of the students were 26 or younger; approximately two-thirds were 32 or younger.

By informing the computer that you want statistics to help you interpret the frequency distribution (in SPSS you would choose "Analyze" and from that pull-down menu choose "Frequencies"), you can obtain the following additional information for the variable "Age of Graduate Sample."

Range	Minimum	Maximum	Sum
32.00	23.00	55.00	1590.00

The first set of statistics provides us with the lowest (minimum) and highest value (maximum), the variable's range (the distance between the lowest and highest value plus one), as well as the sum of all the values added together. The second set of statistics is often more useful. These **measures of central tendency** (the mean, median, and mode) allow us to understand the average response for that particular variable. We learn that the average (**mean**) age for our sample of graduate students is 31.8 years and that the most frequently reported age (the **mode**) is 27, because there were six students of that age.

Mean	Standard Error	Median	Mode	Standard Deviation
31.8	1.1700	29.00	27.00	8.2734

The **median** is the exact midpoint of all the values and is not affected by extreme maximum or minimum values. The median is computed by taking the number of valid cases and dividing by 2. In this example, 50 divided by 2 is 25—so the midpoint is that place located either by counting down 25 cases from the lowest value of 23 *or* 25 cases up from the highest value of 55. Try it. The 25th case is found within the group of three persons who were 29 years of age.

The mean, median, and mode do not always align themselves perfectly on the same value. This is partly explained by the fact that the mean is pulled in the direction of extreme scores while the median is unaffected by them. And the job of the mode is to report the "most popular" response.

The frequency distribution in Table 13.2 shows what happens when the original data are slightly altered. In this new example, there are no graduate students older than 45, and there are a few more 27-year-olds. As a result, the median and mode are now the same. The mean is slightly lower, but still pulled in the direction of the oldest students. We can grasp this by realizing that 44 and 45 are quite a bit further from the median than the minimum of 23 and so they exert more numerical "weight."

Note, too, that the **standard deviation** has grown smaller—from 8.27 in the first example to 5.7 in the second one. The standard deviation is an indicator of how much variation there is in the data; that is, how closely the individual scores cluster around the mean. The standard deviation represents the average distance between scores and the mean. The smaller the standard deviation, the less variability there is and the more similar the values are to each other.

Table 13.2 | Frequency Distribution with No One Older Than 45

Value	Frequency	Percent	Valid Percent	Cumulative Percent
23.00	4	7.7	8.0	8.0
24.00	4	7.7	8.0	16.0
25.00	4	7.7	8.0	24.0
26.00	5	9.6	10.0	34.0
27.00	10	19.2	20.0	54.0
28.00	2	3.8	4.0	58.0
29.00	3	5.8	6.0	64.0
30.00	1	1.9	2.0	66.0
31.00	1	1.9	2.0	68.0
32.00	5	9.6	10.0	78.0
33.00	2	3.8	4.0	82.0
34.00	1	1.9	2.0	84.0
35.00	1	1.9	2.0	86.0
37.00	1	1.9	2.0	88.0
39.00	1	1.9	2.0	90.0
40.00	1	1.9	2.0	92.0
41.00	1	1.9	2.0	94.0
43.00	1	1.9	2.0	96.0
44.00	1	1.9	2.0	98.0
45.00	1	1.9	2.0	100.0
Total	50	96.2	100.0	
Missing 99.00	2	3.8		
Total	52	100.0		

Statistics: Measures of Central Tendency for Table 13.2

Mean	Standard Error	Median	Mode	Standard Deviation
29.5200	.8158	27.00	27.00	5.7685

Range	Minimum	Maximum	Sum	
22.0	23.00	45.00	1476.00	

Table 13.3 shows one of the many possible configurations of data that would result in the mean, median, and mode having the same numerical value. Observe that, once more, the standard deviation has become smaller as the extreme values were eliminated from the sample.

Levels of Measurement Variables are like most things in that they can be subdivided into different types. **Nominal variables** are easily identifiable because they are discrete, named categories. For instance, *male* and *female* are the attributes of the variable gender. Similarly, a student could be *full time* or

Table 13.3 | Frequency Distribution with No One Older Than 35

		Frequency	Percent	Valid Percent	Cumulative Percent
Valid	23.00	6	11.5	12.0	12.0
	24.00	6	11.5	12.0	24.0
	25.00	7	13.5	14.0	38.0
	26.00	5	9.6	10.0	48.0
	27.00	10	19.2	20.0	68.0
	28.00	2	3.8	4.0	72.0
	29.00	3	5.8	6.0	78.0
	30.00	1	1.9	2.0	80.0
	31.00	1	1.9	2.0	82.0
	32.00	5	9.6	10.0	92.0
	33.00	2	3.8	4.0	96.0
	34.00	1	1.9	2.0	98.0
	35.00	1	1.9	2.0	100.0
Total		50	96.2	100.0	
Missing	99.00	2	3.8		
Total		52	100.0		

Statistics: Measures of Central Tendency for Table 13.3

Mean	Standard Error	Median	Mode	Standard Deviation
27.12	.4657	27.00	27.00	3.2928

Range	Minimum	Maximum	Sum
12.00	23.00	35.00	1,356.00

part time; clients might be *first-time offenders* or *recidivists.* Symptoms might be understood in terms of whether they are *acute* or *chronic.* Another key feature of nominal data is that you can't average the categories. Thus, you wouldn't try to compute the mean of the males and females; it would make no sense. With nominal data we simply deal with percentages and might say something like, "52% of the sample were males, 48% were females" and that suffices. If there were multiple categories (like marital status) we might mention the modal category and say, "Typically, clients were unmarried."

Variables like age, weight, height, income, and test or scale scores that are continuous with equal intervals between each value are called **interval variables.** Measuring data at the interval level allows us to get accurate measurements—to measure change in small increments. For example, we might note that clients who participated in a bereavement group were 17% less depressed at posttest than a control group. Phobic individuals may have reduced their anxiety scores by 25 points after six weeks of intervention.

Researchers usually strive to obtain interval data because the more sophisticated statistical procedures require it. This is why it is important to give a great deal of thought to how you want to analyze your data as you are developing your research methodology and instrumentation. Suppose you design a questionnaire and ask your clients:

HOW MANY YEARS OF EDUCATION HAVE YOU COMPLETED?

a. eighth grade or less
b. ninth to twelfth grade
c. some college

The problem with this scheme is that it is impossible to know exactly how many individuals finished a specific grade; furthermore, you wouldn't have any idea as to the *average* number of years of education completed. This problem could have been avoided if you had asked the question this way:

How many years of education have you completed? _____ years

By not supplying the categories but asking open-ended questions, you will obtain interval level data. The exception, of course, is that some variables (like gender) are always nominal variables. A rule of thumb: Interval data can be transformed into categorical data, but not vice versa.

Here's why you need to know the difference between interval and nominal data: The computer can, on occasion, supply you with garbage data if you don't know the differences between the two.

Table 13.4 shows a frequency distribution for the variable *gender* when, to save time, I coded females as 1 and males as 2, and then asked the computer to furnish the mean, median, and mode. While the percentages are accurate, the mean in this instance has no real meaning. After all, what is the distance or interval between males and females? Would you think it appropriate to report that for this sample of 52 graduate students the average for the variable of gender was 1.52? Or would that be nonsense?

Table 13.4 | Frequency Distribution for Gender

		Frequency	Percent	Valid Percent	Cumulative Percent
Valid	1.00	25	48.1	48.1	48.1
	2.00	27	51.9	51.9	100.0
Total		52	100.0	100.0	

Statistics: Measures of Central Tendency for Table 13.4

Mean	Standard Error	Median	Mode	Standard Deviation
1.5192	6.996E-02	2.00	2.00	.5045

Table 13.5 | Frequency Distribution for Gender

		Frequency	Percent	Valid Percent	Cumulative Percent
Valid	Female	25	48.1	48.1	48.1
	Male	27	51.9	51.9	100.0
Total		52	100.0	100.0	

In Table 13.5, the attributes of gender have been entered as "male" and "female." Note that there are no statistics other than percentages being reported even though I asked SPSS to supply mean, median, standard deviation, and so on. The software didn't supply these statistics because the data were entered as "male" and "female," and you can't average words.

The **ordinal** level of measurement sometimes resembles nominal categories in that they are named categories. For instance, staff morale might be categorized as "good," "fair," or "poor"; clients might be designated as "highly motivated," "moderately motivated," slightly motivated," or "not at all motivated." However, the two client satisfaction items below are ordinal variables.

Overall, how satisfied are you with the services you received?

Very Satisfied	Mostly Satisfied	Mildly Dissatisfied	Quite Dissatisfied
3	2	1	0

How would you rate the quality of the services you received?

Excellent	Good	Fair	Poor
3	2	1	0

The secret of recognizing ordinal data is that there is a ranking; the scale is *directional* so that positions on the scale have a relative meaning associated with higher or lower values. With ordinal data there is a presumption that the distance between the categories are equal and that data from these scales can be treated as interval level.

The thing that's a little bit tricky about ordinal data is that sometimes the researcher may use the categories as if the data were nominal and at other times the data may be treated as if they were measured at the interval level. We'll talk more about this in the next section, but for now imagine that 129 clients have given an average rating for the quality of a respite service for families with Alzheimer's as 2.88 on a 0 to 3 scale. That suggests while the agency got a lot of "3" responses, they didn't get 100% agreement—or else the average score might have been a 3.0. The 2.88 would be even easier to interpret if we saw what percent of the families rated the services "Excellent," "Good," "Fair," and "Poor"—or, if we could see improvement from lower ratings in prior years. Another rule of thumb that may help you: When you are trying to decide if data are being treated as if they were nominal or ordinal, see if percentages are being reported. If so, the data are probably treated as nominal data. If there are decimals, as in the example of mean satisfaction ratings of 2.88, then the data are being treated as if they were interval.

Realize, too, that items such as the two client satisfaction items are often combined with other items to constitute a scale. What is important is not the client's response to any one item but the combined or aggregate score. Thus, with a hypothetical 10-item client satisfaction questionnaire and a 0 to 3 rating scale, a respondent could rate the agency anywhere from 0 to 30—creating a dependent variable (overall satisfaction score) that could be analyzed as a continuous or interval level variable.

Whether your data are measured at the nominal, ordinal, or interval level, univariate analysis of data lends itself to graphic portrayals. Graphs, pie charts, histograms, and polygrams can be prepared almost effortlessly once you have entered your data into the computer and have access to a statistical software program. Figure 13.1 provides a few examples of the various ways data can be visually presented.

Both the pie chart and bar chart give the viewer a quick way to assess the portions represented by the various categories associated with a nominal or ordinal variable. Notice that in the pie chart I included a missing data category (those who didn't report their marital status), but I removed those individuals from the bar chart. There's no real hard and fast rule here; however, the reader should be informed if there is a large number of cases with missing data.

Univariate analysis allows the researchers to become acquainted with patterns in the data—among other things, to understand who is included and who might have been excluded. Thus, if you were conducting a study within your agency and noticed that none of the clients in your samples were 65 or older, then you might want to hold off further analysis until additional data could be added. In other words, univariate analysis could inform you when you

A. Pie Chart

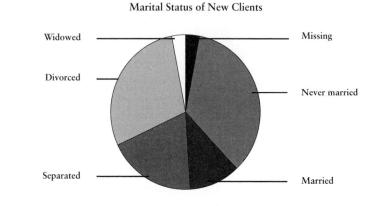

B. Bar Chart

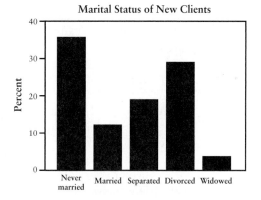

C. Line Chart

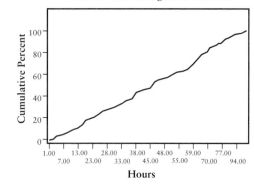

Figure 13.1 | Graphic Portrayals of Univariate Analysis

might have experienced some sort of selection bias in your sampling procedures. Once you have examined your data one variable at a time and decided that the sample or data is adequate, then you are ready to begin to test hypotheses.

Step 4: Hypothesis Testing

Hypotheses can be either simple or complex. Hypothesizing that there may be more female clients than male clients in a certain program is too simplistic to be real research. The social work researcher would want to know why there might be differences in admissions by gender. And he or she might think of any number of relevant questions or hypotheses. For example, if there are more women than men clients, is this true for all income and educational levels? When men enter treatment, do they drop out sooner than women? Do they have more severe diagnoses on admission? Are they more likely to have alcohol or drug histories?

Let's say you have an idea that, for whatever reason, men don't feel as welcome in the agency as women. You draw a sample of 35 clients and ask them the question, "If you were to need help again, would you return to our agency?" You discover that 67% of the women but only 60% of the men say that they would return. Is this a real difference? Can we say that it is a statistically significant difference?

By preparing a table like Table 13.6, we can visually attempt to understand the data. However, it is impossible by simply "eyeballing" the numbers to know whether or not the differences are real or might have been produced by chance. If it is important for us to know whether males and females are significantly different in their responses about returning to the agency, then we compute a **chi-square** (χ^2). We obtain this statistic either by calculating it by hand or by asking the computer to perform a **cross-tabulation.** The crosstabs procedure allows us to examine the dependent variable (willingness to return to the agency) by the independent variable of gender and is performed with categorical, not interval data.

Table 13.6 | Cross-Tabulation of Willingness to Return to Agency by Gender

			Females	Males	Total
	Would Return	Count	10	12	22
		%	66.7%	60.0%	62.9%
$\chi^2 = .16, p = .69$	Wouldn't Return	Count	5	8	13
		%	33.3%	40.0%	37.1%
	Total	Count	15	20	35
		%	100.0%	100.0%	100.0%

In our example, SPSS calculated the chi-square and found it to be .16. That number won't mean a whole lot to you. In the days before computers, it meant a lot more. You would have had to consult a table in an appendix at the back of a statistics book to learn whether or not the chi-square was statistically significant. But today, the software program informs us that the probability (p) of the data falling into those cells the way they did by chance alone was .69 or many times larger than the 5 times in 100 cutoff standard that social scientists most frequently use to determine statistical significance. Probabilities larger than .05 ($p > .05$) are not generally considered significant. So, even though there is about a 7% difference between men and women, that is not a real difference. In this example, males and females are more similar in their patterns of responding than they are dissimilar. One should not look at percentages and from them alone make a pronouncement about whether there are significant differences.

Note: Even though $p < .05$ is the accepted standard, on occasions when it is critical to reduce the role of chance even more than what is normally tolerated, investigators may adopt a more stringent criterion for accepting significance only if $p < .01$. This would be a conservative approach if there was some risk that the intervention might not be helpful or could have some adverse side effects. Once in a while you may find that the standard is lower—as when there is a report of exploratory research with a small sample. Under these conditions it is acceptable to raise the cutoff to $p < .10$.

What would a statistically significant difference look like? Using the same idea of a small survey of our clients, let's imagine that this time we find that only 30% of the males but 80% of the females indicated that they would return.

When we once again go to the computer and order crosstabs of the dependent variable ("would return to the agency") by gender, we find a much larger chi-square (8.58) but, more importantly, a probability or significance level of .003 (see Table 13.7). In other words, the tendency for women clients to indicate they would return and for male clients to indicate that they probably wouldn't is a real finding that very likely did not occur by chance. Yes, it could

Table 13.7 | Cross-Tabulation of Willingness to Return to Agency by Gender

			Females	Males	Total
	Would Return	Count	12	6	18
		% Within	80.0%	30.0%	51.4%
$\chi^2 = 8.58$, $p = .003$	Wouldn't Return	Count	3	14	17
		% Within	20.0%	70.0%	48.6%
	Total	Count	15	20	35
		% Within	100.0%	100.0%	100.0%

be a fluke, but chance alone would explain the data falling this way only 3 times in 1,000. So, 997 times out of 1,000 independent samples with this population, you would be safe in expecting women clients to indicate a greater likelihood of returning.

The simplest chi-square table is the 2 × 2 (two variables each with two attributes). However, the crosstabs procedure will allow you to create tables that are 2 × 3, 3 × 3, 3 × 4, 4 × 4, and so on—you are not limited to a set number of rows or columns. At the same time, if more than 20% of the cells in any one cross-tabulation have an expected frequency of five or less, the Pearson chi-square produced by the computer will not be accurate, and you will need to combine or collapse categories so that you have fewer cells with more respondents in them. For example, if you were using a Likert scale with "Strongly agree," "Agree," "Undecided," "Disagree," and "Strongly disagree," then it would be logical to combine the "Strongly agree" and "Agree" categories into one grouping (the "Agree" category) and then to combine the "Disagree" and "Strongly disagree" into another (the "Disagree" category). Note that while we started with ordinal data, we end up treating it as discrete or categorical (nominal) data. Chi-square is appropriate only for categorical data.

If there are few respondents in the "Undecided" category, another possibility would be to run crosstabs without the "Undecided" cases. In this situation, a 5 × 2 table (gender by a 5-point Likert scale) could become a 2 × 2 (gender 3 agreement/disagreement) crosstab. Most statistical software programs will inform you of the number and percentage of cells that do not meet the minimum expected frequency of 5.

Even with combining categories, it is still possible to have more than 20% of the cells not meeting the minimum expected frequency if you started with a very small sample. In such case, the best solution is to add to your sample. However, there is another chi-square statistical procedure called Fischer's Exact Test that SPSS will produce for 2 × 2 tables when the expected value in one or more cells is small. Although it is somewhat more conservative, it is interpreted the same way as the basic chi-square test (the Pearson chi-square).

THE *t* TEST

What are you to do if your questionnaire used a 10-point scale and you obtained the following data with this item: "How would you rate our program?" (1 = Very Poor, 10 = Excellent)?

It wouldn't make sense to analyze the data in Table 13.8 with the chi-square procedure. For one thing, the ratings don't constitute categories in the same way that you've learned to think about nominal data. Second, there are so many different "categories" or value positions that it's tempting to think of these being equal intervals between the values. And third, had you tried to conduct a chi-square, the software program would have informed you that 100% of the cells failed to meet the minimum expected frequency—making the chi-square statistic useless.

Table 13.8 | Program Ratings by Gender of Clients

Ratings	Men	Women
1	1	0
2	2	0
3	2	0
4	4	0
5	2	3
6	3	1
7	1	6
8	2	3
9	2	1
10	1	1

Table 13.9 | Initial Statistics Produced by the *t* Test Procedure

VAR00001	N	Mean	Standard Deviation	Standard Error Mean
Women	15	7.0667	1.4376	.3712
Men	20	5.3000	2.5772	.5763

		Levene's Test for Equality of Variances	
		F	Significance
VAR00002	Equal variances assumed	7.124	.012

When you have a normally distributed dependent variable measured at the interval level, and a nominal level independent variable, you can look for differences between groups with the statistical procedure known as the *t* **test.** This statistic compares the mean scores for the two different groups and provides a *t* value and a probability statement. The *t* test is appropriate even for small samples of about 30 individuals.

Using the data from the 10-point scale, your statistical software program produces several tables and informs you in the first one of the means for the two groups (Table 13.9).

The next set of data provides an intermediate stage statistic that tells you which *t* value to use in your research report. The Levene Test for Equality of Variances directs you to the best estimate for the standard error of the

Table 13.10 | Independent Samples *t* Test

				t Test for Equality of Means		
		t	*df*	Significance (2-Tailed)	Mean Difference	Standard Error Difference
VAR00002	Equal variances assumed	2.38	33	.02	1.7667	.7406
	Equal variances not assumed	2.577	30.833	.015	1.7667	.6855

difference between the two means. When the significance level is less than .05 for the heading "Equal variances assumed," then the assumption is that the variances are not equal. In this case, $p < .05$ suggests that the variances are very different (as you might expect when the means appear very different), and so you go to the next table (Table 13.10) and look for the heading "Equal variances not assumed." Reading across, you learn that the significance for unequal variances is .015 (or $p < .05$). In other words, there is a real, statistically significant difference in the way that men and women rank the program. Had the Levene's Test been $p > .05$ under "Equal variances assumed," that would have meant the variances were approximately equal, and you could have used the *t* value and probability associated with that estimate.

The *t* test reported in Table 13.10 requires a dependent variable measured at the interval level or ordinal data that can be treated as interval. Using the SPSS software, I clicked on "Statistics" then "Compare Means" and then informed the computer that I had **independent samples**—that is, the groups being used for the analysis were from different individuals (males and females). Had I wanted to compare pretest self-esteem scores with posttest self-esteem scores after an intervention for the group of 35 individuals, then I would have had to inform the computer that we wanted a "**paired samples**" *t* test. This procedure would have matched John Client's pretest with John Client's posttest, Susie Patient's pretest with her posttest, and so on. With the paired samples procedure, you are examining for the average change or improvement by comparing the individuals with themselves.

Both versions of the *t* test are limited to comparing only two groups at a time (i.e., pretest scores versus posttest, or something like males versus females). If you want to compare three different groups and have interval level data, that procedure is **one-way analysis of variance** (sometimes referred to as **ANOVA**). Instead of a *t* value, this method of analysis provides the *F* ratio. However, it is also computed from group means and interpreted much like the *t* test, as can be seen in Table 13.11.

In this example, our agency study has been broadened to include a group of teenagers who are participating in an after-school program. The previous subjects were all men and women over the age of 21; this new group consists of

Table 13.11 | One-Way Analysis of Variance: Mean Ratings from Men, Women, and Teens

Group	Mean	SD	*n*
Women	7.07	1.44	15
Men	5.30	2.58	20
Teens	4.17	2.46	18

		Sum of Squares	*df*	Mean Square	*F*	Significance
VAR00002	Between Groups	69.235	2	34.617	6.718	.003
	Within Groups	257.633	50	5.153		
	Total	326.868	52			

mostly male teens age 13 to 18. When asked the same question, "If you were to need help again, would you return to our agency?" the teens had lower mean ratings than the other two groups. The table produced by ANOVA informs you that the probability that these means occurred by chance was 3 times in 1,000 ($p = .003$). In other words, the three groups are not similar in their ratings of the agency. In fact, there are statistically significant differences in the way men, women, and teens view the agency. However, you cannot say from the one-way findings that there is a statistically significant difference between the way men and teens think about the agency. In order to be able to make that statement, you would need to compute a *t* test for independent samples and compare the men's ratings against the teens' ratings. (In this case, it was not significant: $p > .05$). One-way analysis of variance simply allows you to test the hypothesis that the means of several groups are similar. Like the chi-square statistic, the one-way procedure can easily process three, four, five, or even more groups.

CORRELATION

Even though we've been discussing the differences among three or more groups, do not lose sight of the fact that we're still involved with bivariate analysis—employing two variables, one dependent and one independent.

Still another way to analyze bivariate data is to examine the strength of relationships between variables using correlation coefficients. A **correlation coefficient** is a statistic that ranges between 0 and 1.00. In a perfect correlation, movement within one variable is matched by a corresponding movement in the other. In Table 13.12, students' exam scores increased by 10 points for every hour that they studied. Note that both variables would be measured at the interval level.

Table 13.12 | Distribution of Data, a Perfect Correlation

	Hours of Studying for Exams	Exam Score
Edna	10 hours	100
Bill	9 hours	90
Wanita	8 hours	80
George	7 hours	70
Brooke	5 hours	50

Pearson correlation coefficient = 1.00

Table 13.13 | Distribution of Data, Zero Correlation

	Hours of Studying for Exams	Exam Score
Martha	1	70
Micki	2	75
Waldo	3	80
Kenneth	4	85
Earl	15	90
Heather	6	90
Jennie	7	85
Bob	8	80
Nadine	9	75
Rondell	10	70

Pearson correlation coefficient = .00

The closer the correlation coefficient is to one end or the other of the range, the stronger the relationship between the two variables. (This does not mean, however, that one variable was the cause of the other variable. A high correlation between the amount of street crime in a city and the number of police officers does not mean that law enforcement causes the crime.)

Usually, however, it is not so easy to predict one variable from knowing the other. In Table 13.13, the pattern of increasing scores with additional study time holds for only half of the students. For the other half, scores declined with more study time. In a sense, there were offsetting differences. Can you guess what the correlation will be? A correlation coefficient of 0 indicates that there is absolutely no relationship between the two variables—that it is not

Table 13.14 | Distribution of Data, a Slight Correlation

	Hours of Studying for Exams	Exam Score
Rennie	1	70
Debra	2	75
Betty	3	80
James	4	85
Edward	5	90
Pam	6	90
Donald	7	100
Robin	8	90
Glenna	9	80
William	10	70

Pearson correlation coefficient = .24

possible to make any kind of a prediction about one from knowing the other. In Table 13.14, there is a slight tendency for grades to improve with additional study time for some students.

In these examples, the plus sign is understood. A plus sign indicates a positive direction—as one variable goes, so goes the other variable. If one variable tends to increase, so does the other. A negative sign in front of a correlation coefficient indicates an inverse relationship—the variables go in opposite directions. As one variable increases, the other decreases.

By squaring the correlation coefficient (multiplying it by itself), it is possible to determine the strength of the relationship between two variables. This tells you how much of the variance in the two variables is shared. Thus, a coefficient of .24 allows you to explain about 6% of the variance between the two variables. Saying this another way, knowing a value for one of the variables would allow you to predict the corresponding value on the other variable with only 6% accuracy.

$$.24 \times .24 = .0576 \text{ (or 6\%)}$$

Correlations as high as .70 are rarely found in social science research, and, more typically, are .40 or less. There's something else you also need to know about correlations—they aren't always statistically significant. The earlier examples of a perfect 1.00 correlation with a sample of 10 students produced a probability of .50. This means that you shouldn't place a lot of confidence in the finding because of the small sample size. However, it is also true that you can ensure correlations will be significant if you make the sample large enough.

Table 13.15 | Correlation Matrix with Four Scales

	Homophobia Scale	Empathy Scale	Fear Scale	Social Distance Scale
Homophobia Scale	1.00	−.63	.60	.66
Empathy Scale	−.63	1.00	−.55	−.68
Fear Scale	.60	−.55	1.00	.67
Social Distance Scale	.66	−.68	.67	1.00

A **correlation matrix** is presented in Table 13.15. This matrix resulted from correlating four scales—Homophobia, Empathy, Fear of AIDS, and Desired Social Distance from AIDS Victims—with each other. It produces some perfect correlations (when a scale is correlated with itself) as well as some positive and negative correlations. As you look at these correlations, do you understand why some have a negative sign in front of them while others do not? Why would Empathy correlate negatively with Fear of AIDS?

It is possible to obtain correlations that are statistically significant but because of their low magnitude they may not suggest any implications for practitioners or policymakers. If planning a correlational study, don't forget to control for extraneous variables that may be influencing the correlations.

THE ELABORATION MODEL

Imagine that you have conducted a survey that produced the results in Table 13.16. About a third of the respondents did not feel they were "well-informed about AIDS." At this point, you have conducted only a univariate analysis. But, suppose you introduce another variable. You ask: Is there a difference in how men and women view their knowledge about AIDS? Now you would conduct a bivariate analysis of the dependent variable (knowledge about AIDS) by the independent variable of gender. Table 13.17 shows virtually no difference in the percentages between males and females (and there was no statistically significant difference either, $p = .84$) when χ^2 was computed.

Suppose there is a third variable that might have some explanatory power. Could knowledge of AIDS vary between men and women depending on the type of community in which they live? You can tell from Table 13.18 that male city dwellers rate their knowledge of AIDS higher than small town or rural dwellers and that this same pattern also holds for female respondents. Using the crosstabs procedure again, you could determine if there were statistically significant differences by community of residence when you control for gender.

Table 13.16 | Frequency Distribution

("I am well-informed about AIDS.")

Category Label	Absolute Frequency	Relative Frequency (%)	Adjusted Frequency (%)
Strongly disagree	18	2.4	2.4
Disagree	228	30.6	30.7
Undecided	36	4.8	4.9
Agree	386	51.7	52.0
Strongly agree	74	9.9	10.0
No answer/refused	4	0.5	Missing data
Total	746	100.0	100.0

Table 13.17 | Cross-Tabulation of Knowledge About AIDS by Gender

("I am well-informed about AIDS.")

	Female	Male
Strongly agree/Agree	291	169
	(66%)	(65%)
Strongly disagree/Disagree	153	93
	(34%)	(35%)
Column totals	444	262

Table 13.18 | Knowledge of AIDS by Community Type and Gender

("I am well-informed about AIDS.")

	Female			Male		
	Rural	Small Town	City/Suburb	Rural	Small Town	City/Suburb
Strongly agree/Agree	73	105	112	48	59	60
	(59%)	(65%)	(71%)	(53%)	(65%)	(76%)
Strongly disagree/Disagree	51	56	45	42	32	19
	(41%)	(35%)	(29%)	(47%)	(35%)	(24%)
Totals	124	161	157	90	91	79

■ **Tip for Interpreting Correlations**

Correlations smaller than .20 are often described as slight or inconsequential, those between .20 and .40 are low correlations, correlation coefficients between .40 and .70 are moderate correlations, and anything above .70 is said to be a strong correlation.

You would simply select which variable should be the row variable and which the column variable, and then indicate the control variable. In this case, two different chi-squares would be produced: one for women respondents and one for male respondents.

In this example, there are no significant differences among the female respondents ($p = .09$). However, there were significant differences by community of residence for the male respondents ($p = .009$).

The elaboration model typically begins with the original findings from a survey and then explores relationships between two variables before introducing a third. The search is for causal explanations that, unlike laboratory experiments where the investigator has a greater ability to regulate the influence of extraneous variables, must be controlled by statistical procedures. This notion of controlling variables is the basis on which multivariate analysis rests.

MULTIVARIATE ANALYSIS OF DATA

Multivariate analysis is any statistical procedure that involves several, sometimes many, independent variables and at least one dependent variable, although there may be more than one dependent variable as well.

Multiple regression is a term used when a researcher is interested in using an array of independent variables to find out which ones make the best predictors for a specified dependent variable measured at the interval level. Through complex statistical procedures, beta weights are computed and tested for significance. The researcher can choose to allow them to enter the regression equation simultaneously or one at a time. Often, researchers let the computer do the selecting of the best predictor variables based on those that have the highest correlation with the dependent variable. Multiple regression produces R^2, which reports on the percent of variation in the dependent variable explained by the predictor variables.

There are many more statistical procedures and ways to go about analyzing data than there were 20 years ago. But the best news is that it is also a lot easier now than it has ever been. The goal in writing this chapter was not to tell you everything you need to know about data analysis but to help you understand how you might begin to go about looking for patterns and trends in the data you collect. Admittedly, it is a little scary when you don't know all of the vocabulary and may not know how to proceed at times, but dive in! There is no shortage of useful guides to consult. Data analysis is at least as important as conceptualizing the study and collecting the data. Don't rely on others who may not understand the data as well as you do (or understand what you want to accomplish)—to decide how your data should be examined or what constitutes your main findings.

A FINAL NOTE

Most of the techniques described in this chapter (for example, chi-square, *t* tests, one-way analysis of variance) are commonly used in **ex post facto** research. This is research that takes place after the data have been gathered, generally when unexpected findings generate new hypotheses or research questions. Ex post facto research occurs frequently in analyzing the results of surveys when, for example, the investigator might wonder if individuals who differ on some attitudes are also different in terms of income level or education. Ex post facto research may involve the elaboration process.

A cautionary note: It is entirely possible to put too much importance on statistical significance. For instance, suppose you are running an after-school program for delinquent youth. At the end of the school year you find that those in the intervention group have seen their grade point average rise from 1.40 to 1.65. A *t* test reveals this to be statistically significant at $p < .05$. You feel good about this "important finding" until someone points out that practically speaking, there has been no major improvement—that most of the group is still having academic problems. In the same way, a group of persons receiving intervention for depression might show some statistically significant reduction in symptoms but still be depressed and in need of treatment. The point here is that researchers should not be so swept away by the finding of significance that they forget about other considerations: Are the results also practically or clinically significant?

KEY TERMS

raw data	mean	chi-square (χ^2)	ANOVA
case	mode	cross-tabulation	correlation coefficient
code	median	*t* test	correlation matrix
codebook	standard deviation	independent samples	multivariate analysis
univariate analysis	nominal variables	paired samples *t* test	multiple regression
frequency distribution	interval variables	one-way analysis of variance	ex post facto
measures of central tendency	ordinal		

SELF-REVIEW

(Answers at the end of the book)

1. Which measure of central tendency is affected by extreme scores?
   a. median
   b. mode
   c. mean
   d. stetactic harmony

2. Labeling clients' progress after intervention as "improved" or "not improved" would be using what level of measurement?

3. Labeling clients' progress after intervention as "major improvement," "slight improvement," or "no improvement" would be using what level of measurement?

4. A frequency distribution would be most useful to a researcher at what level of analysis?
   a. multivariate
   b. bivariate
   c. univariate
   d. trivariate

5. A cross-tabulation is associated with which level of analysis?
   a. multivariate
   b. bivariate
   c. univariate
   d. trivariate

6. Juanita runs an outpatient clinic for teens with substance abuse problems. She claims that 60% of the clients are "improved" after six visits and that only 40% are "not improved." What statistical procedure would she use to see if males made more improvement than females?
   a. chi-square
   b. *t* test
   c. one-way analysis of variance
   d. frequency distribution

7. In a self-esteem group Sue was leading, the participants' mean score at pretest was 35.6 and posttest 41.1. She wants to know if this is a statistically significant improvement. With this interval data, Sue would use what statistical procedure?
   a. chi-square
   b. *t* test
   c. one-way analysis of variance
   d. normal distribution

8. Sue wants to examine her clients' improvement by the variable of attendance. She divides her clients into three groups: those with "good" attendance, those with "average" attendance, and those with "poor" attendance. Using the same instrument as in exercise (7) but with three groups instead of two, what statistical procedure should Sue employ?

    a. chi-square

    b. *t* test

    c. one-way analysis of variance

    d. standard deviation

9. How much variation between two variables does a correlation coefficient of .35 explain?

    a. about 30%

    b. about 20%

    c. about 12%

    d. less than 5%

10. T or F. Using the appropriate statistical test, Carolyn obtained a probability of .90. This indicates that her findings are statistically significant.

11. What does $p > .05$ mean?

    a. a statistically significant difference

    b. differences between or among means was not statistically significant

    c. that the odds of obtaining approximately the same means could happen by chance more than 5 times in 100

    d. both b and c are correct

    e. none of the above are correct

QUESTIONS FOR CLASS DISCUSSION

1. While charts or graphs can help readers grasp a study's findings, what is the problem with solely using charts and graphs to understand a study?
2. What are the limitations associated with doing correlational research?
3. What are the statistical software packages used at your college or university? What are students' experiences with these programs?
4. Why is it important for social work researchers to be able to conduct their own statistical analyses?
5. Is it possible to write a credible, professional evaluation of a program's effectiveness without using statistical analysis? Under what circumstances?
6. Which facet of statistical analysis is most difficult to understand? Which is the easiest?

RESOURCES AND REFERENCES

Blanksby, P. E., & Barber, J. G. (2006). SPSS for social workers: An introductory workbook. Boston: Allyn & Bacon.

Girden, E. R. (1996). *Evaluating research articles from start to finish*. Thousand Oaks, CA: Sage.

Kanji, G. P. (1993). *100 statistical tests*. Newbury Park, CA: Sage.

Montcalm, D., & Royse, D. (2002). *Data analysis for social workers*. Boston, MA: Allyn & Bacon.

Nunnally, J. M. (1994). *Psychometric theory*. New York: McGraw-Hill.

Shlonsky, A., D'Andrade, A., & Brookhart, M. A. (2002). JSWE submission suggestions for statistical methods. *Journal of Social Work Education, 38*, 5–13.

ASSIGNMENT 13.1: Analyzing Data

Objective: *To obtain firsthand experience with entering data and performing statistical procedures on the computer.*

Before beginning this assignment you will need to collect some raw data. If you are interning in a social service agency perhaps you can look at the last 50 admissions to the agency in terms of age, gender, race, etc. Or, there may be some other project that needs your assistance. Of course, it will be important to get your supervisor's permission if you are using real client data as it will be important to protect their personal information. Alternatively, your research methods instructor may direct you to conduct a small survey of classmates using either the scale you created in Assignment 5.1 or the instrument that you discussed in Assignment 5.3. If SPSS or SAS or other statistical software are not available to you, a comprehensive collection of interactive statistical computation pages are maintained by John Pezzullo at http://statpages.org.

1. State a hypothesis:

2. What is your dependent variable? Is it nominal, ordinal, or interval/ratio?

3. What variable or variables will you use to analyze the dependent variable? (For each variable named, identify the level of measurement.)

4. What statistical procedure(s) will you be performing?

5. What are your findings? (Your instructor may also want you to submit a printout of your table or findings.)

ASSIGNMENT 13.2: Analyzing Data

Objective: *To obtain firsthand experience with entering data and performing statistical procedures on the computer.*

Enter the data from the next page into the statistical software that you intend to use. If SPSS or SAS or other similar software are not available to you, a comprehensive collection of interactive statistical computation pages are maintained by John Pezzullo at http://statpages.org. Once you have entered the data, you can test hypotheses that there are differences, for example, in:

- clients' ratings of services by gender, age, income, or marital status

- clients' ratings of case managers by gender, age, income, or marital status

- clients' incomes by gender, age, or marital status

- clients' ages by gender, marital status, or income

- clients' willingness to recommend the agency to friends by program type, gender, or marital status

- program participation by gender, age, marital status, or income

You might also want to see if there is a correlation between age and income. Your instructor may tell you which statistical procedure to use or possibly which hypothesis to test. Follow these instructions:

1. Write your hypotheses here.

2. What is your dependent variable? What is its level of measurement?

3. What statistical procedure did you use? Why?

4. Describe your findings.

Data for Assignment 13.2

Service	Gender	Status	Age	Reported Income	Rating of Services	Would Recommend Agency	Rating of Case Manager
Case Manage.	Male	Married	86	$12,000	Good	Yes	4
Case Manage.	Male	Married	83	$17,000	No Info.	No Info.	No Info.
Homemaker	Male	Widowed	77	$15,000	Good	Yes	4
Homemaker	Female	Divorced	65	$11,850	Excellent	Yes	5
Meals	Male	Separated	92	$10,000	Excellent	Yes	5
Transport.	Female	No Info.	78	$9,775	Good	Don't Know	3
Transport.	Female	Separated	68	$14,000	Fair	No	2
Case Manage.	Male	Widowed	69	$17,000	Excellent	Yes	5
Case Manage.	Female	Widowed	70	$13,680	Good	Yes	4
Case Manage.	Female	Widowed	75	$13,500	Fair	Yes	4
Case Manage.	Male	Divorced	85	$19,950	Poor	No	1
Transport.	Female	Separated	71	$18,100	Good	Yes	4
Meals	Male	Divorced	84	$13,000	Excellent	Yes	5
Meals	Male	Widowed	90	$17,750	Excellent	Yes	5
Meals	Female	Married	68	$14,000	Good	Yes	4
Case Manage.	Male	Married	83	$13,000	Good	Yes	4
Transport.	Male	Divorced	73	$18,000	Poor	No	2
Transport.	Female	Married	79	$14,333	Fair	Don't Know	3
Homemaker	Male	Separated	87	$17,250	Excellent	Yes	5
Homemaker	Female	Widowed	66	$14,400	Excellent	Yes	5
Transport.	Female	Widowed	74	$14,800	Good	No Info.	3
Transport.	Female	Separated	83	$12,565	Good	Yes	4
Meals	Female	Married	75	$19,000	Good	Yes	4
Meals	Female	Separated	66	$16,000	Good	No Info.	3
Transport.	Male	Separated	67	$18,000	Fair	Yes	3
Transport.	Female	Widowed	87	$12,000	Good	Yes	4
Homemaker	Male	Divorced	68	$10,000	Good	Yes	4
Meals	Male	Widowed	65	$9,000	Excellent	Yes	5

Service	Gender	Status	Age	Reported Income	Rating of Services	Would Recommend Agency	Rating of Case Manager
Meals	Male	Married	84	$20,000	Poor	No	1
Homemaker	Male	Separated	74	$19,000	Fair	Yes	2
Homemaker	Female	Widowed	80	$22,000	Good	Yes	3
Homemaker	Female	Widowed	82	$11,950	Excellent	Yes	4
Case Manage.	Male	Married	81	$17,600	Good	Yes	5
Case Manage.	Female	Married	72	$20,250	Good	Yes	4
Case Manage.	Female	Married	76	$22,000	Excellent	Yes	4
Case Manage.	Female	Married	82	$17,800	Good	Yes	5
Case Manage.	Female	Married	90	$15,000	Fair	No Info.	No Info.
Meals	Male	Divorced	72	$14,000	Fair	Yes	4
Meals	Male	Widowed	79	$11,000	Excellent	Yes	4
Transport.	Female	Married	70	$12,050	Fair	Yes	2
Meals	Female	Widowed	80	$12,000	Fair	Yes	5
Meals	Female	Widowed	78	$11,600	Good	Yes	4
Homemaker	Male	Widowed	79	$11,300	Excellent	Yes	5
Homemaker	Female	Widowed	77	$12,900	Good	No Info.	3
Homemaker	Female	Divorced	68	$10,800	Good	Yes	4
Case Manage.	Male	Divorced	71	$10,400	Good	Yes	4
Case Manage.	Female	Widowed	70	$10,200	Excellent	Yes	5
Case Manage.	Female	Widowed	77	$9,600	Excellent	Yes	4
Case Manage.	Female	Divorced	66	$9,800	Good	Yes	4
Transport.	Male	Widowed	64	$10,900	Fair	No	2
Case Manage.	Female	Separated	65	$20,000	Fair	No	1
Case Manage.	Female	Widowed	70	$10,800	Excellent	Good	5

Professional Writing

CHAPTER 14

Proposals, Research Reports, and Journal Articles

Although it may seem strange to have a chapter with a focus on writing at the end of a book on research methods, there are three good reasons for this. First, it is very likely that at some point in your career as a social worker you will want to apply to a funding source for monies to develop some new intervention or expand services. The larger the scale of the effort you have in mind, the greater the likelihood that you could benefit from external funding. Grant writing often falls to staff who are knowledgeable about research since funding sources usually expect an evaluation component to be built in to the proposal.

Guess what? Having completed a social work program that required at least one research course makes you "knowledgeable." That is, because your knowledge is more recent, in some cases it may be viewed by your supervisor as more relevant and valuable than that of other staff with even more work experience.

Second, social workers (particularly those with MSW degrees) not uncommonly find themselves on committees or assigned to projects that must report the results of some kind of data collection. For example, these reports may be about the characteristics of clients who are utilizing the agency's services or who have received special services, or may involve studies of staff utilization and caseload changes over time. If a formal report is expected, you'll need to know the standard conventions for presenting this information.

Third, you may need to write a thesis or dissertation some day, or perhaps you'll be a part of a group interested in drafting a manuscript for a professional journal. At any rate, because social work research is *applied,* it is necessary to communicate the findings of your project to others. These people may include academic types (e.g., your advisor or dissertation committee) or your supervisor, the staff in your agency, perhaps the agency's board of directors. You may want to share results with the larger professional community. But whether you are writing a grant proposal or reporting the results of a program evaluation, the elements that you must address are very similar. This chapter presents an overview of the important components needed when planning for or reporting a research effort.

WRITING GRANT PROPOSALS

Most research grant proposals require that your application addresses the various components of a research report that we discuss in this chapter. Not only do you need good written communication skills to write a persuasive grant application, but you also need to understand the role of the **principal investigator (PI)** and how to prepare timetables, work plans, and budget justifications.

The information in this section is presented to help you prepare for the time when you will be asked to write a grant proposal. A successful grant proposal has three essential components: a compelling idea, a funding source interested in that idea, and a plan or statement of methodology explaining how the project will be carried out.

What is a compelling idea? Generally, grant writers must convince the prospective funding source that there is a real problem of some kind and that the organization or PI has an approach that stands a reasonable chance of making an impact. Often foundations and large state or federal agencies announce their intentions to fund research or programs designed to address specific problems. These announcements are known as **requests for proposals** and are generally referred to as **RFPs.** These RFPs usually contain all of the instructions that you need for preparing a grant proposal—giving precise details as to what the funding source is and is not willing to fund, as well as information such as how long particular sections of the proposal may be. When no current RFP has been issued, researchers and program developers often write letters of inquiry to logical funding sources to determine if the agency or foundation would be willing to receive a proposal regarding the specific idea. A compelling idea may be an innovative program or new research; it may also be an idea that has been around for a while that has been given a fresh twist. Once you have a good idea that warrants further development and a firm funding source that may want to underwrite the expense of your project, then your next step is to begin thinking about writing the grant proposal. If you have enough time, forming a community advisory group could provide useful guidance and feedback.

These are the elements that typically go into a grant proposal:

Problem statement: This section of the proposal describes the magnitude of the problem that your compelling idea would address and furnishes background information about the reason for the funding request. It will be important to be very knowledgeable about the literature on the program or problem. You are expected to be an expert and well informed about the efforts of others with regard to this problem. It will be necessary to include statistics showing the extent of the problem as well as statements from local, state, or other prominent authorities. Describe the target population and define these individuals in terms of prominent characteristics. If your project involves the creation of a new program or service, it will be important to conduct a needs assessment to show which needs in the community the proposal would address. Reviewers of your proposal will want to know who will benefit from your program and what impact it is expected to make on the problem. Generally speaking, new and original ideas will get a lot further in the process than ideas that have been around for a long while. Make sure that the innovative facets of your project stand out. It is critical that your project's purpose be clearly stated and, further, that it be consistent with the RFP guidelines or the funding source's priorities.

Qualifications of the organization: The RFP may require that you address the capacity of your agency to deliver the proposed program or to conduct the research. Accordingly, you may want to discuss your agency's mandate for services, the variety of programs offered, geographical service area covered, the make-up and qualifications of staff, their accomplishments, and such details that would convince the funding source of the agency's ability to launch and support the project. List any agency accomplishments or achievements and summarize any outcome evaluation studies or reports that relate to the effectiveness of existing programs. If the proposal will be taking the agency in a different direction or to a different clientele, it will be important to show how this activity will complement the agency's long-range goals or new emphasis. You may want to provide a description of board members or key personnel—particularly if their experience or credentials add to the credibility of your agency. If your agency has a great deal of experience with this type of problem or client group, make sure to highlight it. Readers of your proposal will be looking for indications of the agency's competence and capacity. Working relationships and partnerships with other agencies are generally a plus, as is a history of success in securing prior grants. Sometimes it is essential to describe your agency's facilities.

Proposed goals and objectives: List the goals and measurable objectives associated with the project, along with dates showing when key events or activities will take place. The goals and objectives must relate to what you hope to accomplish with the project. Don't create a set of inconsequential tasks that roam away from the project; they should be directly related in a meaningful way. Be realistic in your plans.

Methodology: In this section you fully describe what will take place if you receive funding. If the proposal is a research-oriented one, this section will detail the research design, research procedures to be followed, how subjects will be recruited, and discuss such matters as the instrumentation to be employed, operationalization of dependent variables, data analysis, and so forth. If the proposal centers on expansion of services or development of a new program, this section will address the activities necessary for increasing service delivery or producing the program. Consequently, you'll need to discuss such items as hiring new staff, acquiring new facilities, how the program will be implemented, how prospective clients will be informed, etc. You may be asked to provide a flow chart showing who has what responsibilities. It may also be necessary to write narrative describing the rationale for your plans—particularly if they are creative or somewhat out of the ordinary. You must convince sometimes skeptical readers about the feasibility of your project.

Evaluation: Almost all federal agencies expect a program evaluation plan. Many other funding sources do also. They may require an outcome evaluation where you would discuss how you plan to measure the project's success (or lack of success). This section builds on and benefits from clearly stated objectives that you previously listed. If, for example, you will be surveying clients (e.g., a client satisfaction study) or reviewing records in order to document subsequent problem behaviors, this is the place where you will be discussing your evaluation plan and methodology. It is a good idea to give thought to the questionnaires or instruments that will be needed as a part of this effort so that you can append them to your proposal (if required by the RFP). Consider, too, the way that data will be collected and analyzed. The RFP might also require a process evaluation, which is a narrative description of how the project unfolded, the key decisions that were made, the activities that took place, and what resulted. Your proposal must demonstrate accountability for the funds received.

Budget: Every proposal will need to contain a budget that identifies all major expenses (e.g., staff salaries and benefits, rent, supplies, photocopies, utilities, office furniture, etc.). It will also likely be necessary to list in-kind contributions (i.e., what your agency donates in the way of staff's salaries and benefits, office space, equipment, etc., as well as what volunteers or others in the community may donate).

Future funding: The RFP may ask about your agency's plans to continue the project after the grant funding period ends. What plans are there for future funding needs?

In addition to the key components already identified, it is often necessary to show that you have community support from agencies and professionals in prominent positions. Letters of endorsement are particularly important from those providing in-kind support such as the contribution of staff or clients to the project. Once your proposal has been drafted, it might be a good idea to get someone not involved with the project to read and critique your efforts so that you can revise it and make the best possible presentation. Take care to be neat and eliminate all spelling and grammatical errors. Make sure that it is delivered to the right location prior to the submission deadline. Finally, make sure that you have followed all of the directions exactly, made the proper number of copies, and written an interesting cover letter to accompany the proposal. Then you wait, sometimes several months, before announcements are made about the funding awards. If you are among the lucky ones, then you can start developing and testing your ideas. Later you will probably be required to write a report to communicate what you learned from the implementation of your project.

WRITING RESEARCH REPORTS

Let's imagine that you have conducted some exciting research and want to communicate your findings. Even if the results didn't turn out quite as expected, you might be prompted to write about your research because the agency executive asks you to draft a report on your project, or because the grant or funding source requires an evaluation. Your audience may run the gamut from coworkers inside your agency to citizens in the community, from nitpicking professors to federal bureaucrats. What would you need to tell them? What format would you follow? The purpose of this section is to show you how to conceptualize and prepare a report of research findings. Please note that the essential elements of a research report with quantitative data are the same as required in a thesis, dissertation, or professional journal article with some minor differences in emphasis or depth. Qualitative dissertations as a rule usually follow this model as well in terms of the main components. However, reports of qualitative research may not conform to this outline. Each of these major categories of presentation will be explained in more depth.

COMPONENTS OF A RESEARCH REPORT

1. Introduction
   a. description of problem
   b. statement of research question or hypothesis
   c. significance of problem and rationale for studying it
2. Literature review
   a. theoretical and historical perspectives
   b. identified gaps in literature
   c. reiteration of purpose of study
3. Methodology
   a. research design and data collection procedures
   b. characteristics of subjects

c. sampling design
d. description of instrumentation
e. data analysis procedures
4. Findings (results)
    a. factual information presented
    b. statistical and practical significance discussed
    c. tables, charts
5. Discussion
    a. brief summary of findings
    b. explanation of unexpected findings
    c. applications to practice
    d. weaknesses or limitations of research
    e. suggestions for future research
6. References
7. Appendices

Introduction

The purpose of the Introduction of the report is to present the research question or problem and to place it within some context or frame of reference. This generally entails describing the problem and its extent. For instance, if your project is about developing services for adolescent parents, a logical starting place would be recent estimates of the number of teenaged girls who become pregnant each year. Is it 100,000 or 1,000,000? Has it been increasing lately or falling off? Your reader should understand the scope of the problem and the kinds of difficulties experienced by teen parents.

There are many different ways to begin a report, and the nature of your topic may suggest an approach. In a content analysis of social work literature, Sutphen (1997) opened with a question:

> How involved is social work in the juvenile justice field? Several social work scholars have questioned the extent of the profession's involvement in this field (Roberts, 1983; Spake, 1987) and have suggested that it is less involved today that it has been in the past (Corcoran & Shireman, 1996; Ezell, 1996). A 1991 survey of more than 87,000 NASW members seems to provide some substance to these claims. The survey revealed that merely 1,025 (1.2%) social workers were working in the justice area, and only 500 listed it as a secondary area of practice. These are results that are virtually unchanged from 1972, and they stand in contrast to a field such as mental health that attracts one out of three NASW members. (Gibelman & Schervish, 1993; McNeece, 1996)

View the Introduction as an opportunity to stimulate the readers' interest in your topic. Tell readers how your research or program is different and why innovative methods are needed. You might start with what is known about a problem and then move to what is not known about it. Controversies work, too. Briefly present the debate as it serves as the stage from which your research emerges.

When you have finished writing the Introduction, read it over to make sure that you have:

1. Articulated some problem or issue
2. Identified your specific research question or hypothesis
3. Offered a rationale for your study

The easiest research reports to read are those that engage the reader's interest. Williams and Hopps (1988) have noted, "Getting off to a good start truly is three-quarters of the battle" (p. 456). One way to do this is to present the problem early in the Introduction instead of burying it toward the end. Material discussed in your Introduction makes more sense when the reader has a clear understanding of the problem prompting your investigation. Don't be afraid to let your enthusiasm for the topic (or your concern about the significance of the problem) be revealed. There's no point in writing so dispassionately that no one will care about your conclusions.

Review of the Literature

The Literature Review section of a report or journal article is where relevant studies and theoretical explanations of the problem or phenomenon of interest are summarized. You need not describe every study that has ever been conducted on your topic. Cite only those pertinent to the issues with which you are dealing. Inform your readers about the major findings from other research. For example, consider the following fictitious excerpt:

> While relatively little has been written in the social work literature about shoplifting, it is a topic of interest to those who work in the criminal justice system because of the seemingly complex dynamics involved. Financial need does not always appear to be a significant factor. Almost all of the studies have shown that poverty is not a major explanation for shoplifting (Mills, 1996). Shoplifters tend to come from all economic classes (Hunt, 1994), and the overwhelming majority of persons caught shoplifting do not intend to resell the item (Book & Vurm, 1997). It has also been noted that in only a minority of cases is shoplifting associated with mental illness, and the majority of arrested shoplifters do not have any psychotic features (Doktor, 1995). Recent studies have shown that shoplifters are not apprehended differentially by race, sex, or age when control variables are employed (Mills, 1996; Vurm, 1996).

From this brief example we can learn that theories based on economic deprivation or mental illness have not been found to explain shoplifting. Further, explanations involving a greater level of absentmindedness among the elderly do not seem to be viable. Since these theories have been tested and then discarded, the way is open for a new theoretical explanation—perhaps that shoplifting is a help-seeking activity unconsciously motivated by high levels of stress.

This passage also demonstrates how quite a few studies can be summarized in a short amount of space. Learn to summarize succinctly other studies and articles. Don't provide irrelevant information. For example, it is usually inconsequential whether the studies were conducted in Idaho or Missouri. It is more important that the literature review show trends in the major findings of these studies. However, the location, methodology, sample size, and other facets of the earlier research can take on more importance if you are replicating a study or want to note how your study is different from or similar to that of other research. Your study may correct problems found in a previous study. Generally, though, do not go into great detail regarding the methodology and *each* finding in all of the prior studies mentioned in your review of the literature. Also, avoid citing lengthy passages.

In reviewing the literature, you may find a number of competing theories. Even though you may not subscribe to all of them, you still owe it to your readers to give a balanced presentation and to acknowledge rival theories or explanations. This background helps provide some of the controversy or interest that can make reading your article or report more enjoyable.

Since new research is usually conducted on those topics on which there is not much literature, the review of the literature section helps justify your research by pointing out gaps in the knowledge base. Unless you are replicating someone's study, you are likely to be conducting research in an area where not much is known. This gap in knowledge provides a major impetus for research. See, for example, Royse (1999):

> There has been little investigation of the effectiveness of efforts to engage first-time blood donors more substantially in the process of maintaining the community's blood supply and thus produce more committed donors. Similarly, there has been no research on how incentives or efforts designed to increase self-identity as a blood donor actually affect subsequent donations. This research was planned to test the effectiveness of an incentive and two different foot-in-the-door techniques designed to foster greater self-attribution as a blood donor as measured by the number of units donated by first-time donors. (Royse, 1998)

After you have reviewed the relevant literature and noted the gaps in knowledge on a particular problem or topic, it is helpful to restate the purpose of your study. The reader may not be as familiar with the problem area as you are, and restating your hypothesis or research question will assist the reader in assimilating the potpourri of literature to which he or she has just been exposed.

When you have finished writing your review of the literature section, look it over to make sure that you have:

1. Covered all of the major studies in the field
2. Included the most recent studies (there shouldn't be a large period of time without any studies; if you discover that all of your references are dated between 1988 and 1995, then you probably need to look a little further)
3. Summarized what is *not* known about the problem you have been studying and reminded the reader of your specific interest

When you have done these things, then you are ready to begin the methodology section.

The Methods Section

The Methods section of the report describes in detail how you conducted the study. In this section, the reader learns the procedures how you collected the data. Typically, the following are described:

1. *The research design.* Explain whether it was an experiment, a non-equivalent control group design, or a survey of some sort.
2. *The subjects.* How were they recruited or selected? Random or convenience sampling? What was special or unique about the subjects?
3. *Data collection procedures.* Did you use mailed questionnaires, record reviews, or personally interview the respondents?
4. *The instrumentation.* What instruments did you use? Have the instruments been used in a similar application before? What is known about the instruments' reliability and validity?
5. *Data analysis.* What statistical procedures did you employ?

You should give sufficient information in this section to allow another investigator to replicate the study. Commonly, subsections and subheadings are used to differentiate the various components of the methodology. This is an example of how one author described her research design (Morrow, 1996):

STUDY DESIGN

The research design was quasi-experimental, which has been found to be appropriate for "natural social settings" (Campbell & Stanley, 1963). The design was a derivative of Campbell and Stanley's research design 5. An experimental group was pretested, received the intervention, and was posttested. A comparison group was pretested as a comparison measure for the experimental group. For ethical reasons, including the risk of dropout related to the emotional stress of a waiting period in exploring personal issues related to coming out, the control group received an intervention similar to the experimental group after the pretests without being required to undergo a waiting period for the sake of posttesting. Thus, the pretesting of the control group served as the comparison measure for the experimental group. Additional measurements included within-group comparison of experimental pretest and posttest means on each of the dependent variables. (pp. 649–650)

You will see somewhat different approaches in the way authors describe their subjects. However, your readers will typically be interested in how many subjects you had, how you selected them, and something about their personal characteristics. In their article, Nugent, Champlin, and Wiinimaki (1997) handled it this way when describing the participants in an anger control training program in a group home for adolescents:

SAMPLE

The subjects involved in this study were 102 male adolescents between 12 and 18 years of age. The mean age of the males in this study was 14.7 years ($SD = 3$). Only about 14% of the sample were minorities. All subjects were in custody of the state of Tennessee Department of Youth Development for delinquent and/or unruly behavior. One group of males, nine of whom agreed to participate in this study, was living in a group home (Group Home A) in which ACT was implemented. A second group of males, four of whom agreed to participate in this study, was living in a second group home (Group Home B) in which ACT was not conducted. The four males in Group Home B made up one comparison group. A total of 89 other males in state custody for delinquent and unruly behavior were a random sample drawn as part of a previous study (Glisson, 1994, 1996) and were used as a second comparison group. (p. 448)

Readers will also be interested in the instruments or measures used in the study. Typically, you identify the source reference for the instrument and discuss its reliability and validity, as in the following example (Oktay, 1992):

> The Maslach Burnout Inventory was used to measure burnout (Maslach & Jackson, 1981). This instrument measures three components of burnout: emotional exhaustion, depersonalization ("loss of concern and feelings for clients"), and (lack of) personal accomplishment ("a negative self-concept and negative job attitudes") (Pines & Maslach, 1978, p. 233). The original instrument measured each area for frequency and intensity; however, the instrument's authors have stated that the frequency scale can be used alone, as was done in this study, with acceptable results (Maslach, 1987). The instrument has 22 items, and each is answered in terms of how frequently the feeling is experienced.
>
> Test-retest reliability is reported by Maslach and Jackson (1981) as follows: emotional exhaustion, .82; depersonalization, .60; and personal accomplishment, .80. Internal consistency (alpha) for these subscales is .90, .79, and .71, respectively. Maslach and Jackson also tested the instrument for discriminant and confirmatory validity, with satisfactory results. More recent analyses of the MBI using factor analysis confirm its validity. (Koeske & Koeske, 1989, p. 434)

Usually only a paragraph or two is needed to inform the reader about the way in which the data were analyzed. Here's the first of two paragraphs on the data analysis from an article about adult children with mental illness serving as supports to their mothers in later life (Greenberg, 1995):

ANALYSIS

> Descriptive statistics address the first purpose of this study: to investigate the amount of help that adult children with mental illness provided to their mothers. Hierarchical multiple regression was used to test the major research hypothesis: whether the social support provided by the adult child was associated with a lower level of maternal subjective burden. The study used a hierarchical regression strategy to determine the amount of additional variance the adult child's support explained in subjective burden after controlling for background variables and sources of stress. The control variables were entered in step 2 of the hierarchical regression model. In step 3, the measure of the adult child's support and assistance to his or her mother was entered. (p. 418)

When you have finished writing your methodology section, look it over to make sure that you have:

1. Explained *who* will be involved. (Who are the research subjects? How will they be recruited and informed of their rights?)

2. Defined *what* data will be collected and analyzed. (Make sure key independent and dependent variables are identified as well as all instruments to be used.)

3. Provided the reader with a firm notion about *when* the data collection will begin and end.

4. Stated *where* the data collection will take place and under whose auspices.

5. Clearly explained the need for all portions of the research protocol so that the reader understands *why* you are doing what you are doing. In other words, it should be very obvious how the methodology will serve the research question or hypotheses.

When you have answered these questions, then you are ready to begin the Results section.

The Results

This section of the report or article contains what you actually discovered from conducting your research. The Results section summarizes the data. You do not present the raw data; only report aggregate or average scores. Up to this point, you have not revealed your findings. Now it is time to exhibit your results. Your task in this section is to present the findings factually, without opinion. The facts must stand by themselves.

You can organize your findings in many ways. The most common practice is to present the major findings first. If you have used several hypotheses, report your findings relative to the first hypothesis, then move to the second hypothesis, and so on.

Many researchers and would-be authors often feel overwhelmed because there appears to be too much information for a single research report. This can happen when they have lots of hypotheses or have performed a large number of statistical analyses. Thinking that all findings are equally important may also contribute to a feeling of drowning in data.

Sometimes it is helpful to get a blank sheet of paper and write down what you would report if limited to one major point. Then ask yourself, "What is the second most important finding coming from this study?" This process continues until you have identified all of the important points. Once you have noted all the key findings, begin thinking about how to present them. Tables are helpful in that they visually break up the narrative while providing precise information that makes for dry reading if incorporated into the text.

Most research reports contain tables as a way of reducing verbiage. You should develop at least one or two tables for your research report. However, having too many tables is almost as bad as not having enough. Don't overdo it. When too many tables are employed, it is hard for a reader or reviewer to keep all of the main points in mind; the information tends to run together.

In the Results section you will also report the outcomes of the statistical tests you have conducted. For example, if your studies found that BSW social workers received higher quality assurance ratings than MSW social workers, it will be important to determine if the difference in ratings is statistically significant. Do not allow your readers to conclude that a difference of three points, for example, makes BSW social workers superior to MSW social workers if a *t* test or other appropriate statistical test reveals no statistically significant difference in their scores. Report the average scores, the results of statistical tests, and the associated probability.

Take the time to prepare the tables in such a way that the data displayed can be "digested." Don't throw some numbers together and think you are done, as in the following example:

Scale	Pretest Mean	Posttest Mean	*t* Value	Significance
A	5.308	4.809	2.15	.04
B	4.339	5.900	4.11	.001
C	6.663	5.323	2.84	.01
D	5.777	4.990	1.57	.13
E	6.191	7.42	1.92	.07
F	5.901	6.02	1.85	.80

Although this table might look neat and tidy, notice that it has no heading or caption. The reader has no idea what is being presented or what the scales represent. Do lower posttest mean scores suggest client improvement or do they indicate that clients have gotten worse? The reader should not have to guess whether Scale A represents social maladjustment or if that concept is represented by Scale E.

If you are in doubt about how to present your findings in tabular form, consult the *Publication Manual of the American Psychological Association*, which is widely used by social work journals. The manual also demonstrates how to portray statistical data within the text. For instance, chi-square is shown this way:

There were no statistically significant differences among the four groups by race χ^2 (6, $N = 1,003$) $= 4.41$, $p = .62$, or gender χ^2 (3, $N = 1,003$) $= 1.33$, $p = .72$.

One-way analysis of variance is expressed in this manner:

There were no statistically significant differences in the number of referrals by group F (3, 1,002) $= .75$, $p = .53$.

Sometimes the characteristics of a study's sample are shown in the results section. In an article by Hudson and McMurtry (1997), the authors described their research participants in their Results section this way:

RESPONDENTS

All 311 respondents were either undergraduate or masters-level students in research courses in the seven schools of social work that participated in the study. Demographic information gathered via the background questionnaire is summarized in the second column in Table 1. As the information shows, the respondents were predominantly female (79%), White (80%), and unmarried (59%). The mean age of the sample was 32.4 years, the mean number of years of schooling completed was 16.4, and the mean annual family income of the respondents was about $40,000. The mean number of times married was less than one (0.7), and for those currently married, the mean number of years with the current spouse was 6.1. The average total family size of the respondents was 1.8, and the mean number of children was 0.9. (pp. 87–88)

When you have presented all of the results that merit reporting, then it is time to move on to the Discussion section.

The Discussion

The Discussion section often begins with a brief summary of your findings. It is not necessary to go into a lot of detail—this information was just exhibited in the Results. Just address the major findings or the highlights of your study. Once that is done, you can begin to flesh out the findings. Perhaps you were surprised to find that the BSWs in your study performed better than the MSW employees; here is the place to elaborate the reasons for your surprise. You can reveal any unexpected findings—as well as what didn't go as planned.

Most importantly, the Discussion section should interpret the findings for the reader and address the relevance of these findings for practice. What do the findings mean or suggest to you? Are you recommending that social service agencies hire BSWs rather than persons with other undergraduate degrees? Does additional training seem to be indicated for the type of employee covered in your study? Do social work educators need to reexamine and possibly revise the curricula at their institutions? What implications does your study have for practice or policy? Discuss findings that have practical significance—even if there was no statistical significance. As Reid (1988) has indicated, our findings do not always "prove," "establish," or make a point so strongly that there can be no other interpretation. Usually, Discussion sections contain what he calls "appropriately qualified language" (p. 456)—phrases that indicate that the findings "provide evidence for," "suggest the possibility that," or "raise questions about."

The part of the Discussion section that many researchers do not like to write is the description of what did not go according to the research design. Sometimes secretaries forget to administer questionnaires. Clients drop out of studies or forget to bring needed documentation. Questionnaires were not mailed on time. These glitches are normal in applied social science research. Social workers don't have the same degree of control that laboratory scientists have. So, admit any major departures from planned research procedures. The problems you encountered in collecting your data may well explain why you got the results that you did. For instance, someone forgetting to mail reminder postcards could have caused you to have a lower response rate for one group than for another. A change in agency policies during the middle of your study could have changed staff morale or increased the proportion of employees who felt "burned out"—which in turn could have affected the quality of their work. Also, recognize biases that may have crept into your study or that you discovered too late to do anything about.

Your study may have significant limitations. Perhaps you had hoped for a representative sampling of social workers from all educational backgrounds, but you heard from 75% of the BSWs, and only 8% of the MSWs. In this section you can discuss the extent to which it is possible to generalize your research.

Almost every study has some limitations—perhaps the most common one is some sort of selection bias. If it is hard for you to think of limitations, you may want to review the section in Chapter 5 ("Research Designs for Group Comparisons") on internal and external threats to the validity of a study.

Many authors conclude their research reports and journal articles by indicating areas for future research. As a result of their experiences, they may have suggestions for other researchers about procedures, instruments, the operationalization of variables, sampling techniques, and so on. This can be done even if a researcher does not have plans for further work in that area but wishes others to benefit from what has been learned in the process of conducting the present research.

Here are two examples of how some authors addressed limitations:

> The study design was limited in the use of a matched comparison group, rather than a control group. However, a variety of measures indicated that the GAP (Growth and Achievement Program) clients did have consistent gains toward self-sufficiency over time compared with a similar group. Other studies have not examined similar outcomes in terms of progress towards self-sufficiency, focusing instead on indicators of mental health. The sample studied was similar to the SRO populations described in much of the literature (that is, it had low income and mental and physical health problems). (Shepard, 1997, p. 591)

> Finally, a weakness of this study lies in the relatively small clinical sample as well as the uncertainties regarding general application of the findings. Further research is needed to determine whether the results reported here may be replicated with different samples. Future research on the test-retest reliability of the scale is also important to make sure the scale does not suffer from response decay when used repeatedly on many occasions. These cautions notwithstanding, the evidence in this article provides a strong initial basis for recommending use of the IDI (Index of Drug Involvement) in clinical and research applications concerned with drug abuse. (Faul & Hudson, 1997, p. 572)

After your discussion section, you may want to prepare a separate section called "Conclusion." Whether you write a Conclusion section separate from your discussion section is usually a matter of individual preference. However, if your report is being prepared for a policy or advisory board, they will likely appreciate a listing of conclusions that have implications for actions that they may need to take. They will want to know if the intervention worked as expected. Were clients helped? Be careful not to become too exuberant and make claims that go beyond your data.

References, Appendices, and Abstracts

Whenever other written documents have been cited in your research reporting, they need to be listed in the Reference section at the end of the report or manuscript. References are usually listed alphabetically by authors' names, and there are various styles or ways in which the titles can appear. However, the APA style is both convenient and widely used. You may want to adopt this style unless told to use another.

The Appendix is where you place a copy of instruments, written instructions given to subjects, or important materials that may have been used during the course of your study. Research reports generally are not considered complete without a copy of your instrument.

Abstracts are brief summaries of reports or manuscripts. Abstracts are almost always difficult to write because of the need to compress a complex manuscript into a few paragraphs. When you write an abstract, limit yourself to a paragraph to introduce the study and no more than a paragraph to present each of your major findings. If you get stumped, look at several abstracts in a recent issue of *Social Work Abstracts* for ideas on how to be succinct. An *executive summary* is like an abstract and is prepared to present a quick overview of the project for board members, the news media, etc.

QUALITATIVE RESEARCH REPORTS

Because there are so many different types of qualitative research approaches, DePoy and Gitlin (1998) state that "there is not one single, accepted format for writing a qualitative research report" (p. 291). However, Drisko (2005), the editor of *Families in Society,* has written an essay entitled "Writing up Qualitative Research" for the readers of the journal. He says the qualitative research report ". . . must always tell the story of the project, richly convey the views of others, and detail implications" (p. 589). DePoy and Gitlin (1998) say it this way: "Interpretative schemes are often presented in storylike fashion in which main themes and subtexts unfold as the story is told" (p. 292).

As we have discussed earlier, qualitative research is different from the quantitative tradition and that difference is usually noticeable right away: there is a heavy use of narrative, as well as quotations from participants in their own voices that allow their views to "come alive to the reader" (Drisko, 2005, p. 592). Quantitatively oriented reports tend not to involve quotations from their research participants unless mixed methods of data collection were used, and seldom would quantitatively oriented investigators use quotations to the same extent as qualitative researchers. At the same time, Neale, Allen and Coombes (2005) remind us that the qualitative report authors should not "over-rely on the use of quotations" and "string together quotation after quotation with little comment in between" (p. 1590).

Another way in which qualitative reports differ from quantitative reports is that the qualitative researcher is expected to reveal his personal reactions, values or biases, that he or she may have recognized during the data collection. In fact, the qualitative researcher can write in first person (using "I" or "my" language) while this is not generally seen in quantitative reports.

Quantitative research reports often involve the testing of theory or hypotheses while the qualitative research report may result in the creation of theory. In the first stance, quantitative studies tend to have thorough reviews of the literature, whereas this is not a mandate for qualitative studies because of their inductive approach. Lastly, quantitative reports tend to include statistical analysis and tables; qualitative reports tend not to involve statistical analysis.

Drisco (2005) provides these suggestions of titles for those who need further direction in writing a qualitative research report:

Ely, M., Vinz, R., Anzul, M., & Downing, M. (1997). *In writing qualitative research: Living by words.* Bristol, PA: Falmer.

Golden-Biddle, K., & Locke, K. (1997). *Composing qualitative research.* Thousand Oaks, CA: Sage.

Padgett, D. (2004). The qualitative research experience. New York: Wadsworth.

Wolcott, H. (1990). *Writing up qualitative research.* Thousand Oaks, CA: Sage.

For an example of a qualitative report, you might want to read

R. R. Luquis, & I. J. Cruz (2006). Knowledge, attitudes, and perceptions about breast cancer and breast cancer screening among Hispanic women residing in south central Pennsylvania. *Journal of Community Health, 31(1),* 25–42.

Luquis and Cruz employed eight different focus groups, involving 56 Hispanic women total, and this is how they presented their first paragraph under the "Results" section:

When asked about cancer in general, most women reported that when they heard the word cancer the first thing that came to mind was either "muerte" (death), "temor" (fear), and/or "emfermedad mortal" (fatal disease). For example, a participant said, "death, it is an incurable disease." In another group, a woman stated "the truth is that when you hear about cancer, one gets very scared, and the only thing that one thinks is that death will come soon." Another woman added, "I get very afraid because I have family members who died of cancer." However, a couple of participants acknowledged that cancer could be prevented and treated. (p. 34)

Later in the "Discussion" section the authors draw this conclusion:

[M]ost participants reported that they have received no or minimal information about breast cancer from their health care provider or other sources (i.e., brochures, friends). This lack of information or misinformation might also reduce the likelihood that these women would practice breast cancer preventive behaviors. (p. 39)

Other examples of qualitative studies that would be good examples to read and possibly use as models for writing would be Wahab (2005) and Swanberg and Logan (2005) previously mentioned in Chapters 12 and 11, respectively.

WRITING AS A PRACTICE GOAL

Williams and Hopps (1987) noted that while few social workers "achieve comfort or familiarity with publishing," one of the hallmarks of a mature professional is that verifiable knowledge derived from practice is used to improve its quality, effectiveness, or efficiency. But where does confirmable knowledge come from? It does not flow automatically from work with clients or the conduct of research, but depends on the reporting of the research. All too often, good applied social work research is never "written up," but remains in file folders or on someone's desk until it becomes outdated or is thrown away. For the results of research to guide practice, the findings must be disseminated to colleagues and other professionals.

Writing about the successes and failures of interventions and about the problems of clients is clearly a responsibility of professional social workers. Indeed, the following passage is found in the National Association of Social Workers Code of Ethics (1996):

> 5.01 (d) Social workers should contribute to the knowledge base of social work and share with colleagues their knowledge related to practice, research, and ethics. Social workers should seek to contribute to the profession's literature and to share their knowledge at professional meetings and conferences.

Additionally, writing for professional audiences can also provide a great deal of personal satisfaction as well as recognition for your agency or university.

The basic structure and key elements needed to report research findings are the same whether one is writing a thesis, an evaluation report, or a journal article. Of course, there are some observable differences when we compare these three types of reports. For one thing, theses and dissertations tend to be much longer than journal articles. While manuscripts for journal articles must often be between 16 and 20 pages, research reports written for internal agency consumption and dissertations may have no set limit on the number of pages.

WRITING FOR PROFESSIONAL JOURNALS

This section contains some suggestions for taking a research report and developing it as a journal article. First, when you prepare a manuscript, have a specific journal in mind. Become familiar with that journal. Are its articles written for the practitioner or for the scholar? Journals have different audiences. Those oriented more toward practitioners may expect case examples, vignettes, or suggestions for working with a particular type of client. Other journals expect sophisticated analytical procedures. Some journals want a very detailed literature review, while others don't. You will have more success placing articles in a journal that you are well acquainted with (for example, knowing the style, format, and type of article that the journal tends to publish) than in an unfamiliar journal.

Practically all journals carry a statement informing readers and prospective authors of the type of articles that they would like to see. By reading such statements, prospective authors determine if their manuscripts would be appropriate for the journals. For instance, this statement is found in *Social Work:*

> The journal's purpose is to improve practice and advance knowledge in social work and social welfare. The editorial board welcomes manuscripts that expand and evaluate knowledge of social problems, social work practice, and the social work profession. The editorial board particularly seeks articles on the following topics:
>
> - Research on social problems
> - Evaluation of social work practice
> - Advancement of developmental and practice theory
> - Culture and ethnicity
> - Social policy, advocacy, and administration

Research on Social Work Practice defines its purpose as being

> a disciplinary journal devoted to the publication of empirical research concerning the assessment methods and outcomes of social work practice. Social work practice is broadly interpreted to refer to the application of intentionally designed social work intervention programs to problems of societal or interpersonal importance. Interventions include behavior analysis and therapy; psychotherapy or counseling with individuals; case management; education; supervision; practice involving couples, families, or small groups; advocacy; community practice; organizational management; and the evaluation of social policies.
>
> The journal primarily serves as an outlet for the publication of:
>
> - Original reports of evidence-based evaluation studies on the outcomes of social work practice.
> - Original reports of empirical studies on the development and validation of social work assessment methods.
> - Original evidence-based reviews of the practice-research literature that convey direct applications (not simply implications) to social work practice. The two types of review articles considered for publication are (a) reviews of the evidence-based status of a particular psychosocial intervention; and (b) reviews of evidence-based interventions applicable to a particular psychosocial problem.

Journals want original manuscripts that are clearly written, of timely interest, appropriate to the journal, of the right length, and in the correct style. Journal reviewers look for an adequate literature review, reasonable research design, and the correct use of statistical techniques. But beyond those considerations, reviewers must decide whether or not your manuscript makes a "contribution" to the knowledge base. Reviewers may decide that your manuscript makes no contribution because of severe limitations in its generalizability, or because a more thorough literature review would have revealed the existence of studies similar to the one being reported. A manuscript might even be judged "interesting" but not relevant for that journal.

You will probably increase your chances of publication if you find a journal that, in the last six years or so, has published similar (or somewhat related) articles to the one you are preparing. While this guideline is no guarantee that the journal will publish your article, at least it indicates that the reviewers have had an interest in your topic. Study the articles that have recently appeared in the journal. Observe the reference style, the use of tables, the length of the literature review, and the general level at which the article is written. Keep in mind that the entire manuscript (including references) should not exceed 16 to 20 double-spaced pages.

When you have narrowed down your choice of journals to one or two, study the "Information for Authors." Sometimes the instructions about manuscript preparation and the types of manuscripts that journals are seeking are found in the back of selected issues. Or, you may want to look for that journal on the Internet. Information about the NASW Journals (*Social Work, Health & Social Work, Social Work in Education*, and *Social Work Research*) can be found at http://www.naswpress.org.

After you revise and polish your manuscript to the point where you think it is finished, set it aside. After several days, reread it. Make necessary revisions, and prepare a clean copy. Share it with two or three persons whose opinions you respect. Find helpful readers who can give you constructive criticism without battering your ego. If you know that you are weak in the grammar department, seek a friendly reviewer who knows that subject well.

One thing that you should not do is send your manuscript to more than one journal at a time. Most journals would be very unhappy if you took such an unethical action. If your manuscript is rejected by the first journal you choose, do not be discouraged. A rejection does not necessarily mean that your manuscript is poorly conceptualized or written. It could be that the journal just accepted a similar article on the same topic last week. Or, it may mean that the journal is planning a special issue, and your manuscript does not fit their needs. You may have submitted your article to an inappropriate journal.

Sometimes, busy reviewers may not take the time to read carefully enough to understand what you have written. Reviews are conducted "blind"—that is, you will not know who read your manuscript and will have no way of knowing whether the reviewer knew as much about your topic or your methodology as you do. So, even good articles can be rejected. If your first effort is rejected, dust off your pride and try to objectively read your manuscript again. Repair any problems indicated by the reviewers of the first journal and submit it to the second journal of your choice.

Journal reviewers usually make one of three decisions: they accept the manuscript as it is; they accept it if the author makes certain changes; or they reject it. Don't let your ego deflate if you are asked to make certain modifications and resubmit. Often articles are strengthened by the additional information that a reviewer might request.

Should your manuscript be rejected twice, it still may have a chance at publication. You may want to get Mendelsohn's (1997) *An Author's Guide to Social Work Journals* for suggestions of additional journals that might be interested in your manuscript. Some journals accept proportionately a much larger percentage of manuscripts than others.

If your manuscript has been rejected three times, should you continue trying to get it published? This is the point at which I become frustrated and tired of working with one manuscript, and I quit. However, if you feel that yours is basically a good manuscript, and some of the reviewers have encouraged revision, then you should try it again.

Getting a manuscript published is like most other things in life that require practice. The more you practice, the better you will become at this activity. Canton (1988) says that it is like learning to ride a bicycle. The way to learn is by trying again!

READING AND CRITIQUING RESEARCH MANUSCRIPTS

Students sometimes have a tendency to believe that any research that manages to appear in print is "good" research. Unfortunately, some pretty shoddy research can be found in journals without too much difficulty. As I stated in the beginning of this book, one reason you are required to enroll in a research methods course is to help you recognize poor or inadequate research. Flawed research (if unrecognized) could lead you to conclusions that are not warranted and could be dangerous to your clients.

Using the major content areas of research reports, we can construct a set of criteria to use in evaluating research reports, journal articles, or manuscripts. (These criteria can also be used to double-check your manuscripts.) I'm indebted to Garfield (1984) for his observations and guidelines on this topic.

When evaluating a research report, you should find yourself answering "yes" to most of these questions. Strong research articles will elicit a greater number of affirmative responses; weak articles will receive fewer. You can use these criteria not only to evaluate the research reports prepared by others, but also to check your own report or manuscript to ensure that you have included all of the crucial elements.

This chapter has attempted to provide instruction on key elements in research report writing. Three points cannot be emphasized enough: (1) the importance of studying examples of other research reports and literature; (2) the critical need for social workers to publish their research results; and (3) the necessity to persevere when first efforts are rejected by journal reviewers.

When you publish your research, you contribute to the knowledge base of social work and allow others to build on your research. Knowledge is an incremental process; it moves forward in small steps rather than large leaps. Any movement toward the goal of advancing social work knowledge starts

Checklist for Evaluating Research Reports, Articles, and Manuscripts

- [ ] Does the Introduction provide a clear notion of:
  - [ ] (a) the problem
  - [ ] (b) the purpose of the research
  - [ ] (c) its significance
- [ ] Are the stated hypotheses reasonable? Do they appear to logically follow from the review of the literature?
- [ ] Is the literature review
  - [ ] (a) relevant to the study
  - [ ] (b) thorough
  - [ ] (c) current
- [ ] Is a research design stated?
  - [ ] Do the subjects appear to have been selected without overt bias?
  - [ ] If there is a control group, does it seem to be an appropriate group for comparison?
  - [ ] Is the number of subjects sufficient?

- [ ] Is there enough information on:
  - [ ] (a) the procedures
  - [ ] (b) operational definitions of the variables
  - [ ] (c) the reliability and validity of the instruments
- [ ] Are the findings discussed in terms of their implications and practical significance?
  - [ ] Do the conclusions logically follow from the data?
  - [ ] Is the author guilty of overgeneralizing? Has actual or potential bias been recognized?
  - [ ] Are the appropriate statistical tests used?

with understanding the research process. Since knowledge can become outdated and obsolete with the passage of time, it is vital that social workers not only read research as a way of keeping up with new developments in the field but also engage in research and seek professional outlets for the dissemination of research efforts. Otherwise, as Williams and Hopps (1987) have noted, "the profession does not advance, clients cannot thrive, and practice does not improve" (p. 376).

KEY TERMS

principal investigator (PI)   requests for proposals   RFPs

SELF-REVIEW

(Answers at the end of the book)
1. T or F. The Discussion section of a research report is where the notable theoretical explanations of the problem are summarized.
2. Why are tables included in research reports?
3. T or F. The Results section of a research report contains only the findings the investigator has obtained; this is not the place for speculation or implications.

4. T or F. The study's limitations are presented in the Methodology section.
5. T or F. The Introduction is where a clear statement of the research problem is addressed so that the reader understands the study's purpose.
6. T or F. The usual length of manuscripts submitted to professional journals is 25 to 30 pages, exclusive of tables and references.

QUESTIONS FOR CLASS DISCUSSION

1. Discuss the ways in which a research report is similar to and different from the customary term paper.
2. Discuss what it is about a "good" journal article that makes it interesting or fun to read and what it is about some journal articles that make them dull and uninteresting.
3. How is writing for professional audiences different from writing to relatives or friends?
4. Think about the various sections of the research report. Tell the class what you think would be the most difficult section to write and your reasons for thinking this.

RESOURCES AND REFERENCES

American Psychological Association. (2001). *Publication manual of the American Psychological Association* (5th ed.). Washington, DC: APA.

Beebe, L. (1993). *Professional writing for the human services.* Washington, DC: NASW Press.

Canton, T. O. (1988). Publishing as a professional activity. *Health and Social Work, 13 (Spring),* 85–89.

DePoy, E. & Gitlin, L. N. (1998). *Introduction to research: Understanding and applying multiple strategies.* St Louis, MO: Mosby.

Drisko, J. W. (2005). Writing up qualitative research. *Families in Society, 86(4),* 589–593.

Faul, A. C., & Hudson, W. W. (1997). The index of drug involvement: A partial validation. *Social Work, 42,* 565–572.

Garfield, S. L. (1984). The evaluation of research: An editorial perspective. In A. S. Bellack & M. Hersen (Eds.), *Research Methods in Clinical Psychology.* New York: Pergamon.

Geever, J. C. (1997). *The Foundation Center's guide to proposal writing.* New York: Foundation Center.

Greenberg, J. S. (1995). The other side of caring: Adult children with mental illness as supports to their mothers in later life. *Social Work, 40,* 414–423.

Hudson, W. W., & McMurtry, S. L. (1997). Comprehensive assessment in social work practice. *Research on Social Work Practice, 7,* 79–98.

Mendelsohn, H. (1997). *An author's guide to social work journals.* Silver Spring, MD: National Association of Social Workers.

Morrow, D. F. (1996). Coming-out issues for adult lesbians: A group intervention. *Social Work, 41,* 647–656.

Neale, J., Allen, D., & Coombes, L. (2005). Qualitative research methods within the addictions. *Addiction, 100(11),* 1584–1593.

Nugent, W. R., Champlin, D. N., & Wiinimaki, L. (1997). The effects of anger control training on adolescent antisocial behavior. *Research on Social Work Practice, 7(4),* 446–462.

Oktay, J. S. (1992). Burnout in hospital social workers who work with AIDS patients. *Social Work, 37,* 432–439.

Reid, W. J. (1988). Writing research reports. In R. M. Grinnell (Ed.), *Social work research and evaluation.* Itasca, IL: Peacock.

Ries, J. B., & Leukefeld, C. B. (1997). *Research funding guidebook: Getting it, managing it and renewing it.* Thousand Oaks, CA: Sage.

Royse, D. (1999). Exploring ways to retain first-time volunteer donors: A test of interventions. *Research on Social Work Practice, 9(1),* 76–85.

Ruskin, K. B. (1995). *Grant writing, fundraising, and partnerships: Strategies that work!* Thousand Oaks, CA: Corwin.

Shepard, M. (1997). Site-based services for residents of single-room occupancy hotels. *Social Work, 42,* 585–594.

Sutphen, R. D. (1997). Social work and juvenile justice: Is the literature trying to tell us something? *Arete, 22(1),* 50–57.

Swanberg, J. E., & Logan, T. K. (2005). Domestic violence and employment: A qualitative study. *Journal of Occupational Health Psychology, 10(1),* 3–17.

Wahab, S. (2005). Navigating mixed-theory programs: Lessons learned from a prostitution-diversion project. *Affilia, 20(2),* 203–221.

Williams, L. F., & Hopps, J. G. (1987). Publication as a practice goal: Enhancing opportunities for social workers. *Social Work, 32(5),* 373–376.

Williams, L. F., & Hopps, J. G. (1988). On the nature of professional communications: Publication for practitioners. *Social Work, 33(5),* 453–459.

ASSIGNMENT 14.1: Assessing Grant Proposals

Objective: *To provide "hands-on" experience with evaluating and critiquing grant proposals.*

In the practicum agency where you are interning, try to find an example of a research or evaluation report. Read this report and use the checklist below to assess its various components. (Instructors: You may want to put a copy of a research report on reserve or post it electronically so that every student is reading the same report. Alternatively, a journal article could be used.)

CHECKLIST FOR EVALUATING JOURNAL ARTICLES AND MANUSCRIPTS

Title of the research report or article read:

Who prepared it?

Date?

THE INTRODUCTION

Does its introduction provide a clear notion of

a. the problem   _Yes _No

b. the purpose of the research   _Yes _No

c. its significance   _Yes _No

How could the introduction have been improved?

THE LITERATURE REVIEW

Is the literature review

a. relevant to the study   _Yes _No

b. thorough   _Yes _No

c. current   _Yes _No

Are the hypotheses/research questions reasonable?   _Yes _No

Do they appear to logically follow from the review of the literature?   _Yes _No

ASSIGNMENT 14.1 (*Continued*)

How might the literature review section have been improved?

THE METHODOLOGY

Is a research design stated? _Yes _No

Do the subjects appear to have been selected without overt bias? _Yes _No

If there is a control group, does it seem to be an appropriate
group for comparison? _Yes _No

Is the number of subjects sufficient? _Yes _No

Is there is enough information on

a. the procedures _Yes _No

b. operational definitions of the variables _Yes _No

c. the reliability and validity of the instruments _Yes _No

What additional information about this project's methodology
would you like to have found in the report?

THE RESULTS

Are the appropriate statistical tests used? _Yes _No

Are the findings discussed in terms of their implications and
practical significance? _Yes _No

Do the conclusions logically follow from the data? _Yes _No

Is the author guilty of overgeneralizing? _Yes _No

Has actual or potential bias been recognized? _Yes _No

ASSIGNMENT 14.2: Assessing Grant Proposals

Objective: *To provide "hands-on" experience with evaluating and critiquing grant proposals.*

Obtain a copy of a recent grant proposal that has been written by a social service agency in your community or a faculty member at your college or university. Read this proposal and use the headings and questions below to assess its various components. Elaborate your responses with a reasoned reply. (Instructors: You may want to put a copy of a grant proposal on reserve or post it electronically so that every student is reading the same proposal.)

1. **Problem statement:** Is the problem real? Is the description of the problem compelling?

2. **Qualifications of the organization:** Does this section make a good argument for why this organization is particularly well suited to launch the project? Does it seem to have the necessary resources and staff?

3. **Goals and objectives:** Are the goals and objectives appropriate for the project? In your opinion are they feasible?

4. **Methodology:** Does this section of the proposal clearly explain what the funding will provide in services or how the research will be conducted? Are these plans reasonable and built on best practice models?

5. **Evaluation plan:** Will the plans to evaluate the project provide important process evaluation information or outcome data for concluding whether it succeeded? Is there anything else you would want to know?

6. **Budget:** Does the budget seem realistic, neither overinflated nor too skimpy?

7. **Future funding plans:** Is a practical plan described that would seem to provide for continued funding of this project?

Attitudes About Research Courses (Instrument)

1. Check the following courses that you successfully completed in *high school:*
   Algebra I _____ Geometry _____
   Algebra II _____ Calculus _____

2. What is your age?_____

3. What is your gender?
   Male _____   Female _____

4. Consider for a moment the extent (if any) of your fear of research courses. Indicate your fear on the scale below:

No fear					*Some fear*			*Lots of fear*	
1	2	3	4	5	6	7	8	9	10

5. On the following scale, rate your perception of how useful you think research courses will be to you.

Not very useful					*Some use*			*Very useful*	
1	2	3	4	5	6	7	8	9	10

6. On the following scale, rate your interest in taking research courses.

No interest				Some interest			Lots of interest		
1	2	3	4	5	6	7	8	9	10

In order to better understand your feelings about research, indicate whether the following statements are true or false.

7. T or F   I dread speaking before a large group of people more than taking a research course.

8. T or F   I would rather take a research course than ask a waitress to return an improperly cooked meal to the chef.

9. T or F   My fear of snakes is greater than my fear of taking a research course.

10. T or F   My fear of spiders is less than my fear of taking a research course.

11. T or F   I would rather take a research course than ask a total stranger to do a favor for me.

12. T or F   My fear of research is such that I would rather the university require an additional two courses of my choosing than take one research course.

13. T or F   I dread going to the dentist more than taking a research course.

14. T or F   I fear a statistics course more than a research methodology course.

15. T or F   I have always "hated math."

The following symbols frequently appear in research studies that utilize statistical analyses. To the best of your ability, identify the statistical symbols. If unknown, write "unknown." (Example: The symbol + means addition.)

16. F _____

17. df _____

18. t _____

19. r _____

20. χ^2 _____

21. $p < .05$ _____

22. $\bar{X}, M$ _____

23. SD, S _____

Drug Attitude Questionnaire (Instrument)

Please read each of the following items carefully and rate your agreement or disagreement by checking the appropriate blank to the right of the question.

	Strongly Agree	Agree	Undecided	Disagree	Disagree Strongly
1. Using marijuana or beer often leads to becoming addicted to more harmful drugs.	_____	_____	_____	_____	_____
2. Drugs are basically an "unnatural" way to enjoy life.	_____	_____	_____	_____	_____
3. I see nothing wrong with getting drunk occasionally.	_____	_____	_____	_____	_____
4. Too many of society's problems are blamed on kids who use alcohol or drugs regularly.	_____	_____	_____	_____	_____
5. Even if my best friend gave me some drugs, I probably wouldn't use them.	_____	_____	_____	_____	_____
6. If I become a parent, I don't intend to hassle my kids about their use of drugs or alcohol.	_____	_____	_____	_____	_____
7. Certain drugs like marijuana are all right to use because you can't become addicted.	_____	_____	_____	_____	_____

continued

	Strongly Agree	Agree	Undecided	Disagree	Disagree Strongly
8. It is not difficult for me to turn down an opportunity to get high.	_____	_____	_____	_____	_____
9. Marijuana should not be legalized.	_____	_____	_____	_____	_____
10. It is not okay with me if my friends get high or drunk.	_____	_____	_____	_____	_____
11. I would rather occasionally use drugs or alcohol with my friends than lose this set of friends.	_____	_____	_____	_____	_____
12. Someone who regularly uses drugs or alcohol may be considered a sick person.	_____	_____	_____	_____	_____
13. Most of my friends have experimented with drugs.	_____	_____	_____	_____	_____
14. Personally, use of alcohol is more acceptable than use of drugs.	_____	_____	_____	_____	_____
15. Any addict with willpower should be able to give up drugs on his/her own.	_____	_____	_____	_____	_____
16. Either drug addiction or alcoholism leads to family problems.	_____	_____	_____	_____	_____
17. Most Americans do not heavily rely on drugs.	_____	_____	_____	_____	_____
18. Some experience with drugs or alcohol is important for a teenager in today's society.	_____	_____	_____	_____	_____
19. Kids who use drugs are less popular than kids who do not.	_____	_____	_____	_____	_____
20. Drugs or alcohol provide a good way to "get away from it all."	_____	_____	_____	_____	_____
21. I think the legal drinking age should be lowered.	_____	_____	_____	_____	_____
22. Teachers should place more emphasis on teaching American ideals and values.	_____	_____	_____	_____	_____
23. It is all right to get around the law if you don't actually break it.	_____	_____	_____	_____	_____

Source: Royse, D., Keller, S., & Schwartz, J. L. (1982). Lessons learned: The evaluation of a drug education program, *Journal of Drug Education, 12*, 181–190.

How to Use a
Table of Random
Numbers

Assume that you have 500 clients in the population and you need to select a random sample of 25 from that population. You have already made a list of these persons (created a sample frame) and accurately counted or numbered them from 1 to 500. In order to draw a random sample, you will need to get a random starting place on the Table of Random Numbers. Before you do this, you need to think about a way to encompass every numerical possibility that will occur within your population. If you choose a single-digit number—for example, 9—as the starting place, any number larger than one digit (the numbers 10 through 500) would be excluded. There is no possibility of their being chosen. If you choose a two-digit number, you would still exclude the three-digit numbers. Therefore, you have to look at the numbers in the Table of Random Numbers in groups of three—numbers such as 009, 147, 935, and so on. This will allow the lowest possible number (001) and the highest possible number (500) in your population (as well as all the numbers in between) to have an equal chance of being chosen.

Now you are ready to draw a sample from the Table of Random Numbers. Since the values on the table are arranged in no particular order, it makes no difference where or how you start. You could, for instance, roll a pair of dice. The number of dots on one could direct you to a particular column and the value on the other would direct you to a particular row of random numbers. You can start from the top or bottom of the table and from the left or right side.

You could also shuffle a deck of cards and select two cards, again letting the value of the first indicate a specific column and the value of the second, a particular row.

A third way to find a random starting place would be to shut your eyes and, holding a pencil or pen, let your hand come down somewhere on the page. Start from that point and take the next 25 three-digit numbers. Of course, if you select a number like 947 or 515, you will have to discard them as they fall outside of the range (1–500).

As you look at the Table of Random Numbers, you will notice that they are grouped in sets of six. It makes no difference if you ignore the first three digits and use the last three of each set or vice versa. When you have selected 25 three-digit numbers falling between 1 and 500, you have your random sample!

Please note that the table below is a very abbreviated one just to illustrate what they look like. As an alternative to consulting a table already prepared, you might want to go to an interactive random number generator such as http://graphpad.com/quickcals/randomN1.cfm and produce your own series of random numbers.

Table of Random Numbers

360062	190148	438921	828610	137813	597216	745136	848373	980702	292403
934762	289048	055252	239359	049231	215708	828323	995602	968653	358123
316630	308216	845177	333584	306213	537904	849376	571680	527394	587341
827749	459314	277743	328793	589905	452433	234203	534213	474746	301166
103359	918057	943330	745098	125601	036980	264454	594793	641501	882535
375215	397377	256691	478121	756814	210058	534319	441724	852186	016678
711032	882621	934206	136008	254288	288709	678536	919749	453691	818526
804845	256068	781681	476628	926897	721293	885133	841857	170057	958707
597462	768354	455724	262587	204958	059064	129034	774120	391834	283950
383424	363439	565399	148896	123675	712072	996343	282454	249228	733297
845446	785274	471471	718267	294703	952780	751216	614147	457324	357589
171037	236626	116308	872015	117031	393199	195654	417915	018433	885064
663704	963322	005562	992787	948421	510794	503441	139789	965668	766346
523120	499512	649587	503120	800718	621563	607424	665129	444721	989526
943685	339626	172547	475197	315309	814281	493565	095760	286835	187233
558632	445148	561021	599971	695121	839266	279515	263519	094626	630463
688812	481716	366194	887525	382441	049265	372731	024735	983979	595913
432063	938512	127163	196425	190817	044621	282333	700128	923578	279450
616425	385590	995664	296416	700414	148695	772517	274528	450435	312249
177081	382698	762128	096542	471251	085339	773561	531650	371110	232144
530653	007347	034621	130744	819405	044061	723251	190820	948230	420664

Answers to
Self-Review Questions

CHAPTER 1

1. b. psychology
2. a. to be an informed consumer
   b. to maintain accountability
   c. to meet CSWE standards
   d. to be an ethical practitioner
   e. to contribute fully to the profession
3. To accredit social work programs; to make sure BSW and MSW programs meet standards
4. True
5. Empirically based means to rely on research to guide assessments and the choice of interventions, and to gauge the effectiveness of those efforts. In every facet of practice, to call on and use research as a tool.
6. Social work research is applied. We use it to improve the quality of our clients' lives.
7. Research starts with us and with the questions we have about the world around us.

CHAPTER 2

1. Step 1: Posing a question or stating a hypothesis
   Step 2: Reviewing the literature
   Step 3: Developing a research design
   Step 4: Operationalizing key variables
   Step 5: Collecting necessary data
   Step 6: Analyzing and interpreting the data
   Step 7: Writing the report
2. True. The hypothesis states there is no difference between the two groups.
3. Impulsivity is the dependent variable.
4. They are large-scale efforts that attempt to speak definitely about a population or client group. Usually explorative studies will have been done first and the descriptive study follows because of flaws or problems with the earlier samples or methodology.
5. There are many ways you could have gone about this. Here are a few examples:
   - Students with at least a 3.5 GPA
   - Students with perfect attendance
   - Students who study at least three hours a night
   - Students who take notes and ask questions in class
   - Students who turn in all their assignments
   - Students who make As on all their tests
6. Independent variables could include age, race, income, other prior arrests, marital status, employment status, alcohol/drug use history, and so on.
7. Concept or construct
8. True
9. c. bias
10. True
11. This is a correct interpretation.
12. The first hypothesis is not clear. It does not indicate what groups of people and whether altruism would be expected to be high or low in the groups. There's no direction to the hypothesis. This hypothesis could be stated along these lines: "Persons who have had at least one social work course are more altruistic than those who have never completed a social work course."

    In the second example, a null hypothesis was attempted. A better way of stating this would be to say, "There is no difference in social work values held by BSW and MSW graduates." If you as an investigator had a specific instrument in mind, you might propose, "There is no difference in social work values held by BSW and MSW graduates as measured by the Dorunrun Social Value Inventory." Alternatively, you might propose something like, "First year MSW students will score lower than BSW seniors on the Dooflicky Social Value Inventory."

    The third hypothesis does not contribute new knowledge—don't we already know that smoking is harmful? And also, it lacks specificity by not indicating what health effects would be the target of the investigation.

The fourth hypothesis is not so bad but could be improved by indicating if fatalistic attitudes *decrease* or *increase* survivability rates of persons with cancer.

13. False
14. Qualitative researchers typically do not feel that they must be fully informed about the literature prior to beginning their study. They may conduct some review of the literature but are not expected to master it in the same way that quantitative researchers are.
15. False
16. True
17. Qualitative
18. Quantitative
19. Qualitative

CHAPTER 3

1. True
2. True
3. False. Minors must still assent to participate.
4. False. If there is no scientific merit, IRBs may refuse to grant permission for research.
5. False. (Although IRBs will review these proposals much more closely to ensure there is no possibility of harm and that the research cannot be conducted any other way.)
6. True
7. Protocol
8. Anonymity
9. Confidentiality
10. True
11. Normally a researcher would not be required in a clinical trial to indicate how successful the new intervention has been. If that information was known, there would be no reason to conduct the clinical trial. However, there must be some reason to suspect that the intervention has promise or potential as an intervention or it wouldn't be in the process of being tested.
12. It may be more likely that a participant in a qualitative study could be identified if there was something unique or defining about that person. For instance, gang members might disclose a nickname or characteristic about one of their group that could be recognized by a police officer or other person reading an account of the qualitative study. Quantitative researchers usually report results in the aggregate and combined means as opposed to individual scores or contributions. Also, qualitative researchers use open-ended or unstructured interviews and so they are less sure of what will be revealed or disclosed to them than quantitative researchers are. Finally, qualitative researchers are less likely to be evaluating interventions. They might, however, interview clients or

patients who have received a certain intervention in order to capture their experience with the program or treatment.
13. False

CHAPTER 4

1. True
2. False. Time goes on the horizontal axis.
3. Two
4. ABAB
5. d. $A_1A_2A_3B$
6. Many peaks and valleys, not a straight linear line.
7. a.   They lend themselves to clinical practice.
   b.   They are not burdensome and they complement practice.
   c.   They are primarily visual and do not require statistical expertise.
8. The major problem is one of generalization. Success with one client doesn't mean, for example, that the social worker is successful with all or most of her clients.
9. The baselines for subjects 2 and 3 are longer than for the first subject; intervention with the second subject is not started until it is shown to be effective with the first subject. Intervention with the third subject is not started until intervention with the second subject has also shown to be effective.
10. To determine if clients are making progress.
11. The major reason is probably lack of time to evaluate their practice, but other reasons include settings not amenable to single-system designs (e.g., where there are short stays or rapid turnover of clients), and lastly, the inability to find suitable instruments to measure progress.
12. Independent. The data probably reflect autocorrelation.
13. Internal validity threats are history, maturation, instrumentation, testing, mortality, statistical regression, and contamination/diffusion.
14. External validity is concerned with whether the findings can be generalized to other settings or locales.
15. The greatest threat to external validity is that it usually is not possible to involve random selection of subjects and therefore those in the study may not be truly representative of the client population.

CHAPTER 5

1. No, it would be much more labor-intensive for Marsha to construct 80 different single-system graphs and then have the possible problem of not being able to interpret them in a conclusive sense. Her focus is not on an individual client, but should be on whether the majority of the clients as a group received benefit from the intervention. Does she need to assess their depression weekly? Probably not. In a situation like this, the investigator would normally administer just pretests and posttests.
2. A control group and random assignment.

3. Extraneous
4. True. It would be an experiment even without pretests.
5. True. In 12 months or more children grow up, bodies change, even our thinking about various topics can move one way or the other.
6. False. This would be the threat of testing or practice.
7. True
8. True
9. False. This is a quasi-experimental design.
10. The time-series design or the time-series with control groups.
11. True
12. It is impossible with this design to rule out the threat of alternative explanations. With no control group, it is impossible to say that the intervention created the change observed at posttest.
13. This would be an example of retroactive research.
14. False
15. False. These designs would be likely used because randomization was not possible.
16. False

CHAPTER 6

1. b.   test-retest reliability
2. She would want to keep it; if it correlates with the other items, it will add to/improve the scale's internal consistency.
3. Computing interrater reliability
4. Validity
5. False
6. False
7. False
8. False
9. False
10. True
11. The authors conducted factor analysis, discriminant validity testing (comparing the MPD sample against the college sample), as well as convergent validity work (correlating depression, dissociation and stressful life event scales with the CATS).

CHAPTER 7

1. True
2. False
3. False
4. d.   It is vague.
5. b.   It uses jargon.
6. c.   It asks for unavailable information.
7. d.   It uses inflammatory or loaded terms.

8. a. It is negatively constructed.
9. b. It is all-inclusive.
10. d. It is vague.
11. c. It is leading.
12. contingency
13. Because he is not sure how young adults cope with divorce, it would be better to use open-ended questions.

CHAPTER 8

1. True
2. Convenience
3. Sample frame
4. True
5. a stratified sample
6. True
7. True
8. False
9. available, accidental
10. False
11. True
12. False
13. True
14. snowball
15. Interviewer
16. False

CHAPTER 9

1. b. personal interview
2. True
3. True
4. True
5. a. extremely accurate (less than 3% error)
6. the ability to observe the respondent and the surroundings (e.g., facial expressions and reactions) and also the ability to present visual aids
7. investigation of topics not previously well researched. Because little is known about the subject being investigated, sample size is not a major consideration and samples may be fairly small.
8. These are the advantages: relatively inexpensive, large numbers of respondents can be surveyed in a relatively short period, respondents can look up information if they need to, privacy is maximized, graphics and visuals can be presented (e.g., response sets), can be completed when convenient for the respondent, respondents can see the context of a series of questions, there is no researcher present to bias the respondent's answers or to inaccurately record the responses.
9. False

10. Pilot test
11. False
12. False
13. True
14. c.   personal interview

CHAPTER 10

1. False
2. He or she is limited by the fact that the data may not exist, or if it does, it may not be available for the years or locations in which the researcher is interested. There could be incomplete or sloppy records, or data that has questionable reliability. The researcher using archival data is limited by not being able to create new, original data.
3. True
4. c.   secondary data analysis
5. False
6. True
7. They tend to be relatively inexpensive.
8. Lack of control over the source material/data—because it already exists. The researcher cannot reword questionnaire items to make them less vague or insensitive, and cannot probe like an interviewer to achieve greater clarification. The researcher also cannot introduce new variables.
9. Latent content
10. True

CHAPTER 11

1. a.   quantitatively oriented researchers
2. c.   large sample sizes
3. d.   concern with instruments and measurement
4. a.   quantitative—could be secondary data analysis or survey
   b.   qualitative
   c.   quantitative
   d.   qualitative
   d.   quantitative
5. You might select a qualitative approach: a) if you can't find an appropriate quantitative instrument to use, b) if you want to investigate a "hidden" or "hard-to-reach" population, c) if you want to study a phenomenon in its natural setting, d) when there is little or no literature or previous studies available on the phenomenon, e) when the topic requires great sensitivity to explore it, f) when the investigator wishes to obtain the perspective of participants in their own words and actions and wishes to write a "rich description" of it, g) when the focus is on the process and not the outcome of a program or activity, or h) when the quantitative findings don't go far enough or need more explanation.

6. True
7. False
8. False
9. Theoretical saturation is when new data obtained by the researcher replicates earlier findings.
10. Member checking involves going back into the field after data collection to verify material with one or more participants with regard to an interpretation or finding.
11. True
12. In the Madey (1982) quote, the zooming out to see the breadth or extent of a problem represents a quantitative approach like a community survey where many people and points of view might be obtained. The zooming in (close-up) represents a qualitative approach that could involve in-depth interviewing of a small handful of individuals to learn from their experiences and stories.

CHAPTER 12

1. Patterns of use
2. Formative evaluation
3. a. narrative
4. Consumer satisfaction
5. Outcome evaluation
6. Cost-effectiveness
7. True
8. that client satisfaction studies invariably produce high satisfaction ratings
9. patterns of use
10. Time, resources, audience, purpose
11. A meta-analysis is a study designed to summarize or synthesize findings from other studies—generally examining treatment effectiveness.
12. Large effect size = .56 or greater

CHAPTER 13

1. c. mean
2. Nominal
3. Ordinal (because there is directionality from high to low)
4. c. univariate
5. b. bivariate
6. a. chi-square
7. b. t test
8. c. one-way analysis (because there are more than two groups and interval data)
9. c. about 12%
10. False (anything less than .05 would be significant)
11. d. both b and c are correct

CHAPTER 14

1. False
2. To cut down on the amount of verbiage in a paper
3. True
4. False
5. True
6. False

Index